Unsettled Settlers

Barriers to Integration

Third Edition

Edited by Soheila Pashang

Library and Archives Canada Cataloguing in Publication

Unsettled settlers: barriers to integration, 3rd ed. / edited by Soheila Pashang

Includes bibliographical references and index.
ISBN 978-1-897160-90-9

1. Immigrants--Canada. 2. Canada--Emigration and immigration--Government policy. 3. Emigration and immigration law--Canada.
4. Immigrants--Services for--Canada. 5. Immigrants--Employment--Canada. 6. Multiculturalism--Canada. I. Pashang, Soheila

Publisher: Shivu Ishwaran
Cover Designer: Faranak Pashang

de Sitter Publications
111 Bell Dr., Whitby, ON, L1N 2T1
CANADA

deSitterPublications.com
289-987-0656
info@desitterpublications.com

Acknowledgement

Soheila Pashang

The book, *Unsettled Settlers: Barriers to Integration*, was first published in 2012, by the de Sitter Publications. Three years later, we found the need for two revisions. This need stem from the ever-changing nature of the Canadian citizenship, immigration, and refugee policies, their implications on various migrant populations and the settlement sectors, as well as academic institutions. It has been a three years of celebration and disappointment, resilience and protest, and networking and uniting to make Canada a better place for those in need of protection and for all Canadians who believe in social justice principles. I am grateful for the possibility of publishing the third edition of this book.

The idea of producing a collection of articles arose from a persistent struggle and gap to find an appropriate textbook or anthology that is accessible to college students and applies existing immigration policies, settlement service practices, and front-line work to the experiences of immigrants and refugees throughout their settlement and integration processes. Although, in recent years, scholarly work on the discourse of migration and immigration in Canada has proliferated, the field of social service work has yet to critically engage in such dialogue. This dearth of applied scholarly work directly affects the treatment and services immigrants and refugees receive as they approach human service agencies for assistance.

This work has been made possible through the trust and unconditional support of the authors who contributed their chapters and subsequently agreed to revise them for the second and third edition. In particular, my sincere appreciation goes to peer reviewers for their time and constructive feedback. This appreciation extends to my students (past, present, and future) who take their learning seriously–you are the future leaders in our field. Among them are two exceptional individuals, Dina Ibrahim and Joshua Bowman for working tirelessly to gather their fellow classmates feedback and for joining other new scholars, Aysegul Karakucuk, Sima Hosseinzadeh, Dalia El-Farra, and Matt H. B. Smith to peer review revised chapters.

I owe a depth of gratitude to Jim Rozsa, Northrose Associates for encouraging me to pursue my passion and Shivu Ishwaran at de Sitter Publications for making it happen.

For most, I am appreciative for the involvement of the educator and community member partners who dedicated their time and innovative ideas to the production of this book. In particular, I wish to dedicate this book to Debbie Douglas, Executive Director of the Ontario Coalitions of Agencies Serving Immigrants (OCASI), and Avvy Go, Director of Metro Toronto Chinese & Southeast Asian Legal Clinic. Both Debbie and Avvy were highly engaged in conceptualizing the framework, selecting topics, and reviewing the chapters, and they both contributed key chapters to the book. They are leaders in the sector serving immigrants and refugees in Ontario.

The wide range of topics covered by this book reflect the multi-faceted challenges facing immigrants, refugees, illegalized persons and racialized members in Canada today.

Finally, I wish to acknowledge lifelong contributions of Professor Nicole LaViolette towards the right of refugees and refugees from the LGBT communities. Nicole, who wrote the chapter entitled "Sexual Minorities, Migration, and the Remaining Boundaries of Canadian Immigration and Refugee Laws," passed away on May 22, 2015.

Foreword

Biljana Bruce
Chair, School of Community Services
Seneca College

The third edition of *Unsettled Settlers: Barriers to Integration* provides a wealth of applied scholarly material, which serves as a valuable resource for students of social service work in the areas of migration, immigration and settlement. This book is vitally important now; it addresses a wider range of questions as agencies serving immigrants and refugees face ongoing fiscal constraints and diminishing resources. As a result, they require well-prepared professionals who can navigate a complex, and often oppressive, socio-political system to support their immigrant and refugee clients. Addressing these needs is the primary motivation for this book.

Similar to the previous editions, the collection of essays in this book provides a much-needed resource that illustrates anti-oppressive theory as it applies to the practice of professionals in the settlement services sector. This edition also includes a chapter on youth and on citizenship, and has been updated to reflect legal changes, as well as changes in government and organizational policies. This will equip students with the tools and resources they need to work more effectively with immigrants and refugees on the front line. The editor of this collection, Dr. Soheila Pashang, deserves special acknowledgement. Dr. Pashang is the Program Coordinator for the Social Service Worker – Immigrants and Refugees Program at Seneca College. This book reflects her commitment to providing students with the most current scholarly work from research to evidence-based practice. Her intention for this text is not only to bring insight to the plight of immigrants and refugees settling in Canada, but also to celebrate their resilience and success, as demonstrated historically by their varied accomplishments.

Finally, the writers of the articles contained in this volume of essays are to be praised for their ability to so eloquently balance theory with practice, as they weave their experience, knowledge and skills into their respective chapters. Together, the authors provide the overview required to recognize the many challenges existing in the sector and to plan for a hopeful future.

Table of Contents

Unsettled Settlers: Introduction

Soheila Pashang

Both historical and contemporary patterns of migration and immigration policies in Canada confirm the fact that our trajectory has been a crossroad of socially constructed hierarchies of race, class, gender, religion, nationality, and sexual orientation, among other forms of intersecting oppressions. While Canada has gained an international reputation as one of the best countries in which to live, it has also been forced to issue official apologies for the treatment of Aboriginal communities at various historical and political conjunctures. Canada continues to promote and implement discriminatory immigration, border control, and human service/settlement policies that negatively affect both new and old immigrants. These policies create an inequitable situation that sets the stage for social exclusion whereby certain groups of immigrants are constructed as a threat to national security or else are perceived as an economic burden on both government and taxpayers. These policies in particular have led to increased racism and discrimination against racialized immigrants while simultaneously dividing them into categories of "good" and "bad." At a same time, restrictive immigration policies have created a major barrier for entering Canada legally for many people (through the Point System, difficulties in obtaining a visa, or on account of hurdles in the refugee determination process and sponsorship criteria). This latter group is provided with no choice but to live in Canada without legal immigration visas. Among them are rejected refugees, women and children, trafficked individuals, displaced persons due environmentally induced (mining, toxin) conditions or violence erupted from negative impacts of neo-liberal capitalism and globalization (such as free trade agreements), violence against women and sponsorship breakdown. We refer to this group of migrants as illegalized persons (formerly known as non-status persons). While it is estimated that between half a million to one million illegalized persons live and work in Canada, unfortunately to date no systemic measures have been in place to protect them from exploitation and human rights violation. It is important to note that women, due to their caregiving responsibilities for their children and families in Canada and of those remained abroad have fewer options to further their chances of gaining legal immigration statuses. For this reason, the illegalized population is highly feminized.

The recent changes to the immigration policies, has meant a political agenda that has seen a significant reorientation away from a balance between family reunification and protection towards economic considerations marked by an increased infusion of temporary foreign workers, a significant reduction in family class immigrants – especially parents and grandparents and dependent children – and a trending down of the number of convention refugees. At the same time we have seen the rise of a public discourse that has shifted away from the role of immigration in nation building to one that demonizes refugees and reduces immigrants to labour units while promoting the belief that immigrant families are a drain on the purse of the state. This discourse, at its worst, links immigration to public security and criminal justice concerns manifested in punitive immigration and refugee protection laws designed for forceful removal and return whereby those in need of protection are deemed legally inadmissible.

Within the current political moment, the scaling back of government support for the civil society through the withdrawal of public funds from programs has been a major setback to organizations serving immigrants and refugees. Since the 1990s, the settlement sector has been under pressures to deliver services in an environment that is increasingly about financial accountability, tightening service eligibility rules, a significant reduction in budgeting flexibility, and decreasing grant dollars. At the same time there is an increase in both perceived and actual need on the part of immigrants and refugees for more professional services and interventions to address their complex issues.

In 2010, the immigrant and refugee settlement and integration sector in Ontario experienced significant reductions in funding from the Federal Government. Over $43 million was cut from the sector, which resulted in the defunding of over 35 programs and agencies in Ontario with a significant impact on thirteen grassroots, community development focused agencies within the Greater Toronto Area (GTA) (Ontario Council of Agencies Serving Immigrants [OCASI], March 9, 2011; Keung, February 24, 2011). This significant reduction in funding has a severe negative impact on the capacity of these agencies to continue providing the level of services required by the communities which they serve. It may also compromise the integrity of their programs in the long term.

The decision for this funding reduction originated in a directive from the federal minister of Citizenship, Immigration and Multiculturalism to reduce the national budget by ten percent as part of the federal government's deficit reduction agenda (OCASI, March 9, 2011). While bureaucrats within the ministry had very little room in terms of the directive to cut their budget, ultimately how and where the cuts were made – particularly in the GTA which is a highly immigrant and racialized populated city – speaks volumes about, at best, the institutional disregard for racialized communities and, at worst, discrimination within Canada's immigration, settlement, and integration program. Of the thirteen community-based organizations in the GTA that lost 100 percent of their funding in 2010, almost 50 percent were "ethno-specific" organizations – East African, African-Caribbean, South Asian, Chinese, and Arab (Keung, December 23, 2010). Despite active community mobilization, government and most mainstream media have yet to effectively explore the implications of funding cuts on racialized communities.

In the absence of public outcry or effective political opposition against changes to Canada's immigration laws, policies and programs, this book aims to speak to individuals working with immigrants and refugees and their issues at the individual, community and systemic levels with the hope of raising social consciousness about the lived experiences of immigrants and refugees on the one hand and intervening into the public conversation about immigration patterns on the other. As is generally recognized, with a declining birth rate and an aging population, Canada is in dire need of immigrants in order to meet its labour demand and maintain population growth. Despite this recognition, the legacy of discriminatory immigration patterns continues to be parallel to current ideological discourses in which some Canadians remain reluctant hosts to anyone they perceive as "outsiders." This has led to the marginalization of immigrants and refugees in terms of income, health status, employment and political participation. It is causing a growing segment of settlers who remain unsettled and unwanted irrespective of their length of residence in and ties to Canada.

Even still, before resigning to or accepting the status quo as unchangeable, let us not forget the resiliency of the generations of immigrants and refugees who have come before us. They too, have experienced the same – and sometimes more intense – levels of exclusion from their host country. Many of these pioneers have persisted and overcome what appeared to be insurmountable barriers. In the process, they made Canada stronger and Canadian society a more diverse nation. With their resilient power, they paved the way for new generations of immigrants.

So, while this book serves primarily as a critique of the Canadian state and the policy direction that the country is sadly taking, it also calls on readers to celebrate the immigrants and refugees who, through their successes, have triumphed over the intolerance, discrimination, and racism in a society that largely rejects and marginalizes them.

Thus, not every immigrant's and refugee's story is a "success" story. Systemic discrimination, poverty, and racism, to name a few, are issues that define the day-to-day experiences of all too many of the newcomers to this country, and are precisely the issues that seem to get the least attention from policy and decision-makers. While this book is not a comprehensive depiction of the collective experiences of immigrants and refugees, it does provide a snapshot of the complex social, political, and economic web within which too many immigrants, refugees, and non-status migrants carve out their precarious existence.

The political readings contained in this textbook, concerning the experience of migration, immigration, citizenship, integration and the various policies, programs and laws that govern these, are as diverse as the authors themselves. As academics, community organizers, refugee rights advocates, physicians, lawyers, or students of law or social policy, the writers share with us a diverse set of values, political ideologies, and life experiences. Themes range from immigration policies through the decades to the formal development of the settlement sector and the discussions of citizenship, multiculturalism and belonging. From refugee and immigration policies affecting racialized individuals, children and youth, and members of LGBQT communities, to education, the criminal justice system, violence against women, the response of civil society through the sanctuary movement and health, employment and housing conditions, readers are introduced to ideas, concepts and language that are at times troubling and contradictory but always intellectually challenging.

Any editorial attempt to resolve the conflicting ideas and concepts presented in this book would have been futile. Nor would it have been desirable to select only those writings that might be regarded as being either too critical of or too deferential towards the Canadian state. The various chapters do paint a certain picture of Canada – one that is less than ideal, and where race still plays a role in deciding the life chances of success for immigrants and non-immigrants alike – there are obvious disagreements as to the extent

to which racism and other forms of systemic discrimination influence the political, and socio-economic structures and decision-making in Canada. Given
such disagreement, there is also a lack of consensus as to the kind of solutions – both political and otherwise – that are needed in order to address
the challenges facing immigrants and refugees whose rights and interests
are the primary focus of this project. Being among the first book for college
students in Canada that cover the issues of immigration and integration
within the field of social services (particularly those interested in working with
immigrants and refugees) can be both an advantage and a disadvantage.
Whatever the goals and objectives, and however successful it may be in
achieving them, the hope is for readers to arrive at a realization that there is
no panacea and that the only way forward is by way of further dialogue and
discussion. But the project would not be complete if it had not included the
perspective of front-line workers, activists, and those engaged with the law.
Whether collectively or individually, structurally or personally, the book bears
the responsibility and professional power to achieve societal change. To get
there, however, we need a common starting point, which in turn requires us
to build a common understanding of the language used in this book, especially in discussions of experiences of marginalization, exclusion and oppression and the responses that build towards a social justice agenda.

The use of language particularly in naming groups of people is always
one of negotiation. The naming of historically oppressed peoples speaks to
issues of power – from colonial relationships to the present-day manifestation of the race, class, gender, ability, and sexual orientation hierarchy. Self-
location is paramount to a peoples' sense of power of being. It is the essence
of how one sees her or him self and how one wants to be seen by others.
Yet this negotiation that takes place within the group is open to outside influences, particularly the groups' historical relationships to others. A good
example of this negotiation can be found with people of the African Diaspora.
In the last hundred years or so we have seen an evolution in naming from
"Coloured" to "Negro" to "Black" to hyphenated African ("African-Canadian")
and recently for some, to racialized persons.

It is not uncommon to find that people who have a sense of entitlement
can be determined to denigrate others that they deem to be different from
themselves. Whether in terms of race, gender, ethnicity, or religion, they will
use names (not of the group's choosing) in an attempt to maintain power
and control. But the tension that exists around naming does not always arise
out of malevolent intent. There is an ongoing debate within the communities
of Canada's First Peoples about naming, and the views are as diverse as

the many nations and ethno-cultural groups engaged in the ongoing discourse. This presents a challenge for writers outside of these communities in determining what the appropriate designation should be.

Throughout the textbook, authors refer to all individuals categorized as "visible minority" or "person of colour" as "racialized." This last term is open for debate given its relatively recent introduction into the lexicon. The discourse on race and racism is not new but the framing of this within the language of racialization has only recently entered into common political usage. It is an acknowledgement that individuals or groups of people, depending on their "race" (often physical appearance, especially colour), are treated differentially vis-à-vis their European counterparts. But while the term as an umbrella is politically useful, it should not dismiss the multifaceted challenges faced by non-racialized immigrants nor be used to conflate and blind us to the experiences of the diverse racial, ethnic, and cultural communities into a singular homogenized whole. To do so would be an injustice to the historic and current specificities of experiences and hamper effective policy interventions needed to address particular experiences of discrimination and exclusion. And, though there are many links between struggles of Aboriginal peoples and those of peoples of colour, the book's focus on the experiences of immigrants and racialized members is consistent with the recognition of the Aboriginal Peoples' unique and specific historical relationship with Canada.

Overall, the book is divided into seven thematic sections. The authors of the seventeen chapters have diverse professional and academic expertise with personal interest in the field or study of immigrants and refugees.

The first theme speaks of immigration and refugee policies. Avvy Go's opening chapter, "A Race-Based Analysis of Canada's Immigration Policy," examines the overtly racist history of Canada's immigration policy and contemporary forms of racial exclusion under current law. In chapter two, Geraldine Sadoway describes the situation of immigrant and refugee children in Canada, and of children who are Canadian citizens but whose parents are immigrants or refugees. This is addressed within the context of international human rights documents such as the *United Nations Convention on the Rights of the Child* that deals with the rights of all children in the world, regardless of their immigration status. The conditions of refugee and unaccompanied children and youth continue to suffer from a gap in academic literature as well as policy and professional practices. Through the review of specific case studies, the author draws attention to existing social service programs that are geared towards supporting immigrant and refugee children and their families. While the law affects all immigrants and refugees,

Nicole LaViolette's chapter, entitled "Sexual Minorities, Migration, and the Remaining Boundaries of Canadian Immigration and Refugee Laws," raises a serious concern about the homophobic and heterosexist assumptions faced by gay men, lesbians, bisexuals, and trans-gender individuals (LGBT) in the complex and convoluted world of immigration and refugee determination system. Based on a moral tradition and through the implementation of discriminatory immigration policies many LGBT visitors, immigrants and refugees were barred from entering Canada or upon their arrivals were subjected to forceful deportation. It is mainly the last few decades that members of the Immigration and Refugee Board began to address the human rights of LGBT claimants to the extent that Canada is considered among some of the most desirable destinations for LGBT claimants.

In theme two, the first chapter written by Debbie Douglas and Amy Casipullai aims to historicize the formal Settlement and Integration program. Together, the authors provide a chronological account of the evolution of the "settlement sector," from its early roots as a project aimed at socializing the poor within the urban communities to its present-day incarnation as a structured program that faces real challenges to its social justice orientation. This challenge, from policy to front-line practice, is further explored by Jennifer Clarke who, in her chapter "Doing Anti-Oppressive Settlement Work: A Critical Framework for Practice," provides us with a toolkit for working in our field. By relying on an anti-oppressive frame-work interweaving with her personal experience when working as a front-line settlement worker, she argues that settlement work entails a wide range of strategies from critical analysis and critical self-reflection to advocacy, empowerment and capacity building, conscious-ness-raising, organizing, activism, and social action.

Although most immigrants experience barriers to settlement and integration, the impact of such struggle is much more profound on racialized members. For this reason, understanding their unique experiences require different sets of policy responses and intervention strategies. Theme three takes on the discussions about citizenship, multiculturalism and belonging as well as racial equity and anti-racist education. The first chapter, "Multiculturalism and Citizenship in Canada as Policy and Discourse: Approaches and Challenges" by Salah Hassanpour, introduces the often-complex negotiations that must take place as immigrants and refugees attempt to establish a sense of home and social and political ownership of this home. From there, a chapter by Cornelia Mazgarean explores the idea of citizenship as it relates to exclusion and raises two critical questions: Who gets to belong? Who deserves to belong? These questions are analyzed through the new changes to *Bill C-24*, titled *"Strengthening Canadian Citizenship Act,"* which received royal assent on June 19, 2014. The new law it is argued will keep more people out of the public sphere of participation, with disparate effects on disadvantaged groups, and represents a weakening of the idea of citizenship. Such discourse is also experienced by racialized pupils from the moment of entering into the educational system to their point of exit affecting their learning abilities and livelihoods. In his chapter "The Relevance of Anti-Racist Education," George J. Sefa Dei critiques the discourse of multiculturalism as an official policy of Canada and argues for anti-racist education as a discursive and political practice. He insists that this analysis must place the myriad forms of racism and their intersections with other forms of oppression in societal institutions on the table for discussion. Thus, educators, policy makers and community workers cannot shy away from an engagement with anti-racism if we are to challenge the often-dominant assumptions of who can be a citizen and an active participant in civil society.

In recent years, many activists and healthcare practitioners have argued for the inclusion of immigration status as a social determinant of health and have seek for inclusive and accessible healthcare services. Theme four begins with a chapter by Soheila Pashang, "Putting More 'Social' in the Social Determinants of Health: A Roadmap to an Inclusive Approach," that addresses ways in which Aboriginal Peoples, racialized individuals, and immigrants, refugees and illegalized persons social determinants of health is affected by the process of colonization in its historical and current trends making members of these communities vulnerable to health disparities. Pashang argues for Aboriginal status, racialization and immigration status to be recognized as elements of social determinants of health by the Public Health Agencies of Canada. The next chapter is by Donald Payne entitled "Mental Health Problems of Refugees Who Have Suffered Trauma." According to Payne, many refugees are faced with traumatic events that lead to their displacement, forced migration, and violation of their rights throughout their flight, during their refugee hearings, and while settling in their new homeland. These external conditions lead to psychological stresses such as anxiety, depression, low self-esteem, and grief over what has been lost.

Theme five expands our knowledge about the criminal justice system, and violence against women policies, programs and best practices. In their chapter entitled "Myths and Realities: Intersections of the Criminal Justice System with Immigration Status," Siavosh Pashang and Soheila Pashang examine ways in which the legacy of colonization has criminalized racialized members and immigrants in Canada. The chapter expands on the ways in which the justice system, through discriminatory practices such as racial pro-filing, can negatively affect the lives of refugees, permanent residents, and illegalized persons as they encounter the justice system either as a victim or perpetrator of crime. Angie Arora, in "Violence against Immigrant and Refugee Women," explores the impact of immigration status on the lives of immigrant women. She expands our notion and understanding of safety by analyzing the range of systemic barriers immigrant, refugee, and illegalized women (non-status) experience in the context of intimate partner abuse. This includes amendments to immigration policies which increases the vul-nerability of immigrant and refugee women and their families.

Theme six addresses the housing conditions of various groups of immi-grants. All chapters offer evidence about the coexistence of one's im-migration status and socio-economic conditions with the eligibility criteria attached in accessing safe and affordable housing whereby individual is forced to live in an underground manner or seek refuge from the Church; push for a innovative housing arrangement such as Refugee Houses; or face homelessness. In "The Legitimacy of Canadian Sanctuary: Civil Dis-obedience or Platform for Human Rights Dialogue?", Lisa Min examines the impact of immigration law such as deportation and removal policies in forcing rejected refugees to take shelter inside the premises of faith institutions in order to prevent the execution of an enforceable removal order against them. The author frames sanctuary incident as a resistance and platform for policy changes under two broad legal narratives: juxtaposing impugned and arbi-trary domestic law and international refugee law. In their chapter "Refugee Houses: Addressing the Immediate Housing Needs of Refugees in Toronto," Philip Ackerman, Francisco Rico-Martinez and Loly Rico examine the hous-ing needs of refugees and offer an alternative approach to housing work. The chapter first presents the history of refugee houses as a mode of political resistance in response to the emerging needs of refugees in Canada and offers a client-based best practice model to address housing requirements and integration of refugees. The housing needs of immigrants are further addressed by Emily Paradis in her chapter "Experiences of Homelessness Among Women and Families with Precarious Status in Toronto." By drawing on the findings of several studies, the author reports a higher rate of home-lessness and precarious housing conditions for mothers with precarious sta-tus compared to those who were Canadian-born and those with permanent resident status. Despite this, service providers' strategies for supporting homeless mothers with precarious status reveals an institutionalization of precarity in the absence of state policies to protect the rights and security of these mothers and their Canadian-born children.

Finally, theme seven addresses the Canadian labour market and the issue of employment among various groups of immigrants and racialized members. In "Historical and Current Labour Market Experience of Racialized Immigrants in Canada: Advancing Structural Intervention," Ajamu Nangwaya addresses existing structural barriers, including racism, for immigrants attempting to enter the labour market force. These barriers shape the experiences of racialized people, including indigenous peoples, and affect their overall life chances. The author raises the question of unionization and employment equity practices as proposed solutions. Despite the restrictive immigration selection criteria for skilled immigrants and its relation to the labour market needs of Canada, there seems to be a disconnect between such policy and employability of new immigrants where nearly two thirds of them are underemployed or are pushed to occupy surviving jobs. The employment conditions of foreign-trained professionals are further explored in "Persistent Challenges and Possible Solutions: Skilled Immigrant Employment in Canada" by Sophia Lowe and Kuziva Ziramba. By focusing on the labour market integration of skilled immigrants, the authors examine various employment barriers from lack of Canadian experience and skills and credential recognition, to linguistic and cultural biases inherent in behavioural interviewing style, limited professional networking, and discrimination against racialized members. To address such gaps, the authors introduce various practices and initiatives promoted by all three levels of government and various stakeholders to improve service provision and policy initiatives.

Overall, each chapter offers practical intervention strategies required for front-line practitioners as they work with immigrants and refugees. Throughout the book, readers will be presented with a case study to understand the lived realities of immigrants and refugees and how their status is interwoven in government laws and policies, and organizational practices. However, change must start with ourselves and be reflected in our professional practices as lawyers, academics, front-line social worker and social service workers. This book is but one tool among many to embark on that journey of change.

References

Keung, N. (December 23, 2010). Funding axed for Toronto immigrant agencies, *thestar.com*. Retrieved from http://www.thestar.com/news/article/911205—funding-axed-for-toronto-immigrant-agencies

Keung, N. (February 24, 2011). Ontario offers relief to settlement agencies, *thestar.com*. Retrieved from http://www.thestar.com/news/article/944522—ontario-offers-relief-to-settlement-agencies

Ontario Council of Agencies Serving Immigrants (March 9, 2011). OCASI position on the CIC cuts to Ontario settlement funding. Retrieved from http://www.ocasi.org/index.php?qid=1072

PART 1

IMMIGRATION POLICIES

CHAPTER 1

A Race-Based Analysis of Canada's Immigration Policy

Avvy Go

Introduction

Canadians love the cliché that Canada is built by immigrants and believe that we have always had an open immigration policy. In reality, such a policy was applied on a selective basis. Despite its reputation as a humanitarian country, Canada has a troubling past when it comes to its treatment of refugees and immigrants, especially those who are racialized. Successive federal governments have enacted immigration and refugee policies aimed at deterring immigrants who are deemed undesirable (i.e., racialized and poor) while limiting the rights of those who are already here. While racism has always played a key role in the framing of Canadian immigration policy, those who are engaged in the issue are often reluctant to talk about race. An examination of contemporary immigration policy reveals the continuing presence of many barriers, both systemic and overt, that bar entrance into Canada for the majority of the world's population, especially from the so-called developing countries where migration is taking place on a large scale. And while Canada's future depends on the continuing inflow of immigrants to replace our aging population, their presence here is tolerated only in so far as they remain a source of cheap labour, without the accompanying unwelcome "baggage" such as their families and their claims on Canada's social safety net.

This chapter begins with an overview of the history of Canada's immigration law. It then proceeds to examine how, directly and indirectly, certain aspects of Canada's contemporary immigration policy continue to exclude and screen out "unwanted" immigrants.

History of Canada's Immigration Law

Despite its reputation as a humanitarian country, Canada has a deeply troubling past when it comes to its treatment of refugees and immigrants, not to mention the colonial root upon which this country was founded, a foundation that resulted in the colonization of the First Peoples in Canada.

Black immigrants arrived in Canada as early as the 1600s. Contrary to commonly held belief, Black slavery did exist in Canada for many years. Some of the slaves were brought here by the Loyalists migrating from the United States. While at one point Canada did offer land to Black Loyalists in exchange for their support for the British cause, the number of Black immigrants did not grow and in fact continued to decline from the late 1800s on (Milan & Tran, 2004). This was due in part to the fact that immigration of Black Americans was actively discouraged on the grounds that they were "unsuitable" for the climate in Canada – a tactic used until the 1960s to turn away applicants from the Caribbean and African countries as well.

The Chinese immigrants who came to Canada to build the Canadian Pacific Railway (CPR) also found themselves victimized by this country's racist immigration law. As soon as the CPR was completed in 1885, the government of Canada imposed a head tax of $50 to discourage Chinese immigrants from coming in. The racist head tax was increased to $100 in 1900 and $500 in 1903. When this measure did not stop the flow of Chinese immigration, the government of Canada enacted a series of Chinese exclusion acts, which effectively barred all Chinese from entering Canada from 1923 to 1947. During those 24 years, fewer than 50 Chinese were allowed to come into Canada (Li, 1988). Meanwhile, Chinese in Canada saw many of their civil, economic, and political rights either severely restricted or stripped completely, such as the right to vote, the right to work in certain key industries (most notably mining), and the right to enter various professions including law.

After the *Exclusion Act* was repealed in 1947, restrictions on Chinese immigration continued. Under an Order in Council, the only Chinese immigrants that were allowed were the spouse and under-aged unmarried children of Canadian citizens and permanent residents. In order to circumvent this harsh and racist immigration rule, many Chinese immigrants came to Canada as "paper sons," that is, men who claimed to be the sons of Canadian citizens or immigrants, either by buying the birth certificate of another person or circulating the same birth certificate among prospective immigrants. In total, about 11,000 Chinese paper sons came in during that era.

Chinese were not the only Asian immigrants who were unwanted by Canada. The "continuous passage" regulations was implemented in the early 1900s to prevent immigration from India by requiring that anyone who entered Canada must have come via a continuous passage from the point of departure. Yet when a group of about 200 Sikhs travelling on the Japanese steam liner Komagata Maru arrived at the Vancouver harbour on May 23, 1914 after a long and continuous journey, they were barred from entering Canada. The immigration officials did everything they could to stop the "brown invasion." In the end, all but 24 passengers were deported to India. Many of the laws that were enacted to disenfranchise Chinese were applied with equal force against Canada's First Peoples as well as other Canadians of Asian descent. While immigrants of colour faced decades of legally sanctioned discrimination, the Canadian government opened up the west to thousands of European immigrants. Land was given, for free, to many European groups so that they could settle in Alberta and the Prairies.

Certain groups of refugees coming to Canada hoping for a chance to save their lives were also turned away. During the height of the Second World War, a shipload of Jewish refugees attempted to dock on the shore of Canada in order to escape Nazi persecution. But thanks to an immigration officer who believed that when it came to Jews, "none is too many," these refugees were turned away and sent back to Germany, ultimately to meet their death.

With the reform of *Immigration Act* in 1967 and the introduction of a "point system" which was used to assess on a more objective basis the eligibility of an applicant to immigrate to Canada, it would appear for the first time that many of these racist and arbitrary policies were removed from our law books once and for all. But does that mean that our system has in fact become fair, equitable and above all open? Not so.

Current Immigration System at a Glance

It has been said that immigration law is one of the most complex areas of law not only because of the various rules and regulations that seem to be constantly changing, but also because it is based on categories of various

types of immigrants, each of which are subject to different eligibility requirements and conditions.

The current immigration system – not to be confused with the refugee
determination system – can be broadly divided into two main categories: the
independent class immigrants, and family class immigrants. Prior to June
2014, individuals could also apply under the investors program and the
entrepreneurs program. Both of these programs were terminated as of June
19, 2014, with the passage of Bill C-31, the budget bill, otherwise known as
the Economic Action Plan 2014 Act.

Significant changes have also been made to independent class immigrants. Historically, independent class immigrants were individuals who were
found to meet the so-called "point system" requirements. As stated above,
the point system concept was created in the 1960s to provide for more objective assessment of potential immigrants. Points were assigned to each application against a set of criteria which evaluate the applicant's age,
educational background, skills and work experience, ability to speak English
and French, and the catch-all category of "adaptability" to Canadian conditions. While the framework for the point system had remained more or less
unchanged for over 50 years, the points/weights given to each criterion were
in constant flux, as governments attempted to manipulate the system in
accordance with their stated priority of the day. In more recent times the
points for fluency in English and French had continued to increase to reflect
the greater emphasis on allowing in only those immigrants who could speak
one of the official languages of Canada.

Since 2012, the Federal Government has moved away from the point
system to more targeted programs to attract immigrants with certain skill set
(most notably language) and background. The 2012 federal budget eliminated the Federal Skilled Worker Program (FSWP). Applicants who applied
prior to February 27, 2008 were told, without prior warning that their applications would be terminated and their fees returned without interests.
Affected applicants unsuccessfully challenged the Government's decision
in the Federal Court. In total, about 280,000 applicants were affected by the
program's cancellation.

The Government brought back a new version of the Federal Skilled
Workers program in May 2014, with an overall cap of 25,500 applications
per annum, which includes a cap of 500 applications from PhD students.
There are also sub-caps of 1,000 for each of the 50 eligible occupations.
The caps do not affect people with a valid job offer. Meanwhile, other various
versions of independent class immigrants have sprung up like wild fire: the

Canadian Experience Class, the Provincial Nominee Program, and the Self-employed persons program, just to name a few. The Government wants to move towards a model initiated by countries like New Zealand and Australia, i.e., the "Expression of Interest" (EOI) model. It is based on the idea that employers will indicate the type of skills they need, while perspective immigrants with the matching skill set will be granted permanent resident status. While not yet law, the Canadian Government is taking step to transition into this new system which they hope to be in place by January, 2015. Once the EOI becomes law, private companies – not the state – will determine who Canada should accept as immigrants, and ultimately, who will become citizens of our country.

The last category, family class immigrants, is the one that is the subject of the most controversy. It is also the one category where race and racialization play the most significant role in the public discourse and in policy narratives. Historically, family class immigrants comprised a significant portion of the overall immigration population in Canada. The 1978 Immigration Act made "family reunification" one of the core objectives of the legislation. From that time on until about 20 years ago, the majority of the immigrants who came to Canada every year entered as family class immigrants. Since the early 1990s, however, the percentage of family class immigrants has steadily been on the decline. Currently, family class immigrants make up less than 25 per cent of all immigration to Canada. Increasingly, our immigration selection policy is geared towards the skilled labourers and professionals who come in as independent class immigrants, as well as semi-skilled and unskilled workers who enter with temporary work permits. By 2010, temporary workers have overtaken permanent residents as the main source of Canada's labour force.

Contemporary Forms of Exclusion

If we look at immigration policy today, there remain many barriers, both systemic and overt, that bar access to majority of the world's population, especially from the so-called developing countries, the very places where migration is taking place on a large scale. The following are but a sample of the systemic exclusions at play within the current immigration system.

Application Fees

Introduced as a budget measure in February 1994, the Right of Permanent Residence Fee (RPRF) (formerly known as the Right of Landing Fee) was imposed initially on all immigrants and refugees who applied to become permanent residents of Canada. This fee is charged on top of the application fee of $550, which each adult applicant has to pay. Bowing to pressure from refugee advocates and the public, the government of Canada removed the requirement to pay RPRF from refugees. Immigrants – regardless of their class and country of origin –continue however to be subject to the fee, which some critics have labelled the new "head tax." Initially set at $975 per head, the RPRF was reduced to $490.00 in 2006 by the Conservative minority government as a way to woo immigrants' votes. While immigrants are the only ones who pay the fees, the money collected goes into the general coffer of the Canadian government instead of being earmarked for services that immigrants need or to cover the operating expenses of the immigration system.

Even at $490.00, the fee has a harsh impact on immigrants from the developing world where that kind of money could well represent an average annual household income. Without the fund to pay the fees, an applicant will be denied the right to landing in Canada. In April, 2011, the Federal Court of Appeal dismissed an appeal by an immigrant who sought to challenge the $550.00 application fee although the court also confirmed that the immigration minister has the discretion to waive the fee requirement in "appropriate circumstances," whatever that means.

Visa Office Resource Allocation

While not as obvious as the other measures of exclusion, the inequitable resource allocation across the various visa posts also plays a role in perpetuating systemic barriers to immigration. On a per capita basis, there are far more visa offices in Europe than in Asia, Africa and any other regions of the world. Fewer resources mean more processing time in these regions even for those who are qualified. For instance, while it may take anywhere between one to four years for someone to apply as an independent immigrant from Beijing, China, an applicant with the same qualification could receive an immigration visa several months after he or she submits an application from, say, the Canadian Embassy in Germany. The unequal distribution serves as a control of, if not a deterrence to, immigration from the under-served countries.

Family Class Immigration

By far the most problematic provisions under Canada's immigration law are found in the family class category. The overall trend of the changing immigration pattern over the last two decades has been coupled with specific changes to the definition of "family class" in the regulations and in the processing of such applications by overseas visa offices over time. On the one hand, greater requirements are being imposed on those who wish to sponsor their families. On the other hand, "family class" immigration (with the exception of spouses) has become more and more narrowly defined. So for instance, while in the past, brothers, sisters, and other extended family members were given points for their relationship to a Canadian immigrant or citizen under the point system, today only those who are considered part of the nuclear family are deemed worthy of being granted entry. The age of dependent children have also been lowered as of August 1, 2014, from under 22 to now under 19. This change affects not only family class immigrants, but also other categories of immigrants as well as refugees who wish to bring their dependent children to Canada.

As well, increasingly restrictive financial eligibility requirements effectively bar many low income Canadians from sponsoring their families from abroad. Conveniently, because members of racialized communities and recent immigrants are more likely to live in poverty, the financial eligibility requirement also has a disproportionately negative impact on these communities. And because immigrants from Asia and other parts of the Global South are most likely to apply through the family class stream, and are also more likely than immigrants from European background to adopt an extended family structure, the reduction of the family class quota and the restrictive definition of family class membership have the added advantage – intended or otherwise – of limiting the number of immigrants from these countries. Thus the Canadian government manages to kill three birds with one stone with its redefined family class immigration policy.

The Canadian government's retreat from its commitment to "family reunification" is made most evident under the *Immigration & Refugee Protection Act* (IRPA). For instance, for the first time in our history, the law prohibits anyone who is receiving social assistance to act as a sponsor. Practically speaking, Canadians who wish to bring their families from abroad must also demonstrate that their loved ones fit into the definition of "family class members" and often they must also satisfy the visa officers processing their applications that the relationship in question is a "genuine" relationship.

A. *"Bona Fide" Marriage/Spousal Relationship*

Who are family members and is their relationship *"bona fide"*? On the surface, these are relatively straightforward questions with equally straightforward answers. In the world of immigration law, however, what constitutes

Case Study

Mr. Chen[1] is a citizen of Canada. His parents live in China. Mr. Chen came to Canada in 2002. He went back to China in 2009 to visit his parents. At age 29, Mr. Chen was still not married. His parents were worried that he would be lonely in Canada. They arranged for their son to meet with a young woman, Ms. Zhang. After a brief courtship, Mr. Chen proposed to Ms. Zhang; she accepted. Mr. Chen returned to Canada. Several months later, he went back to China to marry Ms. Zhang. After staying in China for several months, he returned to Canada to file an application to sponsor his wife. While waiting for the application to be processed, Mr. Chen returned to China several times to visit his wife. A year later, his wife became pregnant. Around the same time, Ms. Zhang received a notice from the Canadian visa office to attend at their office for an interview. The officer asked about their relationship. In the end, the officer decided that their marriage was not genuine and turned down Ms. Zhang's application to Canada. Mr. Chen filed an appeal to the Immigration Appeal Division (IAD) of the Immigration and Refugee Board (IRB). Almost two years later, the appeal hearing was held. By then, Ms. Zhang had given birth to their first child, who has since been granted Canadian citizenship because of Mr. Chen's citizenship status. But because the IAD still believes that the marriage was entered into for the purpose of immigration, the appeal was denied.

a "family member" defies one's common-sense understanding of the term. Moreover, the process whereby these applications are assessed is extremely complicated and exceedingly intrusive. With almost unchecked discretion, immigration officers are free to consider almost any factor in determining whether or not a particular relationship is "*bona fide*," that is, whether it has been entered into for the purpose of immigration. They have the power to ask the applicant any question and require the applicant to provide any information to prove his or her relationship with the sponsor. Just as troubling is the fact that the lack of guidelines and accountability means that the determination process is often fraught with prejudices held by officers making the decisions, many of whom do not share the same cultural, racial, social, and/or economic background as the applicants.

To assess whether a spousal relationship is *bona fide*, the officer often asks for information about how the couple met each other, how the relationship began, how often they communicate with each other, whether there was a wedding, who attended at the wedding and whether there were gift exchanges, and so on. The officer may also ask the applicant to demonstrate knowledge of the other spouse, or state the reasons why she or he decided to marry the sponsor.

While seemingly neutral, any one of these questions has to be assessed and interpreted by an officer who operates with his or her own sets of values, assumptions, stereotypes, and cultural norms. Sometimes assumptions are made about the specific culture of the applicant in question; at other times, they reflect the values that the officer holds based on his or her own upbringing or background.

The bottom line: Who is to say whether a relationship is "genuine," and more importantly, what is and is not a "genuine" relationship? In Canadian society, people get married for many reasons other than love: better insurance benefits packages, tax deductions, wealthy husbands, or trophy wives, just to name a few. Here, we allow competent adults to enter into marriage at their own risk for reasons others may find repulsive or morally questionable, and yet we zealously scrutinize the decisions of Canadians who happen to choose a non-Canadian for a spouse. We let visa officers intrude into the lives of these individuals, tear them apart, and place them under a microscope to be examined by the officers' sceptical eyes. And we do all that in the name of promoting family reunification. The result is a biased, intrusive, and frustrating process for both the Canadian sponsor and his or her loved ones overseas, a process that is made ever more frustrating by lengthy processing times and other delays.

Sometimes the process in fact becomes a self-fulfilling prophecy. While the spousal application is in process of being rejected, or as the process becomes so protracted that in the end when the reunification does take place, the marriage sometimes does not last since by then the couple would have been separated for a number of years. Against this backdrop, Canadians who want to sponsor their spouse must also contend with the growing public perceptions that many of these marriages are in fact fraudulent.

In 2010, the Minister of Citizenship and Immigration announced changes to the family class provision in the name of cracking down on so-called fake marriages. As of September 2010, the regulation on *bona fide* spousal relationships was redefined so that even when the relationship is proven to be genuine, the application can still be rejected if one of the purposes for entering into it is to help the non-Canadian spouse immigrate to Canada.

Further, as of October 25, 2012, the Government introduced "conditional visa" for immigrants who enter Canada as sponsored spouses. This new regulation imposes a two-year conditional probation on immigrants who were in a relationship with a Canadian spouse/sponsor for less than two years prior to their application and who did not have a child with their sponsor at the time of the application. As clearly stated in the Notice in Canada Gazette, the proposed measure takes aim at the so-called "marriage fraud" whereby the parties entered into the relationship for the immigration purpose. Yet the same Notice concedes that figures on "marriage fraud" are unavailable, and that not every refusal of spousal sponsorships is based on concerns about bona fide (Canada Gazette, 2011).

Victims of abuse or neglect may apply for an exemption to Citizenship and Immigration Canada (CIC). CIC has released Operational Bulletin 480 to provide guidance to officers on how to assess abuse. The guidelines recognize that there are various forms of abuse including physical, sexual, financial, and psychological. It also broadly defines neglect to include for instance, the failure to provide the necessaries of life, such as food, clothing, medical care, shelter, and any other omission that results in a risk of serious harm. The bulletin further recognizes forced marriage as an indicia of abuse, but it must still be accompanied by evidence of abuse during the two year period.

As many immigrants' advocates have pointed out, while there are no doubt cases in which the sponsor finds himself or herself duped by the person he or she has brought here, there are far too many situations in which the sponsored immigrant – most likely a woman –finds herself in a controlling and sometimes even abusive relationship after landing in Canada. Like most victims of domestic violence, sponsored immigrants often suffer in silence rather than seeking help – in addition to the added fear of losing their immigration status if they do. By characterising the issue as marriage fraud, the government has shifted attention away from the wider systemic problem of violence against women while at the same time fuelling the anti-immigrant sentiment that already exists in our society (Go, Sharman, & Balakrishna, 2011).

Prior to these series of announcements, the Minister of Citizenship and Immigration travelled to India and China to raise his concerns about fake marriages in those countries (Toronto Star: September 10, 2010) leaving little doubt which communities the minister believes are engaged in such activities. Thus, in one broad stroke, the minister has managed to paint an entire group of racialized immigrants as queue jumpers and cheaters who exploit Canada's generosity (even though these communities were presumably among the "very ethnic votes" targeted by the same minister as part of an election strategy). These accusations give the minster the added political mileage he needed to win votes without doing any apparent damage to the relationship he has been cultivating with the Chinese and South Asian communities over the years.

B. *Exclusion from Family Class*

Another barrier to the reunification of family members found in the regulations pursuant to *IRPA* concerns a section that prohibits the sponsorship of family members who were not declared at the time the sponsor submitted their own application to become a permanent resident. The failure to declare family members has resulted in further family breakdown. In particular, there have been a number of cases in which parents are prohibited from sponsoring their own children by application of provisions in the legislation.

Dependent children are sometimes not included on the original applications for various reasons. In some cases, parents give their children up to foster parents for care or for adoption; in other instances, because of strict policies regulating the number of children each family can have in their country of origin. Such is the case in China where the one-child policy is still being enforced. In such cases, sponsors upon arriving in Canada then attempt to sponsor their biological children who have been left in the care of family or friends. They, too, are prohibited from sponsoring their own flesh and blood because of their failure to declare these children in their original applications; essentially being penalized through no fault of their own.

Section 117(9)(d) of the *IRPR* is one of the harshest provision in the immigration legislation. In many instances, this provision has also been used to deny status to women who came to Canada from the Philippines to work as live-in caregivers. Many of these women did not declare that they were previously married and/or have children for fear that this would lead to a rejection of their own application. Not only would the family members not be allowed to come, but more importantly, the immigrants who had failed to declare their family member could face misrepresentation charges and be subject to deportation.

This provision disproportionately affects racialized communities. Yet if we do not consider the racial impact of these provisions, they could easily be justified by the government as a way of protecting the integrity of our immigration system. This provision also causes families to be torn apart, and forces parents to choose between staying in Canada or returning to their home country to look after the remaining family members. This further nega-

Case Study

Ms. Sun and her husband, Mr. Yang, came to Canada as independent immigrants. Both Ms. Sun and her husband used to live in Shanghai, and they both worked for the Chinese government. They have two daughters. But when Ms. Sun was pregnant with her second child, she went to a remote village to give birth out of fear that her work unit would find out about the pregnancy, which violated China's one-child policy. The second daughter was looked after by Ms. Sun's parents, and was not given a hukou (household registration). When Ms. Sun applied to immigrate to Canada, she did not list her second daughter in her own permanent resident application because she was afraid the Chinese government would find out. After Ms. Sun, her husband, and her eldest daughter came to Canada, Ms. Sun then submitted a new application to sponsor her second daughter. But the application was denied because Ms. Sun had not included this child in her own permanent residence (PR) application. In the meantime, in order to care for their daughter (whose grandparents are no longer able to look after her), Mr. Yang has to travel back and forth between China and Canada. Because he spends so much time outside of Canada, he is at risk of losing his own PR status. As well, the relationship between Mr. Yang and Ms. Sun began to deteriorate due to the forced separation, and their eldest daughter is exhibiting mental health symptoms due to strain and instability within the family.

tively impacts on the settlement process of the newcomers, which leads to economic and other social dislocations.

C. *Minimum Income Requirement*

Under *IRPR*, Canadian permanent residents and citizens who wish to be reunited with their families from abroad (other than spouses and dependent children) continue to be subject to a minimum income requirement imposed on family class sponsors. Prior to January, 2014, Canadians seeking to sponsor parents and grandparents were required to have an income which met the Low Income Cut Off (LICO). In addition, there is a provision under *IRPR* which bars persons in receipt of social assistance (for a reason other than disability) from being sponsors.

Case Study

Ms. Sharma was sponsored to come to Canada by her husband. They have two children. Although trained as an engineer in India, Mr. Sharma can only find general labour work in the manufacturing sector. Ms. Sharma, on the other hand, cannot work outside of home due to childcare concerns. She herself is a trained accountant and is hoping to return to the workforce to help support her family. The couple wants to sponsor Ms. Sharma's mother, a widow, to Canada, as she is getting old and is living alone. They also hope that by bringing the mother here, she may be able to alleviate some of the childcare burden on Ms. Sharma by helping her look after the children. But Mr. Sharma does not make enough money to meet the sponsorship requirement. And without the extra help, Ms. Sharma cannot work to boost their family income. Ms. Sharma has not seen her mother since coming to Canada several years ago, and her mother has tried but is unable to obtain a visitor visa to come to Canada.

Immigrant and refugee advocates have long expressed concerns about the financial eligibility requirement under the immigration law and its hindering effect on family reunification. With the above noted prohibitions under *IRPR*, there is a growing concern that family reunification will be beyond reach for those who are most vulnerable.

The minimum income requirement – together with the new provision concerning social assistance – remains one of the key barriers to the reunification of many immigrants and refugees with their loved ones. Because of systemic discrimination, immigrants and refugees are among the poorest in our society. They tend to be over-represented in low-waged, non-unionized jobs, and are under-employed relative to Canadian workers with equivalent experience. Recent studies have shown that the marginalization of immigrants has worsened over the years, and that, other things being equal, on average it takes an immigrant 15 years to reach the economic level of a person born in Canada. As over 75 per cent of all recent immigrants and refugees are persons of colour, they are also affected by racialization of poverty in that racialized people are over represented among those who live below the poverty line.

To make matter worse, after a two year moratorium on sponsorship of parents and grandparents was finally lifted on January 2, 2014, new criteria now apply to parents and grandparents sponsorship which require sponsors meet an income threshold of 1.3 times of LICO. As well, the period of the financial undertaking for parents, grand parents and their dependent is now extended to 20 years instead of 10 years. There is now a cap of 5,000 applications per year. Meanwhile, parents and grandparents who are subject to the 20 years sponsorship period will be barred from applying for such seniors benefits as Guaranteed Income Supplement, Spousal Allowance and Survivor Allowance, although they are still eligible to apply for Old Age Security once they meet the 10-year residency requirement.

Among immigrants and refugees, certain individuals face additional barriers to economic participation. Immigrant women, for instance, fare worse than immigrant men when it comes to labour participation and income earnings. Not only are immigrant women disadvantaged as immigrants, they also face systemic discrimination because of their gender. Single parents are also more likely to turn to social assistance to support themselves and their children, as many are unable to access the limited number of subsidized childcare spaces.

Meanwhile, the continuing denial of family reunification has taken a toll on recent Canadians, immigrants, refugees, and their families. For the families who do manage to reunite after years of separation, the delay in the processing time has too often caused family estrangement as the circumstances of family members change with prolonged separation.

While family reunification still remains in our law as a core principle of *IRPA*, the financial requirement and other measures taken by the government over time has eroded the fundamental rights of immigrants and refugees to be reunited with their families.

The Role of Settlement Workers

For many immigrants, refugees, and even naturalized citizens, community agencies are their first point of contact when they try to seek help, even when the problems they face are legal in nature.

It is important for settlement workers to be aware of the legal and related challenges faced by immigrants, refugees, and racialized communities in general. In the context of immigration law, settlement workers have the added burden of keeping abreast of the ever-changing rules and regulations, as changes are frequently brought in by the government as a response to real or perceived concerns of the public about "bogus refugees," "queue-jumping immigrants," and anyone who allegedly has "abused" the "generous" and "liberal" immigration policy of Canada.

Settlement workers must learn to adopt a critical perspective, one that is informed by an understanding of systemic racism and its permeating influence within the legal system. Immigration law, like any other areas of law, is a product of politics and as such can and is indeed often used as a tool to further goals unrelated to the stated objectives of the law itself.

Knowing that Canada's immigration law has a long history of being used to exclude, restrict and expel those who are deemed undesirable, while appreciating that even today the "undesirables" are still by and large members of racialized communities, is a lesson that settlement workers should take to heart. It is therefore up to all of us, including those who provide direct services to these target communities, to do what we can to advocate for a fairer and more equitable system, both in the context of immigration law and elsewhere.

Note

[1] All names in the case studies throughout the book are pseudonyms.

References

Canadian Council for Refugees (CCR). (n.d.). A hundred years of immigration to Canada 1900–1999. Retrieved from http://ccrweb.ca/en/hundred-years-immigration-canada-1900-1999

Develop your knowledge

- **After reading the case studies, reflect on the following questions:**
  1. What policy issues arise from these case studies?
  2. What are the implications of these policies for racialized communities in general, and racialized women in particular?

- **Can you identify other current immigration policies which may have a disproportionate impact on racialized communities?**

- **What role should settlement workers play in addressing racialized inequities in the Canadian immigration system?**

Citizenship and Immigration Canada. (n.d.) Home page. Retrieved from
     http://www.cic.gc.ca

Chinese Immigration Act, 1923, S.C. 1923, c. 38

Go, A., Sharman, A., & Balakrishna, A. (2011). Marriage of convenience.
     Retrieved from http://oppenheimer.mcgill.ca/Marriage-of-Convenience

Li, P. (1988). *The Chinese in Canada*. Toronto: Oxford University Press.

Immigration and Refugee Protection Act. R.S.C. 2001, c.27.

Metro Toronto Chinese & Southeast Asian Legal Clinic. (n.d.). Road to
     justice: The legal struggle for equality rights for Chinese Canadians.
     Retrieved from http://www.roadtojustice.ca

Milan, A., & Tran, K. (2004). Blacks in Canada: A long history. *Canadian
     Social Trends*. Catalogue no. 11-008. Ottawa: Statistics Canada.
     Retrieved from http://www.statcan.gc.ca/studies-etudes/11-008/feature-
     caracteristique/5018918-eng.pdf

Toronto Star. (2010, September 10). India vows to crack down on
     unscrupulous immigration agents. *Toronto Star*. Retrieved from
     http://www.thestar.com

Toussaint v. Canada (Citizenship and Immigration). (2011). FCA 146.
     (CanLII). Retrieved from http://canlii.org/en/ca/fct/doc/2010/2010fc810
     /2010fc810.pdf

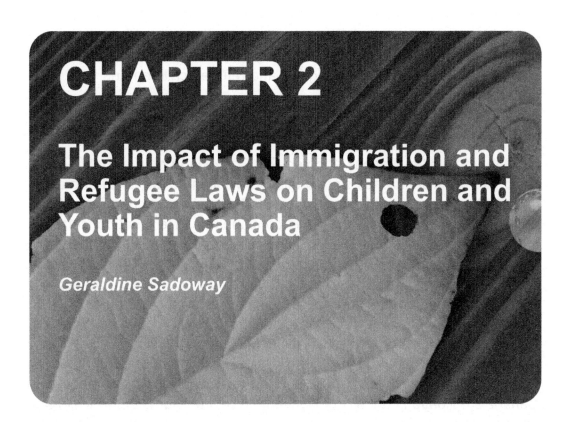

CHAPTER 2

The Impact of Immigration and Refugee Laws on Children and Youth in Canada

Geraldine Sadoway

Introduction

In this chapter I will describe the situation of immigrant and refugee children in Canada, and of children who are Canadian citizens but whose parents are immigrants or refugees. This is addressed within the context of international human rights documents such as the *United Nations Convention on the Rights of the Child* that deals with the rights of all children in the world, regardless of their immigration status. I will explore ways in which Canada has applied the principles set out in this Convention when dealing with immigration and refugee law issues. By providing case studies based on the work of Parkdale Community Legal Services in Toronto, I will show how these laws and policies affect children. The main goal of the chapter is to illustrate how Canada's failure to live up to its promises as the signatory of this Convention impacts the lives of immigrant and refugee families. This is explored through the review of the following policies: 1) family reunification; 2) separated children or unaccompanied minors seeking safety in Canada; 3) Exclusion from the family class; 4) sponsorship breakdown situations when the sponsored persons have "conditional" permanent residence; 5) separation of children from parents through deportation; 6) access to healthcare services; and, 7) access to education rights. From there, the chapter will draw attention to the existing social service programs that are geared towards supporting immigrant and refugee children and their families.

The Legal Framework for the Rights of Children

In 1989, the United Nations adopted the *Convention on the Rights of the Child* (CRC).[1] Canada has signed this Convention in 1991. At the present time, 194 countries are signatory to the CRC, however the conditions of children and youth throughout the world continue to cause great concern due to a failure of many countries, including Canada, to comply with the terms of this Convention. The UN Committee on the Rights of the Child has examined Canada's compliance with the CRC on several occasions, most recently in 2012.[2] The Committee has repeatedly recommended changes to Canada's immigration laws and policies to ensure protection of the fundamental human rights of all children living in Canada.[3]

In the current *Immigration and Refugee Protection Act* (IRPA), which came into force in 2002, there are clear provisions for compliance with Canada's obligations under the *Convention on the Rights of the Child* and other international human rights treaties. Several sections of the *IRPA* refer to the CRC principle of decision-making in the "best interests of the child." For example, section 25(1)[4] of the *IRPA* provides that with regards to a request for an exemption from any requirement of the Act or Regulations on "humanitarian and compassionate" (H&C) grounds, the Minister may grant an exemption "taking into account the best interests of a child directly affected" by the decision. However, Article 3 of the CRC states:

> In all actions concerning children, whether undertaken by public or private social welfare institutions, courts of law, administrative authorities or legislative bodies, the best interests of the child shall be a primary consideration.

On the contrary, section 25(1) of the *IRPA* does not acknowledge "the best interests of any child directly affected" shall be a *primary* consideration in making a decision affecting that child, and the courts in Canada have noted that the "best interests of the child" is one among a number of other factors to be considered.[5]

As evident, despite its commitment to the *Convention on the Rights of the Child*, on numerous occasions Canada has failed to protect the fundamental human rights of children directly affected by our immigration laws. This has caused long-lasting hardship to these children and their families, interfering with their successful integration into Canadian society. The following sections will detail these problems and further provide some recommendations in addressing them.

1. Problems with Family Reunification

One of the most important internationally recognized human rights is one's right to the protection of their family. According to Article 16 of the *Universal Declaration of Human Rights* (1948), "the family is the natural and fundamental group unit of society and is entitled to protection by society and the state." There are similar statements in the *Covenant on Civil and Political Rights* (Article 23) and the *Covenant on Economic, Social and Cultural Rights* (Article 10).

The *Convention on the Rights of the Child* begins with the following statements:

...childhood is entitled to special care and assistance,

...the family, as the fundamental group of society and the natural environment for the growth and well-being of all its members and particularly children, should be afforded the necessary protection and assistance so that it can fully assume its responsibilities within the community,

...the child, for the full and harmonious development of his or her personality, should grow up in a family environment, in an atmosphere of happiness, love and understanding.

Several specific Articles of the *Convention* set out provisions for protecting the unity of the child's family (Articles 7, 8, 9). Article 10 provides for family reunification to be accomplished in a "positive, humane and expeditious manner." With regards to refugee children, Article 22 provides as follows:

1. States Parties shall take appropriate measures to ensure that a child who is seeking refugee status or who is considered a refugee in accordance with applicable international or domestic law and procedures shall, whether unaccompanied or accompanied by his or her parents or by any other person, receive appropriate protection and humanitarian assistance in the enjoyment of applicable rights set forth in the present Convention

and in other international human rights or humanitarian instruments to which the said States are Parties.

2. For this purpose, States Parties shall provide, as they consider appropriate, co-operation in any efforts by the United Nations and other competent intergovernmental organizations or non-governmental organizations co-operating with the United Nations to protect and assist such a child and to trace the parents or other members of the family of any refugee child in order to obtain information necessary for reunification with his or her family. In cases where no parents or other members of the family can be found, the child shall be accorded the same protection as any other child permanently or temporarily deprived of his or her family environment for any reason, as set forth in the present Convention.

Recognition of the right to protection of the family is enshrined in the "objectives" of the *Immigration and Refugee Protection Act*:

- section 3(1)(d) provides that one of the objectives of the Act is "to see that families are reunited in Canada";
- section 3(2)(f) provides that one of the objectives of the Act, with regard to refugees, is "to support the self-sufficiency and the social and economic well-being of refugees by facilitating reunification with their family members in Canada."

These two "objectives" set out at the beginning of the *Immigration and Refugee Protection Act*, indicate the clear intention of Parliament to protect the right of new immigrants and particularly of refugees to be reunited with their families. However, despite this clear intention of the legislation, other provisions of the *IRPA* and the policies adopted by the government have compromised the rights of immigrant and refugee children to live with their families. We see this first of all in the very narrow definition of what constitutes a "family" for immigration purposes.

The "Shrinking Family Class"

The objectives of the *IRPA* which support family reunification are in competition with other objectives of the Act that focus on developing the economic benefits of immigration.[6] Increasingly it appears that the economic goals of immigration are being pursued at the expense of reuniting families in Canada. For example, according to the 2012 immigration department's "Facts and Figures," it is evident that although the actual number of immigrants has remained fairly steady at about 250,000 per year, the percentage of immigrants in the "family class" has decreased from 42% in 1994 to only 25%[7] in 2012. This decrease shows that family class immigration, which allows for reunification of families in Canada, is less important than economic immigration from the perspective of the government. The decrease of family class immigration will continue at a greater pace because of the recent change to the definition of "dependent child." Prior to 2014, a dependent child included children up to the age of 22, or older than 22 if they were still single and attending post-secondary school on a full-time basis. Since August 1, 2014, however, the definition of a "dependent child" is the biological child or adopted child **up to the age of 19**.[8]

There is a special provision that allows for a child over 19 to be considered a dependent child if he or she is "unable to be financially self-supporting due to a physical or mental condition." However, this is a "catch-22" because, if a child is dependent due to a physical or mental disability, that child may be inadmissible on health grounds. According to section 38(c) of *IRPA*, if the child has a condition which "might reasonably be expected to cause excessive demand on health or social services" the child would be inadmissible on health grounds. According to section 42 of *IRPA*, if one member of the family is inadmissible, then the whole family is inadmissible.[9] It is important to note that this inadmissibility under section 42 would not apply in the case of members of the family of a "protected person."[10]

The restrictive definition of the family class regarding dependent children means that some older children will be left behind when a family immigrates to Canada. Even though a son or daughter is over 19, they may continue to be emotionally and financially dependent upon their parents. However, they would have to qualify independently as immigrants in order to join their family in Canada. In the case of refugees, this restrictive definition of dependent child is likely to cause even greater hardship. The older children who are left behind may be in situations of danger, and this will affect the well-being of the entire family. Unlike the situation of immigrants who chose to move to a new country for economic reasons and can decide to immigrate according to when this is the best for their family, refugees flee to a country of refuge due to fear of persecution and they often do not have a choice about when they flee. They flee as soon as they can manage to do so and often refugee families are broken up at the time of flight to safety. In his report to the government on the refugee determination system in Canada, Rabbi Gunther Plaut made strong recommendationsfor laws that would facilitate family reunification for refugees. Rabbi Plaut stated as follows:

Refugees more than anyone else are people in need of roots. Roots are more than genealogical lineages, they are people, and particularly they are the constituents of a person's family.

It is important that we recognize the genuine refugee and accord such a person the status vouchsafed under the *Convention* and our law. But to do this, or to do this and be dilatory about family reunification, is to do only half the job, or to mix involuntary cruelty with voluntary kindness.

What the refugee needs equally badly and without delay is to be reunited with his/her family so that together they can take root in Canada.[11]

Case Study 2.1 – Exclusion from the "family class" due to age

Tsering and Tenzin are a Tibetan couple living in a refugee colony in Nepal with their three children who are now in their teens and attending school in the refugee colony. The parents are illiterate and they work as farmers in the colony to ensure their children go to school. But the children have no future in Nepal because Nepal will not recognize them as citizens and they are discriminated against by the government of Nepal and by some members of the local population. Tsering and Tenzin manage to travel to Canada, leaving their three children in Nepal, with the intention of bringing them to Canada if they are accepted as refugees.

The oldest of the three children, Dolma, is 19 when her parents leave and she is responsible for caring for the two younger children. The refugee process takes about two years to complete and when Tsering and Tenzin are granted Convention refugee status in Canada, they apply for permanent residence and include their three children. However, because Dolma was already 19 when Tsering and Tenzin applied for refuge in Canada, **she is no longer a "dependant"** and is excluded from the family class.

The younger children come to Canada to join their parents but Dolma is left behind in Nepal. The parents are terribly sad and worried about their daughter. Dolma is so devastated that she has become suicidal. The two younger children miss their older sister who was like a mother to them and they are angry at their parents for leaving Dolma in Nepal. Tenzin is so worried about her daughter Dolma that she can't

continued...

keep her job in Canada and she travels back to Nepal to care for Dolma, using all the family savings to make this trip.

Legal assistance

When the family seeks legal assistance at the community legal clinic, they are advised that the only way Dolma can come to Canada – since she does not qualify as a member of the family class – is through an application on "humanitarian and compassionate" (H&C) grounds. This process will take several years and there is no guarantee of success. If the application is refused, there is no appeal since it is not a sponsorship and the only option provided to the family is to apply in Federal Court for judicial review of the visa officer's decision. If the judicial review is successful, the application will be sent back for a new decision by a different visa officer.

Advocacy

The Canadian Council for Refugees (CCR)[12] treats family reunification as a very high priority and might intervene on behalf of this refugee family to support the humanitarian application of Dolma to join her parents and siblings in Canada. The CCR could also provide the family in Canada with referrals to CCR private sponsorship groups that may be able to assist Dolma to immigrate to Canada through private sponsorship if it can be shown that she is in danger in Nepal. Dolma's family in Canada can become a part of the CCR in order to share their experience and work with other refugees to convince the government to allow the family to be reunited in Canada on humanitarian grounds, and to change the law to respond more appropriately to the situation of refugee families.

Discussion of appropriate professional services for this family

Imagine Tsering and Tenzin are seeking support from your agency. How are you going to:
1. Inform family members about the restrictions in the law
2. Partner them with advocacy bodies such as CCR to become involved in the law reform

continued...

3. Refer them to legal and NGO groups to assist with their humanitarian application
4. Prepare documentation on the emotional and economic cost of family reunification – this evidence could be used in the humanitarian application and in the advocacy work to change the law
5. Support the family with the trauma of family separation

Case Study 2.1 illustrates the tragic result of treating refugee families in the same way as our law treats immigrant families. If the family were merely seeking to immigrate for economic reasons, they would do so when it was appropriate for the entire family to immigrate together and no one would be left behind. Refugee families are also more seriously affected by delay in processing that immigrant families, as the following case study illustrates.

Case Study 2.2 – Delay in processing family reunification applications and DNA testing to prove familial relationships

Ruth is a woman who survived the 1994 genocide in Rwanda. Her former husband, his second wife and several of her own children were killed in the genocide. Ruth raised and cared for her own two surviving sons and for the surviving three daughters of her husband's second wife. The two younger girls only knew Ruth as their mother. However, in 2002, Ruth came to know that some of the people who had killed her family members during the genocide had been released from prison and these people knew that she recognized them. She feared for her life and fled to Canada with the help of a religious group. She was granted Convention refugee status in Canada and immediately began an application for permanent residence, including her two sons, the three daughters and her grandson – the child of one of her daughters.[13]

The application was being dealt with through Nairobi, Kenya and was extremely slow due to a backlog of applications and insufficient resources. In the meantime, the situation for Ruth's children in Rwanda was becoming increasingly dangerous. Then Ruth received a request

continued...

to provide DNA evidence that the children were her biological children since she did not have birth certificates for the children. Many identity documents, such as birth certificates, were destroyed at the time of the genocide in Rwanda. The request for DNA[14] proof of relationship would cause a further delay and significant additional costs. But since the three daughters were not her biological children, Ruth also had to deal with the fact that the children might not be permitted to join her in Canada. She advised her lawyer that the three daughters were **not her biological children** but she had raised them as her own since the genocide and the two youngest did not even know that Ruth was not their natural mother.

Since Ruth had not carried out a formal adoption of the children, it was necessary for Ruth to obtain statements from members of the community where she had lived in Rwanda that these were her *de facto* adopted children. She also had to explain to the younger ones what had happened to their biological mother since it was likely that they would be questioned about this by the immigration visa officer. Ruth's lawyer requested that the non-biological children be permitted to accompany Ruth's sons to join Ruth in Canada on humanitarian and compassionate grounds since they were not her biological or legally adopted children.

The process took so long that Ruth's son wrote her a letter accusing her of abandoning them. Ruth's lawyer had to write to him to explain that Ruth was doing her best, that the lawyer was also doing everything possible to arrange for the visas, and that the delay was not Ruth's fault. Receiving this letter from her son was heart-breaking for Ruth as all she could think of and work for was the reunification with her children. In addition, she had been diagnosed with cancer and was undergoing painful chemotherapy treatments. She didn't know if she would ever see her children safely in Canada.

Help from the community

In this case the humanitarian application was successful and immigrant visas were approved for all the children. Then Ruth had to raise $8000 to pay the airfare for her children to come to Canada. Fortunately this money was collected by donations from lawyers and members of the church group that had assisted Ruth to come to Canada. When Ruth's children and grandson arrived in Canada, there was a celebration with

continued...

all the people who had helped them. Those same supporters helped to find a new apartment for Ruth to accommodate the family, and to ensure that all the children were appropriately placed in school. Ruth's two sons, then about 24 years old, quickly got jobs and began helping to support the family while studying at night to improve their qualifications. Ruth's grandson started school and soon became adept at computer skills. A used computer was donated by Ruth's friends and supporters so that he could practice his skills at home.

In an interview about a year after the children had arrived in Canada, they spoke about the period of separation while they were waiting to be permitted to join their mother in Canada. They described how they had to move frequently and take precautions to avoid the people whom they feared. Ruth stated during this interview that if she had known that the process would take five years, she would have stayed in Rwanda and died with her children.

Discussion of appropriate professional services for this family

Imagine Ruth is referred to you for support. How are you going to address the following:

1. counselling for Ruth, counselling for family members during the processing
2. advocacy to change the requirement for DNA testing to prove relationship (was this testing necessary and was it "in the best interests of the children" to show that their mother was not their biological mother?
3. advocacy to reduce the processing time for family reunification for refugees
4. advocacy concerning the serious costs involved in reuniting a large refugee family

2. Separated Children or Unaccompanied Minors Seeking Safety in Canada

There are many examples of children and youth who travel alone or with friends, separated from parents or legal guardians, to reach a safe place such as Canada in order to escape danger in their home country.[15] According to recent estimates, as many as 3000 children who are unaccompanied minors arrive in Canada seeking refugee status every year.[16] Sometimes the children are orphans, or have become separated from their parents due to war or civil unrest. Sometimes the parents, or one of the parents are the source of danger to the child. For example, some young people have fled from their home country due to abuse by a parent or relative. Children may be victims of illegal trafficking groups. Sometimes very young children are sent out of the home country by their parents with friends or relatives or with paid agents, in order to save the life of the child due to serious dangers facing the entire family in the home country. Although there is no single explanation for the fact that children are crossing international borders on their own, it is very clear that such children constitute an extremely vulnerable group of migrants that require special measures of protection.[17]

In the province of Ontario, if a child or youth between the age of 16 and 18 arrives unaccompanied by parents or guardians, the Canadian Border Services Agency (CBSA) contacts the Canadian Red Cross "First Contact" program.[18] Through this program the young person is referred to refugee shelters and other non-governmental services for refugees. Children under 16 arriving in Ontario would be referred directly to the Children's Aid Society. In fact, each of the different provinces of Canada has its own system for caring for children who are in that province without their parents. As a result there is inconsistency in ensuring immediate care and protection for this vulnerable population. The UN Committee on the Rights of the Child has repeatedly made recommendations to Canada to ensure that children arriving alone be provided with guardianship and social services in every province of Canada and that they should not be subjected to immigration detention.[19]

Canadian law provides for the appointment of a "designated representative" to assist any child or youth involved in a refugee or immigration hearing: this is set out in section 167(2) of the *Immigration and Refugee Protection Act*. The Immigration and Refugee Board (IRB) is responsible for appointing a designated representative (DR) for the child to assist them with their hearing.[20] For example, in Ontario the Immigration and Refugee Board has made an agreement with the law firm of McCarthy Tetrault and Pro Bono Law Ontario to provide lawyers from the firm to act as "designated representatives" for unaccompanied minors who have refugee claims in the absence of an appropriate guardian in the community to assist them. The IRB also has a list of potential designated representatives who can be appointed for this purpose. The role of the DR is to ensure that the child has good legal representation and that the child understands the process they are involved in. The DR can also be involved in helping to gather the evidence needed for the refugee hearing. However, the DR is only responsible to help with the hearing process and therefore provincial child welfare authorities and non-governmental charitable organizations are called upon to ensure the protection and care for the refugee child or youth.

Barriers to family reunification for unaccompanied refugee children

If a child is granted "protected person" status in Canada, s/he has a right to apply for permanent residence and should do so immediately.[21] However, unlike an adult who is granted refugee status, child refugees cannot include their parents or siblings in their application for permanent residence in Canada. Section 176 of the *Immigration and Refugee Protection Regulations* permits the protected person to include their "family members" in their application for permanent residence. However under section 1(3) of the *Regulations* a "family member" is defined as the spouse, the child, or the child of the child, of the protected person – not the parent of a child who is a refugee.

The only way that a refugee child can be reunited with parents and siblings in Canada is through an application by their parents to join the refugee child in Canada on humanitarian and compassionate grounds. After the child turns 18 and becomes an adult, she is legally entitled to sponsor her parents, but would have to be an eligible sponsor: i.e. no longer relying on social assistance and earning a significant income in order to ensure that she could support her parents and siblings in Canada.

Case Study III – Barriers to family reunification for unaccompanied minor refugees

Jacques (age 12) fled from Haiti to the United States with his mother Marie. They were living without legal immigration status in the United States and Marie was supporting herself and Jacques by working as a clerk in a store. Jacques was attending school and doing well. Then one day Marie was picked up by U.S. immigration authorities and taken to detention. She sent a message to Jacques to go to stay with friends. Marie was quickly deported to Haiti where she went into hiding. Jacques was taken to the Canadian border by his mother's friends. He crossed into Canada as an unaccompanied minor and made a refugee claim.[22]

continued...

At that point Jacques was 16 years old and still in high school. A designated representative (DR) was appointed for Jacques and the DR found a lawyer to represent him at his refugee hearing. Jacques was not eligible for Children's Aid Society (CAS) care because he was already 16: in Ontario, the CAS is only responsible for children up to the age of 16. However, he was able to get social assistance and there was a non-government agency (NGO) that gave him advice about where to live and how to attend school. Jacques' refugee claim was successful but he was very lonely and depressed without his mother. He had never lived on his own before coming to Canada and didn't even know how to cook for himself. He was shy about asking for help. At his school, his teachers didn't know anything about his personal situation.

Jacques was told that he could not do anything to bring his mother to Canada until he turned 18 and then he would be able to sponsor his mother. As soon as he was 18, Jacques filed the sponsorship papers to bring his mother to Canada from Haiti. He was helped by a community legal clinic that provided free legal services because this is a complicated process. Jacques was still in high school and relying on social assistance. He was no longer doing well in school because he didn't have the support of his mother and he was often depressed and lonely. He was still receiving welfare but after he finished high school, he got a job as a security guard so that he would no longer be on welfare. He also began taking courses at a community college so that he could learn some skills to be able to get a better job in the future. He was having a lot of difficulty trying to work and study at the same time.

The Minimum Necessary Income (MNI) for Jacques to be able to sponsor his mother was about $35,000. He was very depressed about the sponsorship application because he knew he did not qualify to sponsor his mother. His legal advisors made a request that his mother be permitted to come to Canada to join her son on humanitarian and compassionate grounds. The processing took three years. During that time, there was a terrible earthquake in Haiti and for several weeks Jacques did not even know if his mother had survived. Fortunately, she did survive the earthquake. However, Jacques' sponsorship application was refused because he did not have enough income to support his mother.

continued...

Appeal to the Immigration Appeal Division of the IRB

Since Jacques had been granted permanent residence after winning his refugee claim, he had a right to appeal the refusal of his sponsorship application for his mother to the Appeal Division of the Immigration and Refugee Board. The hearing process took about two years. When the hearing finally took place, Jacques was still not earning the MNI to qualify as an eligible sponsor to bring his mother to Canada.[23] Fortunately, the Appeal Board Member who heard his appeal was moved by his obvious distress at being separated from his mother and his continuing emotional dependency on his mother. Jacques' appeal was granted on humanitarian and compassionate grounds. It then took another year for his mother to get the visa to come to Canada and by that time, she and Jacques had been separated for about six years.

Discussion of appropriate professional services for this family

As a professional, how do you address the following concerns:

1. counselling and referrals to appropriate services for Jacques
2. advocacy for consistent and appropriate guardianship for all unaccompanied children upon arrival in Canada
3. documentation of the emotional impact on Jacques of the separation from his mother and lack of adequate assistance – this documentation could be used in the humanitarian application to bring Jacques' mother to Canada
4. advocacy with groups such as the Canadian Council for Refugees to change the law so that accepted refugee children can apply for family reunification
5. advocacy for special humanitarian guidelines to ensure that children can bring parents to join them if that is in their best interests

3. Exclusion from the family class under s. 117(9)(d)

Sometimes an immigrant's spouse or child becomes an "excluded" family member because the immigrant did not include their spouse or their child in their immigration application. Section 117 of the *Immigration and Refugee Protection Regulations* sets out in detail who is included as a member of the "family class" for the purpose of sponsorship to immigrate to Canada. Under the sub-heading of "excluded relationships" section 117(9)(d) provides that:

> (9) A foreign national shall not be considered a member of the family class by virtue of their relationship to a sponsor if...
>
> > (d) subject to subsection (10), the sponsor previously made an application for permanent residence and became a permanent resident and, at the time of that application, the foreign national was a non-accompanying family member of the sponsor and **was not examined**.

The purpose of this permanent exclusion from the family class of a person who was not "examined" at the time of the original application for immigration to Canada of the sponsor is to ensure that all the family members have been examined for admissibility as immigrants, even if all of the family members are not immigrating to Canada at the same time. If one member of a family is inadmissible for any reason, then the entire family is inadmissible to Canada.[24]

If a family member is excluded from the "family class" and subsequently wants to be reunited with the family in Canada, this can only be done through an application on humanitarian and compassionate grounds under section 25 of *IRPA*. This is a discretionary remedy and if the application is refused, there is no appeal available to the Immigration and Refugee Board. The only remedy is to request judicial review in the Federal Court. If the Court finds that the visa officer made a legal error in the decision, then the case is returned to a different officer to make another decision.

Why are family members left off the application?

There are various reasons why a member of the family of an immigrant or refugee might end up being excluded from the "family class" and then be separated permanently from family in Canada as a result. This can occur simply as a result of confusion about how to properly complete the form. Some refugees do not include a family member in the application if they intend to sponsor that person at a later date. In other cases, a child might be born after the immigration application has already been submitted and the immigrant may not realize the importance of correcting the application that is in process.

Case Study IV: Child excluded from Canada because of s. 117(9)(d)

John and Mary are a married couple in China. They have a daughter Linda who is five years old. They applied to immigrate to Canada in the economic class and have been granted visas. The application has taken several years and in the meantime Mary has another child, Donna. Since this child has been born contrary to the one-child policy in China, they do not declare Donna to the Chinese authorities although her birth is registered. They do not disclose the birth of this child to Canadian Immigration authorities because they are afraid that if they now include this second child in the application, their violation of the one-child policy in China will become known to Chinese authorities and this will cause problems for them. When the visa is issued, Mary, John and Linda travel to Canada leaving Donna who is now 3 years old with her maternal grandparents.

After they are landed in Canada they attempt to sponsor Donna but the sponsorship is refused because of Regulation 117(9)(d). Donna is excluded permanently from the "family class" because **she was not examined by an immigration officer at the time of her parents' immigration to Canada**. The grandparents who are caring for Donna did not expect to have the continuing responsibility of her upbringing and they rely entirely on John and Mary for support of Donna. Mary gives birth to a son Peter in Canada. The family travel to visit Donna regularly. She knows who her parents and siblings are and wants to go to Canada with them. They want to bring her to Canada but she is now excluded from the family class. The only way Donna can join her family in Canada is through a humanitarian and compassionate application.

Discussion of appropriate professional services for this family

How are you going to assist John and Mary's family with:
1. counselling for all the family members
2. preparation of documentation by social workers to show the

continued...

impact of the separation on the various family members: this documentation can be used to support the humanitarian application and for advocacy to change the law

3. advocacy for appeal rights to the Immigration and Refugee Board in the case of an exclusion under section 117(9)(d) because the judicial review procedure takes too long and is very uncertain

4. Sponsorship breakdown situations when the sponsored persons have "conditional" permanent residence

In October of 2012, a new regulation came into effect that makes the permanent residence of some sponsored family members "conditional" for two years after their arrival in Canada. The government made this change to protect sponsors from "marriage fraud." Marriage fraud is said to occur when a foreign national marries a Canadian in order to be sponsored as an immigrant to Canada in the family class, and then after arrival in Canada, they leave their sponsor. Under the new rule, if the sponsored person leaves their sponsor within two years of arrival in Canada, then they could face deportation from Canada on grounds that they did not comply with the condition and therefore the marriage is considered be have been fraudulent. If the sponsored person remains with the sponsor for two years, then the condition is fulfilled and they are now really permanent residents.

Many groups oppose this conditional permanent residence on grounds that it could place sponsored immigrants in a situation of danger. If they were abused by their sponsor, they might be afraid to leave the situation of abuse due to fear of deportation from Canada. In response to this concern, the government has issued policy guidelines for an exception to be granted if the sponsored person leaves the sponsor due to abuse.[25]

If the sponsored spouse has a dependent child who comes to Canada with her parent, then that child is also a "conditional" permanent resident for two years. The same exception should apply if the child leaves the home of the sponsor due to fear of abuse.

5. Separation of children from parents through deportation

As noted earlier, there are serious problems in achieving reunification of a family in cases where children are in their country of origin and their parents

Case study V: Sponsorship breakdown due to abuse of child

Michael travels to Ukraine where he meets and falls in love with Alexandra who is a single mother with a daughter Tina aged 15. Michael and Alexandra marry and Michael sponsors Alexandra and Tina to join him in Canada. At first everything is fine and Tina is doing well in school but a year after their arrival, Tina begins to show signs of anxiety and her grades are failing. She confides in a teacher that she and her mother are experiencing abuse from Michael. She doesn't want to live with him but her mother is afraid to leave because she and Tina have conditional permanent residence. Michael has threatened that she and Tina will be deported if they separate from him. Tina is also afraid that if she leaves on her own, she won't be able to support herself, She fears that if she gets social assistance, Michael will be angry and will hurt Tina and her mother if Ontario Works goes after him to repay the social assistance money.[26]

Discussion of appropriate professional services for this family

As a professional working with Tina and Alexandra, how are you going to help them with:

1. counselling about shelters and assistance to victims of domestic violence
2. legal referral for assistance with exception to conditional permanent residence
3. preparation of documentation confirming experience of abuse – to be used in getting the exception, and also to obtain social assistance for Tina or for both Tina and Alexandra, without endangering them by seeking repayment of the social assistance from Michael.[27]

are in Canada. Unfortunately, our immigration laws also cause the separation of children from their parents through deportation of parents from Canada.

All children who are born in Canada (with some exceptions[28]) have a right to Canadian citizenship just because of being born in this country. But if their parents are not Canadian citizens, these parents could be deported from

Canada either with or without their children. The children have no right to keep their parents in Canada. In some cases, the only way the child can continue to live with their parents is to accompany them to their home country. In doing this, the Canadian child would lose the benefit of growing up in Canada.

In general, a person facing deportation from Canada can make an application to remain in Canada as a permanent resident on humanitarian and compassionate (H&C) grounds. Section 25 of the *Immigration and Refugee Protection Act* permits exemptions from any requirement of the Act or the Regulations if there are humanitarian and compassionate reasons for granting these exemptions, "taking into account the best interests of any child directly affected by the decision." A humanitarian application can be made to permit the parent who is a foreign national to remain in Canada. In fact, it does not matter whether or not the child is a Canadian citizen: it may be that both the parent and the child are foreign nationals facing deportation from Canada. If they file an application for permanent residence on humanitarian and compassionate grounds, the officer who decides the case must consider "the best interests of any child directly affected by the decision."

However immigration officers who make these H&C decisions do not always have a good understanding of how to exercise their discretion in a way that gives proper consideration to the best interests of the child. According to the *Baker* decision of the Supreme Court of Canada,

> for the exercise of the discretion to fall within the standard of reasonableness, the decision-maker should consider children's best interests as an important factor, give them substantial weight, and be alert, alive and sensitive to them. That is not to say that children's best interests must always outweigh other considerations, or that there will not be other reasons for denying an H&C claim even when children's interests are given this consideration. However, where the interests of children are minimized, in a manner inconsistent with Canada's humanitarian and compassionate tradition and the Minister's guidelines, the decision will be unreasonable.[29]

6. Access to health care services denied or delayed due to immigration status

The *Convention on the Rights of the Child* is clear that all children, regardless of their immigration status, have a right,

Case Study VI: H&C decision in a case of deportation of a child's parent

Ellen came to Canada from Grenada because she was being seriously abused by her boyfriend. In Canada, Ellen gave birth to Sam. Ellen applied to be granted refugee status in Canada because she feared to return to Grenada where she believed her former boyfriend would continue to abuse her. Her refugee claim was not successful and she then filed an application to remain in Canada with her son Sam, on humanitarian and compassionate grounds. Before the decision was made on the H&C application, Ellen was called in by Canada Border Services Agency (CBSA) and advised she had to leave Canada. Ellen's son Sam suffers from serious asthma and Ellen's legal advisors asked CBSA to defer Ellen's removal from Canada until her H&C application was decided but this request was refused. Ellen arranged for Sam to get his Canadian passport and she took him back with her to Grenada because there was no one who could care for him in Canada.

Ellen was in regular contact with the community legal clinic handling her H&C application in Canada. She told them that she was having great difficulty finding work and could not afford the medications Sam needed. Several times Sam had to be taken to hospital in Grenada because of his asthma. The hot, humid climate aggravated his asthma and he could not be involved in sports activities at school. Ellen's legal advisors in Canada sent all this information about Sam's difficulties in Grenada to the immigration office in charge of the H&C application. Ellen had left Canada with Sam in 2007. In 2011, the legal clinic received the refusal of Ellen's H&C application. The legal clinic filed an application for judicial review of this decision on grounds that the officer had not properly considered the best interests of the child Sam in this decision. The judicial review was successful and in January of 2012, a different immigration officer reviewed Ellen's application and made a positive decision that she could return to Canada as a permanent resident. Since she had been deported from Canada, although she had paid her own way back to Grenada, Ellen had to obtain Authorization to Return to Canada (ARC) and her legal advisers assisted her in making this application. She also had to arrange for Sam's Canadian passport to be renewed which had to be accomplished through the

continued...

Canadian embassy in Trinidad. When everything was in order, Ellen had to seek assistance from a charity to pay for the airfare for herself and Sam to return to Canada. Ellen and Sam returned to Canada in 2014.[30]

In the Federal Court's review of the refusal of Ellen's H&C application, the judge stated as follows:

[63] When assessing a child's best interests an Officer must establish first what is in the child's best interest, second the degree to which the child's interests are compromised by one potential decision over another, and then finally, in light of the foregoing assessment determine the weight that this factor should play in the ultimate balancing of positive and negative factors assessed in the application.

[64] There is no basic needs minimum which if "met" satisfies the best interest test. Furthermore, there is no hardship threshold, such that if the circumstances of the child reach a certain point on that hardship scale only then will a child's best interests be so significantly "negatively impacted" as to warrant positive consideration. The question is not: "is the child suffering enough that his "best interests" are not being "met"? The question at the initial stage of the assessment is: "what is in the child's best interests?"

Immigration officers and visa officers continue to fail in applying the "best interests of the child" test in dealing with H&C decisions. In a recent Federal Court case involving the deportation of the mother of a Canadian child to Philippines, the immigration officer said that whether or not the child accompanied the mother to Philippines was "a parental choice." The Federal Court judge hearing this case was very clear that there was no real choice involved:

"[22] Regarding parental "choice," it was simply never a credible possibility that this single mother would abandon her daughter in Canada, no more than any responsible parent would abandon their child thousands of miles away."[31]

Discussion of appropriate professional services for this family

As professional how do you support the child whose parents are facing deportation:

continued...

1. counselling about effect of separation of child from parent, and of separation of child from other relatives and friends
2. investigation of available supports for child if child accompanies parent being deported
3. legal referral for assistance with humanitarian applications and judicial review of negative humanitarian applications
4. preparation of documentation to show effect of separation of child from parent or from home country
5. advocacy to improve immigration and visa officers understanding of best interests of child determination

to the enjoyment of the highest attainable standard of health and to facilities for the treatment of illness and rehabilitation of health (Article 24).[32]

Canadians pride themselves on universal access to health care free of charge, modelled on health care plans developed in New Zealand (1941) and the United Kingdom (1948). Universal health care was established first in Saskatchewan (1962) and throughout the rest of Canada from 1968 to 1972. Since health care is a provincial responsibility in Canada, there are variations of health care insurance plans across Canada, depending on the province in which the person resides. Yet access to universal health care is not ensured to all persons residing in Canada because it is affected by the immigration status of the person.

Since immigration and naturalization are under the jurisdiction of the federal government, historically the federal government has been responsible for the provision of health care to people in Canada who do not have permanent resident status or citizenship. Since the period following World War II, when Canada began accepting "displaced persons" from Europe and others in refugee-like circumstances, the federal government took responsibility for paying for the medical needs of these immigrants on a temporary basis. The financing of medical care for newly arriving migrants who were in refugee-like situations was provided under an Order In Council signed by the federal government in 1949 (OIC 1949). Subsequently, the OIC of 1949 authorized the Interim Federal Health Plan, which was available to persons seeking refugee status in Canada until they qualified for one of the provincial health insurance plans; or, if their refugee claim was refused, until they were actually removed from Canada. In June of 2012, the federal government passed a new Order In Council which drastically reduced the availability of health care insurance to many refugees, including children.

Health care professionals in Canada took the lead in challenging the OIC 2012: they formed Canadian Doctors for Refugee Care and worked with health organizations across Canada, NGOs and legal advocacy groups to take the government to court on grounds that the restrictions on access to health insurance coverage for refugees in Canada violated their rights under the *Charter of Rights and Freedoms* and was therefore unconstitutional. Justice for Children and Youth, a community legal clinic in Toronto, intervened in this court case and made arguments specifically drawing attention to the violation of Canada's international legal obligations to refugee children under the provisions of the *Convention on the Rights of the Child*.

In July of 2014, Justice Mactavish of the Federal Court found that the OIC 2012 violated sections 12 and 15 of the *Charter of Rights and Freedoms* and she ordered that the IFHP be restored to the way it was prior to June of 2012, to ensure health care protection for all refugees in Canada until they were eligible for provincial health insurance.[33] This was to take place on or before November 5, 2014 but the government has appealed the decision and applied for a stay of the order made by Justice Mactavish. The stay was subsequently refused by Justice Webb of the Federal Court on October 31, 2014.[34] However despite this the government has not fully complied with the court order. Although the government has agreed that all refugees who are children or pregnant women should have access to the IFHP, many refugees are still not covered by the IFHP.[35]

In the decision of June 4, 2014, Justice Mactavish concluded as follows:

[1080] I have found that the affected individuals are being subjected to "treatment" as contemplated by section 12 of the Charter, and that this treatment is indeed "cruel and unusual." This is particularly, but not exclusively, so with respect to children who have been brought to this country by their parents. The 2012 modifications to the IFHP potentially jeopardize the health, and indeed the very lives, of these innocent and vulnerable children in a manner that shocks the conscience and outrages our standards of decency. They violate section 12 of the Charter.

[1081] I have also concluded that the 2012 changes to the IFHP violate section 15 of the Charter inasmuch as it now provides a lesser level of health insurance coverage to refugee claimants from DCO countries in comparison to that provided to refugee claimants from non-DCO countries. This distinction is based entirely upon the national origin of the refugee claimants, and does not form part of an ameliorative program.

Case Study VII: Health care access to refugee children

Helen and Robert are members of the Roma minority group in Hungary. They have two daughters, Ana born in 2002 and Lilian born in 2003. At the time of Lilian's birth, Helen was coerced into signing a "consent" to have a tubal ligation so she would have no more children. Their daughter Ana was born with a congenital heart defect and Robert and Helen were constantly taking her to the heart specialist for treatment. Ana was given medications but no significant treatment and Helen and Robert were accused of trying to exaggerate their daughter's health problems in order to receive more financial assistance from the Hungarian government. In 2009 Helen and Robert sold all their belongings and came to Canada with their two daughters to seek refugee status because they feared that Ana would not survive with her heart condition and they also feared the worsening persecution of the Roma people in Hungary. As refugee claimants the family were eligible in 2009 for the Interim Federal Health Plan (IFHP) and they took Ana to see a doctor in Canada. Ana was referred to Sick Kids Hospital in Toronto and within a few months she had surgery to close the hole in her heart. She quickly became much healthier and stronger and she is now flourishing.

At their refugee hearing in 2012, the history of Helen's forced sterilization at the time of her daughter Lilian's birth resulted in the Refugee Board Member granting refugee status to Helen. But the refugee claims of her husband Robert and the two children Ana and Lilian, were refused as the Board said they suffered discrimination and not persecution. Helen included Robert and her two daughters in her application for permanent residence and in 2014, all four members of the family received their permanent resident status in Canada. At that point they became eligible for OHIP coverage.

Ana was lucky because when she arrived in Canada in 2009, she was eligible for IFHP and this covered the cost of her heart operation. If Ana and her family had arrived in Canada after June of 2012, Ana would not have received IFHP coverage because she came from Hungary which is now a Designated Country of Origin (DOC). Furthermore, since her refugee claim was refused, she would not have been able to get health coverage until her application for permanent residence as a dependent of her mother Helen, was granted. Ana was in

continued...

very poor health when she arrived in Canada in 2009 so her access to health care for the heart surgery may have saved her life.

Discussion of appropriate professional services for this family:

As professional how do you support the child whose family is denied health care:

1. immediate referral to health care and legal services involved in the access to health care campaign for all children
2. counselling about the importance of health care, including preventive care
3. investigation of available free health services: for example, most community health clinics in Ontario provide free health services for uninsured persons, and there is a network of health professionals who also provide services free of charge
4. advising the family that all hospitals are obliged by law to provide emergency life-saving health care treatment, even if the person does not have health insurance coverage or money to pay for the service. [The uninsured person will get a bill from the hospital later but if they cannot pay, the bill due to lack of income, the hospital must absorb the loss; if they are earning income, the hospital will make an arrangement for paying the bill gradually at a rate that is reasonable.]
5. counselling persons who have unpaid bills for medical services incurred when they were uninsured on how to negotiate with the health care provider for repayment over time.
6. documentation of the harm to the family of denial of health care services: their case could be included in the on-going case of the Canadian Doctors for Refugee Care.

7. Access to education rights denied or delayed due to immigration status

Another very important human right for all children, no matter what their status, is the right to free primary and secondary education, and fair access to higher education based on capacity. The *Convention on the Rights of the Child* states the following:

Article 28

1. States Parties recognize the right of the child to education, and with a view to achieving this right progressively and on the basis of equal opportunity, they shall, in particular:

(a) Make primary education compulsory and available free to all;

(b) Encourage the development of different forms of secondary education, including general and vocational education, make them available and accessible to every child, and take appropriate measures such as the introduction of free education and offering financial assistance in case of need;

(c) Make higher education accessible to all on the basis of capacity by every appropriate means.

The *Immigration and Refugee Protection Act* provides under section 30(2) as follows:

30. (1) A foreign national may not work or study in Canada unless authorized to do so under this Act...

(2) Every minor child in Canada, other than a child of a temporary resident not authorized to work or study, is authorized to study at the preschool, primary or secondary level.

However, education, like health care, is under the jurisdiction of the provincial governments so it is very important to look at the education laws in each province to find out whether children who are not citizens or permanent residents of Canada may attend school free of charge. Since many school boards in Canada want the extra money they receive from foreign visa students, they do not like to advertise the rights of all children living in the province to attend school free of charge.

The Ontario *Education Act* has a special provision to ensure that children living in Ontario without any legal immigration status in Canada have a right to attend school: According to section 49.1 of the *Education Act*,

49.1 A person who is otherwise entitled to be admitted to a school and who is less than eighteen years of age shall not be refused admission because the person or the person's parent or guardian is unlawfully in Canada. 1993, c. 11, s. 21.

The Minister of Education of Ontario also developed policy guidelines for the school boards in the province on how to interpret section 49.1 to ensure that parents without legal immigration status in Canada would feel safe about sending their children to school.[36] Furthermore section 49 (7) of the *Education Act* sets out all of the situations in which children who are not permanent residents and not in Canada without legal status, are exempt from payment of foreign student fees. This section makes it clear that children who are refugee claimants, applicants for permanent residence on humanitarian grounds, and the children of temporary workers, are entitled to attend primary and secondary school free of charge in Ontario.[37]

Case Study VIII: Access to school for children with precarious immigration status

Mariana fled from the war in Guatemala to the United States but did not have any legal status in the United States. She gave birth to William in the U.S. in and later in 1997 she fled to Canada with William where she applied for refugee status. Her refugee claim was refused but she then applied to remain in Canada on humanitarian and compassionate grounds. The case took a long time to decide but in about 2004, Mariana and William were granted approval of their humanitarian application. After that they were being processed for permanent residence in Canada.

In April of 2006 an incident occurred in Toronto involving four children who were living in Canada with their parents who had no legal immigration papers. Officials from the Canada Border Services Agency (CBSA) went to two different schools and arrested these four children in their classrooms in front of the other children. The children were taken to the Immigration Holding Centre and told that their parents had to turn themselves in to immigration before the children would be released. The children and their parents were deported soon after. This incident received front page news coverage across Canada. When the incident occurred in Toronto, William was about 14 years old. He refused to return to school, even though at that point he and his mother were soon to receive their permanent resident status. According to a Toronto Social Planning Council Study in 2009, the seizure of the 4 children from their schools in 2006 continued to cause great anxiety to children and their parents for years afterwards: http://socialplanningtoronto.org/wp-content/uploads/2009/02/right_to_learn.pdf.

continued...

> **Discussion of appropriate professional services for this family**
>
> As professional how do you support the child who is being refused admission to school:
> 1. immediate referral to community legal services involved in the access to education, particularly Justice for Children and Youth in Ontario
> 2. contact with school authorities on behalf of the children to explain the policies that exist to ensure that all children have access to school and question why children are being denied access
> 3. counselling about the importance of schooling for all children and documenting the effect of denial of access to school on the children
> 4. advocacy work with groups such as the Sanctuary City, to ensure that the schools are safe for all children:.
>   http://toronto.nooneisillegal.org/sanctuarycity

Conclusion

In this chapter I identified some of the significant problems affecting children who are refugees and immigrants living in Canada. Specifically, I showcased how Canada's immigration laws and policies are failing to respond adequately to the needs of this vulnerable population. There is need for advocacy and law reform to make necessary changes. Immigrant and refugee children living in Canada have great potential to integrate success-fully and to be a source of energy and strength to build Canada's future. To do this, they need recognition of the obstacles they face for successful inte-gration. And they need vigorous and committed support from the profes-sional communities in Canada to help them overcome the challenges they face and to celebrate their achievements.

Notes

1 United Nations Convention on the Rights of the Child; of the 196 coun-tries in the world today, 194 have signed this Convention: http://www.ohchr.org/en/professionalinterest/pages/crc.aspx
2 See UNCRC Concluding Observations on Canada, October 5, 2012:

http://rightsofchildren.ca/wp-content/uploads/Canada_CRC-Concluding-Observations_61.2012.pdf

3   Ibid. sections 71-74.

4   25. (1) Subject to subsection (1.2), the Minister must, on request of a foreign national in Canada who applies for permanent resident status and who is inadmissible — other than under section 34, 35 or 37 — or who does not meet the requirements of this Act, and may, on request of a foreign national outside Canada — other than a foreign national who is inadmissible under section 34, 35 or 37 — who applies for a permanent resident visa, examine the circumstances concerning the foreign national and may grant the foreign national permanent resident status or an exemption from any applicable criteria or obligations of this Act if the Minister is of the opinion that it is justified by humanitarian and compassionate considerations relating to the foreign national, taking into account the best interests of a child directly affected.

5   See *Legault v. Canada, (Minister of Citizenship and Immigration)* (C.A.), 2002 FCA 125, [2002] 4 F.C. 358 at paragraphs 12, 13, and 14: http://reports.fja.gc.ca/eng/2002/2002fca125/2002fca125.html

6   For example, *IRPA*, s. 3(1)(a) "to permit Canada to pursue the maximum social, cultural and economic benefits of immigration" and s. 3(1)(c) "to support the development of a strong and prosperous Canadian economy, in which the benefits of immigration are shared across all regions of Canada."

7   Facts and Figures: http://www.cic.gc.ca/English/resources/statistics/facts 2012/permanent/01.asp

8   Notice: Changes to Definition of Dependent child: http://www.cic.gc.ca/english/department/media/notices/2014-08-01.asp

9   *IRPA*, ss. 38 and 42. Currently "excessive demand" is calculated to be a likely cost to health or social services of over $6,327 per year over a period of 5 years.

10 A "protected person" is a person who is determined to be in need of protection in Canada, either because they are a Convention refugee as defined in section 96 of *IRPA* or because they are at risk of torture or death under section 97 of *IRPA*.

11 *Refugee Determination in Canada: A Report to the Honourable Flora MacDonald*, Rabbi W. Gunther Plaut, April 17, 1985. pp. 152-153.

12 Canadian Council for Refugees: http://ccrweb.ca/family-reunification/

13 According to section 176 of the *Immigration and Refugee Protection Regulations*, a "protected person" can include their "family members,"

defined in section 1(3) of the Regulations as the spouse, dependent child or child of a dependent child, in their application for permanent residence and these "family members" will be processed for permanent residence visas concurrently with the "protected person" in Canada.

14 According to immigration policy, DNA testing to prove relationship should only be required as a last resort if there is no other suitable proof of relationship. The Federal Court stated in the case of *M.A.O. v. Canada*, 2003 FC 1406, at paragraph 84: "I agree with the Applicant that DNA evidence is "qualitatively different" from other forms of evidence. **The intrusion into an individual's privacy that occurs with DNA testing means that it is a tool that must be carefully and selectively utilized**. The visa officer acted as if this evidence was the only way under the former Act that the Applicant could prove his relationship to his children, instead of regarding it as one of several ways that the Applicant could establish his familial relationship to his children." Despite this strong statement by the Court, reflected in the immigration policy manual, Canadian visa officers continue to request DNA testing, particularly in cases of refugees where the applicants do not have birth certificates issued at the time of the child's birth. This causes increased costs and serious delay and may also cause irreparable harm to children and families in situations where unexpected non-paternity is discovered through DNA testing.

15 *Unaccompanied/Separated Children Seeking Refugee Status in Ontario: A Review of Documented Policies and Practices*, M.A. Ali et al, CERIS Working Paper Series, August 2003: http://ceris.metropolis.net/Virtual%20Library/Demographics/CWP27_Ali.pdf

16 T*oronto Star*, "Program helps 'unaccompanied minors' navigate Canada's refugee process" David ays, August 17, 2013: http://www.thestar.com/news/insight/2013/08/17/program_helps_unaccompanied_minors_navigate_canadas_refugee_process.html

17 An excellent new book dealing with children travelling across borders to seek safety and security has recently been published:Jacqueline Bhabha, *Child Migration and Human Rights in a Global Age*, Princeton University Press, 2014.

18 Canadian Red Cross First Contact: http://www.redcross.ca/what-we-do/migrant-and-refugee-services/first-contact/

19 See UNCRC Concluding Observations on Canada, October 5, 2012: http://rightsofchildren.ca/wp-content/uploads/Canada_CRC-Concluding-Observations_61.2012.pdf / Paragraphs 73-74.

20 See IRB guidelines: http://www.irb-cisr.gc.ca/Eng/BoaCom/references/

LegJur/Pages/GuideIdSi07.aspx

21 There is a processing fee of $550 to submit this application and this fee can be a serious problem for the child or youth if they are still attending school and relying on social assistance. Our office has asked the Children's Aid Society, or Community and Social Services to pay this application fee in certain cases.

22 According to the *Safe Third Country Agreement* (2004) between Canada and the United States, Marie and Jacques could not make a refugee claim in Canada together because technically they could have made a refugee claim in the United States – even though Haitians are not usually accepted as Convention refugees in the United States. However there is an exception that allows a child who is living in the United States without his or her parents or guardians, to be permitted to claim refugee status in Canada. Thus when Marie was deported to Haiti, Jacques was able to come to Canada to apply for refugee status because of this exception for unaccompanied refugee children.

23 In fact, Jacques was working 30 hours a week (at night, and on the weekend) as a security guard at minimum wage, while he was attending community college full time.

24 *Immigration and Refugee Protection Act*, s. 42: A foreign national, other than a protected person, is inadmissible on grounds of an inadmissible family member if, (a) their accompanying family member or, in prescribed circumstances, their non-accompanying family member is inadmissible; or (b) they are an accompanying family member of an inadmissible person.

25 Operational Bulletin 480 of June 2014: http://www.cic.gc.ca/english/resources/manuals/bulletins/2012/ob480.asp

26 A sponsor must sign an "undertaking" to provide fully for the sponsored spouse for three years and for any children of the sponsored spouse for 10 years or up to the age of 25, whichever comes first. If the sponsored person receives social assistance during the period of the sponsorship undertaking, the sponsor must repay every cent to the government.

27 See the Ontario Works Policy Directive 3.11 Sponsored Immigrants, for details: http://www.mcss.gov.on.ca/documents/en/mcss/social/directives/ow/0311.pdf

28 Children born in Canada to foreign diplomats temporarily living in Canada do not gain Canadian citizenship by birth as they have the citizenship of their parents.

29 *Baker v. Canada (MCI)*, [1999] 2 S.C.R. 817 at par. 75.

30 See the case of *Williams v. Canada (MCI)* 2012 FC 166.

31 See *Bautista v. Canada (MCI)* 2014 FC 1008.

32 CRC Article 24: http://www.ohchr.org/en/professionalinterest/pages/crc.aspx

33 *Canadian Doctors for Refugee Care, et al v. AG of Canada and MCI,* 2014 FC 651: http://decisions.fct-cf.gc.ca/fc-cf/decisions/en/72437/1/document.do

34 *AG of Canada and MCI v. Canadian Doctors et al* 2014 FCA 252: http://www.cfpc.ca/uploadedFiles/Publications/_PDFs/FedCourt_of_Appeal_Docket_A-407-14_Reasons_20141031-1.pdf

35 Canadian Doctors for Refugee Care and other groups have filed a motion in the Federal Court seeking an order from the Court for the government to immediately comply with the Order of Justic Mactavish.

36 Policy 136: http://www.edu.gov.on.ca/extra/eng/ppm/136.html

37 *Ontario Education Act,* s. 49 (7): http://www.e-laws.gov.on.ca/html/statutes/english/elaws_statutes_90e02_e.htm#BK58

CHAPTER 3

Sexual Minorities, Migration, and the Remaining Boundaries of Canadian Immigration and Refugee Laws

Nicole LaViolette

Develop your knowledge – Ask yourself

The situation of lesbian, gay, bisexual and transgender Canadians has dramatically improved over the last several decades. LGBT Canadians have, for the most part, the same legal rights as all Canadians, including the protection of the *Canadian Charter of Rights and Freedoms* and other federal and provincial human rights legislation. Since 2005, Canada has offered civil marriage rights nationwide to same-sex couples. Social attitudes towards the LGBT community have also improved. In many of Canada's major cities, there are vibrant gay and lesbian communities, neighbourhoods and events.

Given the legal and social progress described above, do you think that LGBT immigrants and refugees encounter any general or specific barriers when migrating and settling in Canada?

Introduction

C anadian immigration and refugee laws have historically discriminated against gay men, lesbians, bisexuals, and transgender individuals (LGBT). Until 1977, homosexuals were listed in the categories of persons to be excluded from Canada along with "prostitutes...pimps, or persons coming to Canada for these or any other immoral purposes" (Immigration Act, R.S.C. 1952, c. 325, s. 19(1)). Gay men and lesbians could not enter Canada as visitors; they could not come to Canada as immigrants seeking permanent residence; and gay men and lesbians who managed to enter into Canada were subject to deportation. Even after the most egregious provisions were repealed in 1977 and gay men and lesbians were no longer barred from entering the country, Canadian immigration law continued to allow only heterosexual Canadians to sponsor their spouses as family class immigrants. Moreover, when individuals fleeing persecution based on sexual orientation or gender identity began to seek refugee status in Canada in the early 1990s, some members of the Immigration and Refugee Board (IRB) rejected their claims based on religious and moral considerations. For instance, a refugee claim by a gay Polish man was rejected on the grounds that, in the view of the adjudicators, the Universal Declaration on Human Rights recognized heterosexuality as the "very foundation of society," and homosexuality was considered clearly incompatible with this established order (Re X. (J.K.) [1992] C.R.D.D. No. 348 (QL)).

To be sure, Canadian immigration and refugee law has evolved significantly in the last twenty-five years. Reform of immigration legislation has removed the bar to sponsoring gay and lesbian partners, and Canada now has some of the most LGBT friendly immigration laws in the world. Refugee law has also evolved to include protection for individuals fleeing persecution based on sexual orientation and gender identity. As a result of this progress, Canada has become an exceedingly desirable destination for many gay, lesbian, bisexual, and transgender immigrants and refugees. For many LGBT refugees and immigrants, settlement in Canada provides the relative protection of a tolerant society and results in improved civil rights and relationship recognition. However, as this chapter will outline, sexual minorities continue to encounter a specific set of challenges when they migrate to and then settle in Canada.

LGBT Migration

There are three primary ways for LGBT refugees and immigrants to settle in Canada. First, when LGBT individuals are facing persecution and are able to travel to Canada, they may make an application for refugee status through Canada's inland refugee determination program. Second, if LGBT refugees are outside Canada, they may be sponsored by government, community groups, or private individuals for resettlement in Canada. Finally, binational same-sex couples can obtain permanent resident status through family sponsorship. Each process will be examined in turn, followed by a discussion of the particular challenges that confront LGBT refugees and immigrants to Canada.

Inland Refugee System

When Kureishi, a gay man from Pakistan, left his home country, he did so in a hurry. He had been arrested and sexually assaulted by the police. His boyfriend Farouk had died in mysterious circumstances. Kureishi knew that Farouk had been sexually assaulted by political opponents a few days before his death. But according to Kureishi, "The police said Farouk shot himself and he left a letter stating that he loved me." The police raided Kureishi's home, arrested him, and told his parents that he was a homosexual. As a result, Kureishi's family considered him a source of shame and dishonour. Upon release, Kureishi changed his name, in part because his family disowned him, and in part to protect himself. Terrified he would be arrested again, Kureishi bought a false passport and made his way to the United Kingdom and then finally to Canada, where he applied for refugee status with the Immigration and Refugee Board.

As Kureishi's story demonstrates, the human rights situation of sexual minorities around the world continues to be alarming. Many countries maintain severe criminal penalties for consensual sex between persons of the same sex, including the death penalty.[1] Sexual minorities also are frequent targets of hate crimes. In several countries, restrictions have been imposed on the freedoms of expression and association of sexual minorities, while in others homosexuality and transexuality are perceived as Western phenomena, or as anti-revolutionary behaviours, crimes against religion, sexually deviant and immoral behaviours, mental disorders, or unacceptable challenges to gender-specific roles.

Egregious human rights violations have compelled some lesbian, gay, bisexual, and transgender people like Kureishi to seek refuge in countries with better human rights protection. This movement has led several states to extend refugee protection to women and men fleeing persecution based on their sexual orientation or gender identity. In the last twenty-five years, decision-makers in countries such as the United States, Canada, New Zealand, Australia, and in several European states have granted refugee status to individuals who fear persecution based on their sexual orientation or gender identity. In Canada, the first reported refugee claim based on sexual orientation dates back to 1991 (Re R. (U.W.) [1991] C.R.D.D. No. 50 (QL)).

The international community codified the rights and status of refugees in two international instruments: the 1951 UN Convention Relating to the Status of Refugees (the Convention) (189 U.N.T.S. 150, entered into force April 22, 1954), and the 1967 Protocol Relating to the Status of Refugees (16 December 1967, 606 U.N.T.S. 267, Can. T.S. 1969 No. 6 [entered into force: 4 October 1967]). By signing the Convention and its Protocol, Canada accepted the primary obligation that flows from the international instrument, which mandates that signatory states will not return any individual to a territory where his or her life or freedom would be threatened. Indeed, Canada has adopted legislation, the Immigration and Refugee Protection Act (S.C. 2001, c. 27.) to implement its international obligations. However, the legal responsibility to provide protection applies only if a person meets the definition of a refugee as provided for in the Convention. Persons seeking asylum must satisfy two main legal tests: first, they must demonstrate a well-founded fear of persecution; and second, they must substantiate that the persecution they fear is on account of their race, religion, nationality, political opinion, or membership in a particular social group. In addition, refugee protection is conferred only if the claimant succeeds in showing that the country of nationality or habitual residence is unwilling or unable to offer protection.

Being a member of a sexual minority has been recognized as a basis for refugee status in Canada, mainly on the grounds that members of these minorities, as members of a particular social group, are persecuted. A Supreme Court decision in 1992 confirmed this approach when it found that sexual orientation and gender constitute the basis of particular social groups as defined in the Convention (Canada (Attorney General) v. Ward, [1993] 2 S.C.R. 689, rev'g [1990] 2 F.C. 667, aff'g (1988), 9 Imm. L.R. (2d) 48). Since then, the Immigration and Refugee Board, the administrative tribunal responsible for deciding refugee claims, has recognized that LGBT claimants can base their fear of persecution on their membership in a particular social group. Indeed, thousands of LGBT individuals like Kureishi have applied for refugee status in Canada.

Resettlement from Outside Canada

When anti-gay hysteria erupted in Uganda, Ayesha was forced to flee the country. Prominent Christian pastors were actively calling for the elimination of homosexuality in the country and the Ugandan Parliament was debating a bill that would impose the death penalty on gay men and lesbians. Terrified by the violent rhetoric, many in the gay and lesbian community went further underground. Ayesha did the opposite. She wrote essays defending her community and submitted them to local newspapers: "They were saying that we were destroying African culture, so I wanted to educate people that gay and lesbian people, we are African people, we are here." One night, armed men kidnapped and brutally assaulted her. She fled across the Kenyan border, but she felt unsafe in the refugee camp to which she was sent by Kenyan authorities. She was surrounded by other refugees with many of the same strict social and religious views she had encountered in Uganda. Ayesha befriended a Canadian refugee worker who encouraged her to seek resettlement in Canada. While the refugee worker offered to help investigate sponsorship options for her, she warned Ayesha that the average processing time for applications at the Canadian embassy in Nairobi was five years.

As with the majority of refugees in this world, LGBT refugees like Ayesha are rarely able to travel to countries where they can make inland refugee claims. According to the United Nations High Commissioner for Refugees (UNHCR), more than 80 per cent of the world's refugees are languishing in developing countries where most are not safe and have no possibility of integration. In 2010, the UNHCR estimated that over the next three to five years more than 805,000 refugees will need to be resettled in countries that are safe and provide a durable solution for displaced individuals (UNHCR, 2010).

LGBT refugees form a fraction of those numbers, and when they flee to countries like Turkey, Kenya, and Egypt, their temporary place of "asylum" is often as homophobic and dangerous as the country from which they fled. In fact, LGBT individuals are often among the most vulnerable asylum seekers and refugees. In addition to the many challenges facing refugees, LGBTs face the common and pervasive intolerance for sexual minorities that exist in most countries to which they flee (Helsinki Citizens Assembly, 2011). As a result, they are often in need of being expeditiously resettled to safe third countries like Canada.

Canada does operate the Refugee and Humanitarian Resettlement Program (RHRP) for people from outside Canada seeking protection. It is estimated that Canada resettles between 10,000 to 12,000 refugees through the two existing streams of the program, the government-assisted and privately sponsored refugee programs. Government-assisted refugees are individuals whose initial resettlement in Canada is entirely supported by the government of Canada. The resettlement of privately sponsored refugees on the other hand is supported by groups of private individuals or by civil society organizations (CSOs) in Canada.

Until recently, LGBT refugees have not benefitted significantly from Canadian resettlement programs. In 2010, then federal Immigration Minister Jason Kenney stated that he had been approached to help Iranian LGBT refugees who had to flee to Turkey. Kenney stated that "we do what we can on a limited basis," but he urged LGBT communities in Canada "to step up" and help LGBT refugees in a more organized fashion, through private and community resettlement programs (Canadian Broadcasting Corporation, 2010). The call to sponsor LGBT refugees has also come from advocates like Vancouver refugee lawyer Rob Hugues, who said:

> We need to look ... at sponsorship programs that can help ... resettle [LGBT refugees] ... That's where we can be more active in the LGBTQ community. All it takes is a group of five individuals to bring them here and provide them with one year of assistance… Organizations that hold a sponsorship agreement with the federal government, churches and religious organizations are also possibilities.

Interest in the resettlement programs has increased significantly since 2010. Individuals from LGBT communities and refugee settlement agencies in Vancouver, Winnipeg, Toronto, Halifax, and Ottawa have now been actively involved in sponsoring LGBT refugees. In March 2011, the federal government announced that it would partner with the Rainbow Refugee Committee, a LGBT refugee advocacy group based in Vancouver, to provide up to $100,000 over three years to help settle gay and lesbian refugees in Canada (Smith, 2011a). The funds, which were renewed for a fourth year in 2014, provide three months of income support for each refugee, while the sponsoring organizations provides refugees with orientation services, accommodation, basic household needs, basic food staples, clothing, and ongoing food needs for the duration of the sponsorship period. These developments are encouraging, but LGBT refugees like Ayesha still face significant hurdles; they have to come out in homophobic environments and face both excessively long processing times and quotas on the number of resettlement applications (Smith, 2011b).

Immigration in the Family Class

Morgan, a student at the University of Manitoba, is anxious to be reunited with her partner Adriana. They met and fell in love when Morgan worked in the northern Mexican city of Ciudad Juárez. Morgan was researching the maquiladora manufacturing industry as part of her doctoral thesis. For the last eight months, Morgan has been travelling back and forth to spend time with Adriana, but this is proving to be expensive and stressful for both women. Adriana has not been able to obtain the necessary permission to travel to Manitoba since the Canadian government imposed a visa require-ment in 2009 on Mexican nationals. Adriana suspects that her applications for a visa are denied because she lives in a town with a high level of gang and drug violence. Canada has stated it wants to reduce the number of Mexican nationals who make refugee claims and Adriana is convinced they think she will make such a claim if she travels to Canada. The couple have been planning to wed, which would allow Morgan to sponsor Adriana to immigrate as her spouse under Canadian immigration laws, but they face a conundrum: getting married would only be possible in Canada, as the state of Chihuahua does not allow for same-sex marriage. Morgan wonders if she could sponsor Adriana as her partner without getting married, but they have not been able to cohabit for a year as common law spouses, and they worry about providing the necessary documentation to prove their commitment is legitimate.

The recognition of LGBT family ties like those of Morgan and Adriana continues to be denied under the laws of a majority of states. Indeed, lesbians and gay men around the world are discriminated against and cannot sponsor their spouses or partners for reunification through immigration laws. In addition, only a minority of states allow same-sex couples to marry; marriage usually facilitates a non-citizen's application to immigrate and remain in a country as a member of a family class. There are, however, close to thirty-five states that have now modified their immigration laws to allow the sponsoring of a same-sex partner for immigration purposes. This includes countries like Australia, South Africa, Iceland, the United Kingdom, Belgium, Brazil, and, since 2002, Canada.

Family reunification has long been a cornerstone of Canadian immigra-tion policy. Indeed, successive laws have allowed citizens and permanent residents to sponsor members of their family as "family class immigrants" and this category constituted an important part of historical and current immi-gration to Canada. However, until 2002, Canadian immigration laws allowed only married, heterosexual Canadians to sponsor their spouses as family class immigrants. The definitions related to conjugal relationships, terms such as "spouse," "fiancé(e)," or "marriage," historically referred only to opposite-sex couples.

This discrimination ended on June 28, 2002, when the Immigration and Refugee Protection Act (S.C. 2001, c. 27) and the Immigration and Refugee Protection Regulations (S.O.R./2002-227) came into effect. The law and regulations have expanded the family class to incorporate common law and conjugal partners in addition to married spouses. Included in these new provisions are gay and lesbian couples. For the first time in Canadian immigration history, gay men and lesbians were now able to formally sponsor their partners.

As a result, same-sex couples who are married or have been in a common law or conjugal relationship are eligible for sponsorship under the Family Class. Common-law partners are defined as conjugal partners who have been living together for at least one year. Common law partners may also include individuals who are in a conjugal relationship for at least one year who are unable to cohabit due to persecution or any form of penal control. Canadian citizens or permanent residents are also permitted to sponsor a foreign national who is their "conjugal partner," a category created to deal with exceptional circumstances where the couple are unable to live together continuously for one year because of an immigration impediment. The "conjugal partner" category might eventually be an avenue for an application by Morgan to sponsor Adriana. Whether an individual is sponsoring a married, common law or conjugal same-sex partner, they must be in a bona fide conjugal relationship for at least one year. Finally, if neither partner of a binational same-sex married or common-law couple is a Canadian citizen or permanent resident of Canada, it may be possible for one to qualify under the Canadian skilled worker category and for the other to apply as a dependent spouse.

Specific Challenges Facing LGBT Refugees and Immigrants

While Canadian laws and programs have been reformed to confer refugee protection and immigration rights to LGBT individuals, sexual minorities nonetheless encounter a specific set of problems during their migration and settlement in Canada. While the full range of legal and social difficulties encountered by sexual minority migrants cannot be covered in this chapter, the following section will highlight some of the most significant challenges facing LGBT refugees and immigrants.

Prejudice Against LGBT

Homosexuality and transexuality remain controversial topics for many Canadians. While the lives of Canadian LGBTs have significantly improved in the last few decades, the level of discrimination, homophobia and violence remains considerable. Many Canadians continue to hold strong views against homosexuality and transexuality. Given this context, there continues to be legitimate concerns that LGBT refugees and immigrants could encounter prejudice and hostility as they navigate the many stages of the migration process. Indeed, when individuals apply for refugee status or to immigrate to Canada, they will have to interact with a host of government officials, civil society agencies, and community groups. This can include dealing with several of the following: visa officers, border and customs personnel, refugee and immigration adjudicators, interpreters, lawyers, immigration consultants, resettlement staff, members of ethnic Diasporas, LGTB organizations, and a multitude of other personnel working in social services and government agencies.

Refugee claims and immigration applications can be negatively impacted if any of the decision-makers involved in the process are insensitive to LGBT issues or rely on stereotypes to make their decisions. Similarly, resettlement efforts can be undermined if agency staff is homophobic or heterosexist. In essence, ignorance, fear, and hostility can lead to poor decision-making and substandard service and support delivery.

In the refugee process, both inland and abroad, the presence of homophobia and heterosexism may lead immigration officials and refugee adjudicators to:

- minimize the importance of sexual orientation or gender identity in a refugee claim;
- devalue a claimant's feelings and experiences;
- deny a claimant protection;
- view claimants strictly in terms of their sexual behaviour;
- assume that celibate adults and adolescents, or ones married to a person of the opposite sex, cannot identity as LGBT;
- conclude that claimants are not LGBT because they fail to meet some arbitrarily and stereotypically defined criterion; and
- perpetuate self-hatred by some LGBT refugees.

Moreover, the use of interpreters can also be problematic if prejudice is present.[2] In both the refugee and immigration context, interpreters may be used to conduct interviews and hearings. In some cases, interpreters and applicants come from the same ethnic or cultural community. As a result, a refugee or immigrant may fear that speaking openly about his or her sexual orientation will result in their sexual orientation being known in the larger community. In other cases, the interpreters have reacted negatively to issues of homosexuality, raising concerns about the reliability of their interpretation. Prejudice against LGBT individuals can also result in the denial of resettlement services and support. For instance, the Canadian state has long relied on faith-based organizations to provide settlement services. While some faith-based sponsoring groups are very supportive of LGBT refugees, some others may refuse to provide settlement services to gay and lesbian refugees (McKinlay, 2008).

It is therefore important that all staff who interacts with sexual minorities reflect on their own prejudices and assumptions about homosexuality and transexuality in order for them to be able to fairly assess refugee claims, immigration applications, or requests for resettlement services. LGBT refugees and immigrants must be "interviewed by trained officials who are well informed about the specific problems LGBT persons face" (UNHCR, 2008, para. 37). Measures should be adopted to ensure awareness of LGBT issues, including targeted training sessions (2008, para. 37). The periodic training conducted by the Canadian Immigration and Refugee Board on sexual orientation and gender identity is certainly among the best practices in this area.[3] However, the vast majority of government and civil society staff involved in the various migration and resettlement procedures have never received LGBT cultural competency training.

Testifying About Sexual Orientation and Gender Identity

It should also be kept in mind that it may be very difficult for lesbians and gay men to speak about their sexual orientation and their lives, particularly to state officials. Many may feel shame, embarrassment, and fear about speaking of something that is so very personal and private. Worse, for some applicants, in order to qualify for a visa, they will be declaring their homosexuality for the first time, and sometimes in countries where such behaviour is against the law. As one gay immigrant stated, he had not been "out" as gay for very long, so "it was very difficult to give such personal details to a government department" (Hart, 2002, p. 48). The United Nations High

Commissioner for Refugees (UNHCR) has recognized this and states that a refugee claimant, for instance, "can be reluctant to talk about such intimate matters, particularly where his or her sexual orientation would be the cause of shame or taboo in the country of origin" (2008, para. 37).

Moreover, in many countries, a governmental investigation of the personal and social lives of gay men and lesbians is not the relatively benign process it may be in Canada. Repression against sexual minorities is state sponsored or encouraged, so it is difficult for many to imagine that state officials could possibly be anything less than hostile to discussions of homosexuality and transsexuality. Some individuals believe that to speak frankly about their sexual orientation or gender identity would only prejudice their case. For instance, some gay and lesbian refugee claimants have suggested that concerns about negative repercussions explain either delays in applying for refugee protection or omissions in first mentioning sexual orientation as a basis for their fear of persecution.[4] For LGBT refugees who have fled to third countries and are waiting for resettlement in Canada, disclosure of their sexual orientation or gender identity can be a risky move if persecution or discrimination against LGBT is as acute in their country of refuge as in their country of origin.

Procedural rules may exacerbate the problem. For instance, under the current Canadian refugee law system, some countries are listed as "Designated Countries of Origin" (DCO) (Immigration and Refugee Protection Act, SC 2001, c. 27, s 109.1(1)). Where a refugee claimant comes from a DCO, he or she is not entitled to the same legal process as refugee claimants from non-designated countries. One of the procedural constraints that distinguished the DCO regime from the regular refugee status determination process is a shortened period to prepare for a hearing (30-45 days) than the time allotted for claimants under the regular determination process (60 days). Such shortened timelines to prepare a hearing have a particularly deleterious effect on LGBT refugee claimants.

One of the reasons accelerated timelines disproportionally impact LGBT refugee claimants is that psycho-social issues act as barriers to timely and full disclosure of the facts of their case and their narrative of self-identity. For instance, among lesbians, gay men, and bisexuals, pervasive societal rejection may cause what is known as "internalized sexual stigma" (also called "internalized homophobia"). Internalized sexual stigma refers to the negative attitudes a person may develop towards one's own homosexuality, others' homosexuality, and disclosing one's homosexuality to others (Gaines et al. 2005, p. 102). Sexual minorities thus often continue to suppress their identity out of a sense of shame, self-hating, stigmatisation, or as a result of long-standing concealment conduct adopted to survive in oppressive environments. In the context of the refugee determination process, they have to overcome these feelings and practices to be able to write out in detail the worst experiences of their lives, and then speak forthrightly about their personal and persecutory history with others, especially with those in positions of authority. Reasonable time delays are thus essential to build the trust required to disclose highly stigmatized self-identities and any traumatic events related to a claimant's sexual orientation or gender identity, particularly to refugee lawyers and adjudicators.

Establishing Sexual Orientation, Gender Identity, and Same-Sex Relationships

LGBT refugees and immigrants may face unusual hurdles in relation to their claims for refugee or immigration status as a family member, specifically when they are required to establish their LGBT status or the genuineness of their same-sex relationship.

In the refugee context, since gay, lesbian, bisexual, and transgender claimants generally assert that they are fleeing persecution because they are members of a "particular social group," one of the legal elements to be satisfied in a refugee claim is the claimant's membership in that group. In order to prove their sexual orientation, gay men and lesbians must present evidence that supports their claim. The refugee claimant bears the onus of proof, and decision-makers must determine whether they believe the claimant's evidence to that effect.

Assessing the veracity of the claimant's sexual orientation or gender identity is a very difficult, sensitive and complex task in the context of an administrative interview or quasi-judicial hearing. Jenni Millbank cites an Australian decision that noted "it is difficult for applicants to substantiate and for decision-makers to evaluate" claims on sexual orientation (Millbank, 2009, p. 392). In particular, the very private and intimate nature of an individual's sexual orientation or gender identity poses real challenges for decision-makers, who are nonetheless required to examine the claimants' personal lives and relationships. The UNHCR suggests that "While some applicants will be able to provide proof of the LGBT status, for instance through witness statements, photographs or other documentary evidence," others may be unable to provide evidence (UNHCR, 2008, para. 35). In the latter cases, the only evidence will be the refugee claimant's own testimony.

Unfortunately, in some cases decision-makers have relied on stereotyp-ical perceptions of sexual minorities in determining their membership in the particular social group, "such as expecting a particular 'flamboyant' or femi-nine demeanour in gay men, or 'butch' or masculine appearance in lesbian women" (UNHCR, 2008, para. 36). Viewing gay men as effeminate or lesbians as masculine reveals prejudicial stereotypes about gay men and lesbians, and a narrow understanding of the construction of masculinity and femininity. Jenni Millbank (2009) has also documented a troubling trend in Australian refugee law where decision-makers doubt or disbelieve the sexual identity of refugee applicants when they do not fit "highly stereotyped and westernised notions of 'gayness'" (p. 392). Barry O'Leary (2008) claims similar problems exist with some UK decision-makers (pp. 89–91) and cases in the United States and Canada have also relied on highly problematic stereotypes.[5]

It is also important to note, as Lee and Brotman (2011) point out, that a refugee's conceptualization of sexual orientation or gender identity can be "fluid and contextual, shifting and changing over time" (p. 254). Human sexu-ality is strongly influenced by social, cultural, religious, and even political environments. Individuals experience and live their sexual orientation in many different ways, depending on their country of origin, gender, culture, social class, education, religion, family background, and socialization. There is no uniform way in which LGBT persons recognize and act on their sexual orientation or gender identity. Therefore, answers to questions about a person's sexual orientation or gender identity will vary widely from one claimant to another. Given this diversity, the credibility of LGBT refugees and immigrants can be undermined if inaccurate, stereotypical and ethnocentric assumptions are made about their lives (see Jordan, 2009, pp. 174–179).

In 2014, the Court of Justice of the European Union outlined some basic principles governing the evidence LGBT refugee claimants are expected to provide to confirm their sexual orientation (A, B, C v. Staatssecretaris van Veiligheid en Justitie, C 148/13 to C 150/13, European Union: Court of Justice of the European Union, 2 December 2014). The Court held that deci-sion-makers must not resort to intrusive questioning about an applicant's sexual acts; nor accept explicit video or photographic evidence documenting intimate sexual conduct; or rely on physical or medical tests purportedly revealing one's sexual orientation. The Court was clear that decision-makers must further avoid relying on stereotypes of sexual minorities. While the deci-sion is not binding on Canadian decision-makers, it does provide a persua-sive interpretation of international refugee law.

In the immigration context, when individuals apply to sponsor their heterosexual or same-sex spouses, common-law or conjugal partners, they will have to prove that their relationships are bona fide. In addition, they will be required to establish the conjugal nature and duration of the relationship. Experience shows that couples tend to demonstrate the bona fide of their relationships in several ways. Prospective immigrants are interviewed by immigration officers, who determine the credibility of the partners. In addition, couples submit supporting documentation: phone bills, letters, plane tickets, boarding passes, visa stamps, photos, and a history of the relationship.

For some gay men and lesbians, it is now possible to prove the genuineness of their relationship by producing marriage certificates, wedding photos, or proof of civil union or partnership registration. If they have cohabited, they can also present rent receipts, joint leases, joint bank accounts, and credit card accounts. Finally, applications are often accompanied by affidavits from individuals with personal knowledge that the relationship is genuine and continuing (Equality for Gays and Lesbians Everywhere, 2003, 110–111).

While it is true that the objective behind Canada's family reunification policy is to facilitate the migration of a particular type of family unit,[6] the inclusion of gay and lesbian families now requires decision-makers to expand their conception of what constitutes the favoured family unit. Many facets of the lives of gay men and lesbians are substantially and significantly different from heterosexual couples. In demanding proof of the bona fide of the relationship, flexibility is required to ensure that inappropriate, discriminatory or heterosexist values are not imposed on same-sex partners.

For instance, it is important to bear in mind that discrimination and persecution often force gay men and lesbians to conceal their relationships, making it more difficult for them to collect the documentation required to demonstrate a legitimate partnership. Some people may not have disclosed their sexual orientation to their family and friends. Such disclosures are often difficult and may have led to hostile and violent reactions on the part of family members. Once someone has come out to themselves, they may or may not seek out other lesbians and gay men. Immigration officials need to contextualize same-sex relationships in order to properly determine the weight to place on the openness or secrecy of the relationship.

Research confirms that many gay and lesbian relationships can be substantively different from traditional heterosexual couples (see Kurdek, 1998; Mackey, Diemer & O'Brien, 2004; Carrington, 1999; Haas and Stafford, 1998). In a study conducted of Australian binational couples, many individuals expressed concern about the models they felt they were forced into by the immigration policy. Here are some of the comments made by gay men and lesbians who experienced the Australian immigration process:

> The models that we were forced into by the department caused a lot of stress. Joint bank accounts, cohabitation, etc. There are other ways to have a relationship. It feeds off and enforces dependency. (Hart, 2002, p. 84)

> I feel I've been expected to be involved in a relationship likened to marriage whereas I'd like to break that mold for a better sort of relationship that has room for growth and individuality. (Hart, 2002, p. 86)

> I feel that the expectations of the Department of Immigration are basing the elements of a relationship on heterosexual standards and are trying to validate and contain lesbian and gay relationships in the same pattern, e.g., living together, lifelong commitment. Sharing bank account, loss of individuality. Does it have to be like this to be genuine? (Hart, 2002, p. 86)

Others spoke of the equality that exists between gay and lesbian partners because of the absence of gender roles:

> Lacking the difference in gender, there is equality between gay partners that is expressed in attitudes toward each other and is exemplified in their maintenance of financial separateness during the early years of the relationship. (Hart, 2002, p. 78)

Thus, there are important differences in how same-sex couples meet, socialize and present themselves to their families, communities, and the world. There may even be individuals in a same-sex partner application that does not identify as "gay" or "lesbian" (Hart, 2002, p. 56).

For prospective gay and lesbian immigrants, the dilemma confronting them is how to form relationships that are personally satisfying while still conforming to government requirements (Hart, 2002, p. 35). For immigration officials, the challenge is to assess the genuineness of gay and lesbian couples without using markers that may only apply in the context of heterosexual relationships.

Proving Persecution

In the refugee system, and in the case of some common law and conjugal partners in the immigration process, an applicant will be required to present evidence that they face a risk of persecution in their country of origin. Such evidence normally includes general evidence of a country's human rights record drawn from governmental, non-governmental, and media reports.

When refugee claims based on sexual orientation and gender identity were first presented in the early 1990s, sexual minorities encountered a specific set of problems in the area of fact-finding (LaViolette, 1996a). First, in many countries, very little information was available on human rights violations against sexual minorities. Governmental and non-governmental organizations were not documenting human rights violations against sexual minorities and thus were not able to provide independent country information. Second, when available information originated from gay, lesbian, bisexual, and transgender organizations, their evidence was sometimes dismissed as biased and unreliable (LaViolette, 2010, p. 309).

The situation has improved as mainstream human right organizations expanded their mandates to include the investigation of discrimination and persecution against sexual minorities. In addition, documentation from sexual minority rights organizations is increasingly regarded as a credible source of information. Nevertheless, documentary challenges remain to this day (LaViolette, 2010; Swink, 2005–06; O'Leary 2008, pp. 91–92; de Jong, 2008).

First, availability of documentation remains a problem. The extent to which mainstream international human rights organizations and sexual minority rights groups are able to uncover worldwide abuses against sexual minorities is still limited. In most countries, stigma continues to attach to issues surrounding sexual orientation and gender identity. This often means that homophobic violence is frequently unreported, undocumented, and ultimately unpunished, making it difficult to investigate the problem.[7] Increased activism has also been met with attacks on gay, lesbian, bisexual, and transgender human rights defenders, which seriously impede their ability to document violations. The particular risks faced by human rights defenders working on issues of sexual orientation have been recognized by the Special Representative of the UN Secretary-General on human rights defenders in 2001:

> Greater risks are faced by defenders of the rights of certain groups as their work challenges social structures, traditional practices and interpretation of religious precepts that may have been used over long periods of time to condone and justify violation of the human rights of members of such groups. Of special importance will be women's human rights groups and those who are active on issues of sexuality especially sexual

orientation and reproductive rights. These groups are often very vulnerable to prejudice, to marginalization and to public repudiation, not only by state forces but other social actors. (United Nations Economic and Social Council [ECOSOC], Commission on Human Rights, 2001, p. 24)

Increasing the risks are the fact that, according to the 2014 State-Sponsored Homophobia report, being a gay man or a lesbian risks jail time in 78 countries and the death penalty in five (Itaborahy & Zhu, 2014, p. 9). Serious risks are therefore involved in investigating, documenting, and reporting human rights violations against sexual minorities, especially if researchers are themselves gay, lesbian, bisexual, or transgender.

Resource limitations also hinder the ability of human rights groups to investigate and publish reliable, current, and comprehensive information. Human rights organizations are not able to produce information about all countries. Moreover, only a fraction of situations, often the most egregious, make it into their documentation. Detailed country reports devoted exclusively to human rights violations against sexual minorities are infrequently released. Moreover, the reports that are produced may not investigate countries from which significant numbers of gay men, lesbians, bisexuals, and transgender persons are fleeing. The Canadian Immigration and Refugee Board has dealt with a considerable number of Mexican gay, lesbian, bisexual, and transgender claimants,[8] yet human rights organizations like Amnesty International and Human Rights Watch do not have a current report on the human rights conditions for sexual minorities in Mexico.

Given the relative absence of reliable independent country information, decision-makers have at times relied on inappropriate sources as substi-

Develop your knowledge – Ask yourself

Given what you have learned about the specific challenges facing LGBT refugees and immigrants, what steps do you think a settlement agency should take to convey to LGBT clients that they have positive policies and attitudes towards sexual minorities? How should they address the prejudice that staff and other clients may display towards LGBT refugees and immigrants?

Develop your knowledge – Online Research

Farid is from Lebanon. He is applying for refugee status in Canada. His claims states that "since the age of thirteen, he has had feminine feelings". As an adolescent, he began to associate with some gay men but he felt very confused about his sexual and gender identity. He was unable to talk to anyone about what was troubling him and after feeling depressed for many years, he tried to commit suicide. He was hospitalized and it is only during his recovery that he accepted that he was a transsexual. He was convinced however that he would not be able to find any help in Lebanon for his situation. On the contrary, he believed that he would be executed if anyone found out he wanted to be a woman. So Farid applied to study in Canada. A few months after his arrival and after reading everything he could find about transsexualism in Canada, Farid decided to try to find a way to stay in Canada and he was told that in order to obtain refugee status, he must show that he has a well-founded fear of persecution if he returns to Lebanon. He did not come to Canada with any documentation that proves that there is persecution of transsexuals in Lebanon.

Using online resources, try to find information about the treatment and situation of transgendered individuals in Lebanon.

1. Are you able to find information about the legal, social and medical situation of transgendered individuals?

2. Do you think that the materials you have found will be considered reliable and credible?

3. What sources do you think a refugee adjudicator would find most convincing: newspapers articles, human rights reports, blogs by Lebanese LGBT individuals, Wikipedia entries?

Develop your knowledge – What's Your Opinion

1. Should lesbian and gay refugee claimants have to prove their sexual orientation when they apply for refugee status in Canada? If so, what kind of evidence do you think they should have to provide to refugee adjudicators? How would you prove your sexual orientation if you had to do so before an administrative tribunal?

2. Should Canadian immigration policy require gay or lesbian couples to have cohabited before they apply to sponsor their partner as a member of the family class? Is cohabitation an unreasonable requirement for LGBT immigrants when they come from countries that discriminate or persecute sexual minorities?

tutes. In 2002, Michael Battista, a refugee lawyer in Toronto, sent a letter to the Canadian Immigration and Refugee Board to complain about material produced for a hearing of a claimant he was representing (Battista, 2002; Dupuis 2003). According to Battista, the package contained material promoting Mexico's gay tourist and travel industry. Battista claimed that such material was inherently promotional and depicted social conditions in the most palatable light. In addition, the information was unreliable, as sources or authors were not identified. Finally, Battista argued that the material was highly prejudicial, as it relied on stereotypical notions of gay men as primarily interested in socializing, parties, and sexual activity (Battista, 2002).[9]

The documentation challenges facing sexual minority claimants remain significant. For refugees, who must prove a well-founded fear of persecution, and same-sex binational couples, who must demonstrate that they have been unable to cohabit because of persecution or penal sanctions, the lack of objective documentation can seriously undermine their chances of gaining protection or immigration status.

Conclusion

This chapter has considered developments in Canadian immigration and refugee law as they pertain to sexual minorities. Canadian borders are no longer closed to LGBT immigrants and refugees. Over the last twenty years, legislative reforms and court rulings have ensured that Canadian laws no longer discriminate against sexual minorities. Refugee protection can be accessed through the inland refugee system while resettlement programs offer opportunities to select LGBT refugees from abroad. In addition, Canadian immigration laws moved from a total ban on gay and lesbian immigration to a formal inclusion of gay and lesbian couples in family sponsorship provisions. The analysis has revealed, however, that while discrimination has been removed from the law, several other challenges confront LGBT immigrants and refugees. In effect, issues arise in the actual application of the refugee and immigration systems, issues that hinder the successful migration of LGBT refugees and same-sex binational couples to Canada. Only when those challenges have been addressed will Canada have true migration equality for lesbian, gay, bisexual and transgendered migrants.

Notes

1   For a survey of laws prohibiting same-sex sexual conduct, see Itaborahy & Zhu (2014).
2   This concern has been raised by several members of the Immigration and Refugee Board during training professional development sessions conducted by the author in 1995, 1999, and 2003. It is also mentioned in United Nations High Commissioner for Refugees (UNHCR, 2008, para. 37).
3   The IRB has conducted professional development training with its members on several occasions since 1995. The author developed and presented these professional training seminars to RPD staff in 1995, 1999, 2003, 2004, 2010, and 2013-2014: see LaViolette (1996b). The training is also mentioned in Jiménez (2007); Lahey (2008).
4   In some cases, claimant's concocted false stories rather than base their refugee claims on sexual orientation; see Re Q.(B.C.) [1993] CRDD No. 207 (QL); Re J.(F.H.) [1994] CRDD No. 77 (QL).
5   See Re Vega Soto, discussed in Hanna (2005); Pischl (2006, pp. 438–439); Trembliuk v. Canada (Minister of Citizenship and Immigration) [2003] F.C.J. No. 1590 (QL).
6   For instance, Canada's family reunification provisions do not allow for the sponsorship of polygamous unions or marriages under the legal age.
7   Louise Arbour, then UN High Commissioner for Human Rights, declared in 2006 that "Because of the stigma attached to issues surrounding sexual orientation and gender identity, violence against LGBT persons

is frequently unreported, undocumented, and goes ultimately unpunished. Rarely does it provoke public debate and outrage. This shameful silence is the ultimate rejection of the fundamental principle of universality of rights" (Arbour, 2006).

8   Mexico was until 2009 the largest source of refugee claimants generally in Canada; see Sarra (2008).

9   Battista (2002). Dauvergne and Millbank have similarly criticised the Australian Refugee Review Tribunal for relying on the Spartacus Guide, a travel guide aimed at gay men, at refugee hearings (Daubergne & Millbank, 2003, pp. 317–320).

References

Arbour, L. (2006, July 26). *Presentation of the Office of the United Nations High Commissioner for Human Rights. Louise Arbour to the International Conference on LGBT (Lesbian, Gays, Bisexual and Transgender) Human Rights, Montreal.* Retrieved from http://www.unhchr.ch/huricane/huricane.nsf/view01/B91AE52651D33F 0DC12571BE002F172C?opendocument

Battista, M. (2002, December 4). Letter to Jean-Guy Fleury, Chairperson, IRB. On file with author.

Lucas Paoli Itaborahy, L.P. & Zhu, J. (2014) State-Sponsored Homophobia - A World Survey of Laws: Criminalisation, Protection and Recognition of Same-Sex Love. International Lesbian and Gay Association. Retrieved from http://old.ilga.org/Statehomophobia/ILGA_SSHR_2014 _Eng.pdf

Canadian Broadcasting Corporation (CBC). (2010, June 6). *Refugees need more help from private groups*: Kenney. Retrieved from http://www.cbc.ca/news/canada/story/2010/06/29/refugee-bill-kenney.html

Carrington, C. (1999). *No place like home: Relationships and family life among lesbians and gay men.* Chicago: University of Chicago Press.

Citizenship and Immigration Canada (CIC). (2010). *Expanding Canada's refugee resettlement programs.* Press release. Retrieved from http://www.cic.gc.ca/english/department/media/releases/2010/2010-03-29.asp

Dauvergne, C., & Millbank, J. (2003). Burdened by proof: How the Australian Refugee Review Tribunal has failed lesbian and gay asylum seekers. *Federal Law Review*, 31, 299–342.

de Jong, A. (2008, September). *An analysis of the coverage of LGBT issues in country of origin information reports produced by the COI service*, UK Border Agency. Retrieved from http://apci.homeoffice.gov.uk/PDF/eleventh_meeting/APCI.11.5%20-%20LGBT.pdf

Dupuis, J. (2003, January 9). *Believe the hype: Refuge evaluated according to tourist info. Xtra!* Retrieved from http://archives.xtra.ca/Story.aspx?s=14751297

Equality for Gays and Lesbians Everywhere (EGALE). (2003). *Outlaws & inlaws: Your guide to LGBT rights, same-sex relationships and Canadian law*. Ottawa: EGALE.

Gaines, S.O. et al. (2005). Cultural value orientations, internalized homophobia, and accommodation in romantic relationships, *Journal of Homosexuality, 50*(1), 97.

Haas, S. M., & Stafford, L. (1998). An initial examination of maintenance behaviors in gay and lesbian relationships. *Journal of Social and Personal Relationships, 15*(6), 846-855.

Hanna, F. (2005). Punishing masculinity in gay asylum claims. *Yale Law Journal, 114*, 913-920.

Hart, J. (2002). *Stories of gay and lesbian immigration: Together forever*. New York: Harrington.

Helsinki Citizens' Assembly–Turkey. (2011, June). *Unsafe haven: The security challenges facing lesbian, gay, bisexual and transgender asylum seekers and refugees in Turkey*. San Francisco: Refugee Advocacy and Support Program, Organization for Refuge, Asylum and Migration.

Jimenez, M. (2004, April 24). Gay refugee claimants seeking haven in Canada. *Globe and Mail*, A7.

Jimenez, M. (2007, February 10). Nicaraguan wins reprieve in bid to remain in Canada. *Globe and Mail*, A12.

Jordan, S. R. (2009). Un/Convention(al) refugees: Contextualizing the accounts of refugees facing homophobic or transphobic persecution. *Refuge, 26*(2), 165–182.

King, D. (2011, March 20). Canada's somersaults in LGBTI resettlement. *Outlooks Magazine*. Retrieved from http://outlooks.ca

Kurdek, L. (1998). Relationship outcomes and their predictors: Longitudinal evidence from heterosexual married, gay cohabiting, and lesbian cohabiting couples. *Journal of Marriage and the Family, 60*(3), 553-568.

Lahey, J. (2008, February 21). *Legal limbo for Canada's gay refugees. Xtra!,* Retrieved from http://www.xtra.ca/public/Ottawa/Legal_limbo_for_Canadas_gay_refug ees-4375.aspx

LaViolette, N. (1996a). Proving a well-founded fear: The evidentiary burden in refugee claims based on sexual orientation. In S. Levy (Ed.), *Asylum based on sexual orientation: A resource guide.* San Francisco: International Gay and Lesbian Human Rights Commission.

LaViolette, N. (1996b). Sexual orientation and the refugee determination process: Questioning a claimant about their membership in the particular social group. In S. Levy (Ed.), *Asylum based on sexual orientation: A resource guide.* San Francisco: International Gay and Lesbian Human Rights Commission.

LaViolette, N. (2010). Independent human rights documentation and sexual minorities: An ongoing challenge for the Canadian refugee determination process. In P. Chan (Ed.), *Protection of sexual minorities since Stonewall: Progress and stalemate in developed and developing countries.* London: Routledge.

Lee, E. O. J., & Brotman, S. (2011). Identity, refugeeness, belonging: Experiences of sexual minority refugees in Canada. Canadian Review of Sociology/Revue canadienne de sociologie, *48,* 241–74.

Mackey, R. A., Diemer, M. A., & O'Brien, B. A. (2000). Psychological intimacy in the lasting relationships of heterosexual and same-gender couples. *Sex Roles, 43*(3-4), 201-227.

McKinlay, C. (2008). Welcoming the stranger: The Canadian church and the private sponsorship of refugees program. *Theses and Dissertations, 104.* Retrieved from http://digitalcommons.ryerson.ca/dissertations/104.

Millbank, J. (2009). From discretion to disbelief: Recent trends in refugee determinations on the basis of sexual orientation in Australia and the United Kingdom. *International Journal of Human Rights, 13*(2–3), 391-414.

O'Leary, B. (2008). We cannot claim any particular knowledge of the ways of homosexuals, still less of Iranian homosexuals ... : The particular problems facing those who seek asylum on the basis of their sexual identity. *Feminist Legal Studies, 16,* 87–95.

Pischl, S. (2006). Circumventing shari'a: Common law jurisdictions' responses to persecuted sexual minorities' asylum claims. *Washington University Global Studies Law Review, 5,* 425-450.

Sarra, S. 2008, (April 16). *New hearing for rejected Mexican. Xtra!* Retrieved from http://www.xtra.ca/public/viewstory.aspx?AFF_TYPE=3&STORY_ID=4 648&PUB_TEMPLATE_ID=9

Smith, D. (2011a, March 24).*On eve of election, Kenney finds $100k for gay refugees. Xtra!* Retrieved from http://www.xtra.ca/public/National/On_eve_of_election_Kenney_finds_ 100k_for_gay_refugees-9931.aspx

Smith, D. (2011b, March 24). *Delays make Canada a poor choice for gay Ugandans.* Retrieved from http://www.xtra.ca/public/National/Delays_make_Canada_a_poor_choi ce_for_queer_Ugandans-9809.aspx.

Swink, A. (2005–06). Queer refuge: A review of the role of country condition analysis in asylum adjudication for members of sexual minorities. *Hastings International and Comparative Law Review, 29,* 251- 266.

United Nations Economic and Social Council (ECOSOC), Commission on Human Rights. (2001). *Report of the Special Representative of the Secretary-General on human rights defenders.* UN ECOSOC, 57th Sess., E/CN.4/2001/94. Retrieved from http://www.unhchr.ch/Huridocda/Huridoca.nsf/0/d6c1b351bf405ad3c12 56a25005109bc/$FILE/G0110638.pdf

United Nations High Commissioner for Refugees (UNHCR). (2008, November 21). *UNHCR guidance note on refugee claims relating to sexual orientation and gender identity.* Retrieved from http://www.unhcr.org/refworld/docid/48abd5660.html

United Nations High Commissioner for Refugees (UNHCR). (2010, July 5). *UNHCR urges more countries to establish refugee resettlement programmes. Press release.* Retrieved from http://www.unhcr.org/4c31cd236.html

PART 2

SETTLEMENT SECTORS AND BEST PRACTICES

CHAPTER 4

History of Settlement Services in Ontario

Debbie Douglas & Amy Casipullai

Develop your knowledge – Case Study

Consider these questions as you read the chapter and following case study:

1. What are the challenges that immigrants would typically experience in their first few weeks after arrival in Canada?

2. What challenges could be attributed to race, gender or class (or economic situation)?

Case Study

Razia Iqbal arrived at Pearson Airport in Toronto on a direct flight from Delhi, with her husband Malik and their four-year-old daughter Shahnaz. Razia's brother met them at the airport and drove them to his home in Markham, Ontario. On the way he briefed them about what they can expect in their new life in Canada. Razia was thoroughly discouraged by what he had to say, especially the information about finding a job in Canada.

Razia was a university professor in India. She knew that she would not be able to teach in Canada, at least not right away. She hoped that she could find a job that would let her use at least some of her skills. But her brother did not sound hopeful about her job prospects. He tells Razia and Malik that he has made an appointment for them at an agency near home, which can advise them on how to get started in their new life. Razia recognizes the name from www.settlement.org, a web site she had encountered in her research about life in Canada.

Razia was one of the 33,085 immigrants that arrived as permanent residents in Canada from India in 2009, and one of the total 259,953 immigrant arrivals in that year (Citizenship and Immigration Canada, 2013).

When Razia and her family go to their appointment at the agency, they will be part of a small but growing number of immigrants who access services outside their network of family and friends upon arrival in Canada (Chui, 2003). They will very likely not use or even become aware of the entire range of sophisticated mix of services that would help to facilitate their settlement process. Instead, they may talk with only one settlement worker who will conduct a needs assessment to discover what they need, and refer them to employment services, language classes, education, skills training, housing services, health-care, and child care services as necessary.

Razia went to the appointment at the agency with Malik and Shahnaz. The first thing they realized is that without access to a baby-sitter for Shahnaz, their prospects for education, training, and employment were almost non-existent. Razia could feel her world shrinking. She hoped the settlement worker could give them some options.

Introduction

The notion of "settlement" derives from Canada's colonial history and the specific mission to establish a White settler colony (Galabuzi, 2006). This laid the foundation for the later marginalization and socio-economic exclusion of Canada's First Peoples as well as racialized immigrants. Canada's colonial project is ongoing. The various manifestations of immigration laws and policies over the years are a component of that enterprise, one in which immigrants are often unwitting but not innocent participants (Lawrence & Dua, 2005).

Galabuzi (2006) notes that the "political system and economy that emerged in Canada were based on the concept of a White-settler society: the building of an 'overseas replica of British society,' complete with dominant culture, values, and institutions that 'mimicked' those of the 'home' country and an internal colonial economy," and that these patterns persisted even as the population demographics changed (p. 76). These replica societies included reformist endeavours, such as the "settlement movement" that emerged in England in 1800. The movement was a response to the growing urban poverty that was a result of the Industrial Revolution (Association of Neighbourhood Houses of Greater Vancouver, 2011). The reformists were highly critical of the prevailing approach to poverty and related issues, one that was centred on a charitable response that treated the poor with condescension and subjected them to moral condemnation. The reformists proposed instead to pursue poverty-elimination strategies while living their life among the urban poor (James, 2001). This approach was based on the notion that community and not the individual was society's fundamental unit. The settlement movement did not question or challenge the ideology and structure of the colonization project, and instead sought social reform from within. While the reformists occupied a physical space in the same geographic community of the people they wanted to assist, they themselves were not poor and therefore had never experienced the same exclusion and deprivation as their neighbours.

Canada's first settlement house was established in 1902 in Toronto. Other houses were set up by different groups, primarily in Toronto but also in other communities such as Windsor and London. Some of the early Toronto settlement houses have endured until today, including St. Christopher House, Central Neighbourhood House, and University Settlement (James, 2001).

Settlement house work was carried out by volunteers who lived in the house. These volunteer settlement workers were White, Anglo, and of a privileged middle-class background. Most of the volunteers in Toronto were Protestant. While many volunteers became involved in settlement work for spiritual reasons, most did not approach it as mission work with a focus on proselytizing. Some settlement houses such as St. Christopher House defined themselves as Christian social settlements and transmitted their principles and values by example rather than making these a condition of accessing their support.[1]

Origins and Evolution of Settlement Programs and Services

The early Settlement Houses were located in urban neighbourhoods among a population that was mostly poor and of immigrant background. Most of the immigrants, while not racialized, were of non-Western European origin, did not speak English, and were visibly different from the White Anglo-Canadians of British origin who constituted the dominant society.

While settlement workers saw themselves as non-traditional reformers, their efforts served to entrench the dominant Anglo colonial ideology that completely denied the history, traditions, treaties, and even existence of Canada's First Peoples and perpetuated the gendered, heterosexual, middle-class values of the colonizer. Although remaining critical of traditional welfare work, settlement workers grounded their reformist efforts in the belief that Anglo-protestant middle-class culture was the Canadian norm (James, 2001). For example, St. Christopher House programs were focussed on providing education and training to local residents dealing with their social and economic conditions and more significantly to "Christianize and to Canadianize" (O'Connor, 1986).

The early settlement programs in Toronto provided education and recreation programs for children. The programs later expanded to include adults and focussed on providing health services, language classes, skills training, libraries, and social opportunities. Domestic science classes for women in hygiene and child-rearing were considered excellent means of transmitting middle-class Anglo values and norms, including the reinforcement of the traditional Victorian gender roles of men as paid breadwinners and women as unpaid domestics in the home (James, 2001). Unlike modern settlement programs, these initiatives were centred on addressing community rather than individual needs and tended to be group activities. While they were not exclusively focussed on immigrant settlement, they were shaped by the realities of the mostly immigrant communities in which they were located.

One of the earliest immigrant-focussed settlement activities stemmed from the efforts of the Jewish Immigrant Aid Society (JIAS). JIAS was established in Montreal in the early 1920s to facilitate the immigration of European Jews. The work included lobbying to counter anti-Semitic immigration policies and settling Jewish refugees and immigrants in Canada (JIAS, n.d.). It was the first example of an ethno-specific agency engaged specifically in facilitating immigrant settlement. Other ethno-specific and religious-based organizations also assisted members of their communities with many issues, including settlement assistance for recent immigrants.

As immigrant communities began to expand and grow, there emerged an increasing number of ethno-specific social clubs, political clubs, sports associations, religious organizations, professional associations, and welfare organizations. Many were a source of help for recently arrived immigrants, but they did not see themselves as providing immigrant settlement services. COSTI and the Italian Immigrant Aid Society (which later merged with COSTI) were early exceptions (Amin, 1987).

JIAS was also the first to hire trained professionals to work with immigrants and the first to develop specialized services (Handford & Tam, 2003). Like the other ethno-specific and religious-based groups, JIAS programs were provided only for the Jewish community. Unlike other agencies involved in helping immigrants, JIAS provided pre- and post-arrival services including sponsoring immigrants, arranging for their travel, and a complete range of social services, language training, and financial assistance for needy families (Amin, 1987).

Between 1948 and 1966, the federal government became directly involved in providing settlement services to help settle Canadian soldiers and their families as well as war-affected refugees (Citizenship and Immigration Canada, 2001). The service was disbanded in 1966 and from then on immigrants were expected to rely on community agencies or on the general social services that were available for all other Canadian residents.

In the 1950s, agencies such as the Red Cross, YWCAs, and YMCAs began providing immigrant settlement programs and services in Toronto as well as in smaller urban centres such as Windsor and London. Churches and settlement houses began taking on more activities for immigrants (Amin, 1987). Amin notes that the arrival of Vietnamese "boat people" in the 1970s led to the development of services for immigrants in small towns.

The Department of Manpower and Immigration was created in 1966 and had its mandate expanded in 1974 to include the provision of settlement and employment services for immigrants. Handford and Tam note that the department also became responsible for the overall co-ordination of the voluntary organizations that were engaged in immigrant settlement work, and this direction resulted in the creation of the Immigrant Settlement and Adaptation Program (ISAP). ISAP was delivered by the federal government through not-for-profit organizations contracted to provide initial settlement services to immigrants upon arrival in Canada, such as providing information and referral to general social services for employment, housing, and other settlement needs (Handford & Tam, 2003).

The Ontario government created Welcome Houses in 1973 to help settle Asian Ugandans expelled by Idi Amin, thus becoming formally involved in immigrant settlement services. The Welcome House service was later expanded in scope to provide assistance to all immigrants and refugees. It was based on a client-centred approach to immigrant settlement. This model provided a broad range of services in one location, including language training, skills training, information and referral, child care services for clients, and a free document translation service. According to Clyde Farnsworth writing in the *New York Times* in 1991, the model was studied by a number of US municipalities as well as government representatives from France, Britain, Sweden, and Norway. The Welcome House service came to an end in 1995 with the election of a Progressive Conservative (PC) government in Ontario. It was to be one of the last, truly comprehensive models for government funded immigrant settlement in Ontario.

Immigrant settlement services and the immigrant and refugee-serving sector have changed considerably over time. These changes were influenced by economic and political factors as well as by the shift in immigration demographics driven primarily by immigrant selection and the corresponding shift in immigrants' expectations. Other elements have changed little, such as the fact that formal service provision is dominated by community-based, not-for-profit organizations, and that immigrants continue to rely on friends and family as the most important source of information and assistance for settling.

History of Settlement Funding

Early settlement services such as those offered by settlement houses were funded through churches and private donations and through fundraising activities organized by volunteers. Later, services were also funded through philanthropic organizations such as the United Community Fund and Community Charities, which later became the United Way (Amin, 1987).

Different levels of government had funded social services in a limited way since before the 1900s, and these were available to immigrants. The inter-dependent relationship between governments and charities developed more fully from the 1960s on. The charitable organizations needed a reliable source of funds to carry out their work, while governments needed certain services to be delivered in a consistent manner and in a particular way (Elson, 2007).

As the needs of their communities grew in scale and became more complex, charitable organizations started to become more and more dependent on government funding in order to expand or intensify their programs. The relationship between the two began to be characterized by growing tension resulting from government limitations on funded activities. Other tensions arose because only the older and more-established organi-zations could get government funding.

From the 1960s on, governments began funding immigrant settlement-focussed services such as language classes, help to find jobs, housing, and access to healthcare. Ontario government investment in language classes became a program known as the Newcomer Language/Orientation Classes (NLOC), which was created in 1978. The federal government increased funding for immigrant settlement services and in the late 1970s formalized the program and named it the Immigrant Settlement and Adaptation Program (ISAP) (Amin, 1987). The program was funded by the Department of Manpower and Immi-gration, which later became Citizenship and Immigration (CIC).

There is an ongoing tension between sector organizations and Citizen-ship and Immigration Canada (CIC). This tension partly results from competing and at times contradictory visions of how the sector sees and characterizes itself and how the Department perceives it. This is captured to some extent in the terminology used by each party. Where the organiza-tions describe themselves as "immigrant-serving agencies" (ISAs) or "immi-grant-serving organizations" (ISOs), government documents including calls for proposals for settlement funding use the terminology "service providing organization" (SPO). The difference is more than mere terminology. Sector organizations provide services to individual immigrants and families, and also serve the community by facilitating capacity building, leadership devel-opment, and opening up opportunities for civic engagement. CIC asks funding applicants to include the full range of activities undertaken by the organization in their proposal, but then persists in reducing them to the totality of CIC-funded settlement programs.

The evolution of government-sector relations in the context of immigrant settlement began in 1975 with the creation of ISAP, when the federal government invited tenders to provide the services. The Ontario Council of Agencies Serving Immigrants (OCASI) was founded in 1978 in the course of a number of settlement agencies trying to convince the government to extend the ISAP pilot and convert it to a permanent program.

OCASI was the de-facto voice of Ontario's immigrant and refugee-serving sector, and engaged in sector-focussed advocacy from its inception. Early activities were centred on advocacy around immigration policy as well as defending and increasing funding for immigrant settlement services. As a result of these efforts, the federal government created an operational grant program for immigrant settlement agencies in 1980, and increased the Ontario budget for Language Instruction for Newcomers (LINC), Refugee Assistance Program (RAP), and ISAP. OCASI also advocated to the Ontario Trillium Foundation and United Way of Greater Toronto for the easing of funding restrictions for immigrant settlement programs and for increasing funding for these initiatives.

Future developments in Canada, particularly federal government fiscal policies under Paul Martin as Liberal minister of finance had a profound impact on Canada's non-profit sector and the organizations that depended on government funding to carry out their activities. Canada responded to the economic recession of the early 1990s like most of Europe and the United States, by reducing investment in social services and moving from core funding for organizations to project funding. One of the more immediate consequences was the loss of resources of non-governmental and not-for-profit organizations to pay for all-important operating costs (Scott, 2005).

Organizations were put in the position of having to use funds from non-government sources that were usually used for advocacy and other activities to pay for operating costs. At the same time, federal government funders introduced new and stringent accountability measures, measures that increased the administrative burden for organizations. These factors significantly affected organizations' ability to carry out advocacy and community-building initiatives. It was the beginning of a shift to a service-only focus of the settlement and integration sector both in Ontario and across Canada.

In 1994–95, the federal government began a process of devolving responsibility for immigrant settlement and integration to the provinces, other than Québec which already had an agreement in place.[2] Ontario organizations that provided services to immigrants became concerned that the provincial government would use settlement dollars as general revenues.

Although Ontario was offered devolution of settlement services in the mid-1990s, the Progressive Conservative provincial government was not interested (Seidle, 2010). Ontario was one of the few major provinces that did not sign an immigration agreement with the federal government. This did not change until 2005, when the governments of Canada and Ontario signed the Canada–Ontario Immigration Agreement (COIA).

Federal government funding for immigrant and refugee settlement services in Canada (except Quebec) was flatlined for more than ten years. A 2003 Parliamentary Committee report on settlement services recommended that overall funding for settlement programs should reflect the increase in immigrant arrivals and should be set at around $3,000 per immigrant for settlement services, based on the funding formula already in effect for Quebec in the Canada–Québec Accord (Standing Committee on Citizenship and Immigration, 2003).

Two years later, immigrant settlement funding in Canada was increased to $1.4 billion over five years to provinces and territories across Canada except Quebec, with almost 60 percent of the funds being allocated to Ontario on the basis of the consistently high immigrant arrivals in the province. The COIA, signed in November of 2005, came with $920 million over a five-year period. Unlike the agreements signed earlier with Quebec, Manitoba, and British Columbia, COIA did not devolve control of the funds to the Ontario government. The responsibility for the administration of the program and the money remained with the federal government (Ontario Council of Agencies Serving Immigrants, 2005).

The significant infusion of funds had an impact on several levels, including expansion of scope and scale of services. Many organizations grew exponentially within a very short period as they introduced new programming, expanded to underserviced areas, and responded to unmet needs within local communities. The new funds also brought new players, dramatically changing the face of the sector. The new players included large public institutions such as boards of education, colleges and universities, hospitals, public libraries, and a smaller number of for-profit entities such as private consultants. Municipalities too received funding from CIC, primarily as the lead applicant in the new Local Immigration Partnership (LIP) initiative. LIPs were created as local planning bodies to allow local stakeholders to collaborate in dialogue and planning on immigrant settlement and integration in their communities (Citizenship and Immigration Canada, 2010).

The new funds also increased the level of wages in the sector. Meeting salary and benefit obligations became a critical factor when CIC imposed funding cuts on the sector in Ontario following the 2008-2010 recession (Ontario Council of Agencies Serving Immigrants, 2011). The organizations that were most affected were the ones where CIC funding was a major percentage of the budget.

Meanwhile, the Canada-Ontario Immigration Agreement came to an end in March 2011. It was extended for one year beyond its original end-date in 2010 to give both governments time to negotiate a new agreement. The Ontario government was much more interested in a new agreement than the federal government. In April 2012, the federal government unexpectedly announced that it was terminating its immigration agreements with the governments of Manitoba and British Columbia so that it could harmonize settlement services across the country (Welcoming Communities Initiative, 2012).

By 2011, the federal government began to phase Ontario into the national funding allocation model that ties the per-province settlement funding to immigrant arrivals. The allocation is calculated on a rolling average of permanent resident arrivals over three-years. While Ontario receives the largest number of immigrants to Canada, the actual number of arrivals and share of the national total has been declining since 2005. Ontario has gone from receiving more than 50% of immigrants to Canada before 2005, to approximately 40% of all arrivals by 2013 (Citizenship and Immigration Canada. 2013). The immigrant and refugee-serving sector in Ontario has been deeply impacted by overall funding cuts to CIC's settlement budget and by the implementation of the national funding formula.

Canada, and particularly Ontario, are continuing the long recovery from the recession. Meanwhile the federal government is pursuing its austerity agenda which is producing further cuts to investment in social services, including to immigrant and refugee settlement. Most sector organizations are vigorously exploring options to diversify funding and other options to resource their work with community organizations.

At the provincial level, the Ontario government in response to the federal cuts created a special fund of half a million dollars to support eight agencies, all located in Toronto, that have been defunded. It also increased funding to all its funded agencies by five percent in 2011.

Settlement Services

The training guide to immigrant settlement counselling defines "settlement" as follows: "Settlement is a long-term, dynamic, two-way process through which, ideally, immigrants would achieve full equality and freedom of participation in society, and society would gain access to the full human resource potential in its immigrant communities" (OCASI, 2000). By definition, settlement services can and should be anything that can further the settlement of immigrants. The guide offers the following explanation:

[settlement services are] a wide range of culturally appropriate essential services to assist a diverse population of immigrants and refugees in the process of settlement and integration. In response to the unique realities and changing needs of communities, volunteers and staff at these agencies have developed unique, culturally sensitive and professional programs. Many of these programs are not available from the larger public service institutions. Some have provided models for these institutions and others have helped these institutions make their services accessible. (OCASI 2000)

The Canadian Council for Refugees' best settlement practices document notes that the range of settlement services depend on "needs, the resources available and imagination" (Canadian Council for Refugees, 1998). The following is offered as one of many ways of describing settlement services:

Initial settlement, including reception & orientation to Canada: counselling, community contact, access to other services, etc.;

Language instruction, from beginners to employment-related;

Employment services, including orientation, job-search skills, job experience placement, employment counselling and placement, and specific skills upgrading and certificate programs;

Long-term integration through education, community development, multicultural, citizenship, anti-racism, organizational change and development. (Canadian Council for Refugees, 1998)

The federal government describes the Immigrant Settlement and Adaptation Program (ISAP) as follows:

ISAP assists immigrant settlement and integration through funding to service providers in order to deliver direct services to immigrants such as reception, orientation, translation, interpretation, referral to community resources, solution-focused counselling, general information and employment-related services, and to provide indirect services that aim to improve the delivery of settlement services. These could include workshops, research projects or staff training programs. (Citizenship and Immigration Canada, 2005)

ISAP services can be accessed by immigrants who are permanent residents and by Convention refugees (individuals determined to be a refugee under the 1951 United Nations Convention Relating to the Status of Refugees). These services are typically focussed on addressing the needs of immigrants who are recent arrivals, but there is recognition that longer-term permanent residents too may need assistance to settle.

The Ontario government funds immigrant and refugee settlement and integration services through the Newcomer Settlement Program (NSP). While this funding envelope is a fraction of federal funding for settlement services, NSP has no eligibility restrictions and is available to anyone that needs the service including refugee claimants, people with precarious status, and citizens. NSP services include the following elements:

- One-on-one settlement and orientation assistance;
- Information about community and government services, and referrals to services such as healthcare, housing, legal assistance, education, and employment, language, and skills training programs and services;
- Information on programs and services to help with finding a job or access to training and skills development programs;
- Interpretation and translation of documents, or help to arrange these services; and
- Help filling out forms and applications.

In addition, the Ontario government funds language training for adults through English/French as Second Language (ESL/FSL) programs and employment supports through various initiatives including "bridge training" and internships programs. These initiatives support the settlement and integration of immigrants and refugees.

Early settlement services, as described by James (2001) and by Amin (1987), were focussed on helping recently arrived immigrants to find food and shelter and jobs, and later to help them access education for children and address the myriad other needs that are part of trying to survive and make a home in a new land. Community organizations did not impose eligibility criteria such as status in the country or length of residence. Amin has noted that factors such as the prevalent economic situation influenced the type of "welcome" new immigrants could expect to receive from the host society. During difficult economic times, settlement house volunteers and settlement workers at other organizations have found themselves dealing with xenophobia and discrimination directed at their clients in the course of addressing typical settlement needs such as arranging food, shelter, and clothing.

The realities that a settlement worker might confront in the course of addressing basic survival needs for a client are not all that different today. Settlement workers may routinely have to address issues of equitable access in the course of assisting a client, whether systemic or situational. These challenges can range from a landlord refusing to rent to a client after hearing the name or seeing the client (often conveyed obliquely by saying the unit is no longer available), or requiring that the client produce references from past landlords in Canada (impossible for someone who arrived recently), to problems arising from the reality that all immigrants in Ontario are excluded from publicly funded health services for three months.

Individual immigrants may face difficulties in their settlement process, but as a group are said to be "remarkable for their resilience" (Canadian Council for Refugees, 1998). Many immigrants may not require more than minimal information and some direction on how to go about settling in a new country upon arrival in Canada. This is not surprising since immigrant selection favours individuals who are perceived to have the capacity to settle with little or no assistance (see discussion of the "points system" in Go's chapter, this volume). Many immigrants, particularly those coming through the Family Reunification stream, arrive to a community of family and friends and typically rely on them for assistance. Refugees are more likely to rely on an external organization for help since they may have specialized settlement needs and since they may not have close friends and family who would be willing to help (Statistics Canada, 2005).

The early forms of settlement services, supported as they were by charitable groups and faith groups, did not exclude individuals on the basis of residence status in Canada. In fact, the entire question of eligibility arose with CIC-funded programs and the Department's insistence on screening clients on the basis of residency in Canada. It was solidified with the introduction in 2001 of the Immigrant-Contribution Accountability Measurement System (ICAMs), CIC's central data collection system.

While no organization turned away an immigrant because of immigration status, most were increasingly hard-pressed to find the resources to serve "ineligible" clients. Organizations found a creative solution by leveraging resources from other funders to bridge the service gap, giving clients access to most if not all the settlement programs they offered.

This became harder to maintain with earlier cuts to the provincially funded NSP program. The increase in Canada's non-status population has strained the capacity of community organizations to respond to the settlement and integration needs of the communities they serve. As Canada increasingly prioritizes temporary migration over permanent migration, more migrant workers are at risk of becoming out of status, swelling the numbers of those who would need and seek assistance from these organizations.

Professionalization, Settlement Workers Role, and Sector Role

James (2001) has noted that the early settlement workers were untrained volunteers. Later volunteers were college-educated women, but they too were untrained for the work they undertook. James reports that settlement houses championed volunteerism while also advocating for formal social service training at University of Toronto (UofT). Their efforts led to the establishment of the Department of Social Services at UofT in 1914, which later became the School of Social Work. The formal training provided at UofT and other post-secondary institutions did not quite address the realities of immigrant settlement, particularly the conditions of systemic discrimination that many immigrants faced.

Following the creation of ISAP, settlement workers were hired first for their language ability and often had little or no formal training to undertake the work (Amin, 1998). Then as now, the sector had a mix of formally trained workers who did not quite understand the social, political, and economic context of their immigrant clients, and workers who had themselves arrived as immigrants but who had no formal training. In this context, the OCASI Professional Development Conference became a welcome resource for settlement workers. First held in the early 1980s, the conference became an annual event funded primarily by Citizenship and Immigration Canada (CIC).

In recent years, the federal government has stopped funding professional development for individual organizations receiving CIC funds for settlement services, and for sector conferences. The government has undertaken a national needs assessment on professional development requirements in the sector and is interested in pursuing a harmonized approach across the country. Many sector umbrella organizations believe that professional development needs are best addressed through a combination of regional training and individual training decided at the organizational level.

Settlement workers also had access to professional development opportunities such as training workshops offered by provincial government ministries, public institutions, and other community organizations that allowed them to remain current with new developments and changes that had an impact on their work. Yet these were not sufficient to address the complex requirements for skills and knowledge among settlement workers that were needed due to factors such as the change in immigration demographics and changes in the social, economic and political environment. Further, settlement workers were increasingly called upon to fulfil functions that were left vacant or orphaned as a result of service downloading by all levels of government. There was a growing recognition of the need for dedicated and sustained investment in sector professionalization, standards, and competencies.

The need to develop service standards and competencies is a long-standing discussion in Canada's immigrant and refugee-serving sector. The Canadian Council for Refugees made the first effort to identify competencies and standards through documenting good practices in settlement service (Canadian Council for Refugees, 1998). The OCASI *Immigrant settlement counselling training guide* (2000) attempted to capture the full scope of settlement work and to formally recognize that the work must be informed by values of equity and anti-oppression. In 2000, the Canadian Council for Refugees worked in collaboration with sector organizations from across Canada to develop a National Settlement Standards Framework. In Ontario, the Ontario Council of Agencies Serving Immigrants (OCASI) developed the Organizational Standards Initiative (2009), which includes a series of standards and an online evaluation tool that agencies use to identify gaps in organizational standards in a variety of areas including governance, finance, administration and operation, human resources, and community development.

To support organizations in meeting the established organizational standards, OCASI instituted various training initiatives with support from government departments and ministries (CIC federally and MCI provincially) and with other funders like the Ontario Trillium Foundation.

The discussion on competencies and standards was continued at the national level at the National Settlement Conference II held in 2003. The discussion covered competencies for settlement workers, and also service standards for organizations providing settlement services. Post-secondary institutions in provinces across Canada have developed or modified existing courses of study in the social sciences, including in social work and community work, to focus on or respond to the experience and needs of immigrants. Several universities and community colleges have now developed degree, diploma or certificate programs with a focus on immigrant and refugee settlement, migration and multiculturalism at various levels of study.

The OCASI conference, while pulling together a broad range of ad hoc professional development opportunities in one space and at one time, also gave settlement workers the opportunity to build a sense of solidarity and community. An early conference became the site for organizing a cross-Ontario settlement workers alliance, later constituted as the Ontario Immigrant Settlement Workers Association (OISWA). Regrettably, the association never quite fulfilled its potential and at the time of writing has ceased to function.

Most importantly, the OCASI conference was a space for peer-learning, networking, and mutual encouragement and support. The conference soon grew into a wildly popular annual event. As the sector grew and as more and more new workers were hired, the conference also became a critically important site for transmitting knowledge and the culture of anti-discrimination and advocacy that is so critical to effective settlement work.

Advocacy became increasingly important in the settlement worker's role particularly in the context of helping immigrants to overcome the systemic barriers that many routinely encounter in the settlement process. While settlement workers will invariably have to advocate with and on behalf of a client to gain access to services, in accordance with rights and entitlements, there is some tension in translating this experience to speaking out or acting out against systemic discrimination.

The tension arises to a large extent from the perceived and real threat of negative consequences for the client, for the worker, and for the organization where the worker is employed. There exists real fear of the possible loss of funding if the worker or the organization were to be "outspoken" in their naming and challenging of systemic discrimination, particularly because this has been the experience of some organizations in recent years (OCASI, 2011). Registered charities face the further threat of potential loss of charitable status.

Today, we are dealing with a range of definitions of settlement work and the settlement worker's role. Umbrella organizations like OCASI encourage settlement workers to envisage their role as facilitating the settlement and integration of immigrants through a critical anti-racism and anti-oppression lens, including taking an advocacy role for and with the individual client and using that experience and analysis to advocate for systemic change (OCASI, 2000).

This expectation of settlement workers as advocates has met with a mix of responses from the agencies that employ them and from the workers themselves. Embedded in this directive to workers is the assumption that as individuals they have developed a critical understanding of the systemic and structural barriers that exist and an analysis of how these barriers can and should be removed.

Even when workers employ a critical anti-racist and anti-oppression analysis of systemic inequalities in their work, they are often operating in environments where this understanding is not shared or where these inequalities are replicated. Our collective challenge is to ensure the creation of a sectoral culture that operates from an anti-oppression framework; where individuals are supported to develop the necessary skills and knowledge to lead systemic change within their agencies and the society at large. It is a political project that makes equity its watchword, and the achievement of progressive social change its goal.

Government Funding and Sector Identity

To deliver on its potential as agents of social change, the immigrant and refugee serving sector must re-vision itself. There is an existing tension, however, that is exacerbated by the funding model that is in place for the community-based, non-profit sector in Ontario and Canada.

To all intents and purposes, the federal government has the largest and most powerful say in immigrant settlement. This means that the "integration" part of the process, one that many would argue is the most important part of the settlement–integration continuum, gets the least amount of resources since this is a secondary consideration in CIC's mandate. After the initial stages of settling post-arrival, immigrants would continue to require assistance to access public institutions and "mainstream" services, usually in the course of trying to access the labour market and also to access rights and entitlements. For effective integration, immigrants must be able to access multiple institutions and opportunities as part of social, economic and political integration and civic engagement; and they may require assistance to do so. They may need assistance in confronting systemic barriers including racism and discrimination (Mwarigha, 2002). Richmond and Saloojee (Richmond & Saloojee, 2005) note that the lack of financial investment in this critical stage of integration, despite recognizing that settlement is a life-long process, is one of the most serious problems with the current system.

Another critical issue with the status quo of the funding regime is the lack of influence of the sector on decision making and lack of a true sense of partnership between government funders and sector agencies. With an increase in influence on policy makers the sector would be able to dictate policy directions that are responsive to the needs of immigrants and refugees but also support a progressive social change agenda. To get to this place, however, the tension between "service provision" versus "community development and advocacy" must be resolved by the various players in the sector resulting in the understanding that it is not an either/or paradigm but a new model that recognizes the complementary relationship between the two activities.

Various initiatives have been undertaken over the years in an attempt to change for the better the relationship between government and the non-profit sector, including the immigrant and refugee serving sector. One such initiative was an attempt to develop a formal government-non-profit sector agreement regarding the funding relationship, through the Voluntary Sector Initiative (VSI) launched by the Jean Chrétien Liberal government in 1999. The CIC engagement in the initiative produced two National Settlement Conferences, in 2001 and in 2003 with the latter focusing on policy.

The VSI produced the Voluntary Sector Accord, the *Code of good practice on funding*, and the *Code of good practice on policy dialogue.* A third document, *From red tape to clear results* – the report of the federal government's Independent Blue Ribbon Panel on Grants and Contribution Programs – resulted from an all-party committee struck to investigate the relationship between the non-profit sector and the federal government after significant complaints from the social services sector in Ontario (particularly in Toronto) about contracting practices by civil servants at Human Resources and Skills Development Canada (HRSDC).

Key federal departments such as HRSDC, Health Canada, Canadian Heritage, Canadian International Development Agency (CIDA), Economic Development Agency of Canada for the Regions of Quebec, and Indian Affairs and Northern Development (IAND) were identified as the leads in departmental implementation of the recommendations contained in the documents. While some of the recommendations were implemented, the majority was not and there remain significant inconsistencies in how federal departments engage with the non-profit sector. The intent to have the sector play a more meaningful role in policy development has not been realized and the government consultation process remains flawed.

Discussions in the sector have increasingly centred on the troubling extent to which service agencies depend on government funding to address the needs of immigrants and refugees with little or no control or say in funding levels, service eligibility, and program priorities. These discussions have become more urgent specifically because of the impact of the significant across-the-board funding cuts in Ontario by CIC in 2011 that resulted in the destabilization of some agencies due to employee lay-offs and the reduction or withdrawal of services (OCASI, 2011).

A more critical discourse is one that explores the impact of the reliance on government funding on collective advocacy by organizations and by extension the communities with which they work. Some of these concerns are explored in "Agency of the Future: Blueprint for discussion" (2013). Many agencies and organizations engaged with community and human services are charities. In fact, there are over 45,000 non-profits in Ontario, many of which are charities. The rules governing these agencies are often prescriptive and stringent, and often restrain advocacy efforts. Yet, over the years there has been recognition by government and the public that advocacy and civic engagement in general is an important and necessary component of the work of these organizations. For organizations providing settlement services, promoting and facilitating civic engagement constituted the "integration" portion of immigrant settlement and integration work. This recognition created the space for organizations to engage in public policy debate, and to respond and to propose political programs all to the betterment of the "public good." But this acknowledgement of the public role of community based organizations in the public sphere is changing as we experience a political shift in how these agencies and organizations are expected to conduct themselves vis-à-vis the political and public policy realms.

This curtailing of organizations' ability to work within their communities on civic engagement and other advocacy projects is the point of tension that the sector must resolve. Civic engagement is integral to immigrant integration and yet is not explicitly funded by CIC, the main settlement services funder, despite being named in the objectives of the Immigration and Refugee Protection Act (2001).

Civic Engagement: The Debate

Civic engagement, sometimes referred to as civic participation, is best described as a set of activities that will benefit individuals and groups. It can include an activity undertaken in an individual context, such as writing a letter to one's Member of Parliament or to a government committee. It can include activities undertaken as part of a group, such as volunteering at a community event or program, to organising around an issue of concern to a community or neighbourhood, to serving on the board of directors of a community organization. It can also include voting in an election, volunteering on the campaign of a political candidate, and standing for election to a political office. The following are some useful definitions.

Ménard has said:

> civic engagement results when citizens acquire behaviours and attitudes that express their will to get involved in their society or community in a manner consistent with democratic principles. This can include involvement in community and volunteer organizations. Civic engagement is broader than political engagement in that it can include service to the community through involvement in health, in education and in charitable organizations. Political engagement is a more targeted aspect of civic engagement and is expressed through voting, demonstrations, signing petitions and work with political organizations. (Ménard, 2010)

Saloojee (2002) notes that civic engagement is a mechanism by which "citizens seek to effect social and political change," including formal political participation and efforts that "seek to bridge the growing gap between them and their political processes and institutions" (p. 34). Saloojee suggests that the discourse of social inclusion and exclusion is a useful lens for analysing the different forms of participation, and raises questions about who is included and whether that inclusion is meaningful. He cites John Veit-Wilson to distinguish between weak and strong versions of the social inclusion discourse. The former is focussed on voting as an indicator of political participation and integration. The latter calls for a consideration of the structural barriers to political participation that marginalized groups such as immigrants and refugees and members of racialized communities would face. The strong version of the discourse focuses on power relations – who is excluded and by whom. It includes an understanding of rights, citizenship, and the restructuring of relations between the excluded and political and other institutions in society (Saloojee, 2002, p. 35).

This social inclusion discourse also suggests that effective immigrant settlement and integration requires full and equal participation in Canada's economic, social, political, and cultural life (Omidvar & Richmond, 2005). Others have raised questions about the discrepancy between expectations of immigrants and expectations of native-born Canadians, and whether the scope and scale of civic engagement is a useful indicator of integration (CCR cited in Public Policy Forum, 2008, p. 8).

Scott (2006) wonders, in light of Canada's growing racial and ethnic diversity resulting in large part from changing immigration demographics, whether immigrants are actively engaged in their communities and whether there are opportunities for meaningful social, political, and economic engagement. But these approaches tend to characterize engagement as essential to individual and community well-being rather than an avenue or mechanism for structural change, the starting point for addressing the fundamental inequities in society. This approach includes volunteerism as a form of civic engagement, the former being an altruistic undertaking to "give back to society" or to strengthen one's community. Volunteerism is also acknowledged to bring the added benefit of personal growth and development and extending one's personal networks for social, political, and economic gain.

Uzma Shakir raises questions about the inclusion discourse, particularly around how inclusion is defined and by whom. She points out that the discourse presumes the existence of a desirable norm, and that we can achieve greater egalitarianism in Canada by including most of the marginalized into that norm. She points out the dangers of conducting the social inclusion discussion in a manner that does not question the fundamental inequities of the existing power structure, and instead focuses on increasing the qualitative and quantitative civic and political engagement of marginalized groups (Shakir, 2005).

The existence of the desirable norm to which all immigrants are expected to conform is demonstrated most powerfully in the Canadian citizenship study guide, *Discover Canada: The Rights and Responsibilities of Citizenship,* updated in 2010. The guide promotes a specific Canadian social and cultural norm, one that relies heavily on references to a particular version of British history and tradition. It refers to the legacy of the Multiculturalism Act stating that a diversity of ethnicity and culture is desirable and valued, and at the same time declares unequivocally that immigrants are expected to

Develop your knowledge – Ask yourself

1. What is an example of systemic discrimination that recent immigrants would routinely encounter in the settlement process?

2. How do race and gender have an impact on the settlement process?

3. What impact would government policies have on settlement services?

4. How do government policies have an impact on the role of the settlement worker?

5. How do government policies have an impact on the activities of the organizations that provide settlement services?

conform to the Canadian norm that is based specifically on a European, White, Anglo heritage.

Civic engagement and political participation do not simply happen, nor are they undertaken in a vacuum. They emerge from and are shaped by a particular social, economic, and political history and context which also impacts on and influences the "actors." A useful critical analysis of civic engagement would take into account the questions raised above, and consider not only who benefits and how, but also why an activity is undertaken, what kinds of activities are legitimized, and in what way the activity does (or does not) question or change the fundamental inequities that exclude immigrants and refugees, particularly women and those from racialized communities.

Conclusion

Settlement services in the years ahead must evolve to keep pace with changing immigration trends, changing needs of newer immigrant cohorts, and Canada's dynamic economy. At present, Canada is one of the few countries in the world where these services are delivered almost entirely by community organizations and funded by government.

Some recurring central themes in settlement work include the tension between government and community organizations, the extent of government funding for immigrant-focussed services, the growing need for national service standards, pressure to diminish the advocacy component in settlement work, the need to invest in the integration component, and the need to maintain a degree of autonomy by seeking and developing alternate resources to sustain sector organizations.

Community organizations that work with immigrants can expect to be challenged on an ongoing basis by the needs of the communities they serve, labour market conditions, and the social, political, and economic environment in Canada. They will need to build a relationship with new and non-traditional players.

Notes

[1]   The resulting tensions and its impact on immigrant settlement services are documented in the descriptive narrative of Toronto's settlement house movement in James (2001).

[2]   The government had already withdrawn from settlement programs in Québec in 1991 and transferred control to the province through the Canada–Québec Accord (Vineberg, 2009).

[3] A framework for occupational competencies was developed in Alberta in 2000 by the Alberta Association of Immigrant Serving Agencies (AAISA), and in British Columbia in 2008 by the BC Ministry of Attorney General. AAISA later launched a settlement worker accreditation program, the only one in Canada at the time of writing.

References

Amin, N. (1987, October). *A preliminary history of settlement work in Ontario: 1900–present*. Toronto: Ministry of Citizenship and Immigration. Retrieved from http://ceris.metropolis.net/frameset_e.html.

Association of Neighbourhood Houses of Greater Vancouver. (2011). *Neighbourhood houses: Past and present*. Retrieved from http://www.campalex.com/pdfs/history_of_neighbourhood_houses.pdf.

Canadian Council for Refugees (CCR). (1998). *Best settlement practices*. Montreal: Canadian Council for Refugees. Retrieved from http://ccrweb.ca/bpfinal.htm.

Canadian Council for Refugees. (2000). *Canadian national settlement service standards framework*. Montreal: Canadian Council for Refugees. Retrieved from http://ccrweb.ca/standards.htm.

Chui, T. (2003, September). *Longitudinal survey of immigrants to Canada: Process, progress and prospects*. Ottawa: Statistics Canada. Retrieved from http://www.statcan.gc.ca/bsolc/olc-cel/olc-cel?catno=89-611-X&lang=eng.

Citizenship and Immigration Canada. (2005). *Evaluation of the Immigration Settlement and Adaptation Program (ISAP)*. Ottawa: Citizenship and Immigration Canada. Retrieved from http://www.cic.gc.ca/english/resources/evaluation/isap/index.asp.

Citizenship and Immigration Canada. (2010). *Annual report on the operation of the Canadian Multiculturalism Act 2009–2010*. Ottawa: Citizenship and Immigration Canada. Retrieved from http://www.cic.gc.ca/english/resources/publications/multi-report2010/intro.asp.

Citizenship and Immigration Canada. (2013). *Facts and figures 2013: Immigration overview – Permanent and temporary residents*. Ottawa: Citizenship and Immigration Canada. Retrieved from http://www.cic.gc.ca/english/resources/statistics/menu-fact.asp.

Citizenship and Immigration Canada. (2010). *Discover Canada: The rights and responsibilities of citizenship*. Ottawa: Citizenship and Immigration

Canada. Retrieved from http://www.cic.gc.ca/english/pdf/pub/
    discover.pdf.

Elson, P. R. (2007). A short history of voluntary sector–government rela-
    tions in Canada. *The Philanthropist, 21*(1), 36–74.

Farnsworth, C. H. (1991, September 15). Helping hands await immigrants
    in Ontario. *New York Times.* Retrieved from
    http://www.nytimes.com/1991/08/15/world/helping-hands-await-immi-
    grants-in-ontario.html.

Galabuzi, G. (2006). *Canada's economic apartheid.* Toronto: Canadian
    Scholar's Press.

Handford, P., & Tan, K. (2003). *Settlement accord discussion paper devel-
    oped for national settlement conference II.* Retrieved from http://inte-
    gration-net.ca/english/ini/vsi-isb/conference2/working-travail/p03-00.htm.

Independent Blue Ribbon Panel on Grants and Contribution Programs.
    (2006). *From red tape to clear results.* Ottawa: Independent Blue
    Ribbon Panel on Grants and Contribution Programs.

Jewish Immigrant Aid Society (JIAS). (N.d.). *Immigrants established JIAS
    so that JIAS could establish immigrants.* Retrieved from
    www.jias.org/history.pdf.

Immigration and Refugee Protection Act. (2001). Retrieved from
    http://laws-lois.justice.gc.ca/eng/acts/I-2.5/.

James, C. (2001). Reforming reform: Toronto's settlement house move-
    ment, 1900–20. *Canadian Historical Review, 82*(1), 1–20

Lawrence, B., & Dua, E. (2005). Decolonizing anti-racism. *Social Justice,
    32*(4), 120–43.

Ménard, Marion. (2010). *Youth civic engagement. Library of Parliament
    background paper.* Publication No. 2010-23-E.Ministry of Citizenship
    and Immigration. (2011). Grants and funding – Newcomer Settlement
    Program. Toronto:

Ministry of Citizenship and Immigration. Retrieved from
    www.citizenship.gov.on.ca/english/grantsandfunding/nsp.shtml.

Mwarigha, M. S. (2002). T*owards a framework for local responsibility:
    Taking action to end the current limbo in immigrant settlement –
    Toronto.* Toronto: Maytree Foundation.

Ontario Council of Agencies Serving Immigrants. (OCASI). (2000). *Immi-
    grant settlement counselling: A training guide* (2000). Toronto: OCASI.

Ontario Council of Agencies Serving Immigrants. (OCASI). (2005). *Frame-
    work for an agreement: Crafting a vision for the sector.* Toronto:
    OCASI.

Ontario Council of Agencies Serving Immigrants. (OCASI). (2011). *OCASI position on the CIC cuts to Ontario settlement funding*. Retrieved from: www.ocasi.org/downloads/OCASI_Position_on_the_cuts_to_Ontario_S ettlement_Funding.pdf.

Ontario Council of Agencies Serving Immigrants. (OCASI). (2011). Background information on CIC cuts. Retrieved from http://www.ocasi.org /sites/default/files/2011,%20OCASI%20CIC%20Cuts%20Back-grounder.pdf.

O'Connor, P. J. (1986). *The story of St. Christopher House: 1912 to 1986.* Toronto: St. Christopher House.

Pathways to Prosperity and Ontario Council of Agencies Serving Immigrants. (2013). Agency of the future: Blueprint for discussion. Retrieved from http://p2pcanada.ca/files/2013/09/Agency-of-the-Future--Blueprint-for-Discussion.pdf.

Richmond T., & Saloojee, A. (Ed.). (2005). *Social inclusion: Canadian perspectives*. Laidlaw Foundation. Halifax: Fernwood.

Scott, K. (2005). *Funding matters*. Ottawa: Canadian Council on Social Development.

Seidle, F. L. (2010). *The Canada-Ontario immigration agreement: Assessment and options for renewal*. Mowat Centre for Policy Innovation Paper. Toronto: University of Toronto.

Standing Committee on Citizenship and Immigration. (2003). *Settlement and integration: A sense of belonging: "Feeling at home."* Ottawa: Citizenship and Immigration Canada.

Shakir, U. (2005). Dangers of a new dogma: Inclusion or else...! In T. Richmond & A. Saloojee. (Ed.). Social inclusion: Canadian perspectives. Laidlaw Foundation. Halifax: Fernwood.

Statistics Canada. (2005). *Longitudinal survey of immigrants to Canada: A portrait of early settlement experiences*. Ottawa: Statistics Canada.

Vineberg, R. (2009). *History of federal–provincial relations in immigration and integration*. PowerPoint presentation to Metropolis Seminar. Retrieved from http://canada.metropolis.net/mediacentre/Rob_ Vinberg_Fed_Prov_Relatns_e.ppt

Walker, B. (Ed.). (2008). *The history of immigration and racism in Canada.* Toronto: Canadian Scholars' Press.

Welcoming Communities Initiative e-Bulletin. (2012). A view on the termination of the Manitoba and B.C. immigration agreements. Retrieved from http://p2pcanada.ca/files/2012/04 /April-2012-e-bulletin_ English.pdf

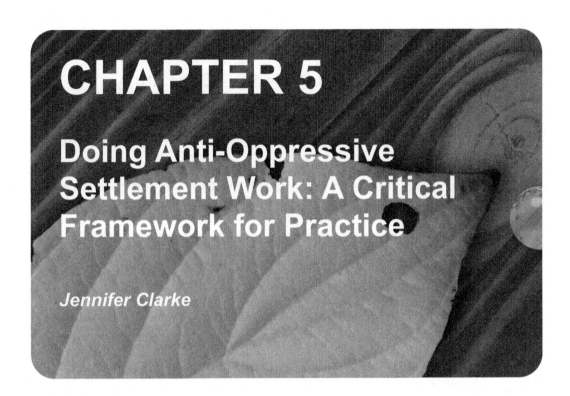

CHAPTER 5

Doing Anti-Oppressive Settlement Work: A Critical Framework for Practice

Jennifer Clarke

Introduction

This chapter was written to share my experiences in the settlement sector with social service students and frontline settlement workers who are searching for ways of integrating anti-oppressive principles and strategies in their everyday work. Increasingly, settlement workers are called upon to provide services to immigrants of diverse backgrounds, but many are unprepared to challenge the systemic and structural oppressions that immigrants experience in Canadian society (Clarke & Wan, 2011; Sakamoto, 2007). Some students and frontline workers are now asking for "checklists" or a "toolkit" of strategies to help them integrate "best practices" in settlement work. Many knowingly and unknowingly reproduce inequality and social injustices in their everyday practices as a matter of routine (Clarke & Wan, 2011). Others have developed strategies for supporting immigrants that include challenging oppression, racism, poverty, and the legacies of colonization (Baines, 2011; Clarke & Wan, 2011). In the current neo-liberal context, restructuring of the non-profit social service and settlement sectors has standardized work practices and processes, which make an anti-oppressive approach more difficult to integrate in settlement work (Baines, 2011).

Develop your knowledge – Case Study

Consider these questions as you read the chapter and following case study:

1. How would you begin to work with the family in the case study? What factors should you consider?

2. What settlement services are available to assist this family?

3. What barriers and challenges might the family experience in the settlement process?

4. What decisions might Thomas and Larissa have to make about their careers?

5. What specific policies and procedures guide your work with this family?

Case Study

Thomas is a recent immigrant to Canada. He and his family arrived from the Caribbean two months ago. He was an accountant in the Caribbean before coming to Canada, and he wants to continue working with in the field. Thomas is very motivated to get back in his field, but he is unsure of how to proceed. His partner Larissa is a nurse and has similar concerns about her career. They have three children ages eight, eleven and fourteen. They are both concerned about getting their children into good schools, and connected to the Caribbean community. The family speaks English but they have no other family in Canada. Tom and Larissa have been on job interviews but have not been able to secure employment since arriving in Canada.

Settlement workers in community-based organizations with few resources are being asked to provide multiple services to clients, in a shorter amount of time, using technocratic and mechanistic approaches to practice (Clarke & Wan, 2011).

Sakamoto (2007) offers an anti-oppression framework that can be applied to settlement work with immigrant families. Her research with skilled Chinese immigrants highlights some of the strategies that settlement workers can use to enhance the settlement and integration of immigrants in Canada. She identifies six areas of focus to distinguish between a traditional social work approach and an anti-oppressive approach to practice: a) social workers; b) immigrants clients/service users; c) immigrant acculturation; d) cultural competence; e) relationships between service providers and service users; and f) structural change (see Table 1). These differences are not viewed as binary opposites but rather as a continuum as settlement workers vacillate between traditional and anti-oppressive approaches to practice (Clarke & Wan, 2011). The aim is to broaden the knowledge and skills of students and settlement workers and illustrate how anti-oppressive strategies can be integrated into settlement work.

Social Work–Settlement Work and Anti-Oppression: Unsettling Colonial Projects

The discussion of settlement work and anti-oppression must be grounded in the history of colonization in Canada. Canada's colonial history of immigration and settlement began over 500 years ago "with the Basque and with French, British, Russian, and other European colonial powers" (Johnson, Tamburro, & Clark, 2012, p. 138). For the past 500 years, Canada's First Peoples have been forced off their lands and displaced from their culture, language, and traditional healing practices by European settlers (Johnson, Tamburro, & Clark, 2012; Lawrence & Dua, 2005; Sinclair, Hart, & Bruyere, 2009). The forced assimilation of Aboriginal peoples has led to children being removed from their families, the outlawing of cultural practices and ceremonies, the loss of life, and overall, much material poverty in First Nations communities (Johnson, Tamburro, & Clark, 2012; Dei, 2006).

Social work and settlement work, like other human service professions, are implicated in the ongoing colonization of Aboriginal peoples in Canada and elsewhere. "According to the Royal Commission on Aboriginal Peoples (RCAP), social work and human service workers were active participants in

Table 1: Ideas underpinning the traditional approach and the anti-oppressive approach to social work with immigrants		
	Traditional Approach	**Anti-oppressive Approach**
Social worker	Assumed to be from or have assumptions of culturally dominant group (e.g., middle class, white)	Can be from any background and have intersecting identities
Immigrants clients/service users	Cultural and/or dissimilar other, who may be traumatized	Service users with multiple identities, who may have transnational ties
Immigrant acculturation	Needed and promoted through information, education, and training	Goals of acculturation are discussed with immigrants, who are referred to corresponding services
Cultural competence	Dominant worker learning about the cultures of cultural minorities	Focus on intersecting identities and oppression. Culturally dominant service providers as well as cultural minorities need to raise consciousness, avoid "race to innocence"
Relationship between service provider and service user	Expert helping novice in the society. Reminiscent of the charity model	Service provider strives to become co-learner, catalyst, and ally in the process, while acknowledging that power differences between service providers and service users can be oppressive
Structural change	Not addressed	Advocacy and social action toward systemic changes to society in integrating immigrants
Adapted from Sakamoto (2007)		

the placement of Aboriginal children in Indian Residential Schools (IRSs) until the 1960s" (cited in Johnson, Tamburro, & Clark, 2012, p. 140). Social work and social workers are implicated in colonial oppression of Aboriginal peoples for their involvement in and activation of church and state legislation and policies, which resulted in the "Sixties Scoop" (Johnson, 1983) and the transracial adoption, racism, and issues with identity that Aboriginal adoptees sometimes experience (Sinclair, 2009).

An anti-oppression approach is a constellation of theories and perspectives including anti-racist, anti-colonial, feminist, Marxist, critical, post-modernist, Indigenous, post-structuralist, and critical constructionist ones (Baines, 2011). It is an integrated model that helps people critically "analyze how power works to oppress and marginalize" and how to fight it (Baines, 2011, p. 26). Healy (2005) describes an anti-oppressive approach as a practice framework that includes critical reflection, empowerment, minimal intervention, and partnership. Sakamoto and Pitner (2005) describe anti-oppressive social work practice as the "eradication of oppression through institutional and societal changes" (p. 436) and propose changes at the micro, meso, and macro levels of intervention. For Dominelli (2002), anti-oppression is "a form of social work practice, which addresses social divisions and structural inequalities in the work done with 'clients' or workers" (p. 6). Barnoff (2005) and Sakamoto, Wei, and Truong (2008) argue for individual and organizational change efforts in integrating anti-oppression. Healy (2004), Valtonen (2001), and Cemlyn (2000) provide us with international perspectives and frameworks for anti-oppressive practice. Overall, an anti-oppressive approach provides us with strategies for working with individuals, families, groups, organizations, and communities of diverse backgrounds and interests (Baines, 2007; Barnoff, 2005; Barnoff & Coleman, 2007; Barnoff & Moffatt, 2007; Clarke & Wan, 2011; Sakamoto, Wei, & Truong, 2008).

The ideas underlying anti-oppression are widely debated and contested. This debate helps to redefine it in new ways for changing populations, "addressing new tensions, social problems, as well as underlying structural factors" (Baines, 2007, p. 4). An anti-oppression framework provides us with critical strategies for shifting our practice away from oppressive, traditional, and colonial approaches to one that is grounded in the theories of anti-racism, anti-colonialism, and decolonization and other social justice strategies. Settlement workers must understand the historical legacy of colonialism and racism in Canada and its impact on Aboriginal people and people of colour and work to promote Aboriginal well-being and healing, values, worldviews, and cultural practices (Freeman, 2011; Laenui, 2000; Sharma & Wright, 2008–9).

Social workers and settlement workers must also understand the history of racism in Canada, specifically how immigration laws and policies have and continue to exclude certain groups of people (Henry, Tator, Mattis, & Rees, 1995). They must also understand how the settlement of new immigrants in Canada is implicated in the ongoing colonization of Aboriginal peoples (Lawrence & Dua, 2005). With this background, social workers and settlement workers must work to "make Aboriginality foundational" in their everyday practice as the struggle against racism must "attend to the specificities of the oppression of people constituted as indigenous" (Lawrence & Dua, 2005, p.122). An anti-oppressive approach requires settlement workers to critically analyse power, domination, privilege, structural inequality, and other forms of oppression, and engage in advocacy and social action for structural change (Baines, 2010; Sakamoto, 2007).

The Social Worker–Settlement Worker: Identity and Difference

The multiple and intersecting identities of current social worker–settlement workers disrupt the traditional image of the social worker–settlement worker of the past who came from the dominant, White, middle-class culture (Sakamoto, 2007). The settlement sector has moved away from the tradi¬tional approach of hiring White, middle-class women as social workers–settlement workers (James, 2001) to one where they "can be from any background with intersecting identities" (Sakamoto, 2007, p. 528). For example, I identify as a Black female of Caribbean background, who speaks the dominant, colonial language – English, as well as the language of the local people in Jamaica – Patois, which is not well understood or recognized as a language in the Canadian context. On the other hand, I am able-bodied, and have a university education and heterosexual privileges that allow me to move easily in society without being attacked by homophobic remarks or actions. These multiple and intersecting identities both privilege and oppress me. Understanding feminist intersec¬tionality theory and how aspects of my identity both privilege and oppress me, is very important in examining power, privilege, and oppression. Therefore, while diversity and equity strategies in organi¬zational hiring policies and practices have created space for racialized workers in the settlement sector, there is much work to be done in the move towards transformative actions.

One common anti-oppressive strategy that has helped to change the settlement sector is the practice of hiring immigrants, particularly racialized women at various levels of the organization. Traditional settlement work was also highly gendered, classed, and raced with middle-class White women doing the work (James, 2001). Today, settlement work continues to be gendered but racialized immigrant women dominate the frontline and racialized men and White women dominate middle and upper management (Clarke & Wan, 2011; James, 2001). Another anti-oppressive strategy that has helped to increase the diversity of the settlement sector is the practice of hiring workers who speak certain ethno-specific languages to work with new immigrants who have limited English language skills (Sakamoto, 2007). Increasing the diversity of settlement workers at various levels of the organization is a critical anti-oppressive strategy that allows immigrants to receive services in their first language and from practitioners who understand and respect the cultural values, beliefs, and practices of the clients they serve (Clarke & Wan, 2011; Sakamoto, 2007).

Develop your knowledge – Ask yourself

1. What are your multiple and intersecting social identities?

2. Why do you think it is important to increase the diversity of staff in an agency?

3. How is the traditional approach to settlement work different from an anti-oppression approach?

Immigrant Clients–Service Users: Multiple and Intersecting Identities

Every year approximately 120,000 immigrants from different socio-economic, ethno-racial, professional, religious, and linguistic backgrounds arrive in the province of Ontario (Citizenship and Immigration Canada, 2009). This is a shift from the past where the goal of Canada's exclusionary immigration policies was to continue the colonial project of establishing a White settler society (Galabuzi, 2006; George, 2002; Lawrence & Dua, 2005). From this colonial perspective, the view of immigrant clients–service users is that of the "cultural and/or dissimilar other[s] who may be traumatized" (Sakamoto, 2007, p. 528). Though some immigrant clients–service users are survivors of torture, trauma and violence, many are educated and experienced, but continue to face barriers to settlement such as "getting [their] credentials recognized or entering the labour market" (Baines, 2011, p.32).

Some social workers–settlement workers continue to have difficulty seeing immigrants as individuals with competencies, strengths, and resiliency, and who also have complex, multiple and intersecting identities (Kumsa, 2007). Influenced by deeply embedded colonial and racist discourses, as well as medical and psychological discourses of trauma, deficit, and pathology frame how immigrant clients–service users are perceived and the kinds of services they receive (Clarke & Wan, 2011; Sakamoto, 2007). These discourses of immigrant client–service users are evident in the media, the boardrooms, at the water cooler, and in our everyday interactions. For example, discourses of immigrants as welfare cheats, non-status, terrorists, lazy, and so on need to be deconstructed and reconstructed in new ways that change perspectives, policies, procedures, practices, and dominant power relations (Clarke & Wan, 2011; Fook, 2002). Although there have been significant gains in the settlement sector, remnants of the traditional approach remain as some social workers–settlement workers continue the process of trying to "Christianize" and "Canadianize" immigrants (O'Connor, 1986). An important anti-oppression strategy is to deconstruct these assumptions and discourses about immigrants that frame everyday practice.

From an anti-oppression perspective, immigrant client–service users are perceived as individuals with agency, and complex, multiple and fluid identities (Clarke & Wan, 2011; Kumsa, 2007; Sakamoto, 2007). This requires settlement workers to understand multiple and intersecting identities as opportunities for challenging oppression in the settlement sector and the broader society (Clarke & Wan, 2011). Recognizing and respecting the diversity among immigrant clients–service users are important steps for frontline settlement work and long-term organizational and institutional change (Barnoff, 2005, 2011; Clarke & Wan, 2011). One of the strategies that frontline settlement workers can engage is to reframe immigrant clients–service users "as competent individuals with agency ... multiple identities and ... transnational ties" (Sakamoto, 2007, p. 528). Doing anti-oppressive settlement is therefore learning to reframe cultural differences and diversity as strengths for challenging oppression and promoting transformative action at the front line and organizational levels (Barnoff, 2011). From this approach, settlement workers can embrace the opportunity to involve immigrant clients–service users in their everyday work, such as developing new programs and services, reviewing and creating organizational policies and procedures, and in shaping everyday practice.

Doing anti-oppressive settlement work requires settlement workers to promote social justice and social change (Barnoff, 2011; Benjamin, 2007). An effective anti-oppressive strategy is to listen to the stories of immigrant clients–service users and seek their perspectives as you work to improve and change your practice. Imagine a practice where you are able to work with immigrant clients–service users as partners and as knowledge creators in the settlement process. Where you are able to listen to their stories and perspectives with the goal of helping to shape and change your work as a practitioner. Imagine a practice where the multilingual skills, education, and other social identities of immigrant clients–service users are perceived as strengths – not pathologies, deficiencies, or risks (Solomon & Clarke, 2008). Imagine a practice where you can engage with immigrant client–service users authentically, that is "being present, being fair ... being real, being non-judgmental, being honest with regard to who you are, and being truly open to all of who your service users are" (Barnoff 2005, p.17).

Develop your knowledge – Ask yourself

1. How is diversity recognized and respected in your organization or placement?

2. Why is it important to recognize the multiple and intersecting identities of clients?

3. What anti-oppressive strategies do you use in your everyday practice with immigrant clients/service users?

4. What are some of the challenges in implementing anti-oppressive strategies in your organization?

Settlement Work: Anti-Oppressive Strategies for Practice

The Contexts of Settlement Work

Settlement work has a long history in Canada (James, 2001). From the reformist settlement movement of the early 1800s to today, settlement work and settlement workers are part of the colonial Canadian fabric (O'Connor, 1986; James, 2001; Lawrence & Dua, 2005; Sakamoto, 2007). From its early charitable beginnings with White, middle-class, female volunteers, settlement work concentrated on several key areas: education and training, recreation, social and health services, skill building, language training, employment and advocacy on behalf of immigrants (Clarke & Wan, 2011; James, 2001; Sakamoto, 2007). Much of these services continue in new forms and varying degrees for targeted populations.

Current settlement work is practised "within the context of neoliberalism, globalization, and restructuring" (Baines, 2009, p. 19). For instance, new funding structures have reorganized settlement work and services so that many programs and services are delivered by part-time, contract workers, limited in scope, few in numbers, and difficult to access due to a narrowing of eligibility criteria (Baines, 2007; Clarke & Wan, 2011). The neo-liberal agenda has infected the settlement sector, and changed the nature and quality of services that settlement workers can now provide to immigrants. For example, in the past, new immigrants would be eligible for the universal Ontario Health Insurance Plan (OHIP). Today, new immigrants must wait a period of three months before they are eligible OHIP. Similarly, new immigrants are no longer eligible for many services after obtaining citizenship which usually occurs after three years in Canada.

Settlement workers have assumed many roles and responsibilities over the years. Their roles have shifted drastically from moral and cultural educators and trainers to advocates and political activists working with and on behalf of immigrants. In recent years, their advocacy role has been diminished by neo-liberal government funding priorities. Many settlement workers and managers fear for their jobs and the threat of losing their organization's charitable status if they engage in advocacy work. I was warned by my supervisor to be careful about the level of advocacy I engaged in with newcomer youth. When pressed for a reason, I was told that advocacy could no longer be tracked as a legitimate settlement activity on monthly reports to funders. Therefore, the amount of time spent advocating for and on behalf of newcomer youth needed to be reduced or eliminated. As social workers– settlement workers move forward in the current neo-liberal context, there are several anti-oppressive strategies that can be utilized.

Immigrant Acculturation: Processes and Voices?

From the standpoint of a traditional approach, acculturation is an important process in the settlement and integration of immigrants (Berry, 1997; Liem, Lim, & Liem, 2000; Sakamoto, 2007). These scholars propose varying perspectives on the concept of acculturation – from a linear process of change in immigrant attitudes, values, and beliefs towards the host society to processes of "*integration* (accept old culture, accept new culture), *assimilation* (reject old culture, accept new culture), *separation* (accept old culture, reject new culture), and *marginalization* (reject old culture, reject new culture)" (Sakamoto, 2007, p. 519). Through settlement services such as "information, education, and training," settlement workers help to facilitate the acculturation process (Sakamoto, 2007, p. 528). Other programs and services such as English Conversation Circle, job search workshops, befriending, and Newcomer Orientation Workshops (NOWs) help new immigrants learn skills, "expand their social networks but also facilitated the acculturation process by teaching [them] ... to be 'Canadian' in speech, dress, and behaviour" (Clarke & Wan, 2011, p.19). Many settlement services are delivered uncritically to new immigrants, promoting assimilation rather than integration (Clarke & Wan, 2011). Stated differently, settlement workers engage in practices that promote "assimilation under the guise of integration" (Clarke & Wan, 2011, p. 20). The failure of acculturation processes to address structural issues or the pathologization of immigrants who may acculturate differently, make settlement workers complicit in the oppression of the service users with whom they work (Sakamoto, 2007).

An anti-oppression framework challenges social workers–settlement workers to discuss the goals of acculturation with new immigrants and refer them to appropriate services (Sakamoto, 2007). This requires settlement workers to critically reflect upon the process of acculturation, and listen to the voices and perspectives of new immigrants in their decision making. Dumbrill (2011) and Freeman (2011) point to the importance of the worker understanding the clients' perspectives and experiences and incorporating these in the work they do with them. It is equally important for clients to understand their own situation from their perspective and viewpoint (Larson, 2012). Rather than the worker making expert decisions about the services that are best for new immigrants or delivering pre-packaged programs and services, settlement workers are encouraged to talk openly with immigrants about the goals of acculturation, and allow them to make choices that meet their needs (Clarke & Wan, 2011). An anti-oppressive approach allows settlement workers to question and challenge traditional, top-down understandings and generic practices of acculturation that are part of their everyday routine. When settlement workers "work within clients' views, cultures, and understandings" (Larson, 2012, p.74), they can raise critical consciousness and build the capacity of immigrants to empower themselves towards the goals of acculturation (Clarke & Wan, 2011).

Cultural Competence or Consciousness-raising and Structural Competence?

The traditional approach to settlement work requires workers from the dominant culture to learn about the cultures of cultural minorities in an attempt to become culturally competent (Sakamoto, 2007). While understanding culture is important for practice, and having knowledge of populations helps in the engagement and assessment processes, these are not sufficient for a critical reflexive practice. In fact, cultural tensions abound in the social work literature (Chung Yan, 2008) and by extension in settlement work. Given the complex web of social relations that frame settlement work, cultural competence is not achievable or desirable in practice. Individuals, families, and communities carry many different sets of cultures and are too diverse and complex to be explained away by cultural competence alone. Further, individuals are situated in different social locations with multiple and intersecting identities that must be considered in the helping process. Therefore, the traditional approach to settlement work "promotes an absolute view of culture and is a form of new racism" (Pon, 2009, p. 60). So what are settlement workers to do – cultural competence or consciousness-raising? I build upon Sakamoto's anti-oppressive framework by arguing for an expanded understanding of consciousness-raising to include structural competence in settlement work.

As a young settlement worker, I recall participating in cultural competency training to gain knowledge about the cultures of the different populations I was working with. Training about the culturally different "Other" was added to my "toolbox" for practice. Though cultural competency training fits well within the neo-liberal context of efficiency and standardization, I quickly learned that it did not prepare me for working effectively with service users who had multiple and intersecting identities, of which culture was only one part. In fact, in many ways the training reinforced stereotypes about different cultures and ignored the power dynamics that shape the worker–client relationship and the structural inequalities that exist in society. Further, although cultural competency and sensitivity training are lauded in settlement work, simply considering these sensitivities does not change the oppressive structures that exists in societal institutions or the unequal power relations between workers and clients. Similarly, when mainstream service providers position settlement workers as cultural interpreters, it reinforces the idea that the challenges new immigrants experience in the settlement process lies in their culture and not in structural inequalities. Settlement workers are thus implicated in maintaining and reproducing the status quo, which leaves structural inequalities and oppression intact.

An anti-oppressive approach takes a critical perspective to understanding cultural competence. From this perspective, cultural competence is deconstructed and reconstructed in new ways that challenge settlement workers to "pay a closer attention to understanding individuals' intersecting identities and multiple oppressions" (Sakamoto, 2007, p. 528). From an anti-oppressive approach, cultural competence is turned on its head to reveal the underlining issues of power, privilege, domination, and hegemony that frame the worker–client helping relationship. Similarly, issues of racism, sexism, homophobia, Islamophobia, anti-Semitism, and so on are openly discussed in all settlement work training. Rather than learning about the "Other," an anti-oppressive approach encourages settlement workers to become border crossers (Girouz, 2005) who continuously interrogate difference, "not only the socioeconomic structures that marginalize particular communities, but also the structures that privilege others" (Solomon, Khattar-Manoukian & Clarke, 2007, p. 81).

Settlement workers from cultural minority groups must think critically about issues of power, privilege and oppression and how these shape the working relationship with immigrant clients–service users. An anti-oppressive settlement worker reflects on and is aware of the ways in which power is exercised and maintained in the service user–service provider relationship and acknowledges this power in their everyday practice. Critical reflection is an approach that allows settlement workers to subject their practice to a critical gaze (Fook, 2002). Settlement workers from cultural minority groups are encouraged to reflect upon and ask critical questions about their shared affinity with immigrants, as this does not exempt them from engaging in oppressive practices. They are also challenged to raise their own consciousness and the consciousness of new immigrants with whom they work to avoid falling into the trap of the "race to innocence" (Fellows & Razack 1998). Critical reflection raises consciousness and spurs action.

From an anti-oppression approach, consciousness-raising is the politicization of "everyday personal experiences [and how these] are part of [the] larger political, economic, cultural and social structures" (Baines, 2011, p. 86). It is also about politicizing practice – that is, helping to educate new immigrants about the host society, raising their consciousness about rights, laws, policies, the economic, social and political structures, and the relationship of these to their everyday realities. Politicizing practice also means engaging new immigrants in the struggle for social justice. Also important in consciousness-raising efforts is an understanding that "the personal is political" (Baines, 2011, p. 86) and involves both reflection and action for social change (Mullaly, 1997). The traditional approach of depositing knowledge uncritically to service users through education and information sessions must be challenged in settlement work. Instead, settlement workers are encouraged to provide critical, politicized information and education to service users about their own and others oppression and how they can be engaged in the change process. Consciousness-raising is therefore about empowerment and capacity building of immigrants rather than depoliticized information sharing. These anti-oppressive strategies offer settlement workers and organizational leaders a structural framework for practice that involves consciousness-raising, critical reflection and political action for social transformation.

The Service Provider–Service User Relationship: Expert or Co-Learner?

Establishing a trusting and caring relationship with service users is important in social work and settlement work. In the traditional approach, settlement workers are perceived as *experts* who help immigrants navigate various systems in the settlement process (Sakamoto, 2007). The role of expert carries a certain degree of power which can let clients feel disempowered and reinforce their sense of powerlessness. The power differential between the immigrant client–service user and the settlement worker is legitimized by the agency, by legislation, and through professional discourses. For example, settlement workers' access to agency resources gives them legitimate power, which they can use to provide or deny services to new immigrants. They also have the power to carry out state mandated directives, prioritize services, and impart knowledge produced by state agencies such as Citizenship and Immigration Canada (CIC) and public school boards.

The quality of the relationship between settlement workers and immigrant clients–service users is critical to the helping process. The traditional approach reinforces the expert power of settlement workers and denies agency and voice to immigrant clients–service users (Sakamoto & Pitner, 2005). When power is exerted over immigrant clients–service users, there is generally resistance. Clients show resistance to worker power in ways that include challenging the worker, postponing appointments, showing up late, or requesting a new worker. Often these resistance strategies upset settlement workers who sometimes exert more power over service users, and even enact disciplinary actions such as exclusion from services or events. The settlement worker-service user relationship must be critically examined for the ways in which it is paternalistic and punitive, and must be reframed in more empowering ways.

In the current neo-liberal context, the opportunity for settlement workers to share power with immigrant clients–service users is further diminished by managerial practices of control on populations and problems (Baines, 2011). In this context, settlement workers are completing more paperwork, and in some cases frequently updating electronic records and databases, and providing more standardized programs and services to immigrant clients–service users with much less resources than in the past. More and more they are expected to document and report their interactions with service users, track the number of clients served for monthly reports and record the services rendered, including the number of referrals made to other service providers. Technology is being used more frequently to monitor the behaviours and actions of social workers, settlement workers and clients, especially in the school setting. The challenge for settlement workers is to understand the changing nature of practice and find creative ways to share power with immigrant clients–service users and work together to resist the neo-liberal agenda.

An anti-oppression approach encourages settlement workers to think of advocacy and social action as part of settlement work (Baines, 2011). It requires settlement workers to practice differently and "regard those utilizing immigrant services as co-learners and allies in the process of locating necessary services rather than seeing them as dissimilar other" (Sakamoto, 2007, p. 529). From an anti-oppressive approach, settlement workers must engage in ongoing critical reflection about the role of expert, and examine their own subjective identity and power in the relationship with immigrant client–service user (Healy, 2005). Sakamoto and Pitner (2005) encourage settlement workers to be vigilant in "addressing the needs and assets of service users, challenging the oppressive structures and, most importantly, critically challenging the power dynamics in the service-provider/service-user relationship"

(p. 435). During my years as a settlement worker, I was often challenged to reflect my own power and privilege and the dynamics in the worker–client relationship. This was important in order for me to work in solidarity with service users from different socio-economic, religious, racial and cultural backgrounds. It is important for settlement workers to understand how their own power and privilege reproduce oppression for new immigrant clients–service users in everyday practice.

Settlement workers must also strive to be co-learners and allies with immigrant clients–service users. To do this, settlement workers need to critically interrogate their role as experts and be comfortable with "not knowing" everything about service user populations, problems, or cultures (Fook, 2002). An anti-oppressive approach encourages settlement workers to ensure that clients–service users' voices are present in the assessment process and that they are fully engaged in helping to find solutions to the problems they experience. When power is shared, both clients–service users and settlement workers learn from each other and contribute knowledge to the helping process (Baines, 2011). The settlement worker who establishes congruence with clients–service users is also able to build alliance for a good working relationship (Dumbrill, 2011).

Engaging in critical self-reflection and reflexive practice are key strategies of an anti-oppressive approach (Clark, 2012; Fook, 2002). It is important for settlement workers to look at their own practice approaches, frameworks and discourses from critical lenses to see how they are implicated in reproducing oppression. In the "doing" of settlement work, they are encouraged

Develop your knowledge – Ask yourself

1. What have you learned about the processes of immigrant acculturation?

2. Why is the service provider-service user's relationship so important?

3. How do you now understand cultural competence in settlement work?

4. What are some of the challenges and opportunities of engaging in advocacy and social action with new immigrants?

to share power with service users in ways that deconstruct the role of expert to a more humble position as co-learners in the helping process (Clark, 2012). Through critical self reflection, settlement workers learn how to value the stories, knowledge, and experiences of service users and become comfortable with sharing power in the professional relationship. In order to develop a critical reflexive practice, settlement workers must engage in ongoing critical analysis and reflection about power, privilege, and oppression and seek to develop the skills necessary to bring about much needed change in frontline practice and organizational structure and culture.

Structural Change: Advocacy and Social Action

The traditional approach to settlement work ignores structural change and does not recognize that individual newcomer needs are rooted in broader structural issues – the "'personal is political'" (Mullaly, 1997). The traditional focus on immediate needs rather than an integrated model that includes client advocacy and long-term structural change keeps new immigrants on the margins and excluded from full participation in society. Currently, when a settlement worker meets with a new immigrant, the focus is on providing information and referral to help the service user navigate the complex web of social services including education, employment, housing, health, recreation, and other services. While it is important to help new immigrants meet their basic immediate needs, it is equally important to engage in advocacy and activism to challenge the structural barriers that keep immigrants on the margins. From an anti-oppressive approach, settlement workers are encouraged to politicize their practice so that settlement services are delivered with the goals of equity, human rights, and social justice being met. For example, settlement workers are encouraged to critically reflect upon the services they provide to new immigrants and be able to identify and discuss the gaps and barriers that exist (e.g., user fees, long wait times) in services. Simply providing new immigrants with a list of services, many of which no longer exist due to funding cuts, or glossy brochures that promote services with eligibility criteria they cannot meet, is not good settlement work and is in fact an unethical practice. Settlement workers need to understand the impact of the current neo-liberal agenda on their work with new immigrants and openly share this information with them.

From the traditional perspective, settlement workers are not required to engage in social action or advocacy on behalf of immigrant clients–service users. Although some workers engage in individual-level advocacy, this is not sufficient to bring about transformation in state agencies and other oppressive social institutions. As I recall, settlement workers were discouraged from engaging in advocacy, especially in the education system. As noted earlier, I was once told by a supervisor to keep my activist practice to myself as this was perceived as a threat to the program's funding renewal. Because of my interest in disrupting the traditional approach to settlement work, I made the decision to move on to an environment where advocacy and activism were an important part of the work and built into the organization's funding structure. In this way, the agency was not at risk of losing its funding and I could engage in advocacy work inside and outside of the employing organization. Mullaly (1997) encourages us to work with and against the system.

Sakamoto calls for structural change and challenges settlement workers to engage in "advocacy and social action toward systemic changes of the society in integrating immigrants" (2007, p. 528). Clarke & Wan (2011) argue for an anti-oppression approach that "requires settlement workers to move beyond direct service provision (e.g., information, referral, assessment, and intake) to advocacy and social action with and/or on behalf of newcomer youth" (p. 22). From this perspective, settlement workers are encouraged to have critical discussions about issues of power and oppression with service users, and continually seek their input and involve them in the work they do. In this approach, settlement workers are also encouraged to listen to the voices of new immigrants and integrate their perspectives in the helping

Develop your knowledge – Ask yourself

1. Which of the strategies discussed do you use in your everyday practice?

2. What are the challenges of integrating anti-oppressive practice in settlement work?

3. How can an anti-oppressive framework change current settlement practice?

4. What changes do you need to make in your everyday work with immigrants?

process. By sharing power and learning from each other, settlement workers and immigrant clients–service workers are both empowered to challenge the oppressive structures that keep them marginalized in society. An anti-oppression approach is thus transformative for both settlement workers and new immigrants. By engaging in advocacy and social action, settlement workers can build a radical, transformative practice that disrupts the traditional approach and advance an anti-oppressive perspective that promotes social justice and social change.

Conclusion

In this chapter, I have shared some of my reflections as a settlement worker and outlined several anti-oppressive strategies that settlement workers can utilize in their everyday practice with new immigrants. I have also discussed the traditional approach to practice, and show some of the challenges that settlement workers experience as they vacillate between the traditional and anti-oppressive approaches. As a settlement worker, I experienced the traditional approach as marginalizing and disempowering for the ways it ignores the voices and experiences of new immigrants as well as the structural barriers they experience in Canadian society and in the settlement process. At the same time, its focus on the worker as an "expert" who exerts power and control over new immigrants in ways that are paternalistic and punitive, makes this an oppressive approach.

An anti-oppression approach, on the other hand, is both challenging and empowering for settlement workers and new immigrants. It is challenging because it takes time, resources, and commitment to implement anti-oppressive strategies in organizations. In many organizations, anti-oppression is not well understood or supported by organizational policies, processes, or mission statements (Barnoff, 2005). At the same time, an anti-oppression approach co-exists alongside a neo-liberal agenda, which makes it more difficult to implement and sustain. However, if settlement workers and organizational leaders are committed to the principles of anti-oppression, then implementing strategies to change organizational culture, policies, procedures, and practices are easier to accomplish. Sakamoto (2007) identifies six key areas of focus that can help settlement workers think critically about and implement anti-oppressive strategies in their everyday practice. These include: (a) social workers; (b) immigrants clients/service users; (c) immigrant acculturation; (d) cultural competence; (e) relationships between service providers and service users; and (f) structural change. These factors have important implications for practice as they raise the consciousness of settlement workers to know differently and practice differently. Anti-oppressive settlement work must therefore occur at all levels of the organization if it is to be sustainable and beneficial to the settlement and integration of immigrants in Canadian society.

An anti-oppression framework provides social workers and settlement workers with an approach to practice that is critical, reflexive, and transformative at the personal, professional, and structural levels (Solomon, Khattar-Manoukian, & Clarke, 2005). Settlement agencies have a responsibility to prepare settlement workers for critical anti-oppressive practice – a practice in which power and oppression are critically interrogated and linkages are made between people's personal struggles and broader structural and systemic issues. An anti-oppression framework requires settlement workers to make the shift from expert to reflexive practitioner, that is, one who continuously reflects upon their practice, and combines critical reflection with consciousness-raising and political action for social transformation. An anti-oppression framework also offers a vision of what settlement work could be, regardless of funding cuts to programs and services and the restructuring of settlement work as part-time, contractual work within the current neoliberal environment.

References

Baines, D. (2007). *Doing anti-oppressive practice: Building transformative politicized social work*. Halifax: Fernwood.

Baines, D. (2010). Neoliberal restructuring, activism/participation, and social unionism in the nonprofit social services. *Nonprofit and Voluntary Sector Quarterly, 39*(1), 10–28.

Baines, D. (2011). *Doing anti-oppressive practice: Social justice social work* (2nd ed.). Halifax: Fernwood.

Barnoff, L. (2005). *Implementing anti-oppressive principles in everyday practice: Lessons from feminist agencies*. Unpublished manuscript. Toronto: Ryerson University.

Barnoff, L. (2011). Business as usual: Doing anti-oppressive organizational change. In D. Baines (Ed.), *Doing anti-oppressive practice: Social justice social work* (2nd ed.). Halifax: Fernwood Publishing.

Barnoff, L., & Coleman, B. (2007). Strategies for integrating anti-oppressive principles: Perspectives from feminist agencies. In D. Baines (Ed.), *Doing Anti-oppressive practice: Building transformative politicized social work*. Halifax, NS: Fernwood.

Barnoff, L., & Moffatt, K. (2007). Contradictory tensions in anti-oppression practice in feminist social services. *Affilia: Journal of Women and Social Work, 22*(1), 56–70.

Benjamin, A. (2007). Doing anti-oppressive social work: The importance of resistance, history and strategy. In D. Baines (Ed.), *Doing anti-oppressive practice: Building transformative politicized social work*. Halifax: Fernwood.

Berry, J. W. (1997). Immigration, acculturation, and adaptation. *Applied Psychology: An International Review, 46* (1), pp.5-68.

Cemlyn, S. (2000). Assimilation, control, mediation or advocacy? Social work dilemmas in providing anti-oppressive services for travelers' children and families. *Child and Family Social Work, 5*, 327–41.

Chung Yan, M. (2008). Exploring cultural tensions in cross-cultural social work practice. *Social Work, 53*(4); 317–328.

Citizenship and Immigration Canada (2009). Language instruction for newcomers to Canada: Client profile and performance indicators. Retrieved from: http://www.cic.gc.ca

Clark, N. (2012). Beyond the reflective practitioner. In J. Drolet, N. Clark, & H. Allen (Eds.), *Shifting sites of practice: Field education in Canada*. Toronto: Pearson Canada.

Clarke, J., & Wan, E. (2011). Transforming settlement work: From a traditional to a critical anti-oppression approach with newcomer youth in secondary schools. *Critical Social Work, 12*(1), 13-26.

Dei, G. J. S. (2006). Introduction: Mapping the Terrain – Towards a New Politics of Resistance. In G.J.S. Dei & A. Kempf (Eds.), *Anti-colonialism and education: The politics of resistance*. Rotterdam, Netherlands: Sense.

Dominelli, L. (2002). Anti-oppressive practice in context. In R. Adams, L. Dominelli, & M. Payne (Eds.), *Social work: Themes, issues, and critical debates* (2nd ed.). Basingstoke: Palgrave Macmillan.

Dumbrill, G. (2011). Doing anti-oppressive child protection work. In D. Baines (Ed.), *Doing anti-oppressive practice: Social justice social work* (2nd ed.). Halifax: Fernwood.

Fellows, M. L., & Razack, S. (1998). The race to innocence: Confronting hierarchical relations among women. *Journal of Gender, Race and Justice, 1*, 335-352.

Fook, J. (2002). *Social work: Critical theory and practice*. London: Sage.

Freeman, B. (2011). Indigenous pathways to anti-oppressive practice. In D. Baines (Ed.), *Doing anti-oppressive practice: Social justice social work* (2nd ed.). Halifax: Fernwood.

Galabuzi, G. E. (2006). *Canada's economic apartheid: The social exclu-sion of racialized groups in the new century.* Toronto: Canadian Scholars' Press.

George, U. (2002). A needs-based model for settlement service delivery for newcomers to Canada. *International Social Work, 45*(4), 465-480.

Giroux, H. (2005). Border crossings: Cultural workers and the politics of education (2nd ed.). New York: Routledge.

Healy, K. (2005). *Social work theories in context: Creating frameworks for practice.* New York: Palgrave.

Healy, L. M. (2004). Strengthening the link: Social work with immigrants and refugees and international social work. *Journal of Immigrant and Refugee Services, 2*(1–2), 49–67.

Henry, F., Tator, C., Mattis, W., & Rees, T. (1995). *The colour of democ-racy.* Toronto: Harcourt Brace.

James, C. (2001). Reforming reform: Toronto's settlement house move-ment, 1900–20. *Canadian Historical Review, 82*(1), 1-20.

Johnson, P. (1983). *Native children and the child welfare system.* Toronto: James Lorimer.

Johnson, S., Tamburro, P. R., & Clark, N. (2012). Indigenous field educa-tion: Protocols and practices. In J. Drolet, N. Clark & H. Allen (Eds.), *Shifting sites of practice: Field education in Canada.* Toronto: Pearson Canada.

Kumsa, M. (2007). A resettlement story of unsettlement: Transformative practices of taking it personally. In D. Baines (Ed.), *Doing anti-oppres-sive practice: Building transformative politicized social work.* Halifax: Fernwood.

Laenui, P. (2000). Processes of decolonization. In M. Battiste (Ed.), *Reclaiming indigenous voice and vision.* Vancouver: University of British Columbia Press.

Larson, G. (2012). Theories and values in action. In J. Drolet, N. Clark, & H. Allen (Eds.), *Shifting sites of practice: Field education in Canada.* Toronto: Pearson Canada.

Lawrence, B., & Dua, E. (2005). Decolonizing antiracism. *Social Justice, 32*(4), 120–43.

Liem, R., Lim, B.A., & Liem, J. H. (2000). Acculturation and emotion among Asian Americans. *Cultural Diversity and Ethnic Minority Psychology Journal, 6* (1), pp. 13-31.

Mullaly, B. (1997). *Structural social work: Ideology, theory, and practice.* Toronto: Oxford University Press.

O'Connor, P. J. (1986). *The story of St. Christopher House.* Toronto: St. Christopher House. Retrieved from www.stchrishouse.org/st-chris/history/TheStoryOfStChristop.php

Pon, G. (2009). Cultural competency as new racism: An ontology of forgetting. *Journal of Progressive Human Services, 20*(1), 59–71.

Sakamoto, I. (2007). A critical examination of immigrant acculturation: Toward an anti-oppressive social work model with immigrant adults in a pluralistic society. *British Journal of Social Work 37*, 515–35.

Sakamoto, I., & Pitner, R. O. (2005). Use of critical consciousness in anti-oppressive social work practice: Disentangling power dynamics at personal and structural levels. *British Journal of Social Work, 35*, 435–52.

Sakamoto, I., Wei, Y., & Truong, L. (2008). How do organizations and social policies "acculturate" to immigrants? Accommodating skilled immigrants in Canada. *American Journal of Community Psychology, 42*, 343–54.

Sharma, N., & Wright, C. (2008–9). Decolonizing resistance, challenging colonial states. *Social Justice, 35*(3), 120–38.

Sinclair, R. (2009). Identity or racism? Aboriginal transracial adoption. In R. Sinclair, M. Hart & G. Bruyere (Eds.), *Wicihitowin: Aboriginal social work in Canada.* Black Point, MB: Fernwood.

Solomon, R. P., & Clarke, J. (2008). *Engaging community: Teacher preparation for urban diversity.* Video. Toronto: Urban Diversity Program, Faculty of Education, York University. Retrieved from www.yorku.ca/foe/rpatricksolomon/udvideo.html

Solomon, R. P., Khattar-Manoukian, R., & Clarke, J. (2007). Pre-service teachers as border crossers: Linking urban schools and communities through service learning. In R.P. Solomon & D. Sekayi (Eds.), *Urban teacher education and teaching: Innovative practices for diversity and social justice.* Mahwah, NJ: Lawrence Erlbaum.

Solomon, R. P., Khattar-Manoukian, R., & Clarke, J. (2005). From an ethic of altruism to the possibilities for transformation in teacher candidates' community involvement. In L. Pease-Alvarez & S. Schecter (Eds.), *Learning, teaching and community: Contributions of situated and participatory approaches to educational innovation.* Mahwah, NJ: Lawrence Erlbaum.

Valtonen, K. (2001). Social work with immigrants and refugees: Developing a participation-based framework for anti-oppressive practice. *British Journal of Social Work, 31*, 955–960.

PART 3

MULTICULTURALISM, RACIAL EQUITY AND ANTI-RACIST EDUCATION

CHAPTER 6

Multiculturalism and Citizenship in Canada as Policy and Discourse: Approaches and Challenges

Salah Hassanpour

Case Study

Suaad Hagi Mohamud is a single mother of Somali descent who lives with her young teenage son in the Greater Toronto Area (GTA). A first-generation Canadian immigrant as of 1999, she acquired Canadian citizenship in 2009. In May of that same year, Mohamud made an emergency visit to Kenya to visit her sick mother. While attempting to return to Canada after two weeks, both a KLM airline employee as well as the Canadian High Council in Nairobi decided that the picture in Mohamud's passport did not look like her: Specifically, it was deemed that her lips did not match her appearance and her glasses were not the same.

For the next three months, Mohamud desperately attempted to prove her identity by producing many more proofs of her Canadian citizenship while spending time in a flea-ridden, guarded guesthouse in Nairobi, charged with being an imposter and scheduled to be deported

continued...

to her native Somalia. Canadian officials during this time ignored all her efforts to prove her citizenship and identity.

If not for Suaad Hagi Mohamud's friends, family, and lawyer bringing her story to the Canadian press (which resulted in weeks of prominent coverage on *CBC* and in *The Toronto Star*), Canadian officials would very likely never have considered accepting the results of a DNA test which, finally, established with 99.99% certainty Suaad Hagi Mohamud's relationship with her son (who was living with family friends far longer than originally planned) (Sheppard & Goddard, 2009).

Introduction

The horrible ordeal that Suaad Hagi Mohamud underwent is certainly unique: Her case is not being brought up at the start of this chapter to claim (or even infer) that this type of scenario happens to Canadians who travel to other countries on a regular basis. However, her story highlights certain forms of discrimination against immigrants, especially those who are also racialized.

The most obvious form of discrimination in Mrs. Mohamud's case is racial profiling, in terms of the overzealous and distorted scrutiny of her photo ID by both commercial airline and government staff but also the racist presumption that people from Africa (and, apparently, Somalis in particular) are likely engaging in imposter scams in order to travel illegally.

To be sure, the Canadian government has mechanisms to aid citizens who travel abroad and encounter problems with foreign authorities. For instance, Mrs. Mohamud could have notified Foreign Affairs and International Trade (FAIT) (via their Registration of Canadians Abroad initiative) of her travel destination and duration of her trip prior to leaving the country. However, doing so would not have guaranteed that her ordeal would have been avoided. This is because, from a social justice perspective, the lack of response from Canadian officials in this case flies in the face of how Canada's often-celebrated multicultural society ought to operate, revealing instead a culture of discrimination and latent racism. Mrs. Mohamud's case more specifically puts into question the value of citizenship when it comes to Canadians who are racialized members: How can immigrants and other so-called "minority groups" possibly cultivate a sense of belonging to a nation that is unwilling to come to their aid or, more generally, to provide necessary supports?

This chapter will introduce two key concepts: multiculturalism and citizenship, which are closely related to each other in terms of official Canadian government policy.[1] These two concepts will be discussed specifically in relation to the challenges faced by newer, increasingly racialized immigrants (and their children) in Canada, not only in terms of economic and political difficulties that are experienced, but also social hurdles, such as their sense of feeling welcome in today's Canadian society when faced with discrimination and marginalization by other Canadians. The role of mass media in Canada will also be analysed, specifically in relation to how and why multiculturalism is either celebrated in some cases, or critiqued in others.

Important aspects of the concept of multiculturalism in Canada will also be criticized here, especially considering that racialized immigrants in particular continue to face systemic challenges despite existing policies that are meant to assist them overcome those very same problems.

Multiculturalism: A Brief History

For many Canadians, especially those of us who happen to live in large urban centres, the notion that we live in a multicultural society probably strikes us as an obvious and unsurprising fact, an idea that many of us may have already taken for granted.

It is important to realize, however, that the *concept* of multiculturalism is a relatively new one in Canadian history. In fact, the Canadian government first used the term in an official manner in 1971 (Driedger & Burnet, 2002). At the time, the official policy of bilingualism only reflected the linguistic and cultural diversity of Canadians who were descendants of European settlers, from France and Britain specifically (and who are sometimes referred to as the "Charter groups") even though Blacks (loyalists and those escaping slavery in the United States), Chinese, Japanese, and individuals from the Indian subcontinent were present in Canada throughout the 1800s and immigrants and refugees from continental and Eastern Europe started to appear in the country in greater numbers after the Second World War (Kobayashi, 1993, p. 205). The country then experienced even larger waves of immigrants appearing from the rest of the world (the Asian subcontinent and South America in particular) from the late 1960s to the present day.

Multiculturalism and Aboriginal Peoples

Of course, immigrants are not the only group in Canada to which the concept of multiculturalism applies. After all, prior to European settlement, Canada was home to many First Nations and Inuit peoples. Today, the term Aboriginal peoples is a "catch-all" category that refers not only to First Nations and Inuit peoples, but includes a third group that have emerged since contact with European settlers: namely, the Métis. Aboriginal peoples constitute a group of distinct ethnicities, each with specific cultural practices and beliefs. However, due to a brutal legacy of deliberate neglect, abuse and genocide at the hands of European settlers, the vast majority of Aboriginal populations have perished and are today also considered "minorities" from a population standpoint. Therefore, due to both their cultural distinctiveness as well as their "minority" status, the Aboriginal peoples of Canada are included in Canadian multiculturalism policies,[2] although those policies only supplement pre-existing policies and treaty rights that are specifically created for them.

Québec and "Interculturalism"

Canada's Francophone (i.e., French-speaking) community, in particular the population that constitutes the majority of people born in the province of Québec, has suffered centuries of discrimination at the hands of their British-origin Charter group counterparts in English Canada. Specifically, the English majority was a constant threat to the sovereignty of French-Canadians in terms of the latter group's right to preserve their language, culture, and religion. While this history is much too complicated to delve into here, for our purposes it is worth noting that the previously mentioned policy of bilingualism demonstrates that Québec society and culture has managed to resist assimilation into the majority Anglophone culture, given that the cultural autonomy of French-Canadians has been preserved from a constitutional (which is to say, legal) perspective since Confederation in 1867.[3]

Canadian Francophones for the most part have been protected through a national bilingual policy. However, multicultural policy also acknowledges their distinct culture and minority status.[4] In contemporary Québec, the majority Francophone society to a large extent determines their own policies when it comes to multiculturalism, which, compared to English Canada, can be characterized as more restrictive. Many scholars, most notably the government-sponsored Bouchard–Taylor Commission, have termed Québec's form of multicultural policy "interculturalism," a form of multiculturalism that "seeks to reconcile ethnocultural diversity with the continuity of the French-speaking core" (Bouchard & Taylor, 2009, p. 19). What this state-ments means is that the first priority for Québec is to ensure that immigrants become Francophones and adopt French-Canadian culture. Accommoda-tion for the practices, beliefs, and activities of immigrants' ethnic origin is of a secondary concern.

In sum, the Canadian state's official recognition of multiculturalism appears a few decades after the end of the Second World War, but more importantly, after a centuries-old racist legacy of immigration policies. Furthermore, due to the fact that European settlers not only occupied this land by tearing it away from its native inhabitants but also fought each other for domination of it, the basis of multicultural policy is the recognition of the status of Aboriginal peoples and French-Canadians.

Citizenship: Two Types

A cornerstone requirement of a democratic society which aims to fulfill its obligation to treat all its residents equally and without discrimination is affording people the chance to become citizens of the nation. Nurse and Blake (2009) suggest that the concept of citizenship has two components: One legal, the other symbolic.

"Legal" Citizenship

According to Nurse and Blake (2009), the legal component of citizenship refers not only to the everyday legal obligations that we must abide by, but also the rights that are specific to citizens (such as voting). As well, "only citizens are entitled to full and complete participation in the political and economic dynamics of the nation" (p. 14). This aspect is crucial: The key advantage of citizenship from a legal perspective has everything to do with being able to engage in Canadian politics and economy with as little restric-tion as possible.

It is worth noting that new immigrants on arrival do not have citizenship status. However, citizenship can be obtained (and over 80 percent of immi-grants do so) after three years of Canadian residency. It is important to note that legal citizenship does not address in any significant way the differential experience of racialized groups, or more specifically, the systemic forms of disadvantage and discrimination that racialized immigrants in particular encounter, especially in the workplace.

"Symbolic" Citizenship

In many ways, the second, symbolic component of citizenship constitutes practices and actions that reside in the social sphere: In sum, it is "a ritual confirmation of identity, establishing the boundaries of a national community. Many people who live in Canada are not citizens and many Canadian citizens live abroad. Citizenship frames and limits the national community, determining who is and who is not part of that body" (Nurse & Blake, 2009, pp. 14–15).

As we will see, the symbolic component of citizenship addresses the differential experience of racialized immigrants to an extent that the legal component is unable to do (as described earlier). As well, the symbolic component of citizenship involves practices, beliefs, behaviours, activities, and actions that can occur prior to attaining citizenship status. However, because the symbolic component of citizenship is, by definition, much more abstract than the much more straightforward legal one, some concrete examples will help us better understand what is being said above, especially regarding somewhat vague concepts such as "identity" and "national community."

"Sense-of-Belonging" Among Canadian Youth

James's (2010) interview with his own students on the question of what constitutes a "Canadian" suggests that many young people continue to believe that the word is synonymous with being White: White Canadian students for their part tend to refuse the concept of "ethnicity" or "culture" when describing their identity (p. 153), whereas non-White Canadians feel obligated to make a distinction between their citizenship and their ethnic origins (or, in the case of first-generation immigrants, their country of birth) (p. 155). Gallant's (2009) survey, while not representative of all of Canada, nevertheless suggests that "nearly ten times more people declared 'feeling Canadian' with respect to citizenship than with respect to identity" (pp. 218–219).

The contradictions that young Canadians feel regarding their legal status as citizens versus how they express their identity (and what role their ethnicity plays in describing it) mirrors the split between the legal and symbolic components of citizenship. While immigrants are afforded opportunities to be productive members of society in terms of their work skills and political engagement (legal citizenship), clearly many of them do not believe their ethnicity plays a strong (positive, inclusionary) role in their civic lives outside of their ethnic communities (symbolic citizenship).

Limitations of Civic and Economic Engagement

This contradiction is one of the main factors that explain the so-called "ethnic enclave" phenomenon, in which a community that shares the same ethnic origin comes to densely inhabit, over a span of time, at least one specific neighbourhood in major urban centres. One outcome of organizing life based on ethnic origin in this manner is that some racialized members will never feel the need to learn the language, customs, social expectations, and rights of the dominant (mainstream) culture of their adoptive country, even though this attitude inevitably comes at the cost of those members restricting their mobility and civic autonomy.

Even the most heavily entrenched racialized immigrant will nevertheless find that they are not able to sustain or import all their cultural practices once they find themselves in Canada. Some of these practices are no longer available to them for a whole set of practical reasons, but often the reason has more to do with practices being incompatible with the Canadian mainstream culture's limited tolerance towards and acceptance of behaviours that are deemed disruptive or, more broadly, different:

> Essentially, while there has been some accommodation of certain cultural beliefs and practices of immigrants and minorities, particularly with regards to cuisine, cultural festivals, style of dress, and celebrations, most often what is accommodated tends to fit within the context of European Christian tradition or does not stray too far away from prevailing practices. (James, 2010, p. 149)

It is important to emphasize that Canadian mainstream society is only interested in immigrant cultures and ethnicities so long as they restrict their practices to the realm of commercial exchange, and even then chiefly via the selling of consumable commodities (e.g., food, clothing) and artistic events, or short-term public displays and observances (e.g., celebrations).

What is being inferred here is that ethnicity other than western European is only tolerated in Canada if it is used in service of generating financial profit: As Joshee, Peck, Thompson, Chareka, and Sears (2010) suggest, "it is important to note that what citizens are being included in, then, is not citizenship in the ethnic or sociological sense of belonging to a community but, rather, they are being included in the community of those who participate, who join in a process" (p. 10). The authors go on to critique this narrow-minded way of thinking about citizenship, specifically because it reduces the notion of multiculturalism to "a potential economic asset" (p. 11) wherein "there is a recognition of diversity but there is no attention to social justice" (p. 12). Therefore, in such instances, the legal component of citizenship, which indicates that racialized group members and immigrants are free to use their ethnic culture for financial gain (which appears to be a positive prospect), actually undercuts the capacity for racialized group members and immigrants to enjoy unrestricted access to the symbolic component of citizenship.

The Failure of Legal and Constitutional Reform

Furthermore, any endeavour that might result in more substantial freedoms, such as altering Canada's Charter or Constitution to accommodate religious observances, legal arbitrations, banking methods, and other practices that operate from principles that derive from ethnic communities outside of Canadian mainstream society, will likely find itself in contradiction to not only the European, Judeo-Christian basis of almost all Canadian institutions and jurisprudence, but more specifically to those who would seek to maintain that *status quo*:

> In claiming that multiculturalism provides opportunities for integration, while still holding tight to white, Anglo-Franco traditions, we ultimately reinforce, protect, and grant legitimacy to the existing ... structure. Consequently, the racism and discrimination that are barriers to minority groups' integration and full participation in our society remain in place. By providing programs and policies (which by their nature are destined to fail) we allow members of society to conceptualize racism as a "problem" of individuals and not a structural issue. (James, 2010, p. 161)

Of course, some cases of denial of ethnic minority rights (such as the failure to establish sharia law in Ontario, which led to the removal of all religious-based arbitration in the province) are by no means simply a function of racist intolerance on the part of Canadian civil society or Canadian law's stubborn adherence to a specific historical-cultural perspective. Instead, the argument for the denial of those proposed rights suggests that they directly contradict pre-existing fundamental (and legally binding) rights that have been established over the span of centuries to ensure equality for all Canadians, regardless of gender, race, ethnicity, age, ability, or religion (in the case of sharia law, it has been argued that women's rights in particular would have been substantially compromised, in the form of an exception for the sake of a few ethnic groups' claims for enhanced freedom of religion).

Second-generation Immigrants and the Perceived Failure of the Integration Model

Researchers and scholars have more recently become interested in studying young Canadians' "sense-of-belong" (i.e., identity plus citizenship) due in large part to recent world events. Since the deadly London Underground bombing of King's Cross station in July of 2005 and the alleged involvement of the so-called "Toronto 18" in a similar terrorist conspiracy the following year, mainstream media attention has been focussed on the unsuccessful integration of many second-generation immigrants (especially of Muslim backgrounds) in so-called "Western democracies," given that in both cases, both actual and alleged conspirators had full-citizenship status and many were second-generation immigrants. During this time, the mainstream press as well as domestic security branches of both the United States and Canada frequently adopted "the terms 'home-grown terrorism' and 'home-grown extremism' [both of which] became major parts of international public discourse" (Wong & Simon, 2009, p. 7).

This broader public discourse that had emerged regarding second-generation immigrants suggested that they had come to experience a profound sense of alienation that is more or less the polar opposite of the model of integration, which multicultural policy has deemed a desired outcome. More specifically, the so-called "straight-line theory of more complete assimilation with each successive generation" (Wong & Simon, 2009, p. 7) – which is the idea that subsequent generations of immigrants, starting with the second, "would be more likely to have a strong sense of belonging to Canada than the immigrant or first generation" (p. 7) – has been proven to have been nothing more than a complete falsehood for some communities.

A particularly negative outcome of such a popular discourse has been a rise in Islamophobic sentiments which, with various degrees of frequency have permeated both mainstream and social media since September 11, 2001. This phenomenon has in turn created an ideal atmosphere for some naturalized Canadians and non-racialized immigrants who hold such beliefs to more freely and comfortably express their racist prejudices about racialized groups (regardless of whether the groups that the prejudice or hatred is directed towards are of Muslim origin or not).[5]

Multiculturalism in Canadian Mainstream Media

Mainstream and social media in Canada has the capacity to reinforce racist stereotypes about racialized immigrants in particular; immigrants almost always appear in the news only when they find themselves run afoul of the legal system. What is worth emphasizing here is that this type of portrayal overwhelmingly occurs in journalism (both television and print) and also on talk-radio and social media (websites, blogs, Facebook groups), and is motivated in many instances by anti-immigrant, anti-racialized communities' political position associated with conservative and far-right political leanings.

However, other forms of Canadian media tend to feature a different approach when it comes to representing Aboriginal, racialized, and immigrant subjects. Multiculturalism is shown to be a problematic social phenomenon, for example, in the domain of cinema. Directors such as Deepa Mehta (*Heaven on Earth* [2008]), Charles Officer (*nurse.fighter.boy* [2008]), Clement Virgo (*The Planet of Junior Brown* [1997]), Atom Egoyan (*Ararat* [2002]), Denis Villeneuve (*Incendies* [2010]), and Philippe Falardeau (*Monsieur Lazhar* [2011]), among others, have, to various degrees and in very different ways, portrayed racialized characters who struggle with their identity, as well as their sense of alienation with mainstream society, while facing economic and legal problems, all of which strongly resemble the systemic difficulties that racialized members and immigrants face in Canada. Similarly, in recent years there have been a few films made by and/or about Aboriginal peoples of Canada that have been successful outside the country. Such films include Zacharias Kunuk's *Atanarjuat* (2001), Bruce McDonald's *Dance Me Outside* (1995), and Yves Simoneau's *Bury My Heart at Wounded Knee* (2007).

As well, some prominent popular musicians such as K'naan and Shad (who are hip-hop artists of Somali and Rwandan background, respectively) feature lyrics and compositions on their albums that not only emphasize their cultural origin but also reflect on a range of disadvantages and discrimination that they, their family, or people in their community have had to overcome (or are overcoming, or have been unable to overcome).

Theatre has been one artistic medium wherein racialized members in particular have managed to flourish in Canada in terms of play-writing, directing, and acting. What accounts for this phenomenon is that plays are fairly economical to write, produce, and mount: They can be staged in relatively smaller venues (community centres, schools, outdoors, etc.); they can be short; production companies tend to charge audiences inexpensive admission compared to other types of live performance; and finally, theatre can feature as few as one actor. Notable racialized playwrights in Canada include Trey Anthony (*Da Kink in My Hair* [2001]), George Elliott Clarke (*Whylah Falls* [1999]), Wajdi Mouawad (*Forêts* [2006]), and Rahul Varma (*Land Where the Trees Talk* [1989]).

However, it is important to note that the vast majority of these films, plays, and albums were produced in the last twenty years. What this fact indicates is that Canadian state funding has been a very recent phenomenon in terms of media that prominently feature racialized members, Aboriginal peoples and immigrants in their stories, especially in contemporary and urban settings. In fact, according to Peter S. Li (1990), the vast majority of state funding for the arts earmarked for racialized members in the mid-1990s emphasized

> the authenticity of customs and costumes of ancient times and foreign origins rather than experimenting with new cultural expressions and forms beyond the stereotypes of multiculturalism. There [wa]s little incentive to create and to develop minority art works that would reflect the contemporary reality of people; little attempt [wa]s made to convert the traditional art forms into an expression of the modern life of minorities in Canada. Minority art [wa]s relegated to the margin where, at best, only the form of an ancient folk culture is retained; it is a form that is devoid of the contemporary essence of lived experiences. This stagnant state of minority culture in Canada [wa]s nurtured within the institutional parameter of multiculturalism, within which the endorsement and the success of minority cultural products depend[ed] largely on their ability to be colourful and entertaining, and not necessarily aesthetically gratifying. (p. 365)

The degree to which Li's assessment of government-funded art created by racialized members, Aboriginal peoples, and immigrants is relevant today is to some extent a matter of debate: College, community and local newspapers, magazines, and radio certainly inform members of specific ethnic groups about artistic events. However, these media, as well as the events themselves, tend to cater exclusively to those very same communities, which is to say that so-called "outsiders" are rarely invited to participate or attend. As well, many of these insular events fall into the same "ancient folklore" trap that Li criticizes, as they tend to be scheduled around important national or religious holidays.

Meanwhile, the Canadian Broadcasting Corporation (CBC), which is the national broadcaster, has historically tended to heavily promote a very naïve and vague notion of multiculturalism that emphasizes otherness, difference, and the exotic rather than celebrating commonalities or new artistic expressions by racialized artists that are not beholden to their ethnic origins. Once again, artists whose practice has to do with staging traditional, "indigenous," or folk-art are promoted, although in recent years the CBC's multicultural mandate has also come to emphasize cultural hybridity (which, in general terms, refers to the mixing of two or more cultural traditions to create presumably new artistic syntheses).

Therefore, even in terms of multiculturalism in art and artists in Canada, challenges persist. For example, new immigrants, racialized members, and Aboriginal peoples are under-represented in terms of mainstream print media (journalism, poetry, fiction, and non-fiction), as well as experimental/avant-garde media, digital media, ballet, and contemporary dance.

Positive Interpretation of Canada's Multiculturalism Policy

The large portion of this chapter has criticized the notion of multiculturalism in Canada because as a discourse, it actually tends to limit racialized groups, Aboriginal peoples and immigrants' economic and social prosperity as well as mask the systemic challenges that many are rarely able to overcome. However, it would be disingenuous to present a purely critical view of multi-culturalism and multicultural policy in Canada, especially given that research exists to point out some positive outcomes.

Kymlicka (2010), for example, summarizes statistical data that suggests that when it comes to the legal component of citizenship, Canada continues to out-perform all other so-called "Western democracies:" Canadian immi-grants not only become citizens more often than anywhere else, they also vote, join political parties, and both run for and hold political office in the greatest numbers (pp. 261–262). Furthermore, data suggests that second-generation immigrants (i.e., Canadian-born children of parents born outside of the country) do better in school than children of non-immigrant parents (irrespective of economic status) and Canadian immigrants suffer less prob-lems with acquiring employment than in other Western democracies, due in large part to education policies (p. 262–263).

Of course, education initiatives such as ESL programs are only one of many services offered to immigrants by the Canadian state. When exam-ining the entire immigrant support mechanism,

> research shows that the accommodation that immigrants experience – in other words, the support they receive – in Canada, contributes to favourable integration, and ultimately to their success in the society ... Social supports [also] play a significant role in the health, settlement, and success of immigrants who are routinely faced with systemic challenges, limited resources, and inadequate policies and programs addressing inte-

gration. Generally, accommodation ... ha[s] an overall positive effect, and the result is development of a more cohesive and productive society. (James, 2010, p. 136)

In sum, if we examine multiculturalism in Canada strictly from an institutional basis, the outlook is very good for immigrants: They seem to prosper politically and economically in a way that other countries in North America and Europe seem incapable of matching. This selective view also allows some scholars to suggest that Canadian social institutions (in particular, our education system and social services) seem to be structured in a way that helps immigrants achieve a level of political and economic prospects than are either equal to or greater than those enjoyed by non-immigrant citizens.

Reality Check: Limits of Positive Interpretation

To begin with, we should keep in mind that part of this "success story" is predicated upon Canada's increasingly restrictive immigration policy in recent decades. Also worthy of consideration is Galabuzi's (2006) more specific conclusion that:

> while the average educational attainment of immigrants has risen, partly due to strict skills-based immigration policy requirements, this has not translated into comparable employment and income opportunities. The human quality of many internationally trained professional and tradespeople is devalued, and many end up as part of an educated underclass even as their skills degrade. (p. xix)

Furthermore, the usefulness of comparing Canada to other "Western democracies" is limited at best: The general claim that "Canada is doing better than the rest" is only worthy of celebration when "the rest" are doing very well to begin with, which is certainly not the case. Finally, while it is tempting to believe that "acquiring employment" is a good outcome, we should always ask "What type of employment?" Unfortunately, evidence increasingly points to the fact that today's flexible labour market "expose[s] racialized groups disproportionately to precarious forms of work – contract, temporary, part-time, and shift work with little or no job security, poor and often unsafe working conditions, intensive labour, excessive hours, low wages, and no benefits" (p. xix), conditions which cause racialized immigrants to suffer more mental, physical, and financial problems than established Canadians (Reitz, Breton, Dion, & Dion, 2009, pp. 72–73).

Conclusion

When it comes to the rights and freedoms of Aboriginal and racialized peoples, and immigrants in particular,

> living, learning, working, playing in an ethnically, racially and religiously diverse society presents complex and difficult challenges that individuals must confront ... The tension and conflict found in culturally diverse societies suggests ... that multiculturalism is not working ... [The] problems with multiculturalism ... are, in various ways, a result of variations in political perspectives, a lack of recognition of – and respect for – differences ... and our society's seeming inability to accommodate and adjudicate these differences. (James, 2010, p. 156)

While this perspective may seem pessimistic, to the point where the reader might assume that perhaps the time has come for Canada to abandon its multicultural legacy as a result, it is worth noting that it seems unlikely that any state can alleviate all forms of disadvantage, injustice and discrimination experienced by its constituents in the first place: For example, given that we in Canada (as well as nearly every human society on the planet) operate on the basis of the capitalist mode of production, the phenomenon of class-based disadvantage and inequality will continue to persist unabated as a result.

In other words, some forms of social inequality are both structural and inherent, which is to say that governments are fundamentally incapable of addressing them, especially in the absence of a radical reconfiguration of social, political and economic relations (which from a mainstream democratic perspective can only occur by the will of the majority of citizens).

In the meantime, fundamental shifts need to occur in the future to take into account rapidly changing patterns of migration and immigration in Canada. These include:

- The legal component of citizenship needs to more reliably guarantee access to less precarious and menial forms of employment, especially for new immigrants;
- Education credentials of new immigrants need to be recognized by an equitable vetting system;
- A civic culture needs to be fostered that not only allows immigrants, including racialized members, and Aboriginal peoples in particular, to preserve their ethnic customs, beliefs and practices, but that also enables the capacity for citizens to enthusiastically expose them-

selves to cultural practices, beliefs, and practices that challenge their own culturally-learned attitudes;

- Racialized groups should not feel obliged to emphasize their cultural difference or to present themselves as "exotic" in relation to mainstream Canadian culture in the realm of art. Instead, cultural hybridity needs to be funded above and beyond "folkloric" or traditional manifestations of ethnicity, which tends to marginalize ethnic cultures and stifle or halt cultural development in subsequent generations; and finally,
- Mechanisms should be in place so that government agencies and departments do not fall prey to racist policies and practices, which otherwise end up victimizing racialized citizens such as Suaad Hagi Mohamud.

This list of potential government policy reforms is by no means exhaustive, in part because a discussion of the shortcomings of multiculturalism and citizenship policies is only one manifestation of the wide range of social, political, and economic inequalities that racialized members, Aboriginal peoples, and new immigrants experience in Canada. In fact, multicultural policy in Canada can be deemed as a failed approach precisely on the basis that it operates in isolation from the complete picture of systemic inequality.

Whether or not Canadian multicultural policy should be abandoned completely or whether the policy should instead be sustained or undergo reform or revision is a matter of differing ideological perspectives. This author adopts the standpoint that this either/or formulation (which finds itself in much of the scholarly discourse) is naïve to begin with, since inequality of any kind cannot be overcome so long as the exploitative capitalist mode of production forms the economic basis of so-called "Western democracies" and until such a proposition (i.e., radical reconfiguration of the mode of production) is taken up seriously.

Develop your knowledge – Ask yourself

It is becoming more and more clear that second-generation immigrants (that is to say, children born in Canada whose parents were born in a foreign land) increasingly feel a profound sense of alienation, in which they do not feel they belong to either mainstream Canadian society, nor do they feel they can identify with all of their parents' values, practices or beliefs.

Consider:

1. What changes do you feel need to occur in mainstream Canadian society to ensure a greater sense of belonging within this demographic?

2. At the same time, is there some value in being able to call more than one country home?

Notes.

[1] For instance, those policies, as well as initiatives and publications concerning multiculturalism that exist on the internet are hosted by the Citizenship and Immigration Canada's website.

[2] *Inter-Action* is "Canada's new multiculturalism grants and contribution program" (Citizenship and Immigration Canada, 2010a) and "is administered by Citizenship and Immigration Canada" (2010a). The program's mandate is achieved by "assisting the socio-economic integration of individuals and communities and their contributions to building an integrated and socially cohesive society" (2010a). To this end, "Canadian Aboriginal organizations" (Citizenship and Immigration Canada, 2010b) are eligible for the Inter-Action events grant, while "First Nations and Inuit governments, band councils, and Aboriginal organizations" (Citizenship and Immigration Canada, 2010c) are eligible for the Inter-Action projects grant.

Furthermore, Aboriginal peoples are included throughout Citizenship and Immigration Canada's "Annual report on the operation of the *Canadian multiculturalism act*," whose mandate is to "report to Parliament on the implementation of the *Canadian multiculturalism act* in federal institutions" (Citizenship and Immigration Canada, 2011, p. 2).

3   See section 93(3) and section 133 of the *Constitution Act*, 1867.
4   See section 3(1)(*i*) and 3(1)(*j*) of the *Canadian Multiculturalism Act*, 1988.
5   Obviously, this is not to say that some racialized group members cannot or do not also express Islamophobic sentiments.

References

Banting, K., & Kymlicka, W. (2010). Canadian multiculturalism: Global anxieties and local debates. *British Journal of Canadian Studies, 23*(1), 43–72.

Bouchard, G., & Taylor, C. (2008). *Building the future: A time for reconciliation*. Retrieved from www.accommodements.qc.ca/ documentation/rapports/rapport-final-integral-en.pdf.

Dion, K. L., Dion, K. K., & Banerjee, R. (2009). Discrimination, ethnic group belonging, and well-being. In J.G. Reitz, R. Breton, K.K. Dion, & K.L. Dion (Eds.), *Multiculturalism and social cohesion: potentials and challenges of diversity*. Toronto: Springer.

Driedger, L., & Burnet, J. (2002). *Multiculturalism. The Canadian encyclopaedia*. Retrieved from www.thecanadianencyclopedia. com/index.cfm?PgNm=TCE&Params=A1ARTA0005511.

Galabuzi, G.-E. (2006). *Canada's economic apartheid: The social exclusion of racialized groups in the new century*. Toronto: Canadian Scholars' Press.

Gallant, N. (2009). Feeling Canadian, feeling other: Perceptions of citizenship and identity among Aboriginal people and second-generation immigrants in Quebec. In A. Nurse, & R.B. Blake (Eds.), *Beyond national dreams: Essays on Canadian citizenship and nationalism*. Markham, ON: Fitzhenry and Whiteside.

James, C. E. (2010). *Seeing ourselves: Exploring race, ethnicity and culture* (4th ed.). Toronto: Thompson Educational.

Joshee, R., Peck, C., Thompson, L. A., Chareka, O., & Sears, A. (2010). Multicultural education, diversity, and citizenship in Canada. Working paper for the IALEI workshop on multicultural education, Seoul, Korea. February 17–19. Retrieved from http://www.intlalliance.org

Kobayashi, A. (1993). Multiculturalism: Representing a Canadian institution. In J. Duncan & D. Ley (Eds.), *Place/culture/representation*. London: Routledge.

Kymlicka, W. (2010). Testing the liberal multicultural hypothesis: Normative theories and social science evidence. *Canadian journal of political science/Revue canadienne de science politique, 43*(2), 257–271.

Li, P. S. (1994, November). A world apart: The multicultural world of visible minorities and the art world of Canada. *Canadian Review of Sociology and Anthropology, 31*(4), 365-391.

Nurse, A., & Blake, R.B. (2009). Narrating the nation: An introduction. In Nurse, A. & Blake, R. B. (Eds.), Beyond national dreams: Essays on Canadian citizenship and nationalism. Markham, ON: Fitzhenry and Whiteside.

Shephard, M., & Goddard, J. (2009, August 15). Stranded woman finally home. *Toronto Star*. Retrieved from www.thestar.com/article/681901.

Wong, L.L., & Simon, R.R. (2009). Citizenship and belonging to Canada: Religious and generational differentiation. *Canadian Issues, 14*(3), 3–14.

CHAPTER 7

Canadian Citizenship by Way of Grant: Who Deserves to Belong?

Cornelia Mazgarean

This chapter will explore the idea of citizenship from the perspective of exclusion. Who gets to belong? Who deserves to belong? The chapter will provide a brief overview of the notion of citizenship and further show how Canadian citizenship exemplifies the insider/outsider division, in light of the new *Bill C-24*, titled *"Strengthening Canadian Citizenship Act,"* which received royal assent on June 19, 2014. It is argued that the new law will keep more people out of the public sphere of participation, with disparate effects on disadvantaged groups, and represents a weakening of the idea of citizenship, in general.

On May 23, 1914, a ship called Komagata Maru carrying 376 passengers from British India approached Vancouver's port. They thought they could settle anywhere in the empire, given that they were British subjects same as Canadians. Enforcing the "continuous journey" regulation, Canadian immigration boats kept the ship a half-mile away from the shore, leading to a dramatic standoff that lasted about two months. The Komagata Maru became a floating detention centre for its passengers. On July 23, 1914, the ship was escorted out to the Pacific. When the passengers arrived back in British India, imperial authorities deemed them to be seditious and when they finally landed, British troops opened fire in the confrontation that ensued where twenty-one people were killed. A few weeks before the ship departed the Vancouver harbour the Court of Appeal in an unanimous judgment decided that the continuous journey regulation was violated, since the ship originated in Hong Kong and not India. Most notably, the court also found that, as a self-governing dominion of the British Empire, Canada had the right to determine who got in. The *Times* of London noted at the time that the decision meant a rejection of the idea that "British citizenship in itself confirms an unrestricted right of entrance into any part of the British Dominions" (Kazimi, 2011, p. 93-131). The question to be answered was, in other words: who deserves to belong?

The question of who should belong to a certain state has been subject of debate since ancient time. Citizenship represents "a circumscribed society that effectively rules some people out by the way it rules other people in" (Dauenhauer, 1996, p. 5). The idea of citizenship originated in Greece and was strongly tied to participation in self-government. Aristotle defined citizens as those who "share in the civic life of ruling and being ruled in return," with the caveat that political participation was confined to Athenian adult males (Kostakopoulou, 2008, p. 14-15). Since then, volumes have been written about the meaning, content and definition of citizenship. Different notions have been used: formal citizenship, social citizenship, transnational, global, virtual, multicultural, urban, queer, cosmopolitan, transnational, postnational, postmodern citizenship and the list can continue. The inescapable consensus seems to be that citizenship is "founded on, and sustained through, difference, that is, the insider/outsider distinction" with the goal of excluding the outsider in order to "elicit the loyalty of the citizenry" (Kostakopoulou, 2008, p. 3).

In most part of the world, citizenship can, in general, be acquired in two ways: by birth or by naturalization. Citizenship by birth can be obtained either by being born within the territorial confinement of a state (*jus soli*), or by being born to at least one parent who is already the citizen of that state (*jus sanguinis*). Citizenship through immigration can be acquired either by starting a relationship with somebody who is already a citizen, such as through marriage, or through length of residence within that state (Cole, 2010). Canadian citizenship is no exception to that pattern. Citizenship can be obtained *jus soli, jus sanguinis* or through immigration by first obtaining permanent residency status (whether through marriage or another class of immigration).

Canadian citizenship has played a crucial role since 1947 in developing the Canadian nation. It grants all residents who contribute through work, culture and taxes, the right to become full members of the society while being able to exercise the right to vote. The *Citizenship Act* of 1985 stressed this approach, such as that "in 2005-2006 the share of foreign-born residents aged 15 and older who had become Canadian citizens was 75 percent" (Winter, 2014, p.3). However, this chapter will argue that recent changes to citizenship laws will generate a regress from the original, more inclusive intent of citizenship policy and will weaken rather than strengthen the value of citizenship.

The term "citizenship by way of a grant" refers to ways in which most foreign-born nationals obtain Canadian citizenship. In order to apply for citizenship, certain requirements must be met such as age, permanent residency, criminal prohibitions, language, general knowledge about Canada and the swearing of an oath of allegiance to the Queen. Some of these requirements carry more controversies than others. This chapter will mainly focus on those requirements that are more contentious.

Most people applying for citizenship must be permanent residents of Canada. This requirement applies to both adults and minors (unless adopted by a Canadian citizen). The residency requirement also has a temporal component for adult applicants. As it stands, the temporal residency requirement means that the applicant must have been a permanent resident of Canada for at least three out of the four years before the date of the application. Time legally spent in Canada prior to becoming a permanent resident is counted as half a day for each day, for a maximum of one year. This requirement however can carry challenges for some applicants, which will be explained through the following case studies.

Case Study 1

A came to Canada in 2006 as an international student. A became a permanent resident through the Canadian Experience Class in September 2012 and applied for citizenship in September 2014. A has spent a total of eight years in Canada, but just two years as a permanent resident. Therefore, A needs three years out of the last four to apply. However, because A will be able to also get the maximum of one year for time spent in Canada before becoming a permanent resident, A is eligible to apply for citizenship.

Case Study 2

B came to Canada as a refugee claimant in 2009 and was accepted as a refugee in 2011. In November 2013, B also became a permanent resident of Canada. B would like to apply for citizenship in November 2014. B, however will not be eligible to apply because even if B gets the one year credit for time spent in Canada before becoming a permanent resident, B will still be one year short of the requirement.

Case Study 3

C came to Canada in 2007 as a refugee claimant. C is stateless. C received a work permit shortly before arrival and worked different jobs since then. C received refugee protection in 2009 and became a permanent resident in December 2012. Based on the present requirement, C could apply for citizenship in December 2014. Based on the proposed requirement, C will have to wait until December 2016 to apply for citizenship.

Case Study 4

D came to Canada as a live-in caregiver in 2005 and met all of the requirements of the program. However, she did not have a good relationship with the employer, as the employer was abusing her situation, making her to do jobs she did not have to do and/or work longer hours. She always been under the threat of immigration consequences. Finally, when she asked the employer for proof of the completion of the required hours, the employer refused her request. As such, she applied to stay in Canada based on Humanitarian and Compassionate (H&C) considerations.

Case Study 5

E came to Canada in 2013, as a sponsored spouse. She received conditional permanent residency, meaning that she has to reside with the sponsor for two years since receiving her residency. However, it is not clear in the legislation whether the two years can be counted towards the four years needed for the residency requirement. Since early 2014, E was subject to abuse by her husband but she never called the police fearing its consequences on her immigration case.

Reflective Questions

1. Do you agree A, B, C, D or E fail to "rub elbows" with Canadian on a daily basis since they arrived in Canada?
2. When thinking about these examples, compare their situations with classes of immigrants who receive permanent residency status upon arrival in Canada.
3. As a practitioner, how are you going to support your client at the micro, mezzo and macro levels?
4. In your opinion, how will the changes to citizenship impact C?
5. How will this impact C's family reunification situation?
6. What are some of the challenges to settlement and integration?
7. Since applying through H&C takes much longer than through the regular live-in caregiver program to obtain permanent residency, what are some of the consequences of this process on D's employment conditions?
8. How will this delay affect D's family reunification process?
9. Based on the present requirement, D could apply for citizenship in December 2014. Based on the proposed requirement, she will have to wait until December 2016 to apply for citizenship. How will this affect her overall settlement and integration process?
10. E knows that there is an exception to the cohabitation requirement in case of domestic abuse, but she does not know how she will be able to prove it. As a professional, how are you going to assist E?
11. E is afraid that if Immigration do not believe her story she will lose

continued...

her permanent residency status and possibly, two years towards her citizenship requirement. How will changes to the residency requirement affect E and other sponsored spouses in her situation?
12. If E also had a newborn child, how might that impact her decision to report the abuse? Will your approach change while trying to assist E?

Bill C-24, titled "*Strengthening Canadian Citizenship Act*," which received royal assent on June 19, 2014, aims at changing the residency requirement. At the present time, some sections of the Bill are already in force, but the sections on the residency requirement is still awaiting to receive an order in council which might take place by August of 2015. The new changes will make it harder for people to apply for citizenship. This, according to activists, can present a serious setback to settlement and integration of new Canadians. The requirement will be increased to four out of the last six years, with 183 days of physical presence for each of the four years. Also, no credit will be given to time spent in Canada before becoming a permanent resident. This will have a discriminatory impact on certain groups of immigrants, such as in-Canada spouses, refugees or live-in caregivers. Proponent of the residency requirement argue that the physical residence will ensure the person becomes "Canadianized" by "rubbing elbows" with Canadians "in shopping malls, corner stores, libraries, concert halls, auto repair shops, pubs, cabarets, elevators, churches, synagogues, mosques and temples...wherever one can meet and converse with Canadians" (*Purgassemi*, 1993; *MCI v Naveen,* 2013). Both case studies indicated above will have to wait significantly longer in order to apply for citizenship and will have to make sure that they are also physically present in Canada for 183 days for each of the four years they will want to use towards the four out of six years requirement.

As evident through above case studies, the changes to Bill C-24 such as residency requirements if receive an order in council, are particularly discriminatory and unfair. This can only be attributed to a political will that cares more about electoral profit rather than the people and the prosperity of Canada. This state of affairs seems to discount the fact that citizenship is not only about "legal, political and national identity, but also an emotional and physical experience determined by who is included and who is excluded" (Kakabadse, Kakabadse, & Kalu, 2009, p. 24). Furthermore, citizenship is a catalyst for "community well-being, personal engagement and democratic fulfilment" (Bosniak, 1998, p. 29). This means that permanent residents, although allowed to participate in the private realm of the state, are excluded from the public realm: "they can be subjects of the law, but not sovereigns over it" (Cole, 2010, p. 4). As Michael Walzer argued, "men and women are either subject to the state's authority or they are not; and if they are subject, they must be given a say, and ultimately, an equal say, in what authority does" (1983, p. 61). This is particularly so for individuals who have spent a significant amount of time inside a certain territory, being subjects to the nation's laws.

Exclusion based on criminality

Other exclusions geared toward keeping certain people out pertain to criminality. In Canada, you cannot become a citizen if you:

- have been convicted of an indictable (criminal) offence or an offence under the *Citizenship Act* in the three years before you apply,
- are currently charged with an offence under the *Citizenship Act*,
- are in prison, on parole or on probation (after a conviction); time spent during this time may not be counted towards the residency requirement,
- are under a removal order (Canadian officials have ordered you to leave Canada),
- are being investigated for, are charged with, or have been convicted of a war crime or a crime against humanity, or
- have had your Canadian citizenship taken away in the past five years.

Case Study 6

F came to Canada on October 1, 2011 and received permanent resident status upon arrival. In early 2014, F was charged with theft and received a suspended sentence (conviction) with one year of probation July 1st of the same year. F will need to wait until the expiry of the probationary period and then find out how much more time is needed to wait in order to meet three out of the four years required. Since the time spent on probation will not count, F may have to wait until at least until October, 2015 to apply for citizenship. Had F received a conditional discharge (finding of guilt, but not a conviction) with a one year probation, F might have been able to use the one year of probation towards the residency requirement.

While F will face severe consequences for the crime committed in Canada, the new changes will also look at whether the person has charges or convictions outside of Canada. Canadian-born citizens however do not face the same scrutiny. Read in conjunction with the new changes regarding criminality and loss of permanent residency because of criminality in the *Faster Removal of Foreign Criminals Act,* which received royal assent on June 19, 2013, it seems that belonging, whether as a permanent resident or a Canadian citizen, is viewed as a privilege that is very hard to obtain and easier to lose. Being deserving of belonging becomes a life-long endeavor for naturalized citizens. Simon McMahon noted that "citizenship is understood as a social process, developing and changing over time" (2012, p. 10). While this statement is accurate, we also need to keep in mind that those who ultimately make those calls for change are people in power, responding to shifting electoral concern, whether real, fabricated or imaginary.

Exclusion based on language proficiency

Aside from the issue of criminality, another barrier used to exclude one from obtaining citizenship is language. Since November of 2012, proof of level four English or French language proficiency has become a condition for all applicants between the ages of 18-54 which must be fulfilled when submitting citizenship application.

Proof of language proficiency can be met in three ways:

1. Proof of successful completion of a secondary or post-secondary program conducted in French or English, either in Canada or abroad; OR
2. Proof of achieving Canadian Language Benchmark/Niveaux de compétence linguistique canadiens (CLB/NCLC) level 4 or higher in speaking and listening skills through certain government-funded language training programs; OR
3. Results of an accepted third-party test at the equivalent of Canadian Language Benchmark (CLB/NCLC)/ Niveaux de compétence linguistique canadien-level 4 or higher in speaking and listening either done previously for immigration purposes (acceptable even if expired) or done specifically for citizenship purposes.

In reality though, many classes of immigrants, such as refugees and family class immigrants, face challenges in meeting the language requirement upfront. Since the processing of their application would take two to three years (Winter, 2014), it would have been more accommodating if the test would be required at the end of the process in order to allow for more time for learning and testing. Considering new immigrants, particularly families with young children face more challenges in attending language classes which would offer childcare, and that new immigrants deal with barriers to employment, have higher rate of poverty, and are less likely to afford private English or testing classes, it would be vital to reconsider the language requirement. In addition, evidence shows that language courses available for such classes of immigrants are inadequate and insufficient (Wayland, 2006, p. 11-15). For refugees who have to deal with the pre-migratory trauma including persecution in the country of origin while having to adapt to a new way of life in their new country, learning a new language to the level desired by the government is not without its challenges. This hurdle is at odds with Canada's international obligation in Article 34 of the Convention relating to the *Status of Refugees* which states that, 'The Contracting States shall as far as possible facilitate the assimilation and naturalization of refugees. They shall in particular make every effort to expedite naturalization proceedings and to reduce as far as possible the charges and costs of such proceedings" (p.30).

Furthermore, many of the refugees and family class immigrants live in Canada for many years without applying for citizenship, but functioning very well in society, participating in social and cultural groups, working, studying, building families and forging friendships. They enhance the Canadian society greatly through their contributions to the social, cultural and economic life. They also pay taxes. Despite all of these, it seems that the government does not deem them deserving of the right to vote. While it is certainly desirable for everybody to learn one of the official languages as quickly as possible, some classes of immigrants will be disadvantaged and will not be able to acquire the required level of language proficiency and will be excluded from civic participation (Derwing, 2010).

Exclusion based on the knowledge of Canada test

In addition to the language test, there is another exclusion mechanism which requires every applicant between the age of 18 and 54 to pass the knowledge of Canada test known as *"Discover Canada"* *Citizenship Guide* which can be found online. This test does not have to be submitted upfront. Once the application is submitted, the applicant will receive instructions about the test. For example, applicants must be able to answer questions, such as: What does the word "Inuit" mean? What is meant by the term "responsible government"? Who was Sir Louis-Hippolyte La Fontaine? What did the Canadian Pacific Railway symbolize? What does Confederation mean?

What is the significance of the discovery of insulin by Sir Frederick Banting and Charles Best? What does it mean to say that Canada is a constitutional monarchy? It suffices to say that considerable time and effort might be needed to best the test. The same considerations mentioned in regards to difficulties that certain groups might have when learning the language would apply when it comes to the knowledge of Canada test.

Two further issues need to be addressed when speaking about the language and knowledge tests. One is the issue of waiver and the other one is a change that Bill C-24 will makes to the age requirement for the tests. On the issue of waiver, while the *Citizenship Act* in s. 5(3)(a) provides for an exception to be made on compassionate grounds from the language and knowledge requirements, in its application, the test is not very flexible. It is difficult for people to access appeal processes due to costs, time constraints and emotional investment. This is also in the context in which Bill C-24 already changed the appeal process. Before August 1, 2014, people had an automatic right to ask for a review of the decision in federal court. As of that date, people will have to first ask for leave from the federal court for an appeal to be heard. Seeking leave on an error of law requires legal assistance of experienced lawyers and there is no consistency at the federal level in terms of judicial decision-making. The introduction of the leave requirement is extremely problematic. (For examples of how law works in practice, read these two cases, both appeals: *Ngo (Re)*, [1986] 1 ACWS (3) 306; *Kalkat v Canada*, 2012 FC 646.)

A more workable solution is needed for waivers to be granted to disadvantaged groups. On the issue of age, Bill C-24 provides for an expansion of the age group to 14 to 64. This provision might become enforceable by August 2015, as it is awaiting an order in council. This means that children aged 14 to 17 will now have to provide proof of language proficiency and pass the knowledge of Canada test. They would not be able to provide a secondary school certificate as they will not have completed secondary schooling. Also, they will need to learn more compared to their peers who do not apply for citizenship or are already citizens of Canada. This will take away from the time they have to dedicate to secondary school, and from their childhood years. The test place an additional strain on children and their family in terms of time and cost. It is also concerning that the requirement will be extended to people between the ages of 54 and 64. The suspect, but reasonable inference is that the government is looking to keep this age group outside of the voting group.

The proposed changes to Bill C-24 have raised enormous community concerns. One example, is the Inter-clinic Immigration Working Group (ICIWG), a network of lawyers and community legal workers in Ontario community legal clinics and student legal aid services societies. Clinics are funded by Legal Aid Ontario (LAO) to provide services to low income, disadvantaged and vulnerable people. The ICIWG noted in its written submissions for the Standing Committee on *Bill C-24* (*unpublished*), that a study commissioned by CIC in 2010 found significant difference in English language acquisition results for new immigrants based on their immigration class and their mother tongue: refugees scored the lowest among all immigration classes, and the South Asian and South East Asian language groups had the most difficulty with English language acquisition. Derwing found that "members of East Asia [...] and Southeast Asian language categories appear to have been disadvantaged relative to other language groups," while "refugees received the lowest CBAL scores of all" (2010, p. 19). So the up-front Level 4 proficiency in one of the official languages as a pre-requisite to applying for citizenship has a disparate impact on refugees and on East Asian and South East Asian immigrants, which has an element of racism.

While *the Citizenship* Act in s. 4(3)(b) and (c) contains a waiver of this requirement for minors and persons who do not understand the significance of taking the oath due to mental health challenges, and aside from other exceptions that would apply to a small number of people, everyone else is required to do it. Without taking the oath, the certificate of citizenship will not become effective. The oath needs to be in the form required in the Schedule to the *Citizenship Act*: "I swear (or affirm) that I will be faithful and bear true allegiance to Her Majesty Queen Elizabeth the Second, Queen of Canada, Her Heirs and Successors, and that I will faithfully observe the laws of Canada and fulfil my duties as a Canadian citizen."

Recent litigation about the legality of requiring someone to pledge allegiance to the Queen resulted in the Ontario Court of Appeal upholding the oath. In *McAteer v. Canada (Attorney General)* appellants objected to the following portion of the oath, based on freedom of conscience and religion, freedom of expression and equality: "I will be faithful and bear true allegiance to Her Majesty Queen Elizabeth the Second, Queen of Canada, Her Heirs and Successors." The court rejected these arguments and found that, "Although the Queen is a person, in swearing allegiance to the Queen of Canada, the would-be citizen is swearing allegiance to a symbol of our form of government in Canada. This fact is reinforced by the oath's reference to "the Queen of Canada," instead of "the Queen." It is not an oath to a foreign sovereign. Similarly, in today's context, the reference in the oath to the Queen of Canada's "heirs and successors" is a reference to the continuity of our form of government extending into the future" (para. 54). The judgment might make sense as an academic contortion designed to arrive at a desired result, but it might not hold water with the Canadian public which might find such a strong connection with the Queen in our present times a bit mysterious. It is hard not to conclude that the court used very convoluted historical analysis to arrive at a certain result. It would be unfortunate if the appellants were to decide not to proceed with the case to the Supreme Court of Canada.

While *Bill C-24* brings with it a myriad of other changes, two more should be mentioned as they might bring some controversy in the years to come. Both of these changes are still awaiting an order in council. For example, a Canadian citizen who is a dual citizen and has been found guilty of "treason" or "terrorism," could lose the Canadian citizenship status. Although treason and terrorism are inacceptable, they are already addressed and punished through our criminal justice system. In addition, there have been cases where people have been unfairly branded as terrorists or traitors and have even been subjected to the danger of unfair trials (See the history of Japanese Canadians in *From Racism to Redress, the Japanese Canadian Experience*, a Canadian Race Relations Foundation; Also see the story of Maher Arar who was a naturalized Canadian citizen and a dual citizen, wrongly accused of terrorism. In addition, the story of Canadian journalist Mohamed Fahmy, who was sentenced together with two other journalists to lengthy terms of imprisonment ranging from seven to ten years for terrorism offence in a trial that is considered to have been a sham and who is still waiting for his retrial to commence, without having been granted bail). In addition, as Audrey Macklin notes, "if terrorism truly poses a global threat, removing a suspected terrorist from one location to another seems singularly parochial and even somewhat futile" (2006, p. 47).

A two-tiered level of citizenship would also result through the implementation of a new ground for revoking citizenship for naturalized citizens on the basis of "misrepresentation" of the intention of residing in Canada permanently as a citizen. While it is currently possible to revoke citizenship if it is shown that it was obtained by fraud, this is something quite different which will weaken the value of Canadian citizenship rather than strengthening it. This change will mean that Canadian citizens who are naturalized will not be equal to Canadian-born citizens or who obtained citizenship through their parents. Naturalized citizens might not be able to work, study, travel or live abroad for fear of losing their status in Canada as citizens. Other Canadians will not have to live and make choices that take this type of fear into account. This is why this move discriminates against naturalized Canadians in a world in which dual citizenship is a reality in an increasingly globalized world (Maclin and Crepeau, 2010). Citizenship is a "right to have rights" (Arendt, 1976, 9.296) and should only be revoked for fraud. When reflecting on the Omar Khadr's experience, Audrey Macklin makes that point that "a foreign born citizen may acquire legal citizenship through naturalization, yet remain a second-class citizen in the subjective sense because of his or her foreign origins" (Macklin, 2006. P. 28). This is very much a perpetuation and a worsening of that phenomenon.

Further discussion points:

1. Should permanent residents be allowed to vote?
2. Should a Canadian citizen's status ever be revoked? If yes, for what causes? Does your answer differ between Canadian-born and naturalized-Canadian?
3. How do you think Canadian citizenship will look like one hundred years from now?

Conclusion

The notion of citizenship has been the subject of many debates, some still ongoing. As a fluid concept, sensitive to changes in society, political ideas and world issues, it is expected that the debate over the content and definition of citizenship will continue. The unavoidable conclusion is that, at the present moment, citizenship is not possible without exclusion. This attribute has been present in Canadian citizenship law and it is even more pronounced today. While the Harper government claims that the new rules would strengthened the value of citizenship, the above analysis of the key changes reveals a worrisome pattern of disregard towards disadvantaged and vulnerable groups and a tendency to keep people out of the civic scene for political gains that have nothing to do with the proposed goal of strengthening Canadian citizenship. On the contrary, the new changes will weaken the value of Canadian citizenship, creating an even bigger gap in the insider/outsider divide.

References

Academic Sources

Arar, M. (June June 13, 2011). My rendition and torture in Syrian prison Highlights US reliance on Syria as an Ally. *Democracy Now*. Retrieved from http://www.democracynow.org/

Arendt, H. (1976). *The origins of totalitarianism*. New York: Harcourt Inc.

Bhuyan, R. (2014). *Unprotected, unrecognized: Canadian immigration policy and violence against women, 2008-2013*. Part of the Migrant Mothers Project. Retrieved from http://www.migrantmothersproject.com/report/

Bosniak, L.S. (1998). The citizenship of aliens. *Social Text, 56, 16(3)*, 22-35.

Canadian Race Relations. (n.d.) *From racism to redress. The Japanese Canadian experience*. Retrieved from http://www.crr.ca/divers-files/en/pub /faSh/ePubFaShRacRedJap.pdf

Clooney, A. (August 18, 2014). The anatomy of an unfair trial. *Huffington Post*. Retrieved from http://www.huffingtonpost.com/Amal-Alamuddin/egypt-unfair-trial_b_5688388.html.

Citizenship and Immigration Canada. (2012). *Discover Canada: The rights and responsibilities of citizenship*. Retrieved from *http://www.cic.gc.ca /english/resources/publications/discover/*.

Cole, P. (2010). Introduction: 'Border crossings' – The dimensions of member-ship. *Citizenship acquisition and national belonging: Migration, member-ship and the liberal democratic state*. London: Palgrave Mcmillan.

Damjanovic, J. (2014). *Canada needs a plan to address violence against immigrant and refugee women*. Retrieved from http://www.huffingtonpost. ca/university-of-toronto-news/violence-against-women_b_6171322.html.

Dauenhauer, B. (1996). *Citizenship in a fragile world*. London: Rowman & Littlefield Publishers, Inc.

Derwing, T. et al. (March 2010). *An examination of the Canadian language benchmark data from the citizenship language survey*. Retrieved from http://www.cic. gc.ca/

Kakabadse, A., Kakabadse N., & Kalu, N (2009). *Citizenship: A reality far from rdeal*. New York: Palgrave Mcmillan.

Kazimi, A. (2011). *Undesirables: White Canada and the Komagata Maru, An illustrated history*. Vancouver: Douglas & McIntyre.

Kostakopoulou, D. (2008). *The future governance of citizenship*. New York: Cambridge University Press.

Kouddous, S. (January 1, 2015), Mohamed Fahmy, Canadian journalist jailed in Egypt, to get retrial. *The Star*. Retrieved from http://www.thestar.com/news/world/2015/01/01/mohamed_fahmy_cana-dian_journalist_jailed_in_egypt_to_get_retrial.html

MacMahon, S. (2012). *Introduction: Developments in the theory and practice of citizenship.* Newcastle: Cambridge Scholars Publishing.

Macklin, A. (2006). Exile on main street. *Law and Citizenship.* Law Commission of Canada. Vacounver: UBC Press.

Macklin, A., & Crépeau, F. (June 2010). *Multiple citizenship, identity and entitlement in Canada.* IRPP Study, *No. 6, June 2010,* online resources. York University Online Catalogue.

Walzer, M. (1983). *Spheres of justice: A defence of pluralism and equality.* Oxford: Martin Robertson.

Wayland, S. V., (2006). *Unsettled: Legal and policy barriers for newcomers to Canada (a* Joint Initiative of Community Foundations of Canada and the Law Commission of Canada). *Retrieved from* http://www.cfc-fcc.ca /doc/LegalPolicyBarriers.pdf.

Winter, E. (2014). *Becoming Canadian: Making sense of recent changes to citizenship rules.* Institute for Research on Public Policy (IRPP). Retrieved from http://www.irpp.org/assets/research/diversity-immigration-and-inte-gration/becoming-canadian/Winter-No44.pdf

Caselaw

Kalkat v Canada, 2012 FC 646.

McAteer v. Canada (Attorney General) 2014 ONCA 578.

MCI v. Naveen 2013 FC 972.

Ngo (Re), [1986] 1 ACWS (3) 306.

Pourghasemi (Re) [1993] F.C.J. No. 232.

Legislation

Citizenship Act, R.S.C., 1985, c. C-29.

Faster Removal of Foreign Criminals Act, S.C. 2013, c. 16.

Strengthening Canadian Citizenship Act, assented to June 19, 2014, available online at *http://www.parl.gc.ca/HousePublications/Publica-tion.aspx?doc=C-24&pub=bill&File=24#1.*

UN Refugee Convention, accessible online at http://www.unhcr.org/ 3b66c2aa10.html.

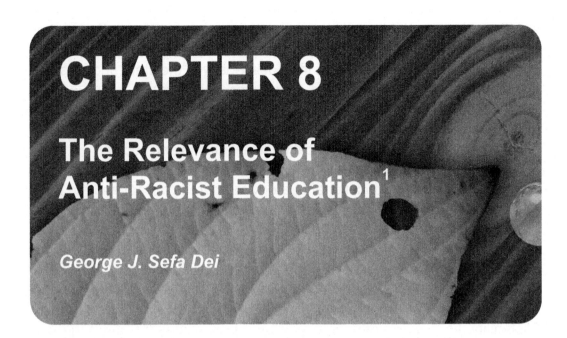

CHAPTER 8

The Relevance of Anti-Racist Education[1]

George J. Sefa Dei

Introduction

This chapter focuses on the applicability of anti-racism for frontline community workers and the important role anti-racist education can play in the settlement of immigrant and refugees and for those working with these communities. Some of the common themes of struggle faced by immigrant and refugee communities relate to questions of belonging, and inclusion into Canadian society. In an effort to address these struggles, this discussion calls on anti-racist education to give voice to the lived experiences of these communities and groups, to situate them at the centre of the discussions around inclusion and belonging. In this, I am not interested in fashionable and seductive discourses of the "limits of anti-racism," rather, the discussion focuses on possibilities for settlement workers and the communities they work with. I will opine that anti-racism as a discursive and political practice places the myriad forms of racism and their intersections with other forms of oppression in societal institutions on the table for discussion. Therefore, researchers, educators, policy makers, and community workers cannot shy away from an engagement with anti-racism as a necessary part of the conversations around official multiculturalism, despite the problematic assumptions that have come to underlay it. In this chapter I ask: What does systemic oppression and the resistances of the marginalized tell us about the concepts of nation, nationhood, citizenship, citizenship responsibilities, identity and belonging? An anti-racist and anti-colonial reading allows us to highlight the material and experiential realities of racialized,[2] immigrant and refugee groups in their dealings with the state and its social institutions (e.g., the school and social work systems). It is argued that without recognition of diverse cultures, histories, identities, and experiences, we (as scholars, educators, and researchers) fail to create room for multiple knowledges to flourish in our educational institutions and society.

Very long ago, informed by the existing literature, I defined anti-racism as an action-oriented educational strategy to address racism and the inter-sections of the myriad social oppressions (e.g., sexism, homophobia, clas-sism, ableism, and ageism) (Dei, 1996). Anti-racism is education about power, privilege, systemic injustices, and social oppression along the lines of race, class, gender, sexuality, language, and religion. It contends that in order to understand the social effects of race we must consider the intersec-tions of race with other forms of difference (class, gender, sexuality, [dis]ability, etc.). For example, how does class or gender affect the way someone is treated if they are a White Canadian or a Black refugee? These social categories are sites and sources of disadvantage, marginality, and exclusions as well as privilege, power, and dominance. The lived experi-ences of refugee and immigrant communities and, in fact many of the front-line community workers, reveal everyday accounts of marginality, exclusion, oppression, dominance, and resistance. For both frontline community workers and racialized, immigrant, and refugee groups it is important we know what anti-racism teaches us, and to apply such knowledge to empower ourselves as we collectively struggle to find a home in a new land and place. Our struggle is about power and resource sharing so that we can define our own collective existence. Our challenge is to trouble, challenge, and subvert the rationality of power and the "logic" of dominance and to define ourselves in contrast to the imposed definitions and identities that are often constructed within the Euro-American imaginary shaped through hegemonic narratives. In the anti-racist struggle for collective existence, knowledge is more than power. Knowledge must compel action and lead to a transformation of our lives. We must understand how we are racialized, what it means to be racial-ized, who has the power to racialize the "Other" as different, and so on, if we wish to challenge such impositions.

Understanding marginality, social exclusions and resisting dominance are all critical aspects of anti-racist work. Marginalization is not synonymous with exclusion. Yet these social practices and experiences are interlinked. In fact, the marginalization and vulnerability of certain segments of our society is a result of established practices of exclusion from access to valued social goods and services needed to participate as an active citizen in society. As has been argued (Rummens & Dei, 2012), any discussion of marginalization must always recognize the different sets of populations and the cultural variations one is working with; the histories and relations of different groups vary and effect the experiences of members of those groups differently. There are racialized youth of immigrant and non-immigrant backgrounds in Canada. We have youth of refugee and resettlement backgrounds. There are Indigenous and Aboriginal populations who have to be acknowledged as having welcomed everyone as immigrants to this land. It is important to note that the trajectories of marginalization, which, while it may be unique to groups, also point to intersections with other oppressed groups. It is also pertinent that we understand marginalization and exclusion as these practices are understood from the vantage point of those who have historically been excluded or disadvantaged in society. It is only through such critical understandings that one can expect that our institutions respond to the multiple needs and concerns of a diverse body politic. Such understandings also allow us to commit to ensuring that all members of our diverse communities develop a sense of entitlement and responsibility, as well as a belonging and connectedness to communities.

Within the educational system, for example, marginalization and exclusions in schooling is about more than omission (deliberate or otherwise) of cultures, experiences, and knowledges. Exclusion is a material, psychological, political, and spiritual practice. Exclusions and marginalization are about spaces and claims to ownership, control, and belonging. Social inclusion, as I conceptualize through anti-racism, is also not simply adding or bringing into an existing order. After all, one can be included while existing on the margins. Inclusion, as described through anti-racism, is about centering, about speaking of equitable outcomes and addressing key questions of power, privilege, and the sense of entitlement that one may have without matching responsibilities. Marginalization and exclusions are real and often felt by youth who express their disenchantment with society in various ways. The ways that typically get attention from the media and policy focus on youth dropping out, or similarly "not playing by the rules," creating a further experience of being marginalized of youth who do not feel they are important members of society. Given the historic inequities that exist in the educational system, the sometimes self-destructive expression by marginalized youths, and the narratives that then surround those youth, a perpetuation of exclusive spaces continues. These practices constitute a waste of knowledge and skills and missed opportunities, and the wider community ends up losing out when youth develop a sense of disconnection, alienation, or even hopelessness in the system. The examples are not limited with the school system; when public and community services face severe funding cuts or out-right elimination by local municipal, provincial, and federal governments these usually result in the further marginalization and exclusions of working-class, racial, ethnic, immigrant, and minority linguistic communities. Usually such elimination and cuts to the funding of local community organizations coupled with the introduction of user fees and privatization of public services place untold hardships on refugee and immigrant resettlement communities who are already struggling to maintain, and claim, their existence in Canada. Thus, targeting the services that benefit the most marginalized segments of our communities creates a sense of hopelessness and lost dreams among some youth and adults, especially those who require employment and social services to make ends meet (see also Rummens & Dei, 2012). Anti-racism discourse is articulating such concerns and acting on them concretely to achieve social justice and fairness. Anti-racism education may not be the panacea to all social ills, but at least it registers such concerns on our collective conscience to act for the good of a common humanity.

Why Anti-racism in a Multicultural Context?

As community and frontline workers and racially disadvantaged groups we need to speak and act on anti-racist practice today more so than ever. Why? In recent months, a number of Western leaders have openly questioned official policies of multiculturalism, arguing that it has failed to meet the challenges of social cohesion and good citizenship. Instead, they argue, the policy has created ethnic enclaves and communities who have stuck hard to their cultures and not adapted or assimilated to the values of their new homelands. It is not at all surprising that such debates and musings will carry over and influence what is happening in Canada. After all, we rightly pride ourselves in having a long-standing, open multiculturalism policy. I admit that I am not a big fan of multiculturalism; yet, I am hesitant to completely dismiss it as a social policy having no relevance. In Canada on July 12, 1988, the passage of Bill C-93 (an Act for the Preservation and Enhancement of Multiculturalism) enshrined multiculturalism into federal law. As an official political doctrine, multiculturalism has promoted cultural diversity as an intrinsic and valuable component of the social, political, and moral order of Canada. The policy also seeks to value racial minorities on the basis of a common humanity and envisions a future assured by goodwill on the part of all. Thus, at the very least, the contributions of different cultures to national well-being and destiny are officially acknowledged.

Many critics argue that, despite many genuine intentions, official multiculturalism has been ineffective in addressing broader questions of structural racism, social oppression, domination, and marginalization of peoples in society. The policy has failed to address profound issues of power and resource sharing as well as working with social identities and the implications of these for knowledge construction (see Price, 1993). There are profound social problems that racialized immigrant communities confront daily in Canadian society – employment, education, housing, law, and the justice system – even under the official multiculturalism stance. These issues are largely connected to integration challenges for newcomers as they are expected to take up and act upon solely Canadian values, leaving behind their cultural values which are socially devalued in the dominant society. This leaves immigrants and newcomers to have to navigate feelings and experiences of alienation in both their cultures and in the new space of Canada. Many immigrant and refugee youth, adults, and Indigenous communities face challenges of poverty; homelessness and displacement, and discrimination in the housing and social services sectors that affect their sense of belonging. Another key issue that multiculturalism does not address, in its official manifestation, is the complex reality of the land of Canada and who has the right to define who can have full access to the land and, simultaneously, be allowed full participation in society. We could, for instance, try to understand this issue through the "Aboriginal lens" and recognize these moments of oppression as deeply embedded within the contexts of racism and colonialism that are weaved into the fabric of Canadian society. Multiculturalism offers limiting conditions in regards to contemporary discussions about Indigenous land rights and self-governance. Celebratory promotions of diversity by the state fail to broach the material needs of Indigenous peoples or address the systems that create these material needs. Multiculturalism, then, comes to appropriate and obscure these important discussions about privilege and systemic power and about the way in which particular groups come to be identified through these discourses and conversations.

Admittedly, the discussion of multiculturalism registers differently in Francophone Canada. In a recent piece in the *Toronto Star*, Jonathan Montpetit points to recent strident critiques of multiculturalism in Quebec, where a growing number of Parti Quebecois politicians have steadfastly been maintaining that "multiculturalism is not a Quebec value." Faced with a troubling anti-immigrant backlash, some scholars in the province have long proposed "interculturalism" as a model of social integration and/or a way to respond to the "accommodation of minorities" (Montpetit, 2011). This model grants the centrality of Francophone culture as a starting point for understanding how to integrate other minorities into the social fabric. The distinction between multiculturalism and interculturalism is very tenuous at best. While interculturalism is different in that it acknowledges the centrality of Fran-cophone or Anglophone culture depending on the social context and location for the discussion, it is ignorant of the racially driven power dynamics that legitimize the White, colonial "settler" narrative in Canada, a narrative that Franco-Canadians are equally complicit within.

Central to the discussion is the question of identity and inclusiveness within Canada; in particular, the ways groups are represented in mainstream media through a co-optation of identity as understood and articulated through the historical cultural narratives of colonialism. The problem lies in the ways in which we make sense of citizenry – questions of who is the imag-ined "Canadian citizen," something that is historically articulated through Anglo-Franco (British/French) nomenclature. In this imagined category of the "Canadian citizen," indigenous peoples and, in fact, anyone other than of White British and French descent, are not included. How the story is told in the history books and mass media suggests that the movement of partic-ular European groups as settlers on this land is simultaneously always already belonging to the land (and conversely, this narrative allows the land to belong to the European settlers). In this telling, the Indigenous and Aborig-inal groups have no claim over the land, and any other (read: non-White European) groups are always positioned as being an "addition" to the nation-state, not as belonging. Both multiculturalism and interculturalism collude in and perpetuate this "logic."

Notwithstanding these extensive limitations, as an anti-racist educator I do see multiculturalism as an allied discourse. We should be careful not to reject it outright and, in the process, remove a valuable first step towards a more critical anti-racist approach. In this light, we must challenge recent high-level critiques of multiculturalism. Recently, I was invited to give an African Liberation Month (African History Month) guest address to a commu-nity group in Edmonton, Alberta. On my way back to Toronto, I picked up a *Vancouver Sun* newspaper at the airport terminal. Glancing through, I read an opinion piece by Licia Corbella (2011). Frankly, it made for an interesting and very troubling read for me. Here, we have leaders of the West –

including Canadian intellectuals of racial minority backgrounds – making such revealing and pointed comments on multiculturalism. In response to immigrant groups who wished to remove their children from certain educational programs on the basis of religious grounds (using the safeguards of the state multiculturalism policy), a university professor who immigrated here from Pakistan is quoted as saying that:

> Immigrants to Canada should adjust to Canada, not the other way around;" the professor adds that, "Canada has an enviable culture based on Judeo-Christian values ... with British and French rule of law and traditions and that's why it's better than all of the other places in the world. (cited in Corbella, 2011)

German Chancellor Angela Merkel is adamant that official multiculturalism has "failed totally." British Prime Minister, David Cameron, is also quoted as saying that

> under the doctrine of state multiculturalism ... we have failed to provide a vision of society to which they [immigrants] feel they want to belong. We have even tolerated these segregated communities behaving in ways that run counter to our values. So when a White person holds objectionable views – racism, for example – we rightly condemn them. But when equally unacceptable views or practices have come from someone who isn't White, we've been too cautious, frankly even fearful, to stand up to them. (cited in Corbella, 2011)

Similarly, French President Nicolas Sarkozy is also quoted as asserting: "We have been too concerned about the identity of the person who was arriving and not enough about the identity of the country that was receiving them" (cited in Corbella, 2011). These comments must be pleasing to the ears of the average person with doubts about multiculturalism, to the persons and groups who believe that inclusion means assimilation, that inclusion means a complete negation of cultural values other than Canadian. Coming from such powerful leaders, these ideas cannot be easily dismissed. I know a large cross section of our communities also share these sentiments.

These statements should also elicit fear and the realization that White, racialized discourses are gaining power and voice in more explicit as well as subtle ways; if multiculturalism, a soft discourse of inclusion is under attack, what does this mean for anti-racism? There is a Ghanaian saying, conveyed in a local song, which goes: "If Jesus Christ, the Messiah himself, was crucified on the cross what do you think they [the crucifiers] will do to the common Pastor? His or her fate will obviously be worse." The sentiment can be appreciated even apart from the Christian faith: If soft multiculturalism is under such attack, you can imagine what is being said of anti-racism, which more explicitly names the power imbalances and oppressive relations that drive Canadian society. But I refuse to engage in cowardliness. I believe that anti-racist and anti-colonial methods of perceiving communities can offer some lessons here. In response to these attempts to consolidate White privilege and further marginalize non-White communities, I intentionally mobilize anti-racist and anti-colonial methodologies to give voice to lived minority experiences and situate them at the centre of the discussions around inclusion and belonging, and I urge community and resettlement workers to do the same.

The push to assimilate ethnic and racial minorities and so-called immigrants into a Canadian/American/European Whiteness or into a society built on a White identity needs interrogation (see also Bedard, 2000). What is troubling in this debate is both the perception of the values of a nation as frozen and immune to the changes happening around it as well as the perceived superiority of Western neo-liberal values. Why does one think that Judeo-Christian values are better than other values or more conducive to inclusivity (as the professor quoted above infers)? Immigrants must learn about the cultures of their new homes but the home country must also adapt to the changes around them, especially when the identities of a nation are continually changing through immigration and through the dynamics of social difference. Why is it necessary to stubbornly conceptualize Canada, America, or Europe as White, Judeo-Christian spaces when these categories purposefully exclude and marginalize many of the people that inhabit these areas? Room must be created within the fabric of Canadian society that is accepting of difference and open to mobility of values. We must not position difference as the problem; rather, we must work with the strength of difference, welcoming difference as an opportunity for us to grow together as a nation/community. We have to be careful how we comply with certain rigid forms of citizenship, which historically has been organized by racial categories. The "global" and the "universal" cannot be presented through a prism of the hierarchy of knowing and privileging of particular ideas, values, cultures, and identities. Furthermore, we must question how the dominant understanding of multiculturalism misreads or ignores race and other forms of social difference as markers of oppression and, in fact, specifically makes race irrelevant in the Canadian/American/European psyche.

Anti-Racism: Resistance and Belonging

As already noted, anti-racism as a discursive and political practice places the myriad forms of racism and their intersections with other forms of oppression in societal institutions on the table for discussion. We cannot shy away from engagement. In fact, given the significance of race as a powerful marker of identification in pluralistic, multicultural communities, it is always important not to lose sight of the saliency and centrality of race in our understandings of multiculturalism. We have to name race (as with gender, class, sexuality, ability/disability) if we are to address the racial problem and, in fact, systemic injustices in general. What does systemic oppression and resistance of the marginalized tell us about the concepts of nation, nationhood, citizenship, citizenship responsibilities, identity, and belonging? Who can claim to be a full citizen and how are a nation's peoples defined? For example, when you think of particular countries, you generally picture a particular raced people; in Canada, the image of a White people is conjured, in Jamaica or Trinidad and Tobago a Black people/bodies come to represent the nation, and yet in all three locations you have peoples from many different racial locations residing.

The anti-racist and anti-colonial gaze seeks to highlight the material and experiential realities of racialized groups in their dealings with the state and its social institutions (e.g., school systems, media, criminal justice system, immigrant resettlement services, etc.). For example, anti-racism acknowledges the meanings and implications of race and racial constructs and how all forms of difference (class, gender, sexual, disability) intersect to script life chances and opportunities. Anti-racism education is involved with learning about the experiences of living with racialized identities and understanding how students' lived experiences in and out of school are implicated in youth engagement and disengagement from school. Anti-racism education also uncovers the ways in which race, ethnicity, class, gender, sexuality, ability, power, and difference influence and are influenced by institutional processes. Anti-racism interrogates the processes of teaching, learning, and educational administration, as well as the ways in which they combine to produce schooling successes and failures for different bodies. Anti-racism holds that questions of power, equity and social difference are significant for learning outcomes and the provision of opportunities for all youth.

Anti-racism broadens the discussion around identity, citizenship, and belonging to include not only the so-called "immigrants" but other racialized, colonized, oppressed, and Indigenous bodies in White-settler contexts. Anti-racism brings questions about the processes of colonization and racialization[3] to the fore, pointing to how citizenship, community building, claims of identity, history, and politics and knowledge as well as power sharing and the distribution of resources are embedded within racialized power relations and mobilized by White privilege to the disadvantage of others. Anti-racism is about power and privilege. It challenges any sense of entitlement, calling for resistance, social responsibility, and collective undertakings to fight oppressions. It is about making claims to self and collective worth that undergird a connection to everyone around us (including social communities as well as our natural environments). This is why an anti-racist body of knowledge would herald the society, culture, and nature interface and point to a spiritual sense of self and place, amplifying interconnections. Anti-racism is bound by connections of inter-dependency and inclusion, with its focus on the relations between people, places, and ideas. In other words, anti-racism works with the understanding that if one aspect is to change, then all the other aspects will (and need) be affected for a holistic transformation.

Anti-racism distinguishes between the notions of "dominant culture/race" from ideas of "majority culture/race." When, in politics for example, we speak of the majority party, it is the party that has the largest contingent, and having been elected it is taken to suggest superiority. With this understanding of "majority", democracy comes to be implicated in the reification[4] of inequitable relations. If the majority party represents what "the largest group" desires, this is where we run into problems of social integration. Thus, a critical anti-racist analysis of the majority–minority dynamic is approached more as a question of power relations rather than sheer numbers. Our understanding of group dynamics and social relations, while acknowledging the existence and presence of majority–minority cultures/groups, will be politically and conceptually flawed if it fails to engage with power and the asymmetrical power relations among groups. In other words, what does it mean when we ask "minorities" to assimilate or integrate into dominant cultures? What is being affirmed and what is being lost? What histories, identities, cultures are we denying and simultaneously, what is being privileged and at what and whose expense? These are critical questions that anti-racist education brings to the table for discussion. Raising these questions is not about fragmenting communities. It is about building, and working with "communities of differences" in which power sharing is a major concern as much as the maintaining of groups identities, cultures, and languages. All groups have rights to maintain their identities, cultures, and languages, but not at others' expense. When there is a loss of individual and group identities, histories, and cultures, the whole goal of social cohesion is lost.

When anti-racism theory is taken up, I sometimes think that the conversation is governed by the assumption that the anti-racist educator is bereft of the Euro-body or the Indigenous body. We must recognize that anti-racism education is not exclusive to a particular group, community, or identity. Therefore, we must come together in the name of community, shared politics, solidarity, social justice, and social change to engage the theory and practice of anti-racism education if we are seeking a harmonious way of life through difference. More importantly, we must ask: What does it mean for the Euro-body to do anti-racism work? Such a question invariably speaks to other concerns: Where does knowledge reside? How do we come to know? What is knowledge and what knowledge counts? How do power and knowledge intersect? These questions are about accessibility and rights. At the same time, we must be cautious about coming to know in ways that reify the historic constituents of colonization. We must avoid a theorizing that accords a particular privileging and discursive authority of minoritized bodies of knowledge while at the same time working with historically contingent variables. In other words, we must work to open spaces for many knowledges to reside rather than simply recreating a different hierarchy of knowledge. This in turn opens up possibilities for discussing the historic specificities and the myriad sites, complexities, and contestations of colonization in relation to the ongoing production of the settler nation-state. The recognition of complexities and contextualization is important because it allows us to move away from reliance on the dogmatization of a particular theoretical framework, the "my way or the highway" conversation (i.e., multiculturalism versus anti-racism). Instead, I invite a theorizing in which all learners can engage in an intellectually honest conversation, allowing for the complicities and complexities of the different historic bodies, as entangled within the politics and representations of settler/citizen/immigrant, to come to the surface. What these issues perhaps tell us then is that, as community workers, we need to extend our focus on the implications of the education of young learners that flow from the policy of multiculturalism/interculturalism onto the possibilities of critical anti-racist educational practice.

Anti-Racism and the Workplace

At this juncture, I would link anti-racist and anti-colonial readings to the challenge of knowledge making in the workplace, schools, media, and other institutional settings. I broach the discussion less as a transition into another discussion and more as an effort to amplify the call to critical workers (including racialized, immigrant, and refugee frontline workers and, in fact, all learners) to mount a spirited defence of anti-racist/anti-colonial intellectual and political stances and, by extension, uphold the discourse and official policy of multiculturalism, notwithstanding the noted limitations. Without recognition of diverse cultures, histories, identities, and experiences, we do not create room for multiple knowledges to flourish in our educational institutions, a stated goal of anti-racism. The failure to offer a counter reading will allow for a "civilisational racism" (Scheurich & Young, 1997) built on the assumptions of the superiority of Western civilization. Furthermore, it will perpetuate the need for other cultures to imitate the particulars of Western "civilization," imbued with Western values, in an effort to be acknowledged as legitimate in global relations.

Furthermore, the Euro-modernist/Euro-colonial project, which rewards racialized bodies that seek legitimation, acceptance or validation in dominant colonial and colonizing spaces, is flawed epistemologically and theoretically. Apart from the dangers of intellectual mimicry, it causes mental, physical, spiritual, and emotional damage to the racialized body. It robs us of our intellectual dignity and inflicts a form of epistemicide and linguicide (see Lebakeng, 2010). By epistemicide and linguicide, I mean to signal the eventual dying out of particular indigenous ways of knowing/knowledge systems (epistemicide) as well as languages (linguicide). We cannot capitulate to the epistemic violence of Western knowledge production and the Western academy that seeks to reject and, ultimately, destroy other forms of knowing. Euro- and Western-centric knowledges, through this epistemicide, locate themselves globally as the one-and-only forms of legitimate knowledge through this non-acknowledgement of other ways of knowing, creating not only a hierarchy of knowledges, but also a stifling and destruction of any knowledges that are differently produced through varying cultures, value-systems, and peoples. Linguicide plays a crucial role in this epistemicide in that it necessitates knowledge to be presented through a particular linguistic organization, again that of Euro- and Western-centric knowledges. As many have articulated previously, language, culture, and identity are closely linked, and when one is required to articulate through a different linguistic system (even if within the same umbrella language), there lies the danger that her or his culture and identity will be lost-in-translation, allowing for a double negation of that culture and identity; one through the epistemic requirements and one through the linguistic requirements of validation.

Consequently, concerns about the current "neo-colonial context" must of necessity be captured as an "anti-colonial moment." This is important so that the project of decolonization is not diluted. Discourses about the intersectionality of social difference (race, class, gender, sexuality, disability, etc. as linked, intersected, integrated, and relational) must never lose sight of such differences as sites of marginality and resistance. It is important to stress and hang on to the notion of the saliency and centrality of particular identities given particular moments and contexts, as well as the relative saliencies of different identities and oppressions, especially as they relate to knowledge production.

For me, it is not a question of arguing that the world is more than simply about subjectivity and identities. Questions of materiality are equally profound. However, it is also about how identities are linked with knowledge production and, particularly, processes of schooling in the distribution of rewards, punishments, and entitlements. For example, I ask: Why are Afri-centric perspectives or anti-colonial discursive frameworks and politics marginalized or even devalued while post-colonialism and post-colonial thought are so lauded? What is it in the terms "post" that make those discourses more comfortable? Perhaps it is the implicit suggestion that society has moved beyond colonialism into an equitable space for all people.

The school or the workplace today is a site in need of anti-racist and anti-colonial readings, interpretations, interventions, disruptions, and subversions. For example, learners of today are, and must be, anti-colonial subjects and agents. The "anti" (in anti-racist/anti-colonial) is not simply oppositional or confrontational but, more importantly, "action-oriented," libratory, productive, and transformational. We must push forward in the recognition of the value of diversity and oppositional knowledges. We must be we willing to interrogate both what we are resisting but also our own resistance, recognizing our multiple positions, and never stopping in our fight against discourses of marginalization and oppression, never losing sight of what we are fighting for. Objective neutrality is not an option.

We must rethink conventional understandings of social justice and the universal learner/subject/worker. Treating everybody the same may be ideal but it is not the only model of social justice. There needs to be recognition of the severity of issues for certain bodies and a conversation around the specific historical contexts that create the varying conditions faced by the many oppressed and marginalized peoples. With these conversations, it is equally important that we do not universalize the experiences of our racialized, immigrant, and refugee populations, communities and learners. The universal may seem reasonable, natural, neutral – it is an approach that works with the notion that a "rising tide lifts all boats" – when, in the face of student experiences, a universal model does not meet all students' needs in the same way. In other words, a rising tide leaves some children gasping for air; some children are left to swim through the effects of epistemicide and linguicide, while others are placed in the boats that rise with the tide! Furthermore, the question of representation and merit/reward procedures is about addressing the challenge of social inclusion. All workplaces want to compete for the "best and the brightest" for a supposedly "shrinking workforce." But what do we mean by the "best and brightest" and how do our definitions denote a "shrinking workforce?" Organizations can only be better equipped to serve a diverse population if the workforce itself is diverse and recognizes the existence of excellence as widely distributed in the population. Our diversity strategy must begin by recognizing the idea of "shared excellence" and the knowledge representations that we may be bringing to "excellence." It is important to increase the pool of candidates from all under-represented groups (racialized and immigrant minorities, Aboriginal, women, people with disabilities, sexual differences, linguistic minorities, etc.). But it is also equally important to ask what happens to these groups when they enter the workplace. How do we address discrimination in the workplace? How do we support all workers against discriminatory practices? Furthermore, we must have the courage to look at the so-called level playing field of the "free market" and face the facts of systemic inclusion of some and exclusion of others. We know the "best and brightest" of our young women, our people of colour and our working-class students, have consistently been kept out of the Canadian dream despite daily assurances that the system works for everyone (a claim which denies what they/we know to be true of the experiences of mothers, fathers, brothers, sisters, and community members).

We must also redefine success more broadly. The North American mythologies of "achievement ideology," the "cult of individualism," fairness, equity, excellence, and what Lewin (2008) calls "standardization recipes" are common, and severely limiting. On this question about "standards," "merit/meritocracy," and "excellence," it is not that marginalized groups do not believe in excellence or merits or that we are not capable of achieving these "standards," but it is the way in which those standards and merits are aligned with particular values from a perspective that does not allow for difference and variety. The contestations are about definitions and contexts. Who is defining and setting the terms? What particular histories shape such constructions that establish the norm/universal? Additionally, while improvements on scores in the standardized EQAO tests in the education of our youth may give us hope, we must measure success beyond test scores to include accounts of how students feel about themselves, the love for learning, their purpose in life and of education, and a commitment to their communities. This is social success.

Working for anti-racist change is to engage the idea of a "Messy Utopia." I work with the term "Messy Utopia" to amplify that Michael Adams' (2007) "Unlikely Utopia" is attainable but it will not be neat, rather, it will be messy and challenging. The search for any utopia is messy and uncomfortable, especially for all who are very much accustomed to the unearned privileges. So by utopian I imply neither easy nor uncomplicated processes, alliances, and efforts. Instead, I refer to the often awkward, challenging, and rewarding collaborations which are needed to affect change in a society which holds among its core values social justice and diversity. Change is never easy and clear. It takes courage to break away from established patterns. We make/create own our histories and futures. Creating a utopia is more than a transformation of the existing order. It may mean that perhaps we replace our workplaces/schools, and so on, with something radically different from what we are accustomed to. It simultaneously needs to remain a work in process; just as the initial legislative act to make multiculturalism a national policy in Canada was a step toward change, the work needs to continue as we bring conversations of multiculturalism and anti-racism together, to support the ongoing change that is necessary.

We must also acknowledge and address our collective implications and complicities. We are all implicated in the very things that we are contesting. By remaining silent we become complicit in our own oppressions, marginal-ization, and social exclusions. There are no neutral positions in the fight for social justice. But, there is a particular responsibility in challenging the idea of a particular subject as the archetype of humanity. This will mean addressing our sense of entitlement without any matching responsibilities. Many of us claim spaces as if we are entitled to these spaces. It is a fore-gone conclusion and yet, what has been the history of struggle to have these spaces in the first place? How is claiming such spaces as entitlements accorded privilege and power that has not been worn or deserved? How do we account for our unearned social advantage? We must all continually ask ourselves such tough questions. I recall a recent incident regarding the proposal of the Toronto District School Board (TDSB) to have a second Afri-centric School open at Oakwood Collegiate in Toronto. Let us forget even the media hysteria and the moral panic and the deliberate conflation of the site/siting of the school with the merits of the Africentric school. Students, parents, and educators of the school who opposed the idea were speaking about how "this is *our* space and we don't want the Africentric school here." Of course, we must hear all voices, but I also ask: Since when do certain parents, students, and educators get to decide on these matters on behalf of others? What about others who want to have access to these spaces? Are we not members of our communities? Interestingly, I am asking you also to think: If there had been a proposal to open a school for White students teaching them classical music, would we need the police officers and security to be around when the proposal is being discussed at a community gathering? I am sure some questions might be raised, but am confident there will not be a moral panic to arouse the necessity for a security detail. Furthermore, I am pretty sure the students will not be quoted at length in the *Toronto Star* as experts entitled to lay claim over the space of the school.

Anti-racist teachings are a way to help create healthy, sustainable, and humane communities. I sincerely believe that any community is as good as we collectively work to make it. There is the oft-repeated African adage, "It takes a Village to Raise a Child." What does this really mean? It is not the idea of the collective in itself. It is about creating and having a community in existence in the first place that everyone can count on. This means working hard to sustain the various communities in which we live in order to create the sense of collective responsibility and sharing of wealth of knowledge, ideas, and practice. We also think in terms of how we come to define and work with our communities. We are "communities of differences" and as such we must define our communities broadly and more inclusively. We must address the asymmetrical relations of power that exists among and within our communities and the unfortunate but deliberate politics of pitting communities against each other. In effect, we must all find ways to ensure all our communities are included at the table. Searching for the "Messy Utopia" must bring us together on many levels as we collectively develop or create a common (if contested) future. Our histories and identities are intertwined. In our frontline community work we must stay connected in the pursuit of social justice and equality for ourselves, our communities, and for the generations to come.

An important Indigenous and Aboriginal teaching is the power of working with a multi-centric knowledge base. Indigenous philosophies conceptualize our worlds holistically, in relations between selves and groups, connecting the body–mind and soul interface, as well as the nexus of society, culture, and nature. These knowings have many lessons to teach all of us. For example, we must begin thinking in circles, rather than in hierarchical binaries, as we seek to co-create the "Messy Utopia." We must seek non-hierarchical, collaborative and collegial relations amongst ourselves and, particularly, in decision-making processes. There is a need for the humanization of our institutions and workplaces. We must begin creating spaces where social interactions and relations serve to humanize us all. This will involve addressing our aversion to spirituality and spiritual knowings and working with embodied knowings. Our equity work must flow from a sense of spiritual understanding which accentuates love, care, and respect but is also revolutionary in terms of pursuit of action to bring transformative change. By spirituality I am not calling for an unquestioned faith in a religion. I am thinking of an understanding of the inner self and connections with group, community, and outer environments. It is about a belief in the power that is beyond the human senses to comprehend. This belief serves to regulate life and social action in service of a common humanity. Spirituality is not fundamentalism. My understanding of spirituality is not to evade power issues, but rather to recognizing that there are different spiritualities and to challenge the "material and non-material" split. Spirituality is about identity, knowing a part of oneself. Just as we speak of racial, class, gender, (dis)ability, language and religious differences, we must also speak about the connections of spiritual identities to who we are as humans or "embodied beings." We cannot ask anyone who has a strong sense of his or her spiritual selves to leave spiritualities "behind." In other words, we cannot conveniently have or create "a spiritual proof fence" (Masseri, 1994) in our institutions, where our spiritual identities must be left at the door as we enter and engage our institutions.

The idea of a multi-centric knowledge base challenges the dominance of particular ways of knowing. For example, educating migrant and immigrant youth to gain access to the "culture of power" is also about helping youth to critique the culture of power for its vested interests, uses, and limitations (see Delpit, 1988, 1995). As Christine Sleeter (2009) notes, knowing the mainstream science as an aspect of the culture of power may help open doors, but it is not the only legitimate/valid way or source of knowing. In other words, the project of anti-racism is not to dismiss Euro-centric knowledge and mainstream education, but rather to understand it as one of many ways to understand our social, physical, and spiritual worlds, and thereby challenge its assumed superiority.

Conclusion

I end with the call for the creation of a "Trialectic Space" (Dei, 2011). This space involves a dialogue among multiple parties, a sort of "dialogic encounter" with an epistemic community. But more importantly, as a mode of anti-racism, it is constituted as a space for all learners to openly utilize the body, mind, and spirit/soul interface in critical dialogues about their existence. It is also a space that nurtures conversations that acknowledge the importance and implications of working with a knowledge base about the society, culture, and nature nexus. Such spaces can only be created when we open our minds broadly to revision schooling and see all social contexts as places/sites and opportunities to challenge dominant and entrenched paradigms and reasoning. It is a space where the core social values highlighted and rewarded are community, responsibility, sense of collective belonging, mutual interdependence, interconnections, inter-relationships, respect, love, and care for all humanity.

Furthermore, the trialectic space is a utopia with a philosophy and "pedagogy of hope" (Dei, 2010) that celebrate the indomitable human spirit teaching love, justice, and healing as important to contesting an over-determined future. A pedagogy of hope allows us to work with emotions in our work and allows for these to propel social and political action. It is about a conviction that there will be success at the end of collective struggles and that hope for a better future can be struggled for and attained. A pedagogy of hope is about coming to know holistically. A pedagogy of hope is teaching about diverse and multiple knowledges, including the active learning of multiple cultures, histories, experiences and knowledges emphasizing the complexities of such knowledges. For example, a pedagogy of hope creates spaces of knowledge and power sharing for family/community involvement in schools (i.e., in areas of pedagogy, instruction, and curricular development) and emphasizes instructional and pedagogic practices that herald collective learning and responsibility by redefining "success" broadly to include academic and social success. Such a pedagogy of hope also promotes political activity that foreground questions of social difference and power relations (race, ethnicity, gender, class, language, [dis]ability, religious, age, and sexuality issues). Working with a pedagogy of hope seeks to heal wounds inflicted by colonizing and oppressive relations and practices and cultivates in all learners agency and the upholding of the virtues of spiritual, emotional, psychological, and (moral) values development of a whole being.

Such a pedagogy of hope assists learners to believe in their power to transform their circumstances and to create a better future for all. This is the critical humanism that Fanon wrote about as the creation of a new social world (Dei, 2010). As this chapter has worked to keep alive the possibilities of transformation through continuing the conversations of multiculturalism and anti-racism, and bringing in conversations of trialectic spaces and pedagogies of hope, I urge those who make up the marginalized communities, as well as those who work with those communities, to join in these conversation as we work toward a nation where all can lay claim to the spaces, communities, and institutions that organize the society.

Develop your knowledge

1. **NARRATIVE:** This chapter amplifies that anti-racism urges for a centering of the lived experiences and narratives of those who have been marginalized. For this activity, write a short narrative about yourself. In one to two pages describe a day at school or a day at work, provide specific details of the events and experiences of the day. Then share your narrative with another classmate and analyze the narratives for a sense of belonging and alienation. The key is that belonging and alienation may not be mentioned explicitly, but consider the ways these feelings present themselves subtly.

2. **GRAPHIC/METAPHORIC REPRESENTATION:** Alone or in groups of two or three, flesh out some of the differences and similarities between anti-racism and multiculturalism. Then create a graphic representation or metaphor to represent the two concepts.

3. **MEMO:** Examine a social practice in the field of social work (either from your work experience, or from your class work) and filter it through the lens of anti-racism. How does this practice reflect the ideas of anti-racism? Can you think of spaces in that practice that are not aligned with the ideas of anti-racism? Write a memo to a supervisor indicating whether this practice should continue, or if it needs to change based on an anti-racist reading.

Notes

[1] This chapter is a much-expanded version of "In defence of official multiculturalism and recognition of the necessity for critical anti-racist education," submitted to *Canadian Issues*, special issue on "Diversity and Education for Liberation: Realities, Possibilities and Problems." I want to thank Eric Ritskes, Marlon Simmons, and Mairi McDermott, all of the Department of Sociology and Equity Studies, Ontario Institute for Studies in Education of the University of Toronto (OISE/UT), for reading and commenting on a draft on the chapter.

[2] When I write and work with terms like racialized or marginalized, I am intending to implicate a system of oppression rather than risking locating the identity as innate to the individuals or groups I refer to.

[3] When writing and speaking of the process of racialization, I intend to amplify the values and attitudes that are attached to particular races through historical, socio-cultural processes that come to shape the identities of people of various races.

[4] To speak of a 'reification' I intend to amplify the process by which the concept of inequity, as an abstract, comes to be made real with material consequences. As anti-racism speaks about the ever-present inequities in present day society, it is important to understand the many ways in which inequities organize our lived experiences.

References

Adams, M. (2007). *Unlikely utopia: The surprising triumph of Canadian pluralism*. Toronto: Viking Canada.

Bedard, G. (2000). Deconstructing whiteness: Pedagogical implications for anti-racism education. In G.J.S. Dei, & A. Calliste (Eds.), *Power, knowledge and anti-racism education*. Halifax: Fernwood.

Corbella, L. (2011, February 14). Time to change the tune on official multiculturalism. *Vancouver Sun*, p. A10.

Dei, G.J.S. (1996). *Anti-racism education in theory and practice*. Halifax: Fernwood.

Dei, G.J.S. (2010). Fanon and anti-colonial theorizing. In G.J.S. Dei (Ed.), *Fanon and the counter-insurgency of education*. Rotterdam: Sense.

Dei, G.J.S. (2011). Keynote Address: Indigenous philosophies and critical education: The African experience. *4th Annual Decolonizing the Spirit Conference, Rebuilding the Community and Reclaiming Our Histories*. March 25. Toronto, Ontario Institute for Studies in Education, University of Toronto.

Delpit, L.D. (1988). The silenced dialogue: Power and pedagogy in educating other people's children. *Harvard Educational Review, 58*(3), 280–298.

Delpit, L.D. (1995*). Other people's children: Cultural conflict in the classroom.* New York: New Press.

Lebakeng, T.G. (2010). Discourse on indigenous knowledge systems, sustainable socio-economic development and the challenge of the academy in Africa. *CODESRIA Bulletin, 1–2*, 24–29.

Lewin, K.M. (2008). *Strategies for sustainable financing of secondary education in sub-Saharan Africa.* Human Development Series, World Bank Working Paper, 136. Washington, DC: World Bank.

Masseri, A. (1994). The imperialistic epistemological vision. *American Journal of Islamic Social Studies 11*(3), 403–415.

Montpetit, J. (2011, March 7). Integrating "interculturalism" in Quebec." *Toronto Star,* A6.

Price, E. (1993). Multiculturalism: A critique. Unpublished paper. Toronto, Department of Sociology and Equity Studies (SESE), Ontario Institute for Studies in Education, University of Toronto.

Rummens, A., & Dei, G.J.S. (2012). Understanding youth marginalization. In K. Kinlock (Ed.), *Marginalized youth: A tranquil invitation to a rebellious celebration.* Waterloo, ON: Wilfred Laurier University Press.

Scheurich, P., & Young, M. (1997). Coloring epistemologies: Are our research epistemologies racially biased? *Educational Researcher 26*(4), 4–16.

Sleeter, C. (2009). Interview with Arvind Mishra: Politics of justice more than politics of recognition. Retrieved from http://deshkaledu.org /Interviews.htm

PART 4

HEALTH CONDITIONS OF IMMIGRANTS AND REFUGEES

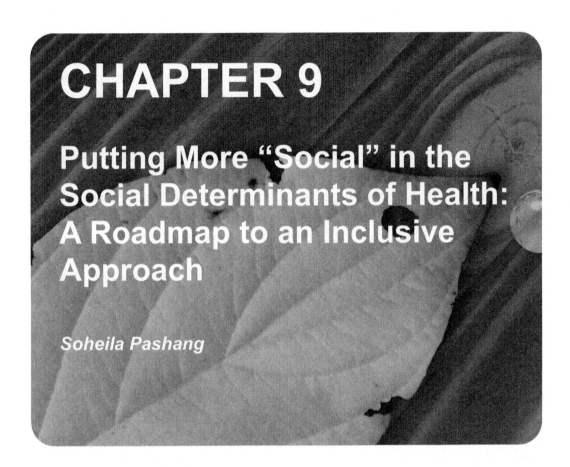

CHAPTER 9

Putting More "Social" in the Social Determinants of Health: A Roadmap to an Inclusive Approach

Soheila Pashang

Introduction

In this chapter I examine the discourse of health as it relates to Aboriginal Peoples, racialized individuals as well as immigrants, refugees, and illegalized persons. For centuries, the notion of **health** has been conceptualized and associated with illness and disease. Today, we recognize that health is influenced by and related to an interconnected set of personal, community and structural factors – from social issues to economic, geo-political and environmental conditions. These factors directly affect the choices and options one might have in their life, or the health concerns, vulnerability to risk factors, barriers and health outcomes that may be present. These overall living conditions are known as the **social determinants of health** (Mikonen & Raphael, 2010).

Social determinants are key to understanding patterns of health and illness as well as ways in which people are equipped to access resources, identify and achieve their personal aspirations, overcome challenges, address their needs, and cope with their environment (Raphael, 2008). The social determinants of health have been enshrined into Canadian government policies since the mid-1970s, with Canada taking a flagship in **health promotion** (Mikkonen & Raphael, 2010). The goal of health promotion policies is geared towards identification and removal of obstacles to healthy public policies beyond the health sectors (Rapael, 2009). This progressive initiative however does not immune all Canadians from health inequities, poverty, gender discrimination, racialization, under-employment, marginalization, food insecurity, housing disparities, and social and political exclusion. Among them are Aboriginals, racialized individuals as well as immigrants, refugees and of those who due to restrictive immigration policies, have been illegalized.

The main focus of this chapter is on social determinants of refugees' and immigrants' health, since 20% of Canada's population by 2017, will consist of racialized peoples with 75% of them being immigrants (Hyman, 2009). Statistics show new immigrants in general, and racialized immigrants in specific have higher educational attainment and are much healthier than their Canadian counterparts, yet they experience greater rates of under-employment, poverty, poor living conditions and discrimination. These systemic factors directly affect their social determinants of health. Discrimination towards immigrants, however, is the result and extension of deeply rooted colonial ideologies against Aboriginals, which extended to racialized individuals and immigrants alike. Despite this, ***Aboriginal status***, ***racialization*** and ***immigration status*** have not been recognized as components of the social determinants of health by the Canadian Public Health Agency.

The main question that will be examined in this chapter is whether the existing Canadian framework of social determinants of health appropriately addresses the health needs of Aboriginal Peoples, racialized individuals and

Discussion

Do you agree or disagree with the following statement:

For as long as racism and discrimination manifest and reproduce itself against Aboriginal Peoples, it will continue to affect racialized individuals including immigrants.

immigrants, refugees, and illegalized persons. Canada's immigration system has evolved over time. In 2013, according to Citizenship and Immigration Canada (CIC, 2013), Canada opened its doors to 258,619 new immigrants including: family class (79,586), economic immigrants (148,037), refugees (23,968), and humanitarian and compassionate cases (7,028) (CIC, 2013). At the same time, many students (293,503) and foreign workers (126,816) have come to Canada with temporary visas. Others, due to the exclusionary immigration and restrictive border control policies are *illegalized* (an estimated of 500,000 to 1,000,000 peoples who live in an underground manner). Among them are rejected refugees, trafficked individuals, sponsorship breakdown, and those who have overstayed their legal visas just to name few.

As a welfare state, all Canadians, regardless of their differences, are to have equal access to medical care and other social support services. However, the intersection of one's immigration status with social programs including the healthcare system has created a two-tiered system restricting some refugees including those from the designated countries of origins (DCO), and other marginalized immigrants from accessing healthcare services. This two-tiered system, along with other systemic barriers engrained within the fabric of Canadian society influences the social determinants of immigrants' health. While inequality directly affects determinants of health of individuals and communities, the immigration, social services and healthcare systems recently became the subject of a reformist push. These reforms simultaneously promote discrimination and the individualization of illnesses and the privatization of healthcare for immigrants, refugees and illegalized persons.

The chapter will first provide a definitional analysis of the social determinants of health and health equity from the perspectives of the World Health Organization (WHO) and the Public Health Agencies of Canada. From there, the chapter will address the social determinants of Aboriginal Peoples from within the legacy of colonization and forced displacement in its past and current forms. Building on the experience of Aboriginals, the chapter argues for social construction of race, racism, and the process of racialization to be recognized as key elements of social determinants of health. Since migration, whether voluntary or through forced displacement, affects determinants of immigrants' health, the chapter further calls for immigration status as another key element of social determinants of health. This discourse is examined by reviewing recent proposed changes to Interim Federal Health (IFH) coverage and social assistance.

Social Determinants of Health and Health Equity: World Health Organization

WHO refers to health as: "a state of complete physical, mental and social well-being and not merely the absence of disease or infirmity" (WHO, 1948, p. 100). This definition however has been the centre of controversy with many proposing reformulation. According to Huber et al., (2011), 'a state of complete physical' as stated by WHO, uses a medical model where medical technologies and pharmaceutical drugs are sought to keep people healthy. In reality, environmental degradation along with increased human mobility and aging populations change the pattern of disease and illness on one hand, and our understanding of health, illness and diseases on the other. This raises a fundamental problem with the WHO's notion of 'complete' which is neither measureable nor operational (Huber et al., 2011). Our physical capacities and understanding of health also vary within populations and from place to place which adds to the complexity of measuring health, interpreting health, and adjusting or recommending a fixed healthy life style.

Nonetheless, the WHO considers social determinants of health as conditions in which people are born, grow, live, work and age through the distribution of economic, power, services and resources at the local, national and global levels where health inequities are rooted (WHO, 4014; Commission on Social Determinants of

Do you Know?

The most comprehensive model of Canadian social determinants of health (although it neglects to recognize immigration status) is presented by Raphael (2009), which contains the following 14 elements:

1. Aboriginal status
2. Gender
3. Disability
4. Housing
5. Early life
6. Income and income distribution
7. Education
8. Race
9. Employment and working conditions
10. Social exclusion
11. Food insecurity
12. Social safety net
13. Health services
14. Unemployment and job security

Health (CSDH), 2008). Therefore, the unequal distribution of health is the result of poor social policies and programs, unfair economic arrangements, and bad politics within and between countries (CSDH, 2008). The health disparities surface through access to health care, school and education, employment and work conditions, leisure, housing, communities and social environment, and life chances (CSDH, 2008). For this reason, the WHO considers health inequities as a matter of social justice (CSDH, 2008). The CSDH (2008) is also concerned about health inequities among Indigenous Peoples for their permanent loss of control over their lives and appropriation of their land, language, culture and livelihood through the process of colonization. This loss, CSDH (2008) suggests is experienced differently among migrant populations since their culture and language is preserved in the country of origin regardless of their movements.

Despite systemic actions and various measures undertaken by the WHO and other international organizations, poverty and social exclusions continue to affect social determinants of health among marginalized communities (Campbell & Jovchelovitch, 2000). This marginalization, particularly in the case of Indigenous Peoples of Canada, suggests a gap between the existing traditional models of development and the need for holistic approaches that respect cultural, social, emotional and economic contexts of Indigenous Peoples lives in relation to the legacy of colonization (Osborne et al., 2013). Some strategies according to Osborne et al., (2013) include the increased role and active participation of Indigenous Peoples in all stages of health research, program development, design, delivery, intervention, evaluation, funding, and short and long term planning (Osborne et al., 2013). The same disparity is presented among racialized members and immigrant populations.

The Public Health Agency of Canada (PHAC) has been criticized for taking traditional and individualistic approaches to health, focusing on behavioral change (such as diet, smoking, physical activities), rather than addressing underlying systemic factors (economic inequity, discrimination, poverty and homelessness) (Raphael, 2003). The following section will put the Canadian healthcare system including the PHAC policies into perspective.

The Canadian healthcare system

Canada is amongst the wealthiest (11th in world) and most powerful nations – a member of Organization for Economic Co-operation and Development (OECD), Group of Seven (G-7), North American Free Trade Agreement (NAFTA), and World Trade Organization (WTO). Canada has also received worldwide recognition for offering publicly funded healthcare, known as *Medicare,* to all its *citizens.* Each year, Canada spends about 10 percent of its Gross Domestic Product (GDP) on healthcare. Nonetheless, disparities and discrimination continue to affect the social determinants of health of many Canadians. For instance, in comparison with other wealthy nations, Canada is ranked as having the highest rate of poverty, with 9.4% of Canadians living below the poverty line and over 16% of them children (OECD, 2008; Statistics Canada, 2006). The poverty rate is particularly higher among racialized persons with two-third of them being immigrants (National Council of Welfare Reports, 2014). Racilaized poverty rate is higher among racialized women (52%) (National Council of Welfare Reports, 2014), as well as Aboriginal children (42.8%) (Citizen for Public Justice, 2012). This clearly indicates that while wealth, economic growth and political power are important indicators of improving population health; they may not necessarily be an indication of health, social and political *equity.* In fact, addressing social determinants of population health requires political will, social justice frameworks, inclusive ideologies, social programs, equitable distributions of resources, and leadership to implement and evaluate measurable outcomes within the healthcare and all other major institutions (WHO, 2005). This includes commitments from all levels of Canadian government and institutions as well as collective engagement of community members to address systemic factors that increase their vulnerabilities towards poverty, oppression, discrimination and poor health.

Reflective Thinking

1. In your opinion, why PHAC has not recognized Aboriginal status, racialization and immigration status as key components of social determinants of health?
2. What are some of the consequences of this lack of recognition on the health and well being of affected communities?
3. How can you raise consciousness about this issue at the micro, mezzo, and macro levels?

The Public Health Agency of Canada (PHAC) takes a **Population Health** approach by viewing health both inside and outside of the health care system. PHAC further acknowledges that at various stages of life, our health is affected by a set of complex and inter-related interactions between social and economic factors as well as the physical environment and individual behavior (PHAC, 2011). These key determinants include:

> 1. Income and Social Status, 2. Social Support Networks, 3. Education and Literacy, 4. Employment/Working Conditions, 5. Social Environments, 6. Physical Environments, 7. Personal Health Practices and Coping Skills, 8. Healthy Child Development, 9. Biology and Genetic Endowment, 10. Health Services, 11. Gender, and 12. Culture (PHAC, 2011).

Raphael (2009) argues that while physical environment (such as health-care system, biology and genetic factors, etc.) is an important indicator, it only accounts for 50% of one's health whereas the other 50% is attributed to social and economic environments (such as distribution of income, housing, food insecurity, employment, housing, and safety). This helps us understand Dr. Halfan Mahler's argument that suggests, *health is politics*, which as Raphael pointed out, justifies why health should be addressed beyond the healthcare system and ministry of health (Raphael, 2009).

In recent years, there has been a perforation of literature on the impact of income inequality and health as well as the widening of the income gap with lowering social cohesion in relation to poor health (Cobum, 2010). Also of concern is the social context of income inequity where in advanced capitalist societies the rise of neo-liberal politics widens the income gap on the one hand, and lowers social cohesion on the other, endangering the **welfare state** (Cobum, 2010). The term welfare state comes from the principles of equal opportunities, equitable economic distribution of wealth, and public responsibility towards all members of the society (Cobum, 2010). Known as a welfare state, the Canadian government has adopted poverty reductionist strategies to address poverty (income security) and promote and protect social well-being (publicly funded education, universal health care system). With the rise of globalization and the shift towards neo-liberal ideologies however, we are now confronted with contradictions in terms of policies that promote transnational and neoliberalism (responsible for the widening of income gap among countries such as Free Trades Agreements, mining), and of those that undermine the welfare state (cuts to social programs, health) (Cobum, 2010; Naverro, 2002; Edwards & Elger, 1999).

By questioning the ethics of the social determinants of health, Jennifer Prah Ruger (2004) interrogates the discourse of justice, fair distribution of goods, as well as equal opportunities (such as investment in basic education, affordable housing, income security and poverty reduction strategies) and further emphasizes an integrated and multifaceted approach to health improvement where people are empowered to help themselves locally and globally (Prah Ruger, 2004). Phelan et al., (2010) on the other hand advocate for policies that encourage medical and health promotion strategies in parallel with strategies that narrow the link between socioeconomic resources (such as money, knowledge, power, and social networks).

Regardless, although the PHAC approach to health promotion as well as poverty reduction strategies rightfully identifies some root causes of health problems (such as gender, income, disability, etc.), as noted earlier, it falls short in addressing the health needs of Aboriginals, racialized individuals, immigrants, refugees, and illegalized populations. This is despite numerous reports addressing ways in which Aboriginal status, race, and immigration status affect the overall life and health and well-being of members of these communities. This inequity is rooted in the legacy of colonization and neo-liberal capitalist relations causing environmental degradation of Indigenous populations, economic and health inequities, conflict, forced displacement, and migration of many peoples overtime. Therefore, the denial of Aboriginal status, racialization, and immigration status as key determinants of health not only increases disparities but also further marginalizes the already vulnerable populations.

Aboriginal Status as an Element of the Determinant of Health

The process of colonization, in its past and present forms, continues to cause displacement and leave intergenerational impacts including health and economic disparities, racism, and criminalization, while creating barriers in accessing appropriate resources. To begin the healing journey from such individual, community, and systemic trauma and discrimination, it is critical to acknowledge **Aboriginal Status** as a key element of social determinant of health. Unfortunately, the Canadian government and PHAC continue to turn a blind eye to such discourse. Many Aboriginal communities have long been advocating for culturally appropriate holistic and community-centered approaches to health that respect Aboriginal wisdoms, knowledge and ways of life. This includes how Aboriginal Peoples understand health and ways in which they prefer to prioritize or address their health concerns, while identifying systemic factors that increase their health disparities as well as barriers that prevent them from accessing the health care system (Graham & Leeseberg Stamler, 2010).

Graham and Leeseberg Stamler (2010) environmental, societal, historical, and political factors influencing health and well-being of Aboriginal

Peoples. Other literature reveals major health disparities between Aboriginal Peoples and non-Aboriginal peoples of Canada (Health Canada, 2006; First Nations and Inuit Health Branch, 2006). At the present time, the PHAC (2013) addresses health inequity within Aboriginal communities under the guise of *"culture,"* and the discourse of dominant cultural values as responsible for increasing the vulnerability of Aboriginals to poor health. For example, in comparison, Aboriginals have higher rates of chronic diseases, child mortality and suicide. However, if we solely rely on statistics or individualize health concerns, we might prematurely conclude that Aboriginal Peoples are not inherently healthy or know how to live healthy lifestyles. This view blames Aboriginals for making unhealthy choices rather than identifying oppressive systems that affect their health or prevent them from thriving. As Graham and Leeseberg Stamler (2010) note, existing research and statistics on Aboriginal health mainly emphasize deficits dismissing the underlying root causes of health disparities, or strength of the community in resisting their oppression.

This persisting gap in health equity is a clear example of the absence of anti-oppressive frameworks and practices in the discourse of social determinants of health, from healthcare system to healthcare delivery, health promotion, and health planning. The anti-oppressive approach understands the intersection of Aboriginal Peoples' health within the context and history of colonization, forced displacement, the trauma of residential schools and the on-going process of racialization. In particular, residential schools have caused the trauma of intergenerational disruptions on one hand and the community member's resistance to such trauma on the other, through claiming agency and the reconciliation process. This tension first requires the dominant culture to acknowledge historical and systemic oppression of Aboriginal peoples, and second, monitor and enforce Aboriginal perspectives of health equity strategies by policy makers, health care programs and healthcare providers.

Indigenous knowledge, according to Lavallee (2009), involves the three important and relational processes of 1) empirical observation (occur in real life situation and setting such as understanding of the medicinal prosperities of plants), 2) traditional teachings (passed from one generation to the next), and 3) revelation (spiritual knowledge). The Health care professionals must acknowledge and respect "Aboriginal ways of life" in health. For example, although spirituality is an integral part of Aboriginal Peoples way of knowledge, colonial racism has presented Aboriginal culture including spirituality as inferior. At the same time, Elders have an integral role in the Aboriginal culture as the carrier of traditional knowledge and therefore they perspectives must be included (Lavallee, 2009).

Many Aboriginal Peoples rely on the Medicine Wheel – a balance between all facets of individuals, families and communities physical, mental, spiritual, emotional and needs in relation to other aspects of human conditions and interactions (Kovach, 2005, Lavallee, 2009). The Medicine Wheel is "an Aboriginal framework in a visual shape of a circle divided into four quadrants; each quadrant represents a direction along with the teachings for that direction" (Roberts, 2005, p 92). For this reason, Aboriginal Peoples must be involved in the design, planning, delivery, and evaluation of their determinants of health. This requires commitment from the health sector and all other sectors and levels of government to consult, train, employ, research, and deliver Aboriginal centered programs with and by Aboriginal Peoples.

As noted earlier, PHAC addresses health inequity of Aboriginals from within the notion of 'Culture" rather than the legacy of colonization in its past and current ways where Aboriginals are racialized. Therefore, the process of racialization is another key element of social determinants of health that has impacted Aboriginal Peoples and extended to non-Aboriginal communities. The existing PHAC model does not account for **Race** and **Racism** as important elements of Aboriginal and other racialized people's health.

Racism as an Element of the Social Determinants of Health

Equal treatment regardless of differences is a fundamental element of human rights enshrined in the Canadian Human Rights Act (Department of Justice, 1985). Despite this, the prevalence of racism and racial discrimination within the fabric of Canadian society at the individual, cultural and systemic levels is high.

In recent years, many scholars, practitioners and activists have argued that racism is a social determinant of health (Graham & Leeseberg Stamler, 2010; Hyman, 2009). The WHO (in participation at the World Conference Against Racism, Racial Discrimination, Xenophobia and Related Intolerance in South Africa) also urged for the link between racial discrimination and health to be recognized (WHO, n.d. noted in Graham & Leeseberg Stamler, 2010, p 15).

Race, is often used as a categorization scheme both in its origin and maintenance (Hyman, 2009) and in its historical, cultural, social, and political forms. For this reason, race like racism, is a social construct. Racism, according to Henry and Tator (2010) occurs on individual, cultural and institutional levels. Galabuzi (2006) refers to the process of **racialization** where certain groups of people are differentiated and are subjected to unequal treatment. Among them are Aboriginals, Blacks, and immigrants who due to the process of racialization are marginalized and excluded from full participation individually and collectively. While belonging to a particular racial group exposes one to racism; discrimination affects social determinants of health of racialized peoples and immigrants. This reality among new immigrants is reflected in the health outcome known as "**healthy immigrant effect**" where their health and well being declines shortly after their arrival in Canada (Access Alliance Community Health Center, 2003; Baiser, 2005). However, racial discrimination by and within the healthcare system is a complex form of exclusion that affects the overall health and well-being of racialized members and immigrants in their efforts to thrive in all aspects of their lives including social inclusion, employment, early childhood development, housing, physical health, social network and political participation, income, gender, and safety and security.

One recent tactic by the Canadian government has been to create socially constructed categories of deserving and non-deserving immigrants based on their immigration statuses. This categorization, disenfranchisement, exclusion and marginalization is rooted in the historical pattern of discriminatory immigration and border control policies that consider individuals as Canadian citizens, permanent immigrants (through skilled workers program and point system), refugees, temporary workers, and illegalized persons. In particular, in recent years, the federal government has restricted the movement of refugees in need of protection through amendments to its *Immigration and Refugee Protection Act* (IRPA).

The following section will draw on root causes of oppression and inequities that cause population movement and increase vulnerability to poor health. This urges us to further conceptualize the relation between forced displacement, population movement and immigration as key elements of social determinants of migrant's health.

Migration, Displacement and Health on the Move

The process of migration, whether by force or voluntary, directly affects immigrants' health during pre-migration, throughout the transition, and while in the host country. During the pre-migrating process, immigrants have less power to control or predict their physical, social and political environments. For example, while in their home countries their activities and livelihoods are endangered by Trade Agreements between local governments with transnational corporations. Trade agreements (such as mining) not only exploit the labour power of local community members, they further appropriate their natural resources, contaminate water, cause pollution, increase illnesses and create economic and socio-political upheavals. We refer to this discourse as **environmental racism** where intentionally or not, marginalized communities are exposed to environmental hazardous (Mohai et al., 2009; Holifield, 2001; Pulido, 2000).

Depending on their socio-political and economic conditions, some groups of migrants may voluntarily leave their homes and travel across international borders as permanent residents, migrant workers, or illegalized persons. The discourse of environmental racism or the social and economic conditions in which various groups of migrants find themselves and their vulnerability to health risk factors, varies among those falling under the category of legal migrants with those who are illegalized. For example, displaced persons and refugees find themselves with no option but to live in highly populated refugee camps with poor social-environments with little access to clean water, sanitation, or health resources. Their physical environment is also under attack by military invasion or rebel attacks, violence, war, poverty, food insecurity, sexual and physical abuse, or lack of access to appropriate resources. Together, they result in forced displacement, refugee crises (both internally and across international borders), and increased vulnerability to poor health. Studies reveal that the process of transition from home country to host country makes refugees more vulnerable to health disparities, mortality and death.

During their post migration and settlement, immigrants and refugees face complex sets of health risks. This begins with discriminatory immigration policies that impact their journey by constraining their livelihoods in detention centers for unknown periods of time, to dealing with individual, cultural and systemic barriers are embedded within the immigration process and the health care system along with all other major institutions.

Discrimination against immigrants overlaps between three major institutions of immigration, health and social programs in the following ways:

1. The exclusionary border control and immigration and citizenship policies
2. New proposed cuts to the IFH coverage for refugees from Designated Country of Origin (DCO)
3. Proposed cuts to social assistance programs for certain group of refugees

Although Canada has gained a reputation for its national healthcare system, differences in life chances are prevalent across genders and among racialized peoples and immigrants with the rest of Canada. Systemic discrimination and differential treatment within healthcare and immigration systems creates health disparities and affect social determinants of health.

Immigration Status as a Social Determinant of Health

Many consider Canada a nation built by immigrants. Since the 1980s, Canada has been the host to over 5 million new immigrants in order to sustain the country's economic and demographic growth. Immigrants, particularly refugees arriving from the global south are believed to be carriers of infectious diseases such as Intestinal Parasites, Hepatitis B, and Tuberculosis (Walker & Barnett, 2007). Yet research suggests that, upon their arrival, new immigrants to Canada have better health than the average Canadians (Laroche, 2000, Access Alliance CHC, 2006). The Immigration Act imposes strict medical examinations in order to determine immigrants' medical admissibility to the country. At the same time, studies show that, despite the "healthy immigrant effect," immigrants' health declines by 30% to 40% six months after their arrival (Access Alliance CHC, 2006). Inadequate healthcare along with other forms of inequities and discrimination directly affects social determinants of immigrants' health.

The condition of refugees however must be contextualized within the framework of state power in relation to the institutions of health as well as Citizenship and Immigration Canada, where policies are formulated (or neglected to be formulated) over issues ranging from eligibility criteria and control of funding allocation. For instance, in 2012 the conservative government suggested amendments to the Interim Federal Health program (IFH) excluding refugees from designated countries of origins (DCO) from certain coverage (Canadian Healthcare Association, 2012).

The proposed changes however resulted in on-going debates and resistance among social justice activists and medical practitioners to the point that the government temporary reinstated its proposed change. Below is a case example that highlights some of the challenges and barriers that immigrants and refugees experience upon arrival in Canada.

The following presents current health coverage for various groups of immigrants:

1. Healthcare coverage for Canadian citizens and permanent residents.

Case Study

Mahin, fears for herself and teenage daughters. They lived in a refugee camp in a conflict zone for a few years before claiming refugee status in Canada. Upon arrival, she is sent to the CBSA detention center where under IRPA she is provided 15 days to complete their personal information form (PIF). Although Mahin was transferred to the shelter for refugees in a timely manner, her social environment in the detention reminded her of the time she visited her husband in jail. He was a political prisoner. For this reason, she experienced anxiety attacks, difficulty concentrating, loss of appetite and insomnia. At the refugee shelter she continue to suffer from symptoms of PTSD including flashbacks, and nightmares with episodes of psychosomatic pain.

Mahin had difficulty concentrating about dates and details of her ordeals including the bombing of her house, execution of her husband, and her torture and abuse while displaced. At the same time, she feared her refugee case was being rejected.

Reflective Questions:

1. If Mahin was from Mexico, escaping armed conflict involving the drug cartel, she could be kept at the detention centre for a long period of time If released she would be ineligible to access certain health coverage and subsequently face deportation. As a front-line practitioner, how do you work with Mahin if she was from Mexico (which is considered a designated country of origin)?
2. If Mahin had arrived in 2015, she could be ineligible to apply for social assistance (under sections 172 and 173 of Bill C-43). How do you help her to survive considering as a new refugee she does not speak English, and has no formal skills or professional training?

    This case study has been adopted and modified from CCR website.

2. The Expanded Health Care coverage for government assisted refugees (GARs)
3. Health Care coverage for accepted refugee claimants and privately sponsored refugees
4. Public Health and Safety Health Care coverage for claimants' from Designated Countries of Origin (DCO).
5. No health coverage for illegalized migrants

The following section will examine the impact of 1) proposed cuts to IFH coverage; and, 2) budget Bill.

1. Proposed cuts to IFH coverage:

One of the most marginalized groups of immigrants is illegalized persons who within the health sector are referred to as *uninsured patients*. Uninsured patients are not eligible to access medical care which at times, contradicts various health policies.

According to the Public Hospital Act, no patient is to be turned away due to financial constraints, however recent reform to immigration and refugee Acts denies refugees from certain countries (designated country of origin) and uninsured persons access Medicare. According to Hynie (2010), the refusal rate is higher among women despite the fact that women are further faced with gender-based health challenges. The health decline of uninsured immigrant women represents the Canadian government's failure to respond to the issue of gender and health where the already marginalized populations are positioned. Within such a system, public healthcare becomes part of the market economy, a development that clashes with the socialist and welfare state principles. It is within this context that healthcare is regulated under the national plan for citizens and other legal residents; and un-regulated and commodified for refugees and uninsured persons. This inequitable system creates a hierarchical system to ensures the submission of refugees and uninsured persons to the institutions of the tiered healthcare system with limited or no standardized guidelines, regulations, or accountability surrounding the admission, optional treatment plans, discharging, and (extra)-billing of uninsured patients.

High hospital costs as evident in the case study of Joel, further contribute to the racialization and feminization of poverty among refugees and uninsured people, particularly those with children. Poverty is exacerbated by other factors, including lack of accessible publicly funded childcare, vicarious employment conditions, poor housing, integration and adaptation obstacles,

Discussion

Joel fell down and broke her leg while at school. She and her mother are non-insured. Although she was admitted at the nearby hospital, her treatment cost over $20.000.00.

1. How do you help the family?
2. Where do you refer Joel for medical and financial support?
3. What happen if her mother is unable to pay the hospital fees?

and other social factors that negatively affect social determinants of one's health, leading to potential mental health challenges.

The most disturbing situation of health disparity is that encountered by pregnant uninsured women. In their case, the foundational principle of the healthcare system—to serve all citizens—is completely compromised due to its intersectionality with immigration status. As a result, pregnant women are ineligible for healthcare services, even though their children will be considered Canadian citizens. This suggests the lack of a health-promotion strategy to invest in pregnant women and their children.

To address disparities to social determinants of immigrants' health and to resist neoliberal and discriminatory practices, in recent years various

Facts

- Refugee claimants are more vulnerable to poor health.
- Majority of refugee claimants (65%) live in Ontario.
- Due to cuts to refugee health care programs, over 30% of Ontario refugee claimants have no access to health coverage outside of public health and public safety coverage.
- The Ontario Temporary Health Program (OTHP) provides access to essential and urgent healthcare services to refugee claimants living in Ontario.

Source: Ministry of Health and Long-erm Care (December 9, 2013). http://news.ontario.ca/mohltc/en

healthcare professionals have developed free health clinics where they volunteer their time to serve uninsured patients. Although this effort, at least for a short term, serves as a Band-Aid solution and further addresses health-care professionals ethical dilemmas of treating all patients in need of medical attention, is not enough on its own to address systemic problems. Social determinants of health must be contextualized beyond charity and compassion, as a matter of human rights and equity.

Furthermore, considering the high poverty rates among racialized communities and the fact that through cuts to healthcare system the Canadian government individualizes the health conditions of various group of immigrants, the federal government's recent proposed Budget Bill which encourages provincial governments to place restriction on social assistance payments to some groups of refugees, place these immigrants at a higher risk of poverty and health problem.

2. Budget Bill:

According to the October 29, 2014 statement by the Canadian Council for Refugees (CCR), the federal government is responsible to fund provinces for their core social services and programs (post-secondary education, child-care and social assistance) through the Canada Social Transfer (CST) (CCR, October 2014). Overall, the Federal-Provincial Fiscal Arrangements Act is responsible for the terms of the CST such as "national standard" with no minimum residency conditions for the Canada Social Transfer. The new proposed Budget Bill (October 2014) under sections 172 and 173 of Bill C-43 is amending the Federal-Provincial Fiscal Arrangements Acts by restricting people without permanent residence status and refugee claimants' income security through the imposition of minimum residency requirements as the eligibility criteria in accessing social assistance benefits.

This means the government is dividing already marginalized migrants into two categories of those with access to income security (Canadian citizens, permanent residents, victims of trafficking on a temporary resident permit and convention refugees) and in contrast, those who do not (refugee claimants, rejected refugees, those under Pre-Removal Risk Assessment (PRRA) and Humanitarian and Compassionate applications, sponsored spouses, temporary residents and individuals living without legal immigration status) (CCR, October 29, 2014). The passage of Budget Bill (sections 172 and 173) will negatively affect the social determinants of health of the former groups resulting in their homelessness, extreme poverty, mental and physical illnesses, poor nutrition and food insecurity, abuse and exploitation. The proposed Bill reduces government responsibility towards migrants, and clearly contradicts the fundamental framework of social determinants of health as well as other legal frameworks such as the Charter of Rights and Freedoms, Canada's obligations towards the International Covenant on Civil and Political Rights, the International Convention on Economic, Social and Cultural Rights, the Convention on the Rights of the Child, and the Convention relating to the Status of Refugees (CCR, October 2014).

The recent amendments to IRPA, and proposed changes to healthcare coverage and social assistance by various group of immigrants and refugees raise serious concerns about the existing social determinants of health. This is particularly the fact as in 2013/2014, Canada's population growth rate was the highest among all G-7 countries with net international migration accounting for 66.5% of such increase (Statistics Canada, 2014). According to statistics, in 2011 alone, Canada's foreign-born population represented 20.6% of the total population with over one million new immigrants arriving between 2006 and 2011 (Statistics Canada, 2011). Despite this changing trend, and in light of Canada's reliance on migrants in terms of population growth, skills, economic prosperities and innovation, immigrants continue to live at the margin of our society where their social determinants of health are shaped by neo-liberal and anti-immigration political claimants in relation with their immigration statuses, race, gender, class, language proficiency, and social networks.

Considering racialization and poverty, barriers to settlement and integration, access to work permits, employment inequity, language barriers, housing, violence against immigrant women, lack of recognition and accreditation of skills and education, cultural differences, and possible trauma as a result of pre-and-post migration challenges, many migrants rely on social assistance to survive their ordeals and move forward with their lives. In comparison to their Canadian counterparts, immigrants are less likely to rely on social assistance or remain on assistance for long period of time.

Conclusion

This chapter examined whether the existing model of Canadian social determinants of health is responding effectively to the conditions of Aboriginal Peoples, racialized members and immigrants, refugees and asylum seekers. The chapter further explored gaps in Public Health Agency of Canada approaches to the social determinants of health, which tend to individualize health rather than challenging underlying root causes of racialization and exclusion of immigrants and refugees. While health is beyond the physical to encompassing social factors, the right to access healthcare and social programs however further divides healthcare and social programs into a two-tier system: one that is inclusive yet inequitable due to the socially constructed discourses of racism, sexism, ableism, ageism, and classism, and another, that is exclusive and ingrained in an artificial sense of nationalism that undermines humanity by placing various restrictive conditions such as immigration status on access to care and healing.

Such a divide is purposely orchestrated through various migration policies, as well as through provincial and federal policies that ensure the categorization of peoples as legal and illegalized immigrants. This is done in order to achieve two goals: first, to avoid acknowledging that these people live in Canada and, second, to avoid taking responsibility for their social determinants of health. As Jiwani (2002) notes, people's access to services is therefore impaired by the degree of legality ascribed to their status. On top of this, segregating people into legal, and deserving groups—in contrast to those that are illegalized, and undeserving—promulgates an artificial fear presenting the latter as a health threat to the public. This discourse further convinces taxpayers that the healthcare system and social programs suffer from the burden of refugees; as a result, it justifies the privatization of health on the one hand, and racism and hate against racialized people, new immigrants, and refugees, on the other.

References

Access Alliance community Health Center. (2003). Best practices for Working with homeless immigrants and refugees: A community based action research project. Execuitve Summary. Toronto.

Anti-Racism Council of Canada (NARCC). Retrieved from http://action.web.ca/home/narcc/attach/NARCC_shadow_ Report_05_ Final_-Oct_11part2.pdf

Beiser, M. (2005). The health of immigrants and refugees in Canada. *Canadian Journal of Public Health, 96*(2), pp. 30-44.

Campbell, C., & Jovchelovitch, S. (2000). Health, Community and development: Towards a social psychology of participation. *Journal of Community & Applied Social Psychology, 10*(4), pages 255-270.

Canadian Council for Refugees. (October 29, 2014). Federal budget will restrict refugee claimant access to social assistance. Retrieved from http://ccrweb. ca/sites/ccrweb.ca/files/billc-43backgrounderoct2014.pdf

Canadian Healthcare Association. (November 2012). Changes to the Interim Federal Health Program: Position Statement. Retrieved from http://www.health carecan.ca/wp-content/uploads/2012/11/IFHP-reform-policy-statement-November-2012.pdf

Cobum, D. (July 2000). Income inequality, social cohesion and the health status of populations: The role of neo-liberalism. *Social Science & Medicine, 51(1),* 135-146.

Commission on Social Determinants of Health. (2008). Closing the gap in a generation: Health equity through action on the social determinants of health. Final Report of the Commission on Social Determinants of Health. Geneva, World Health Organization.

Citizens for Public Justice. (2012). Poverty Trends Scorecard: Canada 2012. Retrieved from http://www.cpj.ca/files/docs/poverty-trends-scorecard.pdf

Citizenship and Immigration Canada, RDM, Preliminary 2013 Data. Retrieved from http://www.cic.gc.ca/english/resources/statistics/facts 2013-preliminary/01.asp

Citizenship and Immigration Canada, Interim Federal Health Program: Information handbook for health care providers, FAS Benefit Administrators Ltd, 2006.

Department of Justice. (1985). Canadian Human Rights Act. Retrieved from: http://digitalcommons.ilr.cornell.edu/cgi/viewcontent.cgi?article=1056&context=gladnetcollect

Graham, H., & Leeseberg Stamler, L. (2010). Contemporary perceptions of health from an Indigenous (Plains Cree) perspective. *Journal of Aboriginal Health*, January, 6-17. http://www.naho.ca/documents/journal/jah 06_01/06_01_01_Contemporary_Perceptions.pdf

Health Canada. (February 1, 2006). First Nations Inuit Health Branch (FNIB). [Fact Sheet]. Ottawa: Author.

Holifield, R. (2001). Defining environmental justice and environmental racism. *Urban Geography, 22(1),* 78-90.

Hyman, I. (March 2009). Racism as a determinant of immigrant health. Policy brief for the Strategic Initiatives and Innovations Directorate (SIID) for the Public Health Agency of Canada. Retrieved from http://canada .metropolis.net/ pdfs/racism_policy_brief_e.pdf

Hynie, M. (February 12, 2010). The relationship between insurance status and presenting complaints of acute care clients in Toronto. Research Conference on Healthcare for the Undocumented and Uninsured:

Systems, Policies, Practices and their Consequences.

Huber, M., Knottnerus, J.A., Green, L., Horst, H.V.D., Jadad, A.R., Kromhout, D., & Smid, H. (2011). How should we define health? *BMJ-British Medical Journal, 343*(6), d4163.

Jiwani, Y. (2002). Race, gender, violence and health care. In K.M.J. McKenna & J. Larkin (Eds.), *Violence Against Women: New Canadian perspectives*. Toronto: Innana Publication and Education Inc.

Kovach, M. (2005). Emerging from the margins: Indigenous methodologies. In L. Brown & S. Strega (Eds.), *Research as resistance* (pp. 19-36). Toronto, Canada: Canadian Scholars' Press.

Laroche, M. (2000). Health status and health services utilization of Canada's immigrant and non-immigrant populations. *Canadian Public Policy – Analyse De Politiques, XXVI*(1). Ottawa, Canada.

Lavallee, L.F. (2009). Parctical application of an indigenous research framework and two qualitative indigenous research methods: Sharing circles and Anishnaabe symbol-based reflection. *International Journal of Qualitative Methods, 8*(1), 21-40.

Mikkonen, J., & Raphael, D. (2010). Social determinants of health: The Canadian facts. Toronto: York University School of Health Policy and Management. Retrieved from http://www.thecanadianfacts.org/

Mohai, P., Pellow, D., Roberts, J. (2009). Environmental justice. *Annual Review of Environment and Resources, 34*, 405-430.

National Council of Welfare Reports. (2014). Poverty Profile: Special Edition: A snapshot of Racialized Poverty in Canada.

Navarro, V. (2002). *The Political economy of social inequalities: Consequences for health and quality of life*. New York: Baywood Publishing Company Inc.

Organization for Economic Co-operation and Development (OECD). (2008). *Growing unequal? Income distribution and poverty in countries.* Paris: France.

Osborne, K., Baum, F., & Brown, L. (December 2013). What works? A review of actions addressing the social and economic determinants of Indigenous health. *Australian Institute of Family Studies*, Issues Paper no. 7, produced for the Closing the Gap Clearinghouse. Australian Government. Retrieved from http://www.aihw.gov.au/uploadedFiles/ClosingTheGap/Content/ Publications/2013/ctgc-ip07.pdf

Edwards, P. K., & Elger, T. (1999). *The Global economy, national states and the regulation of labour.* London: Mansell.

Phelan, J.C., Link, B.G., & Tehranifar, P. (November 2010). Social conditions as fundamental causes of health inequalities. Theory, evidence, and policy implications. *Journal of Health and Social Behavior, 51*(1). Retrieved from http://hsb.sagepub.com/content/51/1_suppl/S28.long

Prah Ruger, J. (September 2004). Ethics of the social determinants of health. *Public Health, 364*, 1092-1097.

Public Health Agency of Canada. (2011). What determines health? Retrieved from http://www.phac-aspc.gc.ca/ph-sp/determinants/index-eng.php

Pulido, L. (2000). Rethinking environmental racism: White privilege and urban development in southern California. *Annals of the Association of American Geographers 90*(1), 12-40.

Raphael, D. (2009). *Social determinants of health: Canadian perspectives*, 2nd ed. Canadian Scholars' Press.

Statistics Canada. (2014). Canada's population estimates: Age and sex. Retrieved from http://www.statcan.gc.ca/daily-quotidien/140926/dq 140926b-eng.htm?HPA

Statistics Canada. (2011). Immigration and ethnocultural diversity in Canada. Retrieved from http://www12.statcan.gc.ca/nhs-enm/2011/as-sa/99-010-x/99-010-x2011001-eng.cfm

The National. (2001). The two faces of Canada: A community report on racism. *The National.*

Walker, P., & Barnett, B. (2007). *Immigrant medicine.* Boston: Elsevier Inc.

World Health Organization. (March 2005). Action on the social determinants of health: Learning from previous experiences. A background paper prepared for the Commission of Social Determinants of Health. Retrieved from http://www.who.int/social_determinants/resources/action_sd.pdf

World Health Organization. (2014). What are social determinant of health? Retrieved from http://www.who.int/social_determinants/sdh_definition/en/

World Health Organization. (April 7, 1948). *Official Records of the World Health Organization, 2*, 100.

CHAPTER 10

Mental Health Problems of Refugees Who Have Suffered Trauma

Donald Payne

Introduction

Refugees arriving in Canada bring their health problems with them and they can have difficulty accessing healthcare in Canada. Refugees have a high incidence of hepatitis, tuberculosis, HIV infection, and dental problems. Psychologically, refugees have to deal with the stress that led them to leaving their country as well as the stress and dislocation of coming to Canada. In addition, there is the stress of being in a new unfamiliar country, often with a different language and culture. The stress of coming to Canada is greatly increased if they experienced the stress of fleeing their country and then on arriving in Canada having the stress of proving to Canadian authorities that they are "genuine refugees," with the marked fear of being returned to their country if they fail to prove their case. The stress of the process of coming to Canada can lead to anxiety, worry, depression, low self-esteem, and grief over what has been lost. How the person deals with these stresses is related to a combination of their personal resources and the community resources available to them.

Refugees can have difficulty obtaining adequate healthcare due to issues including language problems, lack of awareness of available health facilities, social isolation, and delays in obtaining provincial health insurance. Pottie et al. with the Canadian Collaboration for Immigrant and Refugee Health have published evidence based clinical guidelines for recommended investigation and treatment of immigrants and refugees.[1]

The following cases are composite cases of individuals who suffered physical/psychological trauma as a result of political detention and/or war.

Case Study 1 – Ali

Ali, a student in his last year of high school, was angered at the arbitrary restrictions in Iran. Other members of his family had been politically active in opposing the government, and had been detained and tortured. He joined a group of students in putting up posters opposing the government. One night, he was caught while running away after having put up a poster. He was beaten and detained. He was interrogated in a threatening manner in an effort to obtain the names of other students acting with him, for the names of those who had given him the posters and for the location of the printing press. He was kicked, and was beaten with batons on his body and on the soles of his feet. On one occasion, he was told that he was being taken out with others to be executed. He was placed against a wall, was blindfolded, and shots were fired. He collapsed from the shock. When his blindfold was removed, he saw that several of the others had actually been shot and killed. He was told that his execution had been postponed for another day. When he was released after several months, he was very frightened and emotionally distressed with marked fear, anxiety and depression. He remained in hiding at home for a month because of his fear and the need to recover from his injuries. Despite being a very good student, he was not able to continue with his schooling because he was labelled as an opponent of the government. He was very fearful when he saw police or government authorities and tried to avoid them. He knew that he was on the list of government opponents and would be detained again, especially as it was know that his family was politically active. This led him to make arrangement to flee from Iran for his safety.

Case Study 2 – Seyed

Seyed, a teenager, worked on his family farm in Sri Lanka. During the civil conflict, heavily armed members of the Liberation Tigers of Tamil Eelam (LTTE, or Tamil Tigers) came to the farm demanding food and shelter. Shortly afterwards, government forces came to the farm and accused him and his family of supporting the LTTE, as they had let the LTTE stay at the farm. He was beaten and insulted while being interrogated about his involvement with the LTTE. Later, Tamil Tigers returned to the farm, abducted him, and forced him to work for them. He was beaten and made to do heavy labour, such as digging trenches. He was threatened with being shot if he tried to escape. He was very frightened, both for himself and for his family. One night when the camp was being attacked, he managed to escape during the confusion resulting from the fighting. He was very frightened about remaining in Sri Lanka as the Tamil Tigers would be looking for him and the government suspected him of supporting the LTTE. He fled the country for his safety.

Case Study 3 – Alma

Alma, a middle-aged woman from Bosnia, had had a good life before the civil conflict. She and her husband had a good home, which they had just finished renovating, and a summer cottage. She had three children, then in their late teenage years. She worked as a lawyer and enjoyed her work. She looked forward to a good life and a comfortable retirement in the future. Shortly after the civil conflict began, her husband was taken away by the forces that occupied the area. She had no contact with him, not knowing whether he was alive or dead. She was harassed and insulted by the occupying forces, and was worried that her children would be harmed. Her children were able to flee from the area. She had difficulty managing on her own, was constantly insecure, and often had a lack of food and water. She was eventually able to leave the area. It was only after she had left the country that she was able to locate her husband who had been held in a concentration camp where conditions were very bad and where he had been repeatedly beaten and threatened with death. They came to Canada as government-sponsored refugees.

Post-traumatic Stress Disorder

According to a meta-analysis of post-traumatic stress disorder (PTSD) studies, about one in ten refugees living in resettlement countries suffer from PTSD (Fazel, Wheeler, & Danesh, 2005). Experiences of war, of torture, or both increase the likelihood of PTSD. The essential feature of PTSD as described in the current *Diagnostic and Statistical Manual of Mental Disorders (DSM-V)* is the development of characteristic symptoms following exposure to one or more traumatic events (American Psychiatric Association, 2013, pp. 271-280).

The traumatic events include exposure to actual or threatened death, serious injury or sexual violence

The DSM-V divides PTSD symptoms into four groupings: 1) intrusive symptoms related to the traumatic event(s); 2) persistent avoidance of stimuli associated with the trauma; 3) negative alterations in cognition and mood; and 4) marked alterations in arousal and reactivity. A description of these symptoms follows.

1. Intrusive symptoms associated with the traumatic event(s) through intrusive and distressing recollections of the event(s); recurrent distressing dreams of the event; acting or feeling as if the traumatic event were recurring; intense psychological distress at exposure to internal or external cues that symbolize or resemble an aspect of the traumatic event; and physiological reactivity on exposure to cues that symbolize or resemble an aspect of the traumatic event. To meet the diagnostic criteria, the traumatic event must be experienced in at least one of these ways. Refugees who have suffered torture or severe war experiences re-experience their traumatic events in most of these ways.

2. Persistent avoidance includes efforts to avoid memories, thoughts or feelings, closely associated with the trauma; and efforts to avoid external reminders that arouse distressing memories, thoughts of feelings about the traumatic event. Refugees who have suffered torture or severe war experiences typically avoid reminders and situations that trigger reminders.

3. Negative alterations in cognition or mood associated with the traumatic event(s) by two or more of: inability to remember an important aspect of the event(s); persistent and exaggerated negative beliefs or expectations about oneself, others or the world; persistent, distorted cognitions about the cause or consequences of the traumatic event(s) that lead the individual to blame himself/herself or others; persistent negative emotional state; marked diminished interest or participation in significant activities; feelings of detachment or estrangement from others; and persistent inability to experience positive emotions. The last three are common in refugees who have suffered torture or severe war experiences.

E. Marked alterations in arousal and reactivity by two or more of: iritable behaviour and angry outbursts; restless or self-destructive behaviour; hypervigilance; exaggerated startle response; problems with concentration; and sleep disturbances. Refugees who have suffered torture or severe war experience typically suffer most of these symptoms.

The PTSD symptoms have to be present for more than one month and cause significant distress or impairment in social, occupational, or other important areas of functioning.

The Stress of the Refugee Determination System

Individuals who arrive in Canada and claim refugee status here, in contrast to individuals who come as landed immigrants, face additional stressors as they are required to pass though the refugee determination system. The first principle in helping traumatized refugees is to provide them with a safe and secure environment. Although there is a sense of safety in being in Canada, there is no sense of security when a refugee has to confront the realistic fear of possibly being deported back home to face further trauma or death. Many claimants state that they would prefer suicide to the fate that would await them if they were returned.

For an applicant, the refugee determination process entails a re-experiencing of the individual's traumatic experiences and is often a re-traumatization. Claimants have to talk to their lawyer about details of their experiences and also have to talk to doctors about them if medical/psychological reports are required to support their claim. The early scheduling of hearings adds pressure and may not allow claimants time to adequately prepare their cases. They are required to provide oral testimony at their hearings and to be cross-examined on their testimony. Although not intended to be adversarial, in practice it is an adversarial system, with claimants being challenged on their testimony, at times harshly and persistently, and often with the implication that they are lying. This creates increased anxiety and confusion that can lead to poor memory and concentration or to the claimant breaking down emotionally at the hearing. Some claimants experience the questioning as similar to their interrogations in detention back home, at which time they did not have control of their future and were often accused

Case Study 4 – Zahra

Zahra, in her twenties, had been detained for four years because of her suspected political activity. During her detention she was held in a dark and unhygienic cell with many other women. She was frequently taken out to be interrogated under torture. She was sexually insulted and threatened with rape before she would be executed. She was very frightened by this, as she knew detainees were being killed. She could not trust anyone, as she heard that there were spies amongst the detainees. She was freed after her family paid a large bribe to a guard to allow her to escape. Her family arranged for her to come to Canada. She was very afraid while leaving Iran using a false passport, fearing in part that she might be caught and returned to even worse treatment in detention. When she arrived in Canada she was very frightened of immigration officials at the airport, fearing that they would immediately put her back on a plane to be deported. When she contacted her parents, they told her that the authorities had come to their home looking for her. She had difficulty sleeping. She had frequent nightmares of her torture in detention, and of being caught, detained again, tortured, and executed. During the day, she could not keep these thoughts out of her mind. She became instantly fearful when she saw men who looked like the authorities in her country. Even though she rationally knew that police in Canada were not to be feared, she had a conditioned fear of them and anyone in uniform. She had difficulty trusting people, especially people from her country, as they might be spies, and so avoided them, spending much of her time in her dark basement apartment. She was very sensitive to noises, especially at night, having the fear that someone was coming to harm her. She worried about being followed when she was on the street. She felt lonely, with feelings of depression and hopelessness. She was irritable and impatient. Her lawyer referred her to a settlement agency that provided her with some emotional support and practical advice. She

continued...

was referred to a psychiatrist for a report to support her claim at her refugee determination hearing.

She found that preparing for her hearing was very emotionally difficult. She had to repeat the embarrassing and degrading details of her history to her lawyer and the psychiatrist. This process temporarily intensified her PTSD symptoms. Although her lawyer told her that she had a good case, there was still the possibility of being deported, and this is what she brooded about. She was relieved to obtain a hearing date, but as it approached she become increasing anxious about her ability to testify and about the possibility of being deported. At the hearing, she was very anxious, became confused at times, and was not able to remember exact dates. In her anxious state, the repeated questioning about her past made her feel like she was being interrogated in detention. Although she was accepted as a Convention refugee a few weeks later, she had a difficult time dealing with the uncertainty until she received the result of the hearing. The positive result allowed her to start making a life for herself in Canada with the knowledge of being able to remain in Canada in a safe and secure environment.

of lying. Being unable to remember exact dates in the stress of the situation is extremely common. Following the hearing, delays in being informed of the outcome add to the stress and uncertainty.

Helping Refugees Who Have Suffered Trauma

In helping refugees who have suffered from trauma, one needs to consider individuals' lives as a whole rather than focusing primarily on the trauma. Traumatized refugees usually have experienced a long series of traumas over time, including the trauma of their detention and torture, the stressors of life after release or escape from detention, fears of being detained again, the stressors and fears while escaping to Canada, the adjustment to a new country, and often the initial uncertainty about being able to remain in Canada. This situation is very different than that for Canadians who have PTSD as a result of a discrete traumatic event, accident or attack, but for whom the rest of their lives are stable and they carry on relatively unchanged. For in the latter situation, there is a focus in treatment on re-experiencing the event as a necessary component of treatment, but for traumatized refugees, such re-experiencing only increases the symptoms, with the memories becoming more entrenched rather fading away.

McFarlane and van der Kolk (1996, p.419) state that:

> The aim of therapy with traumatized patients is to help them move from being haunted by the past and interpreting subsequent emotionally arousing stimuli as a return of the trauma, to being fully engaged in the present and becoming capable of responding to current exigencies. In order to do that, the patients need to regain control over their emotional responses and to place the trauma in the larger perspective of their lives as a historical event (or series of events) that occurred at a particular time and a particular place, and that can be expected not to recur if the individuals take charge of their lives.

In helping refugees who have suffered trauma, one needs to consider the overall way in which the traumatic experiences have affected the person's life and self-esteem. This includes how being labelled an opponent of the government could have interfered with their schooling and employment, the effect of the traumatic experience on their family, their shame at having been degraded in detention, their fears of re-detention and re-traumatization in their country, their period of limbo in Canada until they know whether or not they can remain here, their social network or lack of it in Canada, and their general problems of adjustment here, such as limited finances and housing. Care would ideally be provided in a centre with a multilingual multicultural staff employing a multidisciplinary approach.

The initial focus must be on helping to stabilize their hyperarousal and affective dysregulation in as secure an environment as possible in Canada. Helping them express their feelings in words can reduce their sense of being overwhelmed by raw emotional feelings. They can be reassured that their symptoms are normal for someone with their experience, and that they are not crazy just because their symptoms are not under their control. If their symptoms are severe or ongoing, they can be referred for medical/psychological assistance. Medication such as selective serotonin reuptake inhibitors (SSRIs) can also be helpful, as well as medication to promote sleep. Although there is a neuro-physiological aspect to their situation, they need to be seen as dealing with a human situation and with human feelings, such as in severe grief, and not an exclusively medical one.

The next focus is on helping them accept their losses and get on with their lives in a productive and meaningful manner. Refugees have lost a great deal and tend to want to start building their lives in Canada rather than being preoccupied with the past. Settlement agencies have developed programs to assist traumatized refugees deal with their limitations in getting on with their lives. These include help with practical matters such as ESL classes, housing and social services, and the use of befriending companions. Once they are established, they may want to explore their experiences and feelings related to their trauma. However, most are more concerned with getting on with their new life than with reliving the past.

Some Factors Resulting in Difficulty in Rebuilding Lives

Difficulty learning English/French: The poor memory and concentration associated with PTSD can interfere with learning a new language and functioning at their previous level of intelligence. This is an increased problem with increasing age. Limitations in speaking English greatly limit the ability to integrate into the larger community and to obtain higher education and/or meaningful employment. There are English as a second language (ESL) programs that will accommodate to refugees' limitations in memory and concentration as well as their restlessness and inability to remain in a classroom for a prolonged period of time.

Social isolation: Refugees may isolate themselves because of their fears of people, their self-consciousness while in the community and/or their shame related to their abuse, especially sexual abuse. The isolation increases their depression and preoccupation with the past. Group programs provide social interaction and help overcome the tendency for traumatized refugees to isolate themselves; these group programs can provide a social environment whereby they can feel accepted and do not have to talk directly about their problems. Art therapy is helpful in providing a method where traumatized refugees can express their feelings and experiences by drawing or painting when they have difficulty expressing them verbally.

Limited family support: Refugees often have the stress of separation from family. This stress is intensified in cultures where families are very important. Even if accepted as Convention refugees, it can take a long time before their spouse and children can join them. In cases of individuals fleeing from war and/or political persecution, family members may end up in different countries, making direct contact between them very difficult.

Lack of employment: Refugees often have difficulty obtaining employment because of their "lack of Canadian experience" and, until they become landed immigrants, because of having their social insurance number (SIN) start with "9," which signals to perspective employers that they are refugees who have not yet obtained status. They may have worked at a professional level in their country, but their professional credentials may not be recognized in Canada, forcing them to work at jobs below their skill level. Having work or other meaningful activity helps the refugee focus on the future rather than being overly preoccupied with the past trauma. Many refugees become preoccupied with the past and become depressed because of this situation.[2]

Limited finances: Refugees, especially those who come to Canada in middle age, may not be able to find employment and are forced to go on social assistance. This is a great blow to their self-esteem, especially if they had a good standard of living in their home country and the satisfaction of a meaningful job. Poverty forces them to live in very inadequate accommodation, have limited money for food and no money for entertainment. They may obtain subsidized housing, but these situations are often very noisy, with visits from the police to the area, adding to their stress and insecurity. With their increased sensitivity to noise, many cannot tolerate apartments next to noisy elevators or garbage chutes.

Ongoing physical problems: Torture, such as from being suspended for long periods or repeatedly beaten on the soles of the feet, can result in ongoing musculoskeletal problems. The damp and cold conditions in detention or during war can contribute to long-lasting arthritic and other muscular-skeletal pain

Co-occurring psychological problems: Some refugees suffer from an ongoing chronic depression. This is more common in refugees in middle age who have not been able to establish themselves at work and have limited social relationships. A few suffer from a major psychiatric disorder that greatly limits their functioning.

Some Factors in Resilience

Age: Younger refugees, up to their mid-twenties, tend to be more resilient in dealing with difficulties and getting on with their lives in Canada. They had less to lose, have more energy, learn English rapidly, and it is easier for them to fit into the Canadian school and work system. Those who were politically involved have good ego strength and a drive to change things. Older refugees, individuals who have had to give up all they had accomplished in life, are often less resilient to stress, have less energy, and have coping resources that may be too depleted to meet further challenges. They find it harder to learn English and to concentrate at school, their work credentials and experience are often not accepted in Canada, and they have little hope of re-establishing a life at the level that they had in the past. Their compensation often comes from their children doing very well in Canada.

Social support: Support from family and the extended community is a very positive factor in assisting adjustment to life in Canada and in limiting social isolation. Pooling of family and community resources can help counter the negative effect of poverty. Beiser et al. (2011, p.338) state:

> nonfamily social relations may be important for reasons other than emotional support. Re-establishing life and social order in a new place – as refugees and their communities must do – calls for the establishment of links to the wider community beyond family and kin.

Coming to terms with their experiences. Coming to terms with their experiences and finding meaning in life helps build resilience. Traumatized refugees have the challenge of coming to terms psychologically with their experiences in a positive, adaptive manner rather than becoming bitter and isolated. Some refugees need to come to terms with having suffered greatly, having wasted many years of their lives, and having lost their country without anything having been accomplished politically. Victims need to find active ways to regain control over their feelings and actions. They are helped by actively exposing themselves to experiences that provide them with feelings of mastery and pleasure. Physical activity or artistic accomplishment can provide gratification which is not contaminated by the trauma.

Ongoing Problems

Refugees need to determine how much of their past is to remain private and how much can be talked about. Younger individuals who are doing well can feel a need to be open about their experiences in order to be understood by friends, but can worry that their friends may be frightened off by their experiences if they are open about them. Parents can disagree over how much of the past to tell their children who were born in Canada; one may feel the children have a right to know about their parents' past while the other person may feel that the children need to be protected from the past. There can problems generated by differences between the country of origin and Canada in terms of family roles and style. This can lead to interpersonal conflict between parents and children and between spouses. In addition, there may be many other psychological issues from the past that traumatized refugees need to come to terms with over time.

Case Study 5 – Anna

Anna, in her early twenties, was not politically active but was detained because of her older sister's considerable political activity. She was detained along with a group of women that included her sister. On several occasions, her sister was taken out to be executed, only to be returned later in the day. On the last occasion, her sister was actually executed. The women in her cell group told her that she had to be strong and not cry so that she would not show any weakness to the guards. Her family paid a bribe for her release and arranged for her to come to Canada. After arriving in Canada, she learned that the authorities had detained her father and interrogated him in detention about her whereabouts. Her father died of a heart attack during the interrogation. She was staying with relatives in Canada, but had difficulty dealing with them as their political views were very different from her own. As well as having to deal with her own ill treatment, she had to deal with her inability to grieve over her sister at the time of her death, her guilt over her father's death, and her own difficulties with her relatives in Canada.

Develop your knowledge – Ask yourself

1. How would you provide assistance to someone who was very anxious in having to face testifying at her Refugee Determination Hearing? In helping her, what factors would you be aware of that could have a detrimental effect on her mental state?

2. What factors would you consider in assisting Anna described in Case 5?

Notes

[1] The guidelines are available at http://www.ccirh.uottawa.ca.
[2] Beiser (1999) has shown that in Vietnamese "boat people" it is the preoccupation with the past that produces depression, rather than vice versa.

References

American Psychiatric Association (APA). (2013). *Diagnostic and Statistical Manual of Mental Disorders*, (5th ed.). Washington, DC: American Psychiatric Association.

Beiser, M. (1999). *Strangers at the gate: The "boat people's" first ten years in Canada*. Toronto: University of Toronto Press.

Beiser, M., Simich, L., Pandalangat, N., Nowalowski, M., & Tian, F. (2011). Stress of passage, balms of resettlement, and posttraumatic stress disorder among Sri Lankan Tamils in Canada. *Canadian Journal of Psychiatry*, *56*(6), 333-340.

Fazel, M., Wheeler J., & Danesh, J. (2005). Prevalence of serious mental disorders in 7000 refugees resettled in western countries: A systematic review. *Lancet*, *365*(9467): 1309–14.

Pottie, K. et al. (2011). Evidence-based clinical guidelines for immigrants and refugees. *CMAJ*, DOI:1503/cmaj.090313.

van der Kolk, B.A., & McFarlane, A.C. (1996). A general approach to treatment of posttraumatic stress disorder. In B.A. van der Kolk, A.C. McFarlane & L. Weisaeth (Eds.), *Traumatic stress: The effects of overwhelming experience on mind, body and society*. New York : The Guilford Press.

PART 5

THE CRIMINAL JUSTICE SYSTEM AND VIOLENCE AGAINST WOMEN

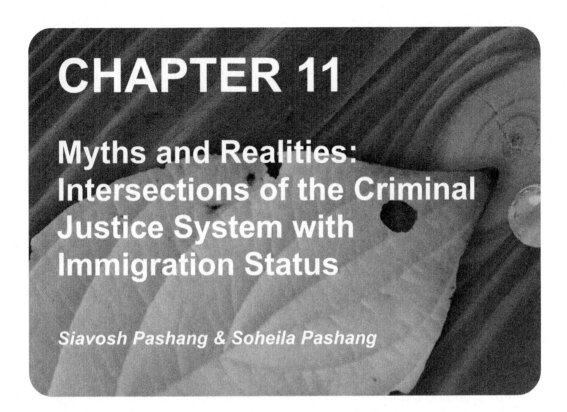

CHAPTER 11

Myths and Realities: Intersections of the Criminal Justice System with Immigration Status

Siavosh Pashang & Soheila Pashang

Introduction

The purpose of this chapter is to highlight the intersectionality between immigration and criminal law principles in Canada. It will review the laws and policies that deem foreign nationals, permanent residents, refugees and illegalized persons inadmissible based on criminality. The chapter will further discuss the consequences that result from an increasing determination to prosecute offences under the *Immigration and Refugee Protection Act (IRPA)* (SC 2001, c. 27). Immigration laws not only deny criminally inadmissible individuals entry to Canada, but also authorize the removal from Canada of foreign nationals and Canadian permanent residents who lost that status. Through case studies, the chapter moves on to discuss how two fields of law – criminal law and administrative law – intertwine with the issues of borders and immigration. From an anti-oppressive perspective, the chapter provides practical perspectives to social workers and social service workers when working with immigrants, refugees and illegalized person after their exit from the justice system.

The Canadian criminal justice system is based on the colonial ideologies and socially constructed relations of power between those who safeguard the law and those who are accused of breaking such law. The fallacy of this relation often manifests itself in the form of racism, sexism, classism, ableism, ageism, homophobia and human rights violations of the individuals encountering the system. These forms of discrimination exist among individual beliefs (through biases, suspicions, stereotypes) and cultural practices (by linking race, culture, religion to a particular crime or community), as well as institutional policies that govern our justice system. While discrimination within the justice system affects many disenfranchised populations, its impact may not be the same for those who are categorized as immigrants, refugees and illegalized migrants. This impact is institutionalized through the practices of two distinct but interrelated institutions, namely, the criminal justice system, on one side, and the Canada Border Services Agencies (CBSA) and Citizenship and Immigration Canada (CIC), on the other side where individual immigrants are situated. They include: Canadian citizens, permanent residents, foreign nationals, convention refugees, and illegalized migrants. The parameters of immigration policies are set by the *IRPA*, accompanied regulations, manuals and ministerial instructions, as well as Canada Boarder Service Agencies policies. Together, they rely on the justice system including the police force for the arrest, imprisonment, and deportation of alleged criminals. IRPA came to effect as a response to often fragmented and piecemeal laws that previously regulated immigration policies in Canada. IRPA's purpose was to combine all immigration and refugee-related matters in a coherent manner within one legislative framework. However, since its passage, the impact of criminality in immigration cases has intensified. The law stipulates that non-citizens of Canada may be inadmissible due to convictions or the commission of criminal acts outside of Canada (*IRPA*, s.36(1)(2)). Anyone seeking a visa (to live, work, study or visit) may be refused entry for facing charges or having been previously convicted of a criminal offence. Those permanent residents or foreign nationals currently residing in Canada may also be forced to leave due to criminality (*IRPA*, s.(1)(a)). The objectives of *IRPA* therefore evidence a balancing of interests that include, on the one hand, permitting Canada to pursue the maximum social, cultural and economic benefits of immigration to enrich and strengthen the fabric of Canadian society, and on the other, protecting the safety of Canadians. Ensuring the safety of Canadians from international criminals falls under the jurisdiction of the Canadian Border Service Agency (CBSA). The CBSA holds the authority of removal of 'illegal' foreign nationals or those who face deportation due to inadmissibility including criminality. The police force and CBSA officers work closely to track down immigrants who have no choice but to live underground or once they are provided with deportation orders by the CIC or by the CBSA itself. The impacts of such intersectionality is examined in the ensuing sections, by showcasing situations in which immigrants, refugees and illegalized migrants find themselves in the justice system.

The Canadian Criminal Justice System and the Definition of Crime

The *Criminal Code of Canada (*R.S.C., 1985, c. C-46) is rooted in colonial ideology and the tradition of English common law in which the definition of all offences originated from legislation in the form of statutes. Under colonial rule, differences between people were used as a mechanism to maintain colonial power. As a result, Aboriginal Peoples along with other undesired immigrants were deemed as inferior and therefore were subject to persecution and segregation. From this time on, colonial rulers continued to rely on the notion of deviant and crime through the practice of deportation of new settlers in order to control the lives of women, homosexuals, individuals with physical and mental health challenges, racialized and immigrants regardless of whether they were charged with an offence or were themselves a victim of crime. With time, the ideological discourse of crime and deportation as a mean of punishment expanded from the expulsion of "fraudulent refugees" to the expulsion of "illegal criminals," and recently as Pratt (2006) notes, to the "crime-security nexus" under the guise of criminality and terrorism. This deeply rooted connection between the process of colonization, migratory movement and the *Criminal Code* is embedded in neo-liberal and anti-immigrant sentiments where immigrants are "othered" along exclusionary lines. As such, the definition of crime has historically meant that those who have been excluded from fundamental social, political, cultural, economic, and human rights are in a category of powerlessness, that is, at the mercy of those who hold power (Griffiths & Verdun-Jones, 1989). It is important to note that individuals who hold power within the justice system are also in the position of shaping and formulating this discourse, whether by passing laws, interpreting those laws, or producing statistics on crime and on those who commit them.

As evident in Chart 1, the justice system might appear to address itself to three separate spheres – those of security (through the police), rights (through the court system), and the management of criminals (through correctional facilities). Consequently, the activities of a particular component

Chart 1: The Criminal Justice System

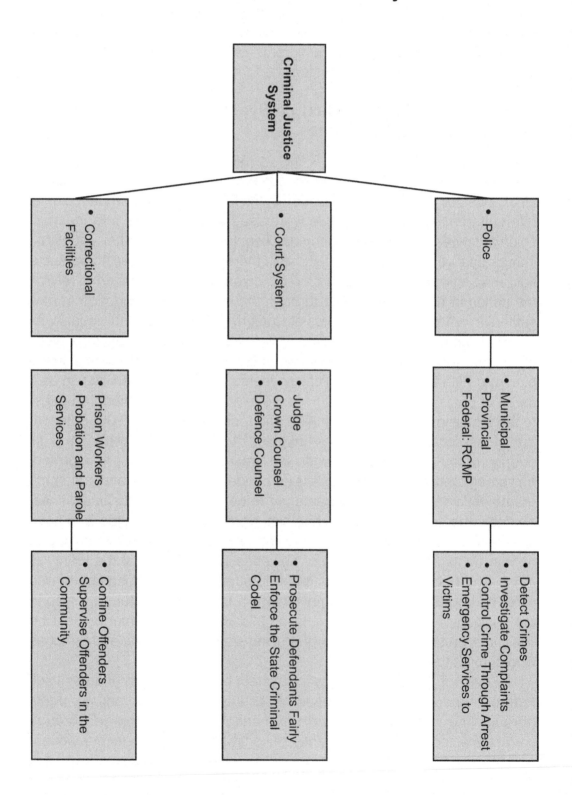

are likely to have an impact upon the others. For instance, the police force's selection of persons facing arrest and charges will determine which cases are presented to Crown counsel for prosecution. In turn, the criminal courts' sentencing practices determine the population within correctional institutions.

Today, all legislation in Canada must comply with the *Canadian Charter of Rights and Freedoms* (Charter) *(The Constitution Act, 1982*, being Schedule B to the *Canada Act 1982* (UK), 1982, c 11). However, despite such constitutional guarantees, unequal treatment continues to exist within our system. Keeping in mind that our justice system is flawed with racial discrimination, when juxtaposed with the immigration system it exposes the already marginalized migrants more vulnerable to additional punishment of the accused. For example, the justice system will work closely with the CBSA for possible enforcement of immigration laws, which may result in confinement within immigration detention centers as well as deportation. In dealing with the arrest of a non-citizen, the police force is further required to report the encounter whether the accused was witness of crime or has committed a crime (NSW Police Force Handbook, 2014; Code of Practice of Crime, 2012). This eventually leads to further immigration investigation by the CBSA which can increase the risk of possible deportation.

In recent years, many refugee claimants waiting their immigration hearings were also kept in maximum-security prisons in the suburbs rather than being placed in the immigration holding centers or sent to refugee houses Friscolanti, October 2, 2014; Bronskill, September 25, 2014). All of these conditions can further explain the potential for overrepresentation of immigrants within the justice system.

Systemic Discrimination in the Criminal Justice System

Amendments to the 1967 immigration point system have changed the face of the Canadian mosaic. Each year, Canada is host to over 200,000 new immigrants, the majority of them from racialized communities. According to the data of 2011 National Household Survey (NHS), Canada had accepted 6,775,800 foreign-born individuals (20.6% of the total population), with 82.4% of them being racialized persons (Statistics Canada, 2011). In 2011, nearly 6,264,800, or one in every five Canadians identified themselves as racialized person (Statistics Canada, 2011). In return, immigrants contribute greatly to the economic prosperity, innovation and population growth of Canada. Despite this fact, many new immigrants - particularly those belonging to racialized communities - continue to face systemic discrimination and marginalization. As Abell and Sheehy (2007) aptly put it, "This level of dominance is created by colonization and structured and enforced through racial and ethnic differentiation and ideologies of choice and individualism" (p. 7).

Criminal Code

- First enacted in 1892, it serves to codify most criminal offences and procedures in Canada.
- Section 91(27) of the *Constitution Act, 1867* establishes criminal law as under the sole jurisdiction of the federal Parliament.

Crime

- Crime is a constantly changing concept relative to the norms of society at a given time. It is a social construct dealing with conformity to these norms.
- Elements of crime include: wrongful acts, convictions, consequences of these acts, and punishment dealing with proven offences.

Criminalization

- Criminalization deals with the legislation that makes something illegal.
- It considers the legislative authorities that define crime and jurisdictional enforcement of offences (federal versus provincial).
- The criminalization of racialized members in Canada starts with issues of colonization, sovereignty, and role of law enforced by white European settlers upon aboriginals.

Over the last few decades, the Canadian justice system has been the subject of controversy suggesting differential treatment against marginalized, racialized and various groups of immigrants. These problems range from a lack of police protection and police harassment to difficulties in accessing legal aid and having fair trials (Henry & Tator, 2010). Systemic discrimination perpetuates a power structure through bias and the unequal treatment especially in patterns of law-making and policy-making where marginalized peoples are targeted. Unfortunately these patterns of behaviours and actions are not isolated mistakes. For example, racialized individuals (including immigrants) are subjected in greater numbers to pre-trial release conditions and coerced into entering guilty pleas, which in turn creates the statistical basis for more frequent arbitrary stops and investigations by the police force. This directly facilitates their re-arrest and return to the justice system (Kellough & Wortley, 2001). More often, the convicted immigrants are also sentenced to longer periods of confinement than members of other communities (Rankin & Powell, 2008). Upon release, members of racialized communities and immigrants are more likely to be caught for breaching their probationary conditions, while guilty pleas often increase the possibility of deportation for immigrant accused who are non-citizens (Kellough & Wortley, 2001). As Razack (1998) indicates, this differential treatment leads to differential legal decisions being among those within racialized communities, from their point of entry into the system to their point of exit. Multiple reports have also established that immigrants are portrayed as a threat to the stability of society (Galabuzi, 2006) by increasing crime (Ismaili, 2011). The 2003 national public opinion survey found that 27 percent of Canadians were in favour of such perception (Ismaili, 2011). This belief creates the discourse of "Otherness" (Henry & Tator, 2010) despite the fact that in comparison, immigrants commit less crime.

Although all new immigrants face settlement and integration challenges, racialized immigrants are confronted with additional challenges due to their intersecting identities. Such disparities push immigrants into segregated and lower-income areas where they are more vulnerable to frequent police surveillance, which in turn increases their likelihood of being wrongfully targeted or caught when breaking the law (Henry & Tator, 2010; Wortley, 2003). Given their economic disadvantage, immigrants also face more barriers in accessing legal services considering recent cuts to Legal Aid. This, along with lack of knowledge about the Canadian legal system and language barriers further places immigrants at risk of becoming victims of abuse by inexperienced or non-registered legal consultants.

Racial Profiling: The Dialect between Over-policing and Under-policing

Systemic discrimination can further be thought of in terms of the concept of racial profiling. Wortley (2003, p.3) defines racial profiling as:

> The members of certain racial groups become subject to greater levels of criminal justice surveillance than other citizens. Racial profiling, there-

fore, is typically defined as a racial disparity in police stop and search practices, racial differences in customs searches at airports and border crossings, increased police patrols in racial minority neighbourhoods, and undercover activities or sting operations which selectively target particular ethnic groups.

Henry and Tator (2010) refer to racial profiling as the "extent to which police use discretion in the surveillance of a community and the apprehension of people in that community" (p. 161).

Racial profiling is prohibited the under Ontario's Human Rights Code (OHRCR.S.O. 1990, CHAPTER H.19); however, its occurrence is a daily reality for many immigrants in the form of carding, unreasonable questioning, requests for identification, retaining personal information, intimidation, searches, aggression and at times, DNA sampling (OHRC, April 2014). For example, in 2013, as part of sexual assault investigations, the Ontario Provincial Police (OPP) engaged in racial profiling by requesting DNA samples from 100 Indo- and Afro-Caribbean male migrant workers near Vienna, Ontario, under the assumption that Black migrant workers are prone to commit criminal behavior (OHRC, April 2014). This raises two important questions: firstly, whether our perception about racialized and immigrants crime rate "may be regarded as information about enforcement rather than

How Can you Help Amy?

Amy who was sponsored by her parents was kicked out of the house upon their disapproval of her new boyfriend. On her way from her part-time job, a bystander rubbed Amy. She called 911. By the time police showed up, many of the witnesses had already gone. The policy asked Amy for an identification card. Amy was arrested and sent to the CBSA holding center for further immigration investigation. Her parents had abandoned her sponsorship application.

1. As a professional, how are you able to help Amy?

2. What kinds of services are available to her?

3. Where do you refer her for assistance?

criminality" (Greenaway, 1980, p. 247); and secondly, whether racialized members or immigrants need police to protect them from crime or in fact they need protection against the police (Henry & Tator, 2010).

While over-policing criminalizes neighbourhoods and individuals living within such proximity, underpolicing, according to Henry and Tator (2010) also fails racialized members and immigrants when they are in need of police protection particularly in the case of violence against women or hate crime. Under-policing occurs in the form of delayed responses which risk eyewitnesses forgetting details or leaving the crime scene. Under-policing can also appear in the form of cultural relativism in terms of attitudes and behaviours of the police towards immigrants (particularly immigrant women) when police uses the issue of culture to explain why men from a particular nationality abuse their partners, or for instance why women from within the same culture may tolerate such action and behaviour. This makes culture as a focal point rather than overall racism, sexism, and patriarchal relations. Therefore, the way in which the police respond to immigrants directly affects the way they perceive the police and the justice system.

Models of Immigrants' Criminality

As mentioned earlier, immigrants commit less crime by comparison. The following presents models of immigrants' criminality (Wortley, 2009, noted in Ismaili, 2011):

The Importation Model: individuals migrate to a new country with the intention of committing crime. Their activities range from international organized-crime to criminal gang, terrorist networks and organizations.

The Strain Model: Immigrants' crime is linked to their exclusion, marginalization, lack of resources and opportunities and systemic discrimination along with inequality embedded in employment, education and housing which together pushes people to commit crime.

The Cultural Conflict Model: immigrants are caught in criminal activities because behaviours that are a norm and legal in their countries may be prohibited in Canada.

The Bias Model: the over-representation of immigrants in the justice system is reflective of discrimination within the justice system.

These dominant ideologies have resulted in restrictive immigration policies against nations that are considered source countries as well as harsher crime control strategies against individuals migrating from these countries (importation model). At the same time, blaming culture (cultural conflict model) as a dividing factor between immigrants and mainstream Canadians perpetuates the existing discrimination and racism against immigrants and racialized members.

In its contemporary form, particularly since post-September 2011, as noted by Yasmin Jiwani (2011), the media has created moral panics and hysteria against immigrants where the problem of terrorism is now linked to the notions of threat and security. The discourse further legitimatizes surveillance, criminalization and illegalization of immigrant Muslim alike. In this context, religion is constructed as politics, law, culture, nationality and the freedom of international movement (Mojab & El-Kassem, 2007). Jiwani further unpacks ways in which violence against immigrant women and the recent reports on honor killing for instance is presented as a form of cultural barbarism and a point of hierarchical divide between certain groups of immigrants with mainstream Canadians.

One clear example is the passage of *Zero Tolerance for Barbaric Cultural Practices* Act (Government of Canada, 2014), which is aimed to protect Canadians from immigrants, mainly Muslims and Blacks stereotyped for their violent cultural practices of polygamy and violence against women including honour killing. However within such neo-liberal and anti-immigrant sentiment the disappearance and murder of over 500 Aboriginal women (Jiwani, 2011) and the femocide and trafficking of Canadian women attract little attention or raise no racial, religious or immigration and security questions. In contrast, the Prime Minster, Stephen Harper argues that the problem of missing and murdered Aboriginal women is not a "sociological phenomenon," but solely an issue of crime against innocent people (Ditchburn, 2014).

Mojab and El-Kassem (2007) construct this notion as cultural relativism within the neo-colonialist-orientalist worldview where the identity of women from the Middle East is homogenized and reduced to a faith that they may or may not subscribe. In this context, while immigrant women's struggle and resistance against patriarchy is dismissed, the debate is further centered on cultural accommodation, cultural polarity, cultural differences and tolerance where images and bodies of Muslim women are used as a sign of liberation or oppression, progression or backwardness.

Cultural relativism according to Mojab and El-Kassem has managed to confront earlier twentieth-century racism that saw Western civilization as superior to all 'others' (including Aboriginals and certain group of immigrants), fall short in confronting the complexity of Islamophobia (2007) or violence against immigrant women. For example, cultural relativism uses the term *differences* rather than *domination,* and rejects hierarchal power structures across genders or within other societal spectrum (Mojab & El-Kassem, 2007). This leaves the discriminatory practices of the justice system against immigrants or the exclusionary immigration system unchallenged. Historically, Canadian criminal law originated within colonial ideologies and continues to intersect with immigration policies in order to maintain white and patriarchal colonial power. This power manifests itself in the form of criminalization and culturalization of racialized members and immigrants and further justifies carding or racial profiling. Racial profiling against immigrants as indicated earlier, juxtaposes their lives with the immigration system and simultaneously increases their vulnerability towards family separation, poverty and potential deportation.

The intersection of the Criminal Justice System with Immigration

This section will discuss how two fields of law – criminal law and administrative law – intertwine with the issues of borders and immigration. The previous sections addressed the challenges faced by those who are within the boundaries of the state yet excluded from protections of the laws due to their socially constructed differences. What happens when the state feels no obligation toward protecting individual foreigners (i.e., refugee claimants, inadmissible immigrants)?

Once known as a country holding high humanitarian values for refugees in need of protection, and for its commitments towards multiculturalism, Canada has recently painted a picture that assumes refugees are "bogus," "illegal" and a threat to national security. In particular, the government has announced a new refugee regime that makes it difficult for refugee claimants from safe designated countries to stay. The two-tier system, as well as ever-increasing border security and restrictive immigration policies, tends to criminalize refugees – especially those who are racialized – upon their arrival in Canada. They may be prosecuted at their port of entry (which leads to their detention or potential deportation), or prosecuted at any point in their efforts at obtaining refugee status. Even once they are granted conventional refugee status, certain criminal act can endanger their chances of obtaining permanent residency or access to full citizenship status. The following section will put this issue into perspective.

Refugees

Following the September 11, 2001 terrorist attacks and the ensuing war on terror, prevailing stereotypes have impelled the majority of Western countries

to take extreme measures against "terrorism," while certain pieces of legislation have simultaneously been passed. These policies directly affect the
conditions of refugees in need of protection who find themselves with no other
option than to rely on human smugglers to reach their destination countries.

In June 2002, under section 118, *IRPA* responded to the issue of trafficking offences such as kidnapping, forcible confinement, extortion, and
assault. Section 117 states that "No person shall knowingly organize, induce,
aid or abet the coming into Canada of one or more persons who are not in
possession of a visa, passport or other document required by this Act" (IRPA,
SC117. (1). The Canadian Council for Refugees (CCR) (April 2014)
considers this action an example of closing its doors on refugees in need of
protection, which contradicts the very foundation of national and international
human rights laws. To oppose the criminalization of refugee aid workers, the
CCR and other community activists organized *Proud to aid and abet
refugees* campaign.

In order to escape their ordeals, refugees are expected to provide proof
of their identities to the satisfaction of immigration authorities. Many refugees
do not have the option of planning their trips; they live in hiding, or find themselves at risk of prosecution if they approach their government to acquire
official travel documents or passports. Similarly, refugees may spend many
years at refugee camps, lose their identification documents, separate from

On September 2007, Janet Hinshaw-Thomas, a refugee worker and
director of PRIME - Ecumenical Commitment to Refugees was
charged with people-smuggling (section 117 of the IRPA). Although
her charges were dropped, in December 2007 Margaret de Rivera,
also a refugee worker was threatened with prosecution for accompanying refugees to the border.

Note: Leave to appeal granted today by the SCC against the judgment of the BCCA in R. v. Appulonappa, 2014 BCCA 163.

In the appeal case, the BCCA set aside the trial judge finding that
the human smuggling provisions of the IRPA violated s.7 of the
Charter by capturing the morally innocent in their scope of criminal
liability.

Two or three other FCA judgments on the human smuggling
provisions are also before the SCC and the appeals will be heard
together.

their family members who hold their documents, or sell them in return for food or safety. Meanwhile, many refugees who manage to flee their countries through human smuggling have been warned to destroy their identification documents while in transit or before arriving on the soil of their destination countries. Adding insult to injury, Canadian embassies often do not operate in conflict zones or countries with high records of human-rights violations. This reality prevents refugees from obtaining legal visas while, at the same time, the exclusionary and class-based immigration policies and practices fail to allow refugees to seek admission to Canada legally and under various immigration categories.

Permanent Residents

The *Strengthening Canadian Citizenship Act* (Bill C-24, Government of Canada) provides immigration officials with the discretionary power to strip citizenship from naturalized Canadians (born abroad) with dual citizenship who are convicted of certain criminal offenses such as terrorism, treason or spying abroad. The Anti-Terrorism Act of 2001 addresses individual suspects, those who

> The labeling of terrorism is highly political. This reality suggests terrorism accusations, prosecutions and convictions are similarly politicized, and subject to political interpretation. Like the case of Nelson Mandela, yesterday's terrorists may be today's honorary Canadian citizens. (Kanji, National Post, February 14, 2014).

fundraise for terrorist organizations, and those who assist or harbor them (Skinnider, 2005).

The CBSA, which is responsible for the enforcement of immigration law, heavily relies on the justice system to ensure border security and the removal of non-citizens. For example, Section 83.28 of the Criminal Code allows the police to approach individuals for questioning or to obtain documentations if they have reasonable grounds to believe a terrorism offence has or will be committed (Skinnider, 2005). At the same time, the police are required to provide information about immigration status of the offenders to the CBSA who then prepare a report to the members of IRB for the 'admissibility hearing' which can lead to a removal order, departure and exclusion of permanent residents and foreign nationals.

As mentioned previously, IRPA may deem non-citizens to be inadmissible due to criminal convictions or the commission of certain criminal acts both inside or outside of Canada.

The types of criminality that can lead to inadmissibility can be grouped into four categories:

1) Convicted *in* Canada;
2) Convicted *outside* Canada;
3) *Committed an "act"* outside Canada; and,
4) *Committed an "act"* upon entering Canada.

IRPA s.36(1)(a) states that a permanent resident or foreign national who is convicted of an offence in Canada is considered inadmissible if:

- The offence carries a maximum term of imprisonment of at least 10 years; or
- For which a term of imprisonment of more than 6 months has been imposed

Foreign nationals carry a heavier burden for less serious offences that do not affect permanent residents. They are deemed inadmissible if:

- An offence is punishable by way of indictment (any hybrid offence is deemed indictable[1]); or
- Any two offences do not arise out of a single occurrence.

For convictions outside of Canada, ss. 36(1)(b) and 36(2)(b) deal with permanent residents and foreign nationals very similarly to the guidelines above (those convicted in Canada) if the offence committed abroad is classified as equivalent to an offence in Canada. The individual may be deemed inadmissible if an officer has "reasonable grounds to believe" that he/she was convicted of one or more offences outside Canada.

The Case of Majd: Putting the Context into Lived Realities

Majd was charged for assaulting his wife. Majd was trained as an engineer in his home country and came to Canada with his wife, a registered nurse, and their two children under the immigration point system. They had waited four years for their application to be processed. Upon arrival, the couple rented a small apartment and Majd found a job as a driver for a local pizza store. However, Majd and his wife while away from their families and friends support system in dealing with challenges to settlement often engaged in arguments over the spending of money, disciplining their children, and other household

continued...

issues. One afternoon, just before Majd left for work, an argument escalated between the couple. Majd, for the first time slapped his wife in front of their children and threatened to hurt her again if she refused to listen to him. That day, Majd was stopped by two police cruisers. His neighbour had called the police.

Note: The subject of this case study, Majd is created with permission to illustrate the experiences of immigrant men charged with assault against their female partners.

Upon his release from prison, Majd was to attend sixteen weeks of a mandatory Partner Assault Response (PAR) program at a local community agency as part of his probationary conditions. While attending his program, he reported being subject to the following treatment:

I was caught at the wrong time – post 9-11. The officer asked me where I am from. I replied, Iran. The officer reprimanded me and said, "You terrorist!" His fellow officer then asked, "How many wives do you have? Muslims have two wives, right?" What hurts me is that I am not Muslim! I am Iranian but not Muslim. Why did he assume my religion and why did he need to put Muslims down anyway? In reality, from the moment of my arrest to the point of exiting the jail, I was dehumanized by the threats of being deported to my country, that my culture is barbaric and patriarchal, and that in Canada, I have no right to hit anyone. I was referred to as "wife beater," "uncivilized," "polygamous Muslim man," and "terrorist." The entire time, I had flashback[s] about the time of my political arrest, torture, and when I was kept in the solitary confinement. (Pashang, 2003, pp. 71–72)

While violence against women is not to be condoned and should be dealt with seriously; however, from the statement above, it is clear that within the context of the criminal system, the discourse of "race" intersects with "Islamophobia" in ways that alter the perceptions of employees of the justice system, which sets the stage for the treatment one may receive. The Canadian Centre for Police–Race Relations (2001) found that police racism against racialized groups casts the racialized group as "Others" and in so doing, creates a sense of fear towards members of these groups.

The intersection of the criminal justice system with issues of immigration status has long been discussed by legal and human-rights activists. In the

Reflective Questions for Practitioners

1. While the arresting officer may have prevented any subsequent violence by Majd against his wife through arrest, what are some of the implications of the discriminatory actions and behaviour (such as discriminatory language) of the officer against Majd?

2. Do you think racial profiling against immigrant men stops violence against women or forces women to remain silent when they are subjected to abuse in order to protect their communities? How can the justice system implement more inclusive strategies to address violence against women and children?

case of Majd, his arrest was concurrent with his process of pursuing citizenship. According to Majd,

> *I was charged just prior to my citizenship examination. My conviction changed the whole process. Everything is still on hold; once you have a criminal record, you're doomed.* (Pashang, 2003, p. 72)

The reality is that a criminal conviction further affects the ability of immigrants to sponsor their family members. In Canadian law, to sponsor a relative, an immigrant must be a Canadian citizen or permanent resident (Community Legal Education Ontario, June 2008). However, criminal charges and convictions can interfere with the processing of one's sponsorship application. For instance, Majd's assault conviction (slapping his wife) and threatening to harm will impact the sponsorship of his parents or other dependent family members wishing to come to Canada. In retrospect, considering the fact that our justice system is not bias-free, any discriminatory practices such as unfair treatment, harsher sentencing, and longer imprisonment terms can directly affect immigrants' family-reunification processes. Finally, the criminal records of men (as principal applicants) intersect with the immigration statuses of their entire families and create innumerable financial, social, and emotional dilemmas for immigrant women. This can cause displacement and forceful deportation conditions under which women become more vulnerable within their existing vulnerability as immigrant women.

Detention and Deportation

Another way that the justice system interacts with the immigration system is the situation of rejected refugee claimants and those awaiting their deportation orders who are placed within the provincial jails. This is against international law where states are required to place immigration detainees with no criminality in facilities appropriate to their non-criminal status. In 2012, according to a report by the Red Cross, an estimated 3,952 immigration detainees across Canada were placed in correctional institutions alongside other inmates, with 288 minors being detained in federal facilities and three in provincial facilities (Friscolanti, October 2, 2014; Bronskill, September 25, 2014).

To resist their conditions, in 2013, over 100 detained migrants in the Central East Correctional Centre in Ontario went on hunger strikes pleading for basic freedoms against 28 months of maximum-security prison. The No One is Illegal which is an international network supporting the rights of non-resident immigrants considers the vulnerability of detained migrants to possible death while crossing international borders or when housed within securitized detention, a colonial ideology embedded in the interlocking relation between prison institutions and exclusionary immigration system (Walia, September 29, 2014). According to an investigation by the Toronto Star (Chown Oved, August 20, 2014), Canada deports over 10,000 migrants annually, including rejected refugees to war-torn countries or countries that Canada has official moratorium on deportation (Haiti, Democratic Republic of Congo, Zimbabwe, Iraq and Afghanistan).

In December 2013, a 42 year old Mexican deportee, Lucia Vega Jimenez detained at the Alouette Correctional Centre for Women, and later removed to the holding center at Vancouver International Airport was found hanging in a CBSA shower stall. Jimenez was stopped by the transit police officer for an unpaid fair who due to her accent turned her to the CBSA members. She was a victim of intimate abuse and at a time of her arrest had physical scars with symptoms of anxiety.

The Role of Social Work Agencies

In recent years, many social-work agencies have found the need for greater involvement in offering crime-reduction programs for convicts and other supportive services to their family members. Such services include spiritual, psycho-social, educational, individual, and group counselling, as well as language and culturally specific programs. Some social workers and settle-ment workers practice within an anti-oppressive framework and engage in an advocacy role, or follow a traditional and therapeutic approach. While interdisciplinary approaches and the involvement of social workers, social service workers and settlement workers with the justice system are highly recommended, one needs to avoid a homogenization of the experiences of immigrants and racialized members during and after their encounters with the justice system. That being said, particular attention must be paid to the ways in which immigrants experience the criminal justice system including the impact on their immigration status. Intervention programs, therefore, must recognize such a complex and multifaceted problem.

Regrettably, in their study titled *Are Social Workers Ready to Work with Newcomers?*, Chung Yan & Chan (2010) found that most social workers in Canada have little knowledge about immigrants and refugees. They also found that social workers do not feel competent working with them, and that their organizations and programs do not address the needs of the ever-growing population of newcomers. This nexus of issues explains the field's shortcomings in responding to the needs of refugees and immigrants dealing with the justice system, and further raises concerns about the impact of social workers' roles and their service provision while serving immigrants from diverse cultural and linguistic backgrounds.

The justice system has rightfully addressed the issue of linguistic and cultural differences by hiring trained professional interpreters. However, while the recognition of linguistic barriers by the justice system represents a major step in addressing the notion of equitable access, when immigrants and members are charged (whether or not they are ultimately proven guilty or found innocent), they often find themselves facing a white judge, Crown attorney, and defence lawyer, and white law clerks and security guards (Henry et al., 2000). Being mindful that the criminal justice system has a long history of discriminatory practices in terms of the hiring practices of police forces, agenda setting, and the ways in which they carry out their activities (Commission on Systemic Racism in the Ontario Criminal Justice System, 1995), the claim of cultural-linguistic accessibility must be addressed more cautiously. Cultural-linguistic interpreters must be provided with anti-oppressive training in order to understand their roles as they work with disenfranchised peoples encountering the justice system. This further includes an understanding of ways in which gender, race, class and immigration status interacts with the justice system.

Thus, language interpretation services can only address the basic needs of immigrants in understanding the justice system, including court proceedings. Interpreters have a passive role solely limited to translating a given conversation, rather than preventing discriminatory practices more broadly. While various mainstream community organizations and health centers have established programs geared towards serving immigrants and refugees, the justice system has yet to implement such specialized services to address the needs of immigrants and refugees who further require settlement and immigration related support. For example, crown attorneys, defence lawyers and probation officers should be educated about the intersectionality of the crime with the immigration status of the individuals in order to provide more accurate information about the option and choice one may make while pleading guilty. This is particularly concerning since the justice system is to report the status of immigrants to the CBSA but not committed to assist their basic settlement and immigration needs. It is, therefore, time for us to go beyond the rhetoric of "empowering" our communities through language and cultural programs. Working from anti-oppression framework, we must examine the notion of power and link it to the discourse of access to equitable services as well as decision-making processes within our social work and social service practices, programs, organizations, and major institutions such as the criminal justice system.

Even though offering programs at various ethno-specific agencies decreases the marginalization of immigrants and racialized members, these agencies are faced with serious threats of cuts to their funding which simultaneously affects their ability to survive and offer adequate programs.

Although the *Charter* guarantees the right to legal counsel upon arrest or detention (s.10(b)), our system is not equipped to address the complex and multifaceted needs of immigrants. Factors such as restrictive eligibility criteria attached to obtaining a legal-aid lawyer, language barriers, unfamiliarity with the existing system, and a lack of access to appropriate legal services hinder this process substantially. Similarly, new immigrants may not know the difference between an experienced lawyer who is familiar with both immigration and criminal laws and a consultant who might charge them enormous amounts of money or provide them with inaccurate advice. This disconnect between the needs and human rights of immigrants accused of crimes will in turn affect the treatment they receive while under custody or upon their release as they encounter regulations of CBSA. Working from an anti-oppression framework therefore requires referral as well as engagement in advocacy role to raise awareness about the various challenges faced by immigrants and refugees within the justice system.

Conclusion

In summary, the discussion above has shed light on how the criminalization of immigrants is a major and continuing problem in Canada. Social workers and settlement workers must pay particular attention to the conditions of individuals who are not Canadian citizens. The role of frontline practitioners, therefore, needs to go beyond delivering supportive or rehabilitative programs. These workers need to remain committed to an anti-oppressive framework while simultaneously increasing their knowledge about the inter-sectionality of criminal justice laws with immigration policies. They should also take on advocacy roles to educate, confront, and eliminate individual, cultural, and systemic barriers.

While the criminal justice system is solely responsible for dealing with crim-inal matters, the arresting officers, Crown prosecutors, judges, defence lawyers, duty counsel, jury members, law clerks, and probation officers all play a part to the extent that their decisions have an effect on the lives of various groups of immigrants. This disconnect makes it more difficult and strenuous to eliminate racism and discriminatory practices against immi-grants and members of racialized communities. To move forward, we need commitment from all level of governments and major institutions. One posi-tive initiative has been the indefinite suspension of police carding proposed by the Toronto police Chief, Bill Blair (CBC News, January 6, 2015). Initia-tives as such are step forward towards ensuring principles of democracy where all members, regardless of their differences can feel safe, and rely on the justice system to ensure their safety. At the same time, we might want to interrogate why carding (or racial profiling) has been tolerated in Canada despite its claim of being multicultural nation.

Note

[1]   A hybrid offence is an offence which can be prosecuted either summarily (less serious) or by indictment (more serious); the majority of criminal code offences are hybrid

References

Abell, J., & Sheehy, E. (2007). *Criminal law & procedure: Cases, context, critique* (4th ed.). Toronto: Captus.

Bronskill, J. (September 25, 2014). Red Cross uncovers problems facing immigration detainees. Newcomers are often held in provincial jails and policies facilities, families are separated. *Canadian Press.* *http://www.macleans.ca/news/canada/red-cross-uncovers-numerous-problems-facing-immigration-detainees*

Canadian Race Relations Foundation. (2001). Racism in the Justice System. Retrieved December 31, 2006, from http://www.crr.ca/Load.do?section =26&subSection=37&id=242&type=2

Canadian Race Relations Foundation. (2005). Legalized Racism. Retrieved December 31, 2006, from http://www.crr.ca/Load.do?section=26&sub Section=37&id=245&type=2

Canadian Charter of Rights and Freedoms. Part I of the *Constitution Act, 1982*, Schedule B to the *Canada Act 1982* (U.K.), c.11.

Canadian Council for Refugees (April 2014). *E-Chronicle*, 9(1). Retrieved from http:// ccrweb.ca/en/chronicle-april-2014

CBC News. (January 6, 2015). Caring suspended 'until further notice' by Bill Blair. Retrieved fromhttp://www.cbc.ca/news/canada/toronto/carding-suspended-until-further-notice-by-bill-blair-1.2891741

Criminal Code of Canada (R.S.C., 1985, c. C-46)

Citizenship and Immigration Canada. *Criminal Justice and the Immigration and Refugee Protection Act:* Facts for Criminal Proceedings. Retrieved from http://www.cic.gc.ca/english/resources/publications/justice.asp

Commission des droits de la personne et des droits de la jeunesse (2011).

Commission on Systemic Racism in the Ontario Criminal Justice System. (1995). *Report of the Commission on Systemic Racism in the Ontario Criminal Justice System.* Toronto: Queen's Printer for Ontario.

Community Legal Education Ontario. (June 2008). *Criminal charges in Canada and your immigration status.* 2001(5). Retreived from http://www.cleo.on.ca/english/six/English/stat-en.pdf

Community Legal Education Ontario. (2008). *Do you want to sponsor your family to join you in Canada?* Retrieved from http://www.cleo.on.ca/english/six/English/spon-en.pdf

Chown Oved, M. (August 20, 2014). Canada deports people to wars, repressive regimes after rejecting their refugee claims, Canada sends people to places like Iraq and Afghanistan in spite of a formal ban on deportations to these countries. *The Star*, http://www.thestar.com/news/gta/2014/08/20/ canada_deports_people_to_wars_repressive_regimes.html

Chung Yan, M., & Chan, S. (2010). Are social workers ready to work with newcomers? *Canadian Social Work, 12* (1), 16-23.

Ditchburn, J. (2014). Reports contradict Stephen Harper's view on aboriginal women victims. *CBC News*. Retrieved from http://www.cbc.ca /news/aboriginal/reports-contradict-stephen-harper-s-view-on-aboriginal-women-victims-1.2754542

Friscolanti, M. (October 2, 2014). A free man on paper. Already under fire after an inmate's suicide, did the Canada Border Services Agency rush to release a critically ill inmate so he wouldn't die in custody? *Macleans*. Retrieved from http://www.macleans.ca/news/canada/a-free-man-on-paper

Galabuzi, G.E. (2006). *Canada's economic apartheid: The social exclusion of racialized groups in the new century*. Toronto: Canadian Scholars' Press Inc.

Government of Canada .(November 5, 2014). *Protecting Canadians from barbaric cultural practices*. News Release. Retrieved from http://news.gc.ca/web/article-en.do?nid=900399

Government of Canada. (2014). Bill C-24 - Strengthening Canadian Citizenship Act. Retrieved from http://news.gc.ca/web/article-en.do?nid=872659

Griffiths, C.T., & Verdun-Jones, S.N. (1989). *Canadian criminal justice*. Toronto: Butterworths Canada Ltd.

Henry, F., & Tator, C. (2010). *The colour of democracy: Racism in Canadian society* (4th ed.). Scarborough: Nelson Education.

Henry, F., Tator, C., Mattis, W., & Reez, T. (2000). *The colour of democracy: Racism in Canadian society*. Toronto: Harcourt Brace & Company.

Immigration and Refugee Protection Act, S.C. 2001, c. 27.

Ismaili, K. (2011). Immigration, immigrants, and the shifting dynamics of social exclusion in Canada. In Perry (Ed.), *Diversity, crime, and justice in Canada*. Oxford University Press.

Jiwani, J. (2011). Meditations of race and crime: Racializing crime, criminalizing race. *Diversity, crime and justice in Canada*. In Barbara Perry (Ed.). Oxford University Press.

Kanji, A. (February 14, 2014). Stripping convicted terrorists of their citizenship leaves all Canadians vulnerable. *National Post*. Retrieved from http://fullcomment.nationalpost.com/2014/02/14/azzeza-kanji-stripping-convicted-terrorists-of-their-citizenship-leaves-all-canadian-vulnerable

Kellough, G., & Wortley, S. (2001). Risk, moral assessment and the application of ball conditions in Canadian criminal courts. Paper presented at the 2001 International Meeting of the American Law and Society Association. July 2-7, Budapest, Hungary.

Mojab, S., & El-Kaseem, N. (2007). Cultural Relativism: Theoretical, Political, & Ideological Debates. *Canadian Muslim Women at the Crossroads: From Integration to Segregation?* Canadian Council of Muslim Women.

New Police Force (2012). Code of Practice of CRIME: Custody, Rights, Investigation, Management and Evidence. https://www.police.nsw.gov.au/__data/assets/pdf_file/0007/108808/Code_CRIME_-_January_2012.pdf

NSW Police Force Handbook .(August 2014). http://www.police.nsw.gov.au/__data/assets/pdf_file/0009/197469/NSW_Police_Handbook.pdf

Ontario Human Rights Code (1990). OHRCR.S.O., CHAPTER H.19.

Ontario Human Rights Commission (April 2014). *Speaking Out.* Submission of the Ontario Human Rights Commission to the Office of the Independent Police Review Director's Systemic Review of Ontario Provincial Police Practices for DNA Sampling. Retrieved from http://www.ohrc.on.ca/en/ohrc-submission-office-independent-police-review-director%E2%80%99s-systemic-review-opp-practices-dna

Pashang, S. (2003). The Canadian criminal justice system: An exploratory study of perceptions and experiences of Iranian men who have participated in partner abuse response programs. Research report, York University, Toronto.

Pratt, A. (2005). *Securing borders: Detention and deportation in Canada.* Vancouver: UBC Press.

Razack, S.H. (1998). *Looking white people in the eye: Gender, race and culture in courtrooms and classrooms.* Toronto: University of Toronto Press.

Skinnider, E. (August 2005). Some Recent Criminal Justice Reforms in Canada – Examples of Responding to Global and Domestic Pressures. Paper presented at The Canada China Procuratorate Reform Cooperation Programme Lecture Series I, Xi'an, Shaanxi Province and Lanzhou, Gansu Province. International Center for Criminal Law Reform and Criminal Justice Policy. http://icclr.law.ubc.ca/sites/icclr.law.ubc.ca/files/publications/pdfs/ES_Paper_Aug05_Conference.pdf

Statistiscs Canada. (2011). Immigration and Ethnocultural Diversity in Canada. National Household Survey. https://www12.statcan.gc.ca/nhs-enm/2011/as-sa/99-010-x/99-010-x2011001-eng.cfm#a2

Statistics Canada, Integrated Correctional Service Survey and the 2006

Census. (2006). Retreived from http://www.statcan.gc.ca/daily-quoti-dien/090721/t090721b1-eng.htm

The Toronto Star. (2002). There is no racism. We do not do racial profiling. *The Toronto Star*, October 19. A14.

Walia, H. (September 29, 2014). Death and despair in Canada's migrant dungeons. No One is Illegal-Vancouver, *rabble.ca*. Retrieved from http://rabble.ca/columnists/2014/09/death-and-despair-canadas-migrant-dungeons

Wortley, S. (2003). Hidden intersections: Research on race, crime, and criminal justice in Canada. *Canadian Ethnic Studies Journal*, *35*(3), 99–117.

Wortley, S., & Tanner, J. (2006). *Criminal organizations or social groups? An exploration of the myths and realities of youth gangs in Toronto*. Unpublished paper. Centre of Criminology, University of Toronto.

Yeager, M.G. (2002). Rehabilitating the criminality of immigrants under Section 19 of the Canadian Immigration Act. *International Migration Review, (*36)1, 178-192.

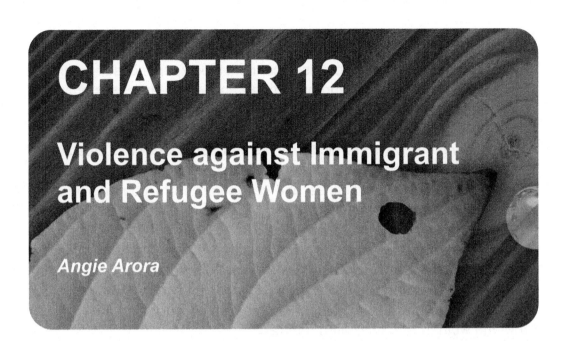

CHAPTER 12

Violence against Immigrant and Refugee Women

Angie Arora

Case Study

Mary, her children, and her husband have come to Canada as refugee claimants. Mary is being physically, verbally, and psychologically abused by her husband. She believes she cannot report the abuse because no one helped her in the past. She is in an unfamiliar country with a different language and legal system. Mary's husband uses this as a way to reinforce his power over Mary and their children. She feels as though she has no one to talk to and her husband constantly threatens that he can have her deported and keep the children with him. Sometimes he says, "I will fail with immigration and they will deport us. Then I will kill you and marry another woman who will look after the kids."

After reading the case study, reflect on the following questions:

1. What barriers are preventing Mary from experiencing safety in her life?
2. Of these barriers, which can be attributed to her status as a refugee woman?

Introduction

The purpose of this chapter is to connect the experiences of immigrant and refugee women who have been abused to larger systemic and structural barriers which can prevent women from achieving safety in their lives. Through the use of an anti-oppression framework, the chapter will explore various ways in which systems and institutions have created and perpetuated obstacles for immigrant and refugee women who have experienced abuse. Various practices and responses from communities and systems are discussed, including but not limited to the criminal legal system, child welfare services, and community services. Violence against women (VAW) is rooted in systemic gender inequalities, is reinforced by structural sexism, and represents serious violations of the human rights of women. The chapter concludes by exploring basic guidelines in supporting women who have been abused, including the importance of safety planning and providing women with facilitated referrals.

When you think of the term violence against women, what images and thoughts come to mind? *Domestic violence*, *wife assault*, or *family violence*? It is important to spend a few minutes looking at these terms as the language we use represents our values and beliefs. Furthermore, the values and beliefs that guide the language used often dictate societal responses – or lack of responses – to violence against women.

For example, *domestic violence* is commonly understood as abuse that occurs between partners in an intimate relationship. It has been criticized for not reflecting the gendered nature of violence in that there is no reference to the fact that the majority of people who are abused are women. Furthermore, the word *domestic* portrays an image that the issue is a private one, one that is better left to the couple to deal with, as opposed to a social issue that requires a societal response. *Wife assault* is a term that was commonly used in the formative stages of the women's movement in North America. It is now widely accepted that *wife* does not capture the range of women affected, as abuse occurs in same-sex, dating, common-law, and former relationships.

For the purposes of this chapter, the term *woman abuse* will be used. This term highlights the gender inequalities which can occur in intimate relationships and recognizes that abuse is the result of the unequal distribution of power between men and women, which can translate into abuse within the family. The gendered nature of abuse is apparent just below in the comparison of incidents of violence against women as compared to men;

this illustrates that abuse is primarily a gendered social issue. As compared to men, women are:

- Six times more likely to report being sexually assaulted;
- Five times more likely to report being strangled;
- Five times more likely to require medical attention, as a result of an assault;
- Three times more likely to be physically injured by an assault;
- More than twice as likely to report being beaten;
- Almost twice as likely to report being threatened with, or having a gun or knife used against them;
- Much more likely to fear for their lives, or be afraid for their children as a result of the violence;
- More likely to have sleeping problems, suffer depression or anxiety attacks, or have lowered self-esteem as a result of being abused; and
- More likely to report repeated victimization. (Department of Justice Canada 1999)

According to Nova Vita Domestic Violence Prevention Services (n.d.):

- One in four Canadian women suffers some form of abuse by her partner;
- Women are at the greatest risk of increased violence – or murder – at the hands of their partner during the time just before or after they leave an abusive relationship;
- Spousal homicide accounts for 15 percent of all homicides in Canada.
- A woman is nine times more likely to be murdered by an intimate partner than by a stranger; and
- Domestic abuse remains an immensely under-reported crime. It is estimated that just 25 percent of domestic violence incidents are reported.

Based on findings from the Ontario Domestic Violence Death Review Committee (2008):

- A total of 253 domestic-violence related deaths occurred in Ontario between 2002 to 2008.
- Of these deaths, 159 were women, 23 were children, and 71 were men.
- Of the 159 women who died, 96% were identified as victims. However, of the 71 men who died, 18% were identified as victims whereas 78% were identified as perpetrators.

It is important to remember that there are other components of women's identities which impact their lived realities, including their race, immigration status, age, ability, sexual orientation, and socio-economic status. While a woman may experience abuse as a result of gender inequity, she may also be experiencing compounding issues of racism, ageism, heterosexism, and/or classism. Using an integrated anti-oppression framework means understanding that a woman's combined identity will impact how she experiences abuse. A racialized immigrant woman living with a disability will experience abuse differently than a young lesbian woman. This does not mean that one woman experiences abuse more or worse than another, however, it does mean that while there are similarities in their experiences, there will also be key differences, because of their different identities. Understanding a woman's intersecting identities also enables us to better understand the resources and options at her disposal to respond to the abuse.

Structural Barriers Impacting Immigrant and Refugee Women

Some people may wonder why a woman stays in an abusive relationship and question why she does not end the suffering by leaving. However, by placing the responsibility on a woman who has experienced abuse, we inadvertently blame her.

> Blaming the victim is an easy way to avoid acknowledging and addressing the many barriers faced by women on a daily basis. The "blame the victim" mentality can seep into the minds of anyone, given the bombarding messages we continuously hear from powerful social outlets such as the media. (Ontario Association of Interval and Transitional Houses, 2010)

If we use terms like domestic violence, for example, we are portraying the message that violence against women is a private matter. By doing so, the social issue continues to be concealed from others and therefore is perpetuated. This belief not only silences women but also removes the possibility of creating community accountability to address and prevent the abuse. Instead of asking why some women remain in abusive relationships, start to explore the structural barriers that prevent women from living their lives free from violence. By shifting our attention to systemic barriers, we begin to focus on societal responses which cause and allow violence against women to continue to occur.

Radhia Jaaber and Shamita Das Dasgupta (2010) have coined the term *social risks* to highlight different factors that prevent immigrant women from securing the safety that they need and deserve. Social risks are practices and responses from communities and institutions which create barriers for women. These barriers can create further situations of marginalization for women. For example, the ways in which systems create barriers can make it more difficult for women to access required services, can place women at higher risk of experiencing homelessness and poverty, and may place her in a situation of living with precarious immigration status. Social risks may not appear visible to others because they are embedded into the way communities and institutions function, but they are very real to immigrant and refugee women experiencing abuse.

Figure 1 helps to contextualize some of the lived realities of immigrant and refugee women caused by structural inequalities. With the woman at its centre, the diagram depicts four examples of systems that women may interact with that can create barriers from living free from abuse: inaccessible services, the immigration and refugee system, the criminal and family law systems, and the child welfare system. Oppressive practices have become embedded into these structures resulting in systemic racism, sexism, ableism, heterosexism, ageism, and classism.

As a result of these systemic inequalities, women may experience social risks including poverty, homelessness, precarious immigration status, isolation, increased dependency on the person who has abused her, and family separation. The ordering of these risks does not indicate their importance. For example, for some women poverty and homelessness may pose the greatest risk if they decide to leave an abusive relationship. Other women may believe that it is their responsibility to keep the family united at all costs. Thus, to risk her beliefs is to potentially risk her family, her social network, and her community supports, risks that she may consider to be of greater consequence than the possible or probable risk of harm from remaining in the relationship.

The following section explores some of these barriers and social risks experienced by immigrant and refugee women in situations of woman abuse. Although these barriers are discussed separately, they are directly linked and often overlap to compound a woman's situation. By understanding the different social risks a woman may face, we move away from viewing her as a victim and instead as a woman with tremendous resilience and strength in surviving the many structural barriers she may encounter. Furthermore, our attention is drawn to structural changes required to eliminate barriers preventing women's safety.

Figure 1:
Structural Inequalities Faced by Immigrant and Refugee Women

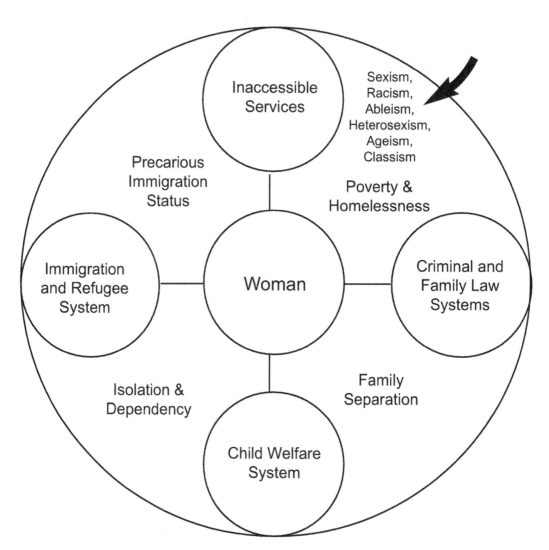

Lack of Accessible Services

Various community-based services exist to support women and children who have experienced abuse. While a range of initiatives exist to educate the public about violence against women in an effort to prevent abuse, the majority of supports that exist are meant to address abuse. Although services such as shelters, housing, and counselling are crucial to promoting women and children's safety, the root causes of abuse are not necessarily addressed by reactionary services.

One way in which services can become inaccessible to women is by not addressing her language needs. A language barrier is much more than not understanding a language. Without proficiency in the dominant language, women lose their confidence in negotiating with the world. They may be frightened that no one will understand them and that no one will help. They are left in the vulnerable position of being easily taken advantage of by family members and those in positions of power. For example, lack of English proficiency means that accessing mainstream systems becomes much more difficult (MacLeod & Shin, 1990). Without accessing mainstream systems, women are left in more vulnerable and vicarious situations of not understanding their rights and options.

It is important to understand that there are structural barriers which prevent women from learning English throughout their settlement experience. One must be eligible to access services such as Language Instruction for Newcomers (LINC); as the funder, Citizenship and Immigration Canada (CIC) has specific eligibility requirements. Because the program is geared towards permanent residents and Convention refugees, Canadian citizens, and temporary residents such as international students and temporary workers cannot access LINC programs. This creates a significant barrier for those who are trying to establish themselves in Canada but cannot simply because of the funder's eligibility restrictions. For example, a woman may be a Canadian citizen but has only resided in Canada for four years. Her partner may have kept her isolated for the first few years and now that she is trying to access services, she is turned away because she does not "qualify."

While various ethno-specific agencies exist to attempt to reduce barriers for women through multi-lingual services and by providing culturally appropriate support, this does not lessen the onus and responsibility for all organizations and institutions to be fully accessible. Furthermore, one cannot assume that a woman will feel more comfortable or able to access services in an ethno-specific agency, as she may prefer to disclose the abuse to those who do not identify with her cultural or faith-based community in order to protect her safety.

Many mothers may only be able to access language instruction services if child-minding or childcare services are in place. Accessing childcare, obtaining supports such as transportation, resources for classroom materials and activities like field trips that enhance the learning process will become much more difficult as these are services which have been affected as a result of the recent CIC funding cuts (Ontario Council of Agencies Serving

Immigrants [OCASI], 2011). Further, "clients, particularly women from low-income populations would be the most affected" (OCASI, 2011). A lack of a national affordable childcare strategy adds to the lack of accessibility for low-income women.

A woman may be coming from a country where services such as shelters and counselling do not exist or where communities have a different under-standing of the roles that systems play in their lives. This could include systems such as law enforcement and child welfare services. There are a number of factors that lead to women being unaware of social support serv-ices available in their community such as: the abusive partner purposefully keeping her isolated so that she cannot learn about her rights and options; outreach material created by non-profit organizations may be inaccessible to some women because of the language they are written in or the format they are created in; and women may not be informed about these services at ports of entry into Canada.

Let's use the example of a women's shelter. You are working with a woman who is in the process of deciding whether she will be leaving her abusive partner or not. In a conversation with the woman, you provide her with the name and contact information of local women's shelters. By assuming she knows what a shelter is, we perpetuate the cycle of creating inaccessible serv-ices. Providing sufficient information to women and creating room for dialogue so that they can make informed decisions is the first step, but it is also our responsibility to advocate for change within systems to promote barrier-free access to services. This discussion illustrates that it is not the person's lack of proficiency in a language which is the problem; it is the various systems that fail to address language barriers which is problematic.

Even if a woman is aware of what services exist, she may not fully under-stand what type of support she can expect. For example, women may not know what to expect from a counselling session or what life would be like living in a shelter. Simply providing a woman with a list of organizations' contact information is not a sufficient way to provide referrals. Providing more effective referrals will be discussed later in the chapter.

Even when women are aware of the services that exist and what type of support they can expect, studies have revealed that the social service sector's response to woman abuse does not provide a range of services that many women have stated are necessary (Arora, 2004). Many immigrant women have reported that services tend to take their strengths away from them rather than promote them, as their familial connections are not recog-nized (MacLeod & Shin, 1990). For example, many of the traditional services provided are available for women once they have left the relationship or work with her to help her leave. The focus tends to be on working with women individually to improve their immediate circumstances without always factoring in the value many women place on their families. The individual focus de-contextualizes the role of cultural, social, and other factors in immigrant women's lives (Weibe, 1985). Individual and confidential support to women is important; however, to rely solely on this as our response isolates women who decide to remain in the relationship but still want support for the entire family in order to end the abuse. Furthermore, the focus on individual, reactionary services restricts our ability to engage communities in concrete actions to prevent violence against women.

Immigration and Refugee System

Families enter Canada in different ways and these different ways carry their own potential barriers when it comes to woman abuse, particularly for women who have not obtained Canadian citizenship. While sponsors may be male or female, women who are sponsored by their male spouses may face particular vulnerabilities. As a sponsor, the spouse has power and control over the initial immigration procedures, making their partner, often the woman, vulnerable to control tactics (Côté, Kérisit, & Côté, 2001). As noted above, the sponsor may coerce the woman to remain in the abusive relationship, threatening that if she leaves, she will be deported from Canada.

It is imperative that service providers and women are aware of what may happen to a woman's immigration status should she decide to leave the abusive relationship. "A permanent resident or a Canadian citizen can leave an abusive partner and her status in Canada will not be affected by that decision alone" (Community Legal Education Ontario [CLEO], 2011). However, women who do not have permanent resident status or Canadian citizenship and decide to leave the abusive relationship can potentially face deportation: "If a spouse or partner withdraws the sponsorship or the couple separates while the sponsorship application is being processed, the woman risks being removed from Canada" (CLEO, 2011). If this sponsorship withdrawal occurs, the woman is no longer eligible to obtain permanent residency. Women in this situation are left in a very precarious situation in addition to potential deportation.

To complicate matters, CIC is attempting to crack down on "fraudulent marriages" by introducing "a 'conditional' permanent residence period of two years or more for sponsored spouses and partners who have been in a relationship of two years or less with their sponsors" (Canadian Council for Refugees, 2011). This regulatory amendment which took effect in October 2012 means that if a partner does not remain cohabitating with their spouse for at least two years after receiving their conditional permanent residence status, they are subject to losing their status and hence, could face deportation.

This places women who are sponsored in a very precarious situation as it allows the sponsor to use the partner's status as a tool for manipulation. While there is a process whereby sponsored spouses being abused can report the abuse and apply for an exemption, not all women know what their rights are, nor do they necessarily feel comfortable reporting the abuse to immigration authorities.

Women face barriers seeking support from the very system that granted them sponsored status. It is imperative that women obtain legal advice immediately as they may be able to apply to remain in Canada based on humanitarian and compassionate grounds. The immigration system can play an important role by providing women with information at ports of entry in accessible formats and different languages. Furthermore, the government must assume responsibility for ensuring that women who experience abuse are able to leave an abusive relationship without risking their immigration status.

They are not able to seek support from the very system that granted them sponsored status. It is imperative that women obtain legal advice immediately as they may be able to apply to remain in Canada based on humanitarian and compassionate grounds.

Women who live as refugee claimants also face particular risks. The abusive partner or family member may withhold her documents or give her wrong information as a way of exerting dominance over her. Think back to the case study at the beginning of this chapter when Mary's husband exerted his power over her with threats of deportation. According to Canadian refugee law, he does not have the power to have her deported. In this situation, because her husband was the main applicant of the refugee claim, Mary can request to have her application processed separately. The result of her claim will depend on the decision made through the refugee determination process, but it is important to note her husband does not have the power he claims to have.

What about women who are living as non-status or undocumented? According to the Rights of Non-Status Women Network, "Women without status face the same forms of gender based violence as all other women, but are at higher risk because of the vulnerable position they live in" (Rights of Non-Status Women Network, 2006). This is because they cannot call the police in an emergency without putting themselves at risk of deportation, as the police have the authority to arrest or detain someone on behalf of Citizenship and Immigration Canada. Furthermore, people who are non-status or undocumented cannot easily access medical services; therefore, they face particular vulnerabilities if experiencing physical or sexual abuse.

Child Welfare Services

Children's Aid Societies (CAS), formerly known as Family and Children's Services, are child welfare agencies mandated by the government of Ontario to protect children from harm by preventing abuse and neglect, improving child safety, maintaining children's health and well-being, and supporting families to care for children (Ontario Association of Children's Aid Societies [OACAS], 2010). Children's Aid Societies investigate and assess suspected abuse and neglect of children and, if necessary, the management of a case when a child is taken from a family and placed in care. CAS workers follow standards and guidelines in order to determine the kind of support required to keep children safe in situations of abuse, neglect, or possible harm.

An abusive partner may threaten a woman with contacting CAS to report her as a neglectful mother and may threaten to gain full custody of the children. Furthermore, calling the police in situations of woman abuse will also result in child welfare authorities being contacted. These situations can induce significant fear in women, especially if she is living with precarious immigration status or if she does not fully understand her rights and the role of CAS: "The predominant fear any woman feels regarding child welfare services is the prospect of losing custody of her children" (OCASI, 2010, Module 1) and as a result, may do everything in her power to ensure authorities do not find out about the abuse.

Some women may believe that it is better for their children to remain in a home where the parents are living together than apart, which is an example of women prioritizing the safety and well-being of their children over their own (Jaaber & Das Dasgupta, 2010). The intention might be to prevent backlash and stigmatization related to divorce on the part of family and the wider community in Canada and possibly on the part of those in her home country as well. Some women may also remain in the relationship because divorce legislation in Canadian family law differs from her cultural and/or religious beliefs. Some religions do not recognize divorce according to Canadian law and may prevent women who have a civil divorce from participating in their religious community or from remarrying in a religious ceremony (Family Law Education for Women [FLEW], 2011).

Some women may believe it is better for her and the children to remain in the relationship so that she does not have to care for the children as a single mother. When a woman has limited personal and financial resources, limited access to subsidized childcare, and is faced with extremely low rates of social assistance, she may feel that she cannot afford to leave an abusive situation: "The sudden loss of financial support leaves many women unprepared for managing households, rent, and mortgages on their own" (Singh, 2010, p. 39).

For immigrant women, the fear of living in poverty is a valid one. New immigrant women experiencing abuse may have even fewer options for leaving an abusive relationship if they are financially dependent on their male relative sponsors in Canada. It is important to note that women's vulnerability to poverty is caused by structural factors. For example, new immigrant women between the ages of 25 to 44 with a university degree and who worked year round, full-time earned on average $14,000.00 less than Canadian-born women in 1995 (Canadian Research Institute for the Advancement of Women [CRIAW], 2005). This is because of overt racism in the workplace including discriminatory hiring practices, but also because the credentials and experience of immigrant women are not recognized. Clearly, education does not reduce the income gap between immigrant women and Canadian-born women.

Woman abuse is a significant contributor to homelessness among women, and as such the experience of abuse is important to understanding homelessness among immigrant and refugee women. Due to a sudden need to leave the abuser, women may find themselves in precarious living situations. Living in inadequate, unsafe, or temporary conditions may lead a woman to return to the abusive situation. Further, "Many shelters and drop-in centres are not accessible for immigrants and refugees due to language barriers and lack of culturally appropriate services" (Shirwadkar, 2004).

Criminal Legal System

As with the involvement of child welfare authorities, immigrant women who are experiencing abuse face specific barriers in contacting the police. The Canadian criminal justice system may be viewed as a potential interference to their way of life, one that threatens family, cultural, and religious values (Baobaid, 2002) Women may internalize the belief that what happens in the family, should stay within the family. The thought of involving external parties may not be seen or experienced as a safe option.

A woman may call the police with the intention of achieving interim safety; however, she may not know what will happen when the police arrive, nor might she realize that by calling the police, she may become involved in a system that will create other challenges in her life. Ontario has had a mandatory arrest policy around physical abuse of women since 1983. This means that when the police arrive, the laying of criminal charges is in the hands of the police, not the woman. The reason behind the policy was to remove the woman's burden of having to choose whether or not charges should be laid, as she may be coerced by the abuser to retract and say that nothing happened. Once charges are laid, the case moves into the hands of the Domestic Violence Courts (DVCs).

DVC staff including police, Crown attorneys, the Victim/Witness Assistance Program (V/WAP), probation and parole, and the Partner Assault Response (PAR) program receives training in issues of woman abuse. The DVC program uses case management procedures to promote a co-ordinated approach to prosecution and to promote early intervention.

However, "whether women are harmed or helped by the police and courts is largely contingent on their social positioning as white or racialized, citizens or immigrants, middle class or poor" (Singh, 2010, p. 38). Immigrant and refugee women or women whose partners are living with precarious immigration status face the possibility of detention and/or deportation, depending on the circumstances, something women may not realize until after contacting the police. This is not to suggest that women should or should not call the police, but rather it points to a systemic flaw which puts women at further risk of marginalization and vulnerability. By becoming involved with a system that is meant to help her, she may end up in a situation which she defines as worse than before. Even if her immigration status or that of her partner's is not in jeopardy, women without familial or social networks face the possibility of isolation if their partners are arrested and removed from the home (Singh, 2010).

Communities that have had negative experiences with police in their home countries, involving such things as torture, persecution, and murder, might carry these memories with them during their settlement process in Canada. It is common for women to experience strong feelings of guilt if they call police (Rafiq, 1991) because of the memories police involvement may trigger and also because of the fear of what will happen next. She is less likely to contact the police if she or members of her family view them as an oppressive institution.

Furthermore, immigrant communities have continued to experience discriminative and racist practices on the part of law enforcement in North America (Jaaber & Das Dasgupta, 2010). Women may hesitate to contact the police to avoid promoting the existing stereotype that racialized communities are prone to violence. The decision not to contact the police is a way of protecting their partners from furthering the racism, stigmatization and criminalization that already afflicts racialized communities.

While the criminal legal system's response is one way to hold perpetrators accountable for abuse, this cannot be the only method used to promote accountability. It is necessary to explore the different ways in which other systems and communities can also help hold abusers socially responsible, with the ultimate goal being to prevent further abuse. Clearly, the criminal legal system can only be one part of the solution, as it alone has not been able to eradicate woman abuse and in some situations can create further barriers for women.

Role of Family and Community

"Family is often the one stabilizing force that enables immigrants to weather the turbulent process of migration" (Shetty & Kaguyutan, 2002, p. 2). There are many challenges associated with the settlement process, but the family support system in particular can help newcomers navigate their new realities. In situations of abuse, partners may isolate women from her family and friends. Furthermore, if family and friends are aware of the abuse, they may blame the woman for staying in the relationship. Other women may experience pressure from their families and communities if they decide to leave the relationship, being blamed for "breaking up" the family unit. "Ultimately, the stigma associated with abuse results in a woman not talking to others about her situation and to a loss of self-esteem, described by many women as a feeling of emptiness, worthlessness, and emotional paralysis" (Horrill & Berman, 2004 p. 5).

The barriers or social risks just described illustrate how issues impacting women are rooted in much broader systems. Therefore, the issue is not a private or familial one, but one requiring both a community and societal response.

Suggestions for Social Service Workers

The barriers that immigrant and refugee women may experience to achieving safety impact the potential roles that social service workers will assume when supporting women. The following section is provides a brief introduction to some of the things to consider when supporting a woman who is experiencing abuse.

Dealing with Disclosures

Not all women will tell you that they are experiencing abuse. Thinking back to the concept of *social risks* will remind you of the many barriers that may prevent a woman from feeling safe to do so. It is through conversation and observation that we are more likely to be able to determine the likelihood that she is experiencing abuse, including various, often interrelated forms, such as physical, sexual, emotional, verbal, psychological, spiritual or financial abuse.

When engaged in a conversation with the woman, there may be signs and indicators of woman abuse through learning about the woman's partner. For example, she might reveal that her partner:

- Confines her or forces her to stay at home;
- Forces her to have unwanted sexual activity;
- Humiliates and criticizes her repeatedly in private or in public;
- Undermines her self-confidence; and/or
- Denies her access to her own money.

These observations create an entry point for more specific conversations with the woman about potential abuse.

You may not know what to say or do when a woman discloses that she is experiencing abuse. The following list provides some guidelines on how to ensure your response to women who do disclose is both sensitive and appropriate:

- Assure her that you believe her story.
- Listen and let her talk about her feelings.
- Do not judge or give advice. Talk to her about her options.
- Physical safety is the first priority. If you believe she is in danger, tell her. Help her plan an emergency exit.
- Respect her right to confidentiality.
- Let her know you care and want to help.
- Allow her to feel the way she does and support her decisions. Let her talk about the caring aspects of the relationship as well. Don't try to diminish her feelings about her partner. Don't criticize her for staying with him, but share information on how abuse increases over time without intervention.

- Give clear messages, including:
  1. Violence is never okay or justifiable.
  2. Her safety and her children's safety are always the most important issues.
  3. Woman abuse is a crime.
  4. She does not cause the abuse.
  5. She is not to blame for her partner's behaviour.
  6. She cannot change her partner's behaviour.
  7. Apologies and promises will not end the violence.
  8. She is not alone.
  9. She is not crazy.
  10. Abuse is not loss of control, it is a means of control.

- Discuss how the violence affects the children.
- Be encouraged that every time she reaches out for help she is gaining the emotional strength needed to make effective decisions. She may be too fearful and immobilized or confused to take any step immediately.
- Although police can be asked to accompany a woman going back home to retrieve personal belongings, encourage her to be prepared for the possibility of leaving home in a hurry. She should have necessary documents or photocopies ready, as well as important items such as:
  11. credit cards, cash, bank books
  12. passport, birth certificates, citizenship papers
  13. house keys
  14. medications
  15. children's favourite toy, clothing, etc.

- An abused woman needs our support and encouragement in order to make choices that are right for her. However, there are some forms of advice that are not useful and even dangerous for her to hear:
  16. Don't tell her what to do, when to leave or when not to leave.
  17. Don't tell her to go back to the situation and try a little harder.
  18. Don't rescue her by trying to find quick solutions.
  19. Don't suggest you try to talk to her partner to straighten things out.
  20. Don't place yourself in danger by confronting the abusive man.
  21. Don't tell her she should stay for the sake of the children. Springtide Resources (2000)

Pay specific attention to the support system a woman does or does not have in her life. If she reveals that she has no support network outside her home, have a conversation about creative ways in which she may be able to create one in a safe way. The fact that she is able to be having a conversation with you is a great starting point to validate her efforts. Ask her if there are things she is able to do without her partner (e.g., shopping, medical appointments, visiting other family or friends) and if these present opportunities for her to get the social support she is looking for. For example, would she be able to attend a LINC class? Would she be able to access parenting-related resources with her children? These may present opportunities for her to begin to receive the social support she is looking for. It is important to have a conversation about her safety when discussing these options.

Safety Planning

The concept of social risks reminds us to keep an open and flexible definition of safety, as what constitutes barriers to safety for one woman may vary for the next. One aspect of safety includes a woman and her children's physical well-being. It is important to work with a woman to assess her safety and plan for ways to increase her physical safety, whether she is in the abusive relationship, plans to leave the relationship, or has left the relationship.

There are many safety plans which have been created by community groups which you can use when supporting women. The purpose of this plan is to identify different ways a woman can increase her safety, including identifying steps to prevent and/or deal with the possibility of further abuse. Spend some time reviewing safety plans which have been created by women's groups.[1]

Facilitated Referrals

Depending on the mandate of the organization you are working in and your role as a worker, you may or may not be in a position to provide women with the ongoing support needed to address her needs and goals. In the event that you need to refer a woman to other community resources, it is important to provide a *facilitated* referral; this means providing a woman with more than just a telephone number. The following list provides general guidelines to follow when making a referral to a woman who you suspect or know has experienced abuse:

- Listen to her and validate her. It is best to have only one person take the responsibility of being with her. This way, she does not have to repeat her story and we show respect for her and her story by maintaining confidentiality.

- Do not make assumptions of what services will work best for her. This decision should be made in conjunction with the woman. For example, just because a woman identifies as Portuguese, does not necessarily mean she wants to be referred to an organization serving primarily people from Portuguese communities for fear of losing confidentiality. Respect her choices.

- Build partnerships with agencies so that you can refer a woman to a specific worker at an agency. For example, you do not want a woman to call a generic number and face a complicated automated system which may prevent her from reaching a person that may be able to provide her support.

- Ensure the woman understands the service you are referring her to. For example, she may not be familiar with the concept of a shelter or counselling. In order for you to fully explain what the service encompasses, be sure you fully understand it first.

- Follow up with the woman (when possible) to see if she contacted the agency.

- Offer her suggestions, information and not advice. It is important that we respect women's choice even if they might differ from our personal beliefs.

- When in doubt of referral sources, call the Assaulted Women's Helpline. This is a 24 hours a day, 7 days a week telephone crisis line for women in Ontario. A telephone counsellor provides immediate crisis counselling, safety planning, as well as referrals to women. Service is provided in up to 154 languages. Deaf and hard of hearing women are served through the TTY line.

Conclusion

This chapter highlighted the structural barriers which impact immigrant and refugee women who have experienced abuse. Systems which have been developed to support women such as the criminal legal system, child welfare services and community services, create and perpetuate sexism and racialization which prevent women from achieving safety in their lives. Having an understanding of these issues better allows social service workers to understand woman abuse as a social issue, not a private or familial matter, therefore requiring a coordinated, societal response. The chapter concluded with introductory guidelines on how to effectively support women who have experienced abuse by exploring safety planning with a woman and providing her with facilitated referrals.

Develop your knowledge – Ask yourself

For each of the following scenarios, determine what social risks the woman is experiencing and reflect on how these barriers may affect her from living a life free from abuse.

1. Julia is a woman who has been experiencing physical, emotional and sexual abuse by her common-law partner for over two years. While she has considered calling the police, she fears that by calling, the Children's Aid Society of Toronto may become involved. One day, she receives a call from her child's school. The teacher tells Julia that her daughter informed the teacher that her "daddy hits her mommy when he gets mad." The teacher sets up a meeting with the parents to discuss the issue. Julia is scared and does not know what to do.

2. Kate is a recent newcomer to Canada. She and her parents have been sponsored in-land by her husband. Kate has experienced severe financial and verbal abuse from her husband. She discloses the abuse to her pastor and is told that it is her duty as a wife to make the marriage work. When Kate decides to talk to her parents, they say the abuse is not right, but that without him, they will not financially survive in Canada. Kate is confused and does not know what to do.

Develop your knowledge – Helpful Weblinks

The purpose of this chapter was to provide introductory information about how abuse affects immigrant and refugee women as well as some things to think about when supporting women. To deepen your understanding of the issue, the following are some helpful websites to support your learning.

- **BOOST: Child Abuse Prevention and Intervention**
  http://www.boostforkids.org/
- **Center for Women's Global Leadership**
  http://www.cwgl.rutgers.edu/
- **Centre for Children and Families in the Justice System**
  http://www.lfcc.on.ca/
- **Centre for Research and Education on Violence Against Women and Children**
  http://www.crvawc.ca/index.htm
- **Family Law Education for Women**
  http://www.onefamilylaw.ca/
- **INCITE! Women of Colour Against Violence**
  http://www.incite-national.org/
- **Neighbours, Friends and Families**
  http://www.neighboursfriendsandfamilies.ca/
- **Ontario Council of Agencies Serving Immigrants: Settlement Workers Against Violence Everywhere (SWAVE)**
  http://moresettlement.org/swave/
- **Peel Committee Against Woman Abuse**
  http://www.pcawa.org/wap3.php
- **Springtide Resources: Ending Violence against Women**
  http://www.springtideresources.org
- **The Metropolitan Action Committee on Violence Against Women and Children (METRAC)**
  http://www.metrac.org/
- **Woman Abuse Affects Our Children**
  http://resources.curriculum.org/womanabuse/
- **Woman Abuse Council of Toronto**
  http://www.womanabuse.ca/
- **Your Legal Rights**
  http://yourlegalrights.on.ca/

Note

[1] See, e.g., Peel Committee Against Woman Abuse (PCAWA) (2005).

References

Arora, A. (2004). *Experiences of front-line shelter workers in providing services to immigrant women impacted by family violence.* Retrieved from http://www.womanabuse.ca/ExperiencesofFrontlineWorkers.pdf

Baobaid, M. (2002). *Access to women abuse services by Arab-speaking women in London, Ontario: Background investigation and recommendations for further research and community outreach.* Retrieved from http://www.crvawc.ca/documents/Final-AccesstoWomenAbuse Servicesb-yArabSpeakingMuslimWomeninLondon_001.pdf

Canadian Council for Refugees (CCR). (2011). *Proposed "conditional permanent residence" for sponsored spouses.* Retrieved from http://ccrweb.ca/files/comments_conditional_residence_proposal.pdf

Community Legal Education Ontario (CLEO). (2011). *Immigrant women and domestic violence.* Retrieved fromhttp://www.cleo.on.ca /english/pub/onpub/PDF/immigration/immwomdv.pdf

Côté, A., Kérisit, M., & Côté, M. (2001). *Sponsorship ... for better or for worse: The impact of sponsorship on the equality rights of immigrant women.* Ottawa: Status of Women Canada.

Family Law Education for Women (FLEW). (2011). *Marriage and divorce.* Retrieved from http://www.onefamilylaw.ca/en/marriage

Morris, M., & Gonsalves, T. (2005). *Women and poverty* (3rd ed.). Canadian Research Institute for the Advancement of Women. Retrieved from http://criaw-icref.ca/WomenAndPoverty

Department of Justice Canada. (1999). *Spousal abuse: A fact sheet. General social survey on victimization.* Retrieved from http://www. phac-aspc.gc.ca/ncfv-cnivf/publications/fvfvirprt-eng.php

Horrill, K. E., & Berman, H. (2004). *Getting out and staying out: Issues surrounding a woman's ability to remain out of an abusive relationship.* Centre for Research on Violence Against Women and Children. Retrieved from http://www.crvawc.ca/documents/FinalGettingOutandStayingOutIssues-SurroundingaWomansAbilitytoRemainOutofanAbusiveRelati_000.pdf

Jaaber, R., & Das Dasgupta, S. (2010). *Assessing social risks of battered women.* Retrieved from http://praxisinternational.org/praxis_lib_ advocacy.aspx

MacLeod, L., & Shin, M. Y. (1990). *Isolated, afraid and forgotten: The service delivery needs and realities of immigrant and refugee women who are battered.* Ottawa: National Clearinghouse on Family Violence: Health and Welfare Canada.

Morris, M., & Gonsalves, T. (2005). *Women and poverty* (3rd ed.). Canadian Research Institute for the Advancement of Women (CRIAW). Retrieved from http://criaw-icref.ca/WomenAndPoverty

Nova Vita Domestic Violence Prevention Services. (2010). *What is abuse.* Retrieved from http://www.novavita.org/statistics.php

Ontario Association of Children's Aid Societies (OACAS). (2010). *Child welfare.* Retrieved from http://www.oacas.org/childwelfare/index.htm

Ontario Association of Interval and Transitional Houses (OAITH). (2010). *A guide to critical reflection: Understanding and using a feminist anti-oppression framework*. Toronto.

Ontario Council of Agencies Serving Immigrants (OCASI). (2010). *Understanding and responding to woman abuse in immigrant and refugee communities: eLearning for settlement workers*. Toronto.

Ontario Council of Agencies Serving Immigrants (OCASI). (2011). *Background information on CIC cuts*. Retrieved from http://www.ocasi. org/downloads/OCASI_CIC_Cuts_Backgrounder.pdf

Peel Committee Against Woman Abuse. (2005). *Creating a safety plan.* Retrieved from http://www.pcawa.org/rp1.php

Ontario Domestic Violence Death Review Committee. (2008). Annual report to the Chief Coroner. Toronto, ON: Office of the Chief Coroner.

Rafiq, F. (1991). *Towards equal access: A handbook for service providers working with immigrant women survivors of wife assault*. Ottawa: Immigrant and Visible Minority Women Against Abuse.

Rights of Non-Status Women Network. (2006). *Non-status women in Canada fact sheet*. Retrieved from http://www.owjn.org/owjn_ 2009/index.php?option=com_content&view=article&id=195&Itemid=67.

Shetty, S., & Kaguyutan, J. (2002). *Immigrant victims of domestic violence: Cultural challenges and available legal protections*. Retrieved from http://www.vaw net.org/applied-research-papers/print document.php?doc_id=384.

Shirwadkar, S. (2004). Canadian domestic violence policy and Indian immigrant women. *Violence Against Women, 10*(8), 860–79.

Singh, R.D. (2010). In between the system and the margins: Community organizations, mandatory charging and immigrant victims of abuse. *Canadian Journal of Sociology, 35*(1): 31–62.

Springtide Resources. (2000). *Friends and family: How to help an assaulted woman*. Retrieved from http://www.springtideresources. org/resources/publications.cfm

Weibe, K. (1985). *Violence against women and children: An overview for community workers*. (2nd ed.). Vancouver: Women Against Violence Against Women/Rape Crisis Centre.

PART 6

HOUSING NEEDS OF IMMIGRANTS

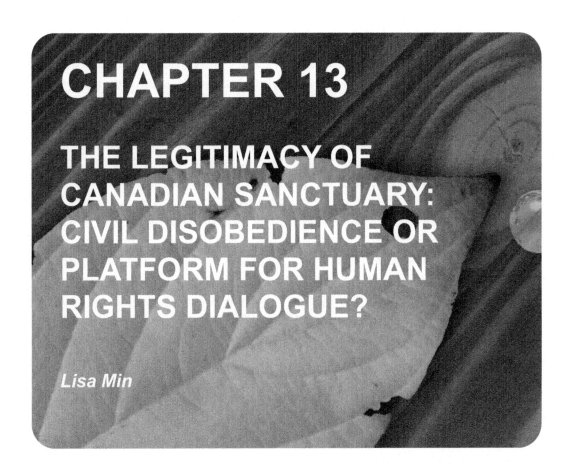

CHAPTER 13

THE LEGITIMACY OF CANADIAN SANCTUARY: CIVIL DISOBEDIENCE OR PLATFORM FOR HUMAN RIGHTS DIALOGUE?

Lisa Min

Introduction

The term "sanctuary" denotes a holy place in which a fugitive, debtor, or criminal is entitled to immunity from his or her pursuer. An extensive historical tradition of sanctuary in offering asylum dates back to the Old Testament (the Hebrew Tanakh); there, God directed Moses to establish "six cities of refuge ... for the Israelites, for the resident or transient alien among them, so that anyone who kills a person without intent may flee there" (United Church of Canada, 2004). These inviolable sites of refuge also trace their roots to ancient Greek and Roman law, medieval European law, and Catholic canon law (Rehaag, 2009). By the Middle Ages, the practice of sanctuary gradually receded in Europe in the face of the growing power of the modern nation-state, and it was formally abolished in Britain by statute in 1624 (Lippert, 2006). Although whether or not sanctuary practices withered completely in Western societies remains a contested issue, it is clear that the sanctuary tradition began to undergo a revival in recent years (Lippert, 2005).

Perhaps the most well-known resurgence of sanctuary activities in a national context, the United States sanctuary movement that commenced in the 1980s has sparked considerable scholarly attention (Lippert & Rehaag, 2009). Established by congregations, secular community members, and human rights activists across the United States as a form of "civil initiative," the sanctuary movement responded to the plight of failed refugee claimants from El Salvador and Guatemala who were fleeing political oppression in Central America (Stastny, 1989). Despite the fact that extended accounts of sanctuary outside the U.S. context have not been documented, contemporary sanctuary is not an exclusively U.S.-based phenomenon. Indeed, throughout the 1980s and 1990s, sanctuary incidents were reported in France, Germany, Norway, Belgium, the Netherlands, Switzerland, and Australia. Furthermore, sanctuary incidents in Canada have become increasingly prevalent in the past two decades, incidents in which churches across Canada have provided sanctuary to unsuccessful refugee claimants subject to deportation orders who have exhausted all opportunities for judicially reviewing their initial refugee determinations. Indeed, the 34th General Council of the United Church of Canada, the largest Protestant denomination in the country, comprised of 3,677 congregations, endorsed "the moral right and responsibility of congregations to provide sanctuary to legitimate refugee claimants who have been denied refugee status" (Lippert, 2005). Although co-operation among religious agents is an identifying characteristic of every sanctuary incident, sanctuary activists are not limited to members of the clergy and congregations. Indeed, many who provide material support and advocate for the legal rights of the migrants include community members, human rights organizations, legal professionals, and student volunteers having no religious affiliation.

Under section 6(1) of the *Canadian Charter of Rights and Freedoms*, non-citizens do not have an unqualified right to enter or remain in Canada. Moreover, an enforceable removal order is made with respect to a claimant whose claim for refugee protection has been rejected by the Refugee Protection Division (RPD) of the Immigration and Refugee Board (IRB). As a result of the constraint of assessing refugee claims against the rigid definition of a Convention refugee under the *Immigration and Refugee Protection Act*, S.C. 2001 (hereafter, the Act), achieving a balance between the opposing imperatives of protecting the integrity of Canada's official refugee determination system and respecting the fundamental human rights of refugees has become progressively difficult. By observing the trajectory of the Canadian sanctuary discourse, this chapter argues that sanctuary practices that connote non-compliance with Canadian state law is not tantamount to illegal acts of civil disobedience that purports to threaten the parameters of state authority. Through a close analysis of the relevant provisions of the Act, one may view sanctuary practices as a means to consolidate Canada's commitments toward refugees under domestic and international law, thereby respecting the rule of law. Specifically, it is plausible to analyse the legitimacy of Canadian church sanctuary practices by situating sanctuary incidents within two broad legal narratives: a juxtaposition of domestic and international law.

Canadian Sanctuary Incidents

Sanctuary in Canada as Isolated Local Incidents

Although no study has sought to produce a comprehensive portrait of sanctuary practices in Canada in the same way accounts of sanctuary have been documented in the U.S. context, we do know that sanctuary incidents have become more prevalent in Canada (Lippert, 2005). In many central ways, sanctuary incidents in Canada share similarities with the United States sanctuary movement that proliferated in the late 1980s. First, in many cases, individuals who take sanctuary inside a church are failed refugee claimants without legal status in Canada who wish to avoid or delay their imminent arrest and deportation. Secondly, the majority of migrants who take sanctuary have exhausted all legal avenues provided for in the official refugee determination process. Thirdly, the Act explicitly prohibits "aiding" and "abetting" foreign nationals to unlawfully remain in Canada in violation of their legal orders. Although sanctuary practices in both the United States and Canada are rooted in humanitarian assistance and charity as a direct challenge to the state's shortcomings in attending to the legitimate needs of refugee claimants, Canadian church sanctuary may also be distinguished from the United States sanctuary movement in several ways. For example, in contrast to the nationwide U.S. movement that was strongly affiliated with the repressive regimes in El Salvador and Guatemala and the foreign policy of the U.S. government in Central America, Canadian sanctuary practices constitute less a national social movement and more an array of regional grassroots efforts that are geographically dispersed. Furthermore, although the United Church of Canada has developed guidelines for local congregations who are considering offering sanctuary, there have not been sustained efforts to organize a broad network of sanctuaries either through regional congregations or in conjunction with other denominations. Indeed, there has only been minor communication among sanctuary providers across incidents, and only one congregation has been involved in more than one sanctuary incident (Lippert, 2005). Thus, Canadian sanctuary incidents occur almost exclusively at a local, community level rather than on a national or regional basis.

Attributes and Prevalence of Canadian Sanctuary Practices

The "Lippert Study" was an empirical study of Canadian sanctuary practices that identified 36 church sanctuary incidents between 1983 and 2003 (Rehaag, 2009). Since the initial study, 14 subsequent Canadian sanctuary incidents have been reported (Lippert, 2009). A televised press conference held on January 20, 1984, in which an ecumenical group of church officials pronounced Montreal's St. Andrew's United Church a sanctuary on behalf of a Guatemalan migrant who began taking shelter inside an unknown church building in December 1983, marked the first documented instance of Canadian church sanctuary. Significantly, within hours of the spectacle generated by the mass media, Canada's Citizenship and Immigration Minister declared a temporary suspension on all deportations to Guatemala and spared the publicized sanctuary providers legal prosecution (Lippert, 2006). Although the Lippert Study identified only one other sanctuary incident in the 1980s, sanctuary became more widespread in the ensuing decades. Indeed, 24 of the 36 sanctuary incidents occurred between 1998 and 2003 (Lippert, 2005). Seven incidents were identified in 2003, the most in any given year since 1983 (Lippert, 2006). Furthermore, the duration of sanctuary incidents has increased significantly since the first case was documented. In the 1980s, the average duration of stay was 19 days, but between 1990 and 1994, the average duration increased to 113 days. In the next five-year period the average was 183 days, and the number increased to 313 days between 2000 and 2004. Most significantly, the average length of time spent in a sanctuary increased to 686 days between 2005 and 2009, which is more than twice the average incident duration in the preceding five-year period and almost four times the average duration of stay in the late 1990s (Lippert, 2009).

All but two sanctuary incidents documented to date involved failed refugee claimants facing deportation orders who alleged that they continued to face serious risks of persecution in their home countries (Rehaag, 2009). Although the illegal entrance and transportation of Central American refugees was a common practice within the United States sanctuary movement, the migrants in all 36 incidents identified in the initial Lippert Study entered Canada lawfully to apply for formal legal status through the official refugee determination process. More than 60 percent of the migrants applied for leave for judicial review to the Federal Court, and 74 percent applied for Humanitarian & Compassionate considerations before requesting sanctuary (Lippert, 2005). Therefore, as stated previously, the majority of migrants turned to church assistance only after they had exhausted all legal options for reviewing their negative refugee determinations.

The denominations of churches that offered sanctuary have been almost exclusively Christian, ranging from the traditionally conservative (Baptist and Pentecostal), liberal (Unitarian), hierarchy-structured (Roman Catholic and Anglican), to decentralized (United) (Lippert, 2005). In two instances, migrants were granted sanctuary inside a Sikh and a Hindu temple (Lippert, 2009). Sanctuary incidents have been reported in sixteen cities across seven provinces, although a disproportionate number of incidents occurred in larger cities such as Montreal, Vancouver, Winnipeg, Calgary, and Toronto (Lippert, 2005). The concentration of sanctuary sites in these cities reflects the fact that larger cities are where regular refugee determination hearings take place whose outcomes may produce an adverse finding against the refugee claimant, and so leading to the issuance of a deportation order. Although cooperation among religious agents is an identifying characteristic of every sanctuary incident, sanctuary activists are not limited to members of the clergy and congregations. Many who provide material support and advocate for the legal rights of the migrants include community members, human rights organizations, legal professionals, and student volunteers with no religious affiliation (Lippert, 2005). Indeed, 27 incidents documented in the initial Lippert Study were initiated by non-secular individuals who made inquiry at local congregations about the possibility of requesting sanctuary (Lippert, 2006).

The 50 Canadian sanctuary incidents reported to date encompass adult refugee claimants between the ages of 18 and 71 from 28 diverse nationalities, including individuals from Guatemala, Chile, Peru, Colombia, Turkey, Iran, China, Bangladesh, Fiji, Poland, Romania, Serbia, Zimbabwe, Algeria, Nigeria, and Somalia (Lippert, 2005). A total of 288 migrants have taken sanctuary in Canada, with a single sanctuary incident comprising between one and seven individuals, reflecting the fact that many migrants took sanctuary as family units. 36 percent of incidents involved males only, and 14 percent involved female migrants exclusively (Lippert, 2009). The average age of an independent adult migrant at the time of their entry inside a church was 37, which represented 23 of 50 sanctuary incidents. The remaining incidents involved migrants with accompanying children, with the overall average age of migrants being 22 (Lippert, 2005).

Legal Outcomes

All documented instances of sanctuary practice have ultimately delayed arrest and deportation of the migrants concerned (Rehaag, 2009). Indeed, during the 20-year period of the Lippert Study, the police and immigration authorities refrained from entering a church to arrest those granted sanctuary for the purpose of enforcing federal law (Lippert, 2005). A majority of the incidents also yielded positive legal outcomes for the migrants in securing immigration status or an otherwise long-term permission to stay in Canada. Specifically, 33 of the 50 incidents accrued permanent legal status or a long-term ministerial grant to remain in Canada. In 12 incidents, the migrants either exited the church to "go underground" and live in concealment or surrendered to immigration authorities and were consequently deported. The outcome was unknown or undecided in the remaining five incidents (Lippert, 2009).

Although a number of migrants in sanctuary were not ultimately able to attain legal status to remain in the country, Canadian sanctuary incidents is an exceptional phenomenon in light of the fact that 90 percent of applications for leave for judicial review to the Federal Court are refused, and the success rate in judicial reviews of negative refugee determinations is merely two percent (Rehaag, 2009). The positive outcome for 66 percent of the migrants who took shelter inside the spatial confines of a church building have significant implications for how the exercise of power is conceptualized within state-based legal systems, as merely acceding to requests for sanctuary does not diminish the legal authority of government officials to enforce removal orders against claimants. Moreover, a majority of clergy members decided to keep church doors unlocked at all times, so it is incorrect to assert that all churches physically impede the enforcement of state immigration and refugee law (Lippert, 2006).

Forms of Power Emanating from Church Sanctuary

Sovereign Power

A nation-state's authority to enact explicit requirements, conditions, and prohibitions in respect of the entry of foreign nationals creates a strong demarcation between included and excluded members of the polity, which has been traditionally viewed as an integral aspect of its sovereignty

(Cunningham, 1998). Under subsection 6(1) of the Charter, only Canadian citizens are conferred the unqualified right to enter or remain in Canada. Accordingly, Parliament has enacted legislation prescribing the conditions under which non-citizens will be permitted to enter and remain in Canada. An enforceable removal order is issued with respect to a claimant whose claim for refugee protection has been rejected by PRD if there is no right to appeal, an appeal is not made, or a final determination of an appeal has been rendered. If a removal order is enforceable, the foreign national against whom it is made must leave Canada immediately. Therefore, failed refugee claimants who take sanctuary in order to prevent the execution of an enforceable removal order are in violation of Canadian law. As section 131 of the Act imposes legal sanctions on anyone who knowingly induces, aids, abets, or counsels any person to contravene a provision of the Act, the law seemingly implies that sanctuary providers who actively assist migrants in evading their removal order are also in breach of the legislation.

However, as suggested by the government's hesitation to enter churches to enforce legal measures provided for under the Act, sanctuary is consonant with the notion that sovereign power emanating from the state is not necessarily coercive. Indeed, no Canadian sanctuary providers have been arrested to date. Although immigration authorities have the legal capacity to arrest sanctuary activists and issue removal orders against claimants who are accorded sanctuary, state sovereignty is confronted by church sanctuary's affinity for spectacle and media attention. The fact that immigration authorities avoid storming the church in order to prevent a political spectacle that illuminates the punitive actions of the state creates a notion of sovereignty that entails exceptions to coercion and exclusion. These exceptions are indeed indicated by the grant of a discretionary Minister's permit to allow the migrants to remain in Canada or other reprieves to those offering and taking sanctuary (Rehaag, 2009). Therefore, sovereign power does not emanate exclusively from the nation-state but may be exercised by the church, as sanctuary practices also connote the control of a protective territory.

Also entailed in the church's exercise of sovereign power is the discretion in deciding who to include and exclude from sanctuary protection by deploying screening procedures that are distinct from but nevertheless analogous to the formal refugee determination procedures and exclusion mechanisms administered under the Act (Rehaag, 2009). It must be remembered that in the vast majority of sanctuary cases, those who request sanctuary are highly traumatized and vulnerable individuals for whom the future is uncertain. However, despite the church's commitment to carry out a ministry of advocacy on behalf of the migrants, congregations must still carefully consider their case and ask themselves whether the case can withstand intense legal and judicial scrutiny. A participant in the Lippert Study who was a member of the Southern Ontario Sanctuary Coalition (SOSC) stated that he received phone calls on a weekly basis from individuals requesting sanctuary but could not accept most of those seeking help. In emphasizing that sanctuary is only granted in exceptional circumstances, another member of SOSC stated:

> We decided that we would be very careful about the cases that we undertake. We would ... not take on any cases that we thought would not be absolutely ironclad ... We did not want to be caught taking on a case that turned out to be obviously filled with distortions and perjury and all sorts of stuff. (Lippert, 2006)

To assist congregations in selecting individuals for sanctuary, a pamphlet prepared by the United Church of Canada for congregations entitled *Sanctuary for refugees? A guide for congregations* (United Church of Canada, 2004) refers to the value of documentary evidence regarding country conditions as well as suggests means of evaluating migrants' testimony (Rehaag, 2009). Therefore, although many sanctuary providers focus on humanitarian assistance to justify church intervention rather than on whether the migrants' plight strictly corresponded to an enumerated ground of persecution under the UN definition of a Convention refugee, protection was not accorded to all migrants in similar predicaments, as the decision to grant sanctuary is based on the unique circumstances of individual claimants. Indeed, only the claimants whose cases are regarded as highly persuasive under the screening procedures are accorded sanctuary (Rehaag, 2009). Consequently, in some cases, the most appropriate response to a request for sanctuary may be to offer emotional support to the claimants to help them prepare to return home, even if supporters feel compelled to offer sanctuary. Where there is anything in the claimant's history that would discredit their claim for refugee protection, it may not be appropriate for churches to encourage such individuals to evade enforcement of immigration decisions by seeking sanctuary.

Pastoral Power

Church sanctuary may also be viewed as an instance of pastoral power that aims to ensure, sustain, and improve the lives of migrants in order to enable them to become self-sufficient, contributing members of society. Pastoral power encompasses compassion, kindness, and continuous care on an individualized basis, which mirror the characteristics of shepherds who attend to the needs of their flocks (Lippert, 2006). Correspondingly, sanctuary providers sacrifice their time, resources, and finance in order to provide for the migrants' needs and to remedy the dire consequences that arise from their precarious immigration status, even in the face of risk of legal prosecution. Therefore, in providing assistance and assurance to failed refugee claimants in a situation of great uncertainty, sanctuary providers personify protective shepherds.

Pastoral power is crucial for claimants taking sanctuary, as they live under the glare of publicity while coping with the physical confines of a church. Although seemingly secondary to the need for protection from deportation, the migrants' needs were many and varied, encompassing not only the provision of basic necessities of life but spiritual, emotional, and psychological care. In many instances, the obvious fear of state authorities that manifested inside churches resulted in a 24-hour rotating surveillance of the migrants, who were deemed incapable of making appropriate choices on their own (Lippert, 2006). A critical element in exercising pastoral power that has been exemplified in sanctuary incidents is the generation of intimate knowledge about individual migrants who remain with their providers for a protracted period of time (Lippert, 2006). A level of intimacy that is maintained between the sanctuary providers and the migrants provides the basis upon which to understand the depth of the migrants' needs. However, it must also be emphasized that the gathering of intimate knowledge may result in a concomitant loss of privacy and an increase in public attention and scrutiny. Therefore, when exercising pastoral power, it is important to be aware of how advocacy efforts made on behalf of the migrants can affect their capacity to exercise autonomy and choice in their lives.

In contrast, the state is prevented from exercising pastoral power under Canada's official refugee determination system. The legislative mandate to fit a refugee claimant into the confines of the Convention refugee definition often overshadows the claimant's need to remain in Canada and their inability to return (or fear of returning) to their home country. Furthermore, the effort to harmoniously process the mass number of refugee applications, reduce the backlog of pending refugee claims, and protect the integrity of Canada's official refugee determination procedures from so-called "bogus" claims can compromise immigration authorities' time and capacity to maintain intensive conversations and continuous contact with every individual refugee claimant. Because intimate knowledge of the migrant's history, thoughts, and feelings are crucial for the exercise of pastoral power, the ability of state immigration authorities to view migrants in sanctuary as real entities in need rather than unfamiliar, distant and failed refugee claimants is significantly curtailed.

The influence of the above two complementary forms of power exercised by the church becomes evident when Canadian sanctuary discourse is understood within two legal narratives: sanctuary incidents as against domestic law before international law..

Interactions between Canadian Sanctuary Practices and the Law

Sanctuary Juxtaposing Domestic Law

One way in which the legitimacy of sanctuary may be understood is to view sanctuary incidents as an act of resistance to oppressive immigration and refugee law, analogous to how participants of the United States sanctuary movement characterized their activities. While the U.S. sanctuary activists acknowledged that they had violated the law and did not contest the legality of the enforcement measures under the American *Immigration and Nationality Act* (INA), they nevertheless denounced the U.S. administration's foreign policy interests that perpetuated human rights violations through the deportation of Central American asylum seekers (Blanke, 2003). Similar to the sanctuary activities in the U.S. context, the moral legitimacy of Canadian sanctuary arises from the risk of serious consequences that many failed refugee claimants may face as a result of removal from Canada. Indeed, the mere fact of an issuance of a removal order does not render its appropriateness self-evident if claimants are subsequently returned home to face serious harm to their lives. Moreover, arguably a large majority of those who request the protection of sanctuary are failed refugee claimants who contend that their claims were wrongfully rejected. They challenge the view that the sanctions enforced by immigration authorities are a legitimate exercise of the law in light of the inconsistency of decision-making by the RPD. There is no guarantee that two individuals with identical bases for their refugee claims will receive the same determination. Among the claimants facing similar predicaments who are equally in need of state protection, a handful of individuals may be sent back to their country of origin to face the possibility of persecution, while a selective few will be deemed to be deserving of refugee protection. Therefore, Canadian sanctuary incidents can be positioned against impugned and arbitrary legislation as a last resort "appeal" mechanism that operates as a means to remedy the errors and delays within the formal refugee determination process.

Canada's current immigration legislation was passed by Parliament in 2001, which set out provisions for a Refugee Appeal Division (RAD) that would allow for a merit-based legal appeal of a rejected refugee claim. However, the sections pertaining to the RAD was not enacted when the Act came into force in June 2002 (Lippert, 2009). Bill C-11, the Balanced Refugee Reform Act, received royal assent on June 29, 2010 and established the long-awaited RAD at the IRB. On December 15, 2012, Canada's refugee determination system underwent significant changes, with the RAD finally coming into force after its notional legislative creation in 2002.The RAD is a quasi-judicial administrative tribunal that is meant to give claimants a chance to prove that the decision made by the RPD was wrong in fact or law or both. While RAD decisions are pending, refugee claimants benefit from automatic stays on removal (Immigration and Refugee Protection Act, s. 49(2)(c)). Although a refugee claimant has several other legal avenues to contest the refusal of his or her claim – namely by way of an application for leave for judicial review at the Federal Court, application for a Pre-Removal Risk Assessment (PRRA), and request to remain in Canada on Humanitarian and Compassionate (H&C) grounds – they are not effective mechanisms to correct errors of fact that may be committed in the initial refugee determination process and do not act as a complete safety net for several reasons. First, appeals to the RAD can be based on a question of fact or mixed fact and law, whereas judicial review is limited to errors of law. Those seeking judicial review must also first obtain leave from the Federal Court, however, 90 per cent of applications for leave for judicial review to the Federal Court are refused, and no reasons for refusing leave are provided. Next, a PRRA is not an effective procedure for correcting errors in the initial refugee determination, as claimants may only raise new evidence that arose after the rejection of their claim. In 2005, only three per cent of PRRA decisions were positive. Thirdly, applications for permanent residence on H&C grounds may not offer an effective recourse for failed refugee claimants as the measure is a discretionary provision with no established eligibility criteria, and a pending H&C decision may not stay a removal order. Without an appropriate procedural framework in the refugee determination system to review the negative decisions that the IRB may mistakenly render, Canada will risk returning a claimant to persecution contrary to the objectives of the Act and in violation of Canada's international obligations.

An appeal mechanism based on the merits of a refugee claim is also crit-ical in light of the fact that there are wide disparities in decision-making within the IRB. While some adjudicators granted refugee status in 95 percent of cases, others accorded refugee status in less than ten percent of cases (Dunlop, 2009). The IRB attributes the inconsistency of the decisions to the manner in which refugee cases are assigned. However, the variance remains significant even when approval rates are adjusted to take into account expedited cases and country of origin (Rehaag, 2007). Although the varying disposition of IRB members combined with the highly individualistic experience of a refugee claimant render refugee determination inherently difficult, the Canadian Council for Refugees (CCR), a non-governmental group representing various organizations supporting refugee advocacy, human rights protection, and refugee resettlement, has argued that credi-bility assessments of refugee claimants is often inaccurate because the IRB may have limited knowledge of the social, political, and economic conditions in the claimant's country of nationality; may demonstrate a lack of affective concern for claimants whose cultural and moral discourses differ from their own; and may dispute the testimony of those who find difficulty disclosing relevant information due to their traumatic experiences (Canadian Council for Refugees, 2006). Without intimate knowledge of claimants' personal experience in fleeing their country of origin, even qualified and well-trained panel members can err in rendering judgement.

Despite the inconsistency in approval rates and delayed implementation of the RAD as part of reforms to Canada's refugee determination system, immigration authorities may nevertheless reject the argument that it is the legal invalidity of migrants' removal orders that authorizes sanctuary practice to exist. This is because most migrants in sanctuary have already exhausted all avenues for judicially reviewing their negative refugee determinations, indicating that their claims would have been systemically rejected multiple times by the time they enter sanctuary (Rehaag, 2009). Even if this argument is accepted, it fails to fully explain whether refugee claims have been accu-rately decided on their merits. Indeed, data obtained from the IRB through an Access to Information Request reveals wide discrepencies in the rate of positive decisions made by decision-makers (Canadian Council for Refugees, 2013). Moreover, it is actually unclear whether Canadian law can render the activities of sanctuary providers illegal. As stated previously, the Act states that it is an offence to induce, aid, abet, or counsel any person to contravene a provision of the Act. Citizenship and Immigration Canada has stated in a documented entitled *Avoiding deportation by claiming sanctuary*,

"It is an offence pursuant to IRPA to aid and abet a person to contravene the Immigration and Refugee Protection Act" (in Rehaag, 2009). In articulating the differences between the terms "aiding" and "abetting" the Supreme Court of Canada in *Regina v. Greyeyes* interpreted "aiding" to mean assisting or helping the actor and "abetting" to include encouraging, instigating, promoting or procuring the crime to be committed. This statement suggests that to the extent that sanctuary providers actively assist migrants in evading legal measures, they commit the offence of "aiding" and "abetting" in violation of Canadian immigration and refugee law. However, neither the Act nor the Supreme Court of Canada clarify what forms of assistance equate to "aiding" and "abetting" in the context of sanctuary practice. On one hand, it may be argued that sanctuary activists who conceal migrants in order to avoid detection by immigration authorities are guilty of committing the offence of "aiding," as they actively facilitate the migrants in circumventing legally enforceable removal orders (Rehaag, 2009, p. 49). However, far from concealing claimants, many sanctuary activists publically notify state officials of their decision to accord sanctuary by holding press conferences, vigils, and protests, and most churches do not impede with the enforcement of a removal order (Lippert, 2006). Furthermore, it is unclear whether "aiding" encompasses the offering of shelter, food, and other physiological assistance as the Act, in contrast to U.S. law, does not explicitly declare it an offence to "harbour" a foreign national who unlawfully remains in the country. The only prohibition on "harbouring" under the Act is found under provisions concerning human trafficking, which is defined by Article 3 of the *Protocol to prevent, suppress and punish persons especially women and children* (the Palermo Protocol) as:

> the recruitment, transportation, transfer, harbouring or receipt of persons, by means of the threat or use of force or other forms of coercion, of abduction, of fraud, of deception, of the abuse of power or of a position of vulnerability of the giving or receiving payments or benefits to achieve the consent of a person having control over another person, for the purpose of exploitation. (UN General Assembly, 2000)

In the context of human trafficking, generally distinct from sanctuary practice, the offence of "harbouring" is distinguished from "aiding" and "abetting." It is also uncertain whether the offering of sanctuary amounts to the offence of "abetting" in light of jurisprudence indicating that "abetting" involves encouraging or instigating the commission of an offence. In exercising non-state sovereign power, congregations deploy selection procedures to decide which migrants' request for sanctuary they can legitimately respond to. As sanctuary is accorded in exceptional circumstances, not all sanctuary providers encourage migrants to evade enforcement measures. Therefore, churches that accede to requests for sanctuary cannot be said to automatically encourage claimants to remain in Canada in breach of the law. It is interesting to note that "in practice, prosecution is discretionary and churches which have been deemed to actively assist persons in evading removals have, to date not faced charges" (Rehaag, 2009, p. 49).

The exercise of pastoral power is deeply embedded within the "sanctuary juxtaposed to domestic law" narrative, as sanctuary providers take a firm stance against the oppressive threats to the lives of needful migrants even as they face risks of legal prosecution that are at most regarded as potentially lawful. In light of the inconsistent and arbitrary application of legislation with respect to both the claimants and providers, even if Canadian sanctuary incidents stand in opposition to the law, church intervention legitimately operates alongside domestic law until the refugee determination system functions with efficiency, consistency, and fairness. Indeed, a judicial remedy that allows unsuccessful refugee claimants to have their initial refugee determinations reviewed on their merits is a legal appeal process that the CCR has been rigorously advocating for (Canadian Council for Refugees, 2006).

Sanctuary under International Law

The second way in which the legitimacy of sanctuary may be understood is to view sanctuary incidents as affirming Canada's international commitment to protecting refugees. The Act contains an interpretive clause that requires the legislation to be applied in a manner that complies with Canada's international obligations. In 1969, Canada signed the 1951 *United Nations Convention Relating to the Status of Refugees* (Convention) and the 1967 *Protocol* (the Protocol), which are the primary human rights instruments for defining who is a refugee, articulating the legal obligations of contracting states, and providing a legal framework on which states can regulate their refugee determination system (Canadian Council for Refugees, 2006). It is important to note that although Article 14 of the *Universal Declaration of Human Rights* confers on everyone the right to seek asylum in other countries, the Convention does not oblige states to grant asylum to all refugees. However, it enshrines the principle of *non-refoulement*, one of the most important protections provided under the treaty. According to article 33(1) of the Convention, a contracting state cannot "expel or return (*refouler*) a refugee in any manner whatsoever to the frontiers of territories where his life or freedom would be threatened on account of his race, religion, nationality, membership in a particular social group or political opinion." In aligning Canadian immigration and refugee law with international responsibilities to refugees, Canada has incorporated into the Act the Convention definition of a refugee and the principle of *non-refoulement.*

Article 3 of the *United Nations Convention Against Torture and Other Cruel, Inhuman or Degrading Treatment or Punishment* (CAT) and Article 7 of the *International Covenant on Civil and Political Rights* (ICCPR) also prohibit state parties from returning an individual to a place where there are substantial grounds for believing that he or she would be in danger of being subjected to torture. As a signatory to the Convention, CAT, and ICCPR, Canada is prohibited from forcibly returning refugees to countries where their physical security could be placed at risk. However, whether or not international treaties have been explicitly incorporated into domestic legislation, the principles reflected in international human rights instruments help to contextualize the interpretation of Canadian law in a manner that is consistent with the intention of the legislature. Accordingly, international human rights documents purport to place a limit on the exercise of state sovereignty, although contracting states are given leeway not to extend the benefit of the principle of *non-refoulement* to persons who are inadmissible on grounds of security, their past violation of human rights, or membership in organized criminality. Nevertheless, Canadian immigration authorities are obliged to act in accordance with not only domestic legal norms but international standards respecting fundamental human rights.

Although migrants who have been issued a deportation order may be said to violate Canadian law if they remain in sanctuary in order to evade enforcement measures, it may also be argued that it is not legitimate for immigration officials to diminish the relevance of *non-refoulment* for the protection of such individuals on the basis that they are not deemed Convention refugees or persons in need of protection. This is because under the Convention, the contracting states are prohibited from deporting to persecution anyone who meets the refugee definition, not just individuals whom states determine to be Convention refugees (Rehaag, 2009, p. 55). If Canada's official refugee determination process fails to identify claimants who have a genuine fear of persecution, the state may be in danger of deporting individuals who require international protection but are determined not to be Convention refugees due to a lack of adequate procedural safeguard in the refugee determination procedure. As such, Canada would be in breach of its international obligation for *non-refoulement.* Another manner in which Canada may be in violation of international human rights is through the application of the Safe Third Country Agreement, which directs a refugee claimant who is seeking entry to Canada at the Canada–U.S. land border ports of entry to return to the United States to seek asylum (Citizenship and Immigration Canada, n.d.). Accordingly, subject to a few exceptions under Section 159 of the *Immigration and Refugee Protection Regulations*, SOR/2002-207, a refugee claim is ineligible to be referred to the RPD if the claimant entered Canada from a designated "safe" country. The United States is the only country that has been so designated to date under the Act. Although CIC has stated that responsibility sharing for refugee protection between Canada and the United States can enhance the orderly handling of refugee claim applications, a designated "safe" country cannot guarantee every refugee claimant protection from persecution. However, Article 33(1) of the Convention prohibits *refoulement* in any manner whatsoever, which is interpreted to mean prohibiting a contracting state from returning refugees to a potentially persecutory place either directly or indirectly. Accordingly, if Canada returns a claimant to the United States who is subsequently extradited to another jurisdiction that imposes a risk to his or her life or freedom, Canada would be equally in violation of its international obligations. Therefore, it can be argued that immigration authorities that apply the provisions in the Act in derogation of international law cannot lawfully prosecute participants in sanctuary incidents who aim to offer meaningful protection to the migrants from persecution and human rights violation in their country of origin. Indeed, the principles of international law governing state responsibility as drafted by the United Nations International Law Commission have implied that a state breaches its international obligations if it takes an obstructive attitude in preventing its citizens from acting in conformity with its international obligations (Matas, 1988).

As sanctuary providers and takers violate domestic law in order to uphold the fundamental rights of refugees accorded under international treaties, the humanitarian causes of church intervention demonstrate the exercise of pastoral power within the boundaries of international law. In an effort to render Canadian immigration and refugee law consistent with international human rights provisions, Canadian sanctuary incidents are positioned before international law in such a way that the church is authorized and legitimized by "higher" legal principles to act.

Conclusion

Despite the disappearance of church sanctuary in the sixteenth and seventeenth centuries, North America has witnessed a revival of sanctuary incidents in the last few decades. Indeed, the practice of church sanctuary continues to exist in Canada to this day, and Canadian sanctuary has become more prevalent in recent years both in terms of the frequency of occurrence and duration of incidents. Although sanctuary practices are criticized as illegal acts of civil disobedience that purport to threaten state sovereignty, it is also plausible to understand the legitimacy of Canadian sanctuary incidents by framing sanctuary discourse within two legal narratives. First, sanctuary addresses oppressive Canadian state law by challenging the lawfulness of deportation orders in light of the risk of persecution that migrants can face abroad. Sanctuary juxtaposes domestic law as a last resort "appeal" mechanism that is necessitated due to the systemic procedural flaws in the formal refugee determination system. The current process frustrates the correction of false negative refugee determinations and prompts the removal of "genuine" refugees. Second, sanctuary stands before international law whereby the church strives to affirm Canada's international obligations to protect refugees and respect their fundamental human rights. Within these narratives, the significance of the church's exercise of

Develop your knowledge – Ask yourself

1. What legal, ethical, and policy issues arise from sanctuary practices?
2. What recommendations would you make to address the shortcomings of the current refugee determination system?
3. What are the positive and negative implications of concealment strategies adopted by sanctuary providers to assist migrants in evading enforcement measures?
4. What are the positive and negative implications of exposure strategies adopted by sanctuary providers to communicate public declarations of sanctuary using mass media?
5. What role should settlement workers play in addressing the mental, physical, and social well-being of migrants who are seeking sanctuary protection?
6. What considerations should sanctuary providers take into account when "screening" migrants for protection? What questions might you ask them before deciding to accord sanctuary?

non-state sovereign power and pastoral power in producing positive legal outcomes for migrants also becomes apparent. Through a close analysis of how Canadian sanctuary incidents interact with the law, one may view sanctuary as a platform for effecting policy changes that aim to consolidate the official refugee determination system with Canada's commitments to refugees under both domestic and international law, thereby upholding the rule of law.

References

Blanke, S. (2003). *Civic foreign policy: U.S. religious interest groups and Central America, 1973–1990*. (Unpublished doctoral dissertation). Freie Universität Berlin, Berlin.

Canadian Charter of Rights and Freedoms. Part I of the Constitution Act, 1982, being Schedule B to the Canada Act 1982 (U.K.), c.11.

Canadian Council for Refugees (CCR). (2013). 2013 *Refugee Claim Data and IRB Member Recognition Rates*. Montreal: Canadian Council for Refugees.

Canadian Council for Refugees (CCR). (2006). *Refugee Appeal Division backgrounder*. Montreal: Canadian Council for Refugees.

Citizenship and Immigration Canada (CIC). (2010). *Processing claims for refugee protection in Canada*. Retrieved from http://www.cic.gc.ca/english/resources/manuals/pp/pp01-eng.pdf

Citizenship and Immigration Canada (CIC). (2011, August 18). Balanced refugee reform. Retrieved from http://www.cic.gc.ca/english/refugees/reform.asp

Convention Against Torture and Other Cruel, Inhuman or Degrading Treatment or Punishment. December 10, 1984. 1465 U.N.T.S. 85, 23 I.L.M. 1027

Cunningham, H. (1998) Sanctuary and sovereignty: Church and state along the U.S.–Mexico border. *Journal of Church and State*, 40, 371.

Dunlop, M. (2009, July 30). Gimme shelter: Refugees who found sanctuary in Canadian churches. *This Magazine*. Retrieved from http://this.org/magazine/2009/07/30/immigration-church-sanctuary

Immigration and Nationality Act, 1952 8 U.S.C. 1324.

Immigration and Refugee Protection Act, S.C. 2001, c. 27.

Immigration and Refugee Protection Regulations, SOR/2002-207.

Lippert, R.K. (2005). Rethinking sanctuary: The Canadian context, 1983–2003. International Migration Review, 39(2), 381–406

Lippert, R.K. (2006). Sanctuary, sovereignty, sacrifice: Canadian sanctuary incidents, power, and law. Vancouver: University of British Columbia Press.

Lippert, R.K. (2009). Wither sanctuary? *Refuge, 26*(1), 57–67.

Lippert, R.K. & Rehaag, S. (1988). Sanctuary in context. *Refuge, 26*(1), 3–6.

Matas, D. (1988). Canadian sanctuary. *Refuge, 8*(2), 14–17.

R. v. Greyeyes. (1997). 2 S.C.R. 825.

Rehaag, S. (2007, August 30). Adjudication lottery for refugees. *Toronto Star*. Retrieved from http://www.thestar.com/comment/article/251233.

Rehaag, S. (2009). Bordering on legality: Canadian church sanctuary and the rule of law. *Refuge, 26*(1), 43–56.

Stastny, C. (1989). [Review of the book *Conviction of the heart: Jim Corbett and the sanctuary movement*]. *Refuge, 8*(3), 11.

United Church of Canada. (2004). *Sanctuary for refugees? A guide for congregations*. Toronto: United Church of Canada.

UN General Assembly, Convention Relating to the Status of Refugees, 28 July 1951, United Nations, Treaty Series, vol. 189, p. 137. Retrieved from http://www.unhcr.org/refworld/docid/3be01b964.html

UN General Assembly, International Covenant on Civil and Political Rights. (1966, December 16). United Nations, Treaty Series, vol. 999, p. 171. Retrieved from http://www.unhcr.org/refworld/docid/3ae6b3aa0.html

UN General Assembly. (2000, November 15). Protocol to prevent, suppress and punish trafficking in persons, especially women and children, supplementing the United Nations Convention Against Transnational Organized Crime. 40 ILM 335 (2001)/UN Doc. A/55/383 (Annex II, p. 53)/[2005] ATS 27.

UN General Assembly, *Universal Declaration of Human Rights*, 10 December 1948, 217 A (III), Retrieved from http://www.unhcr.org/refworld/docid/3ae6b3712c.html

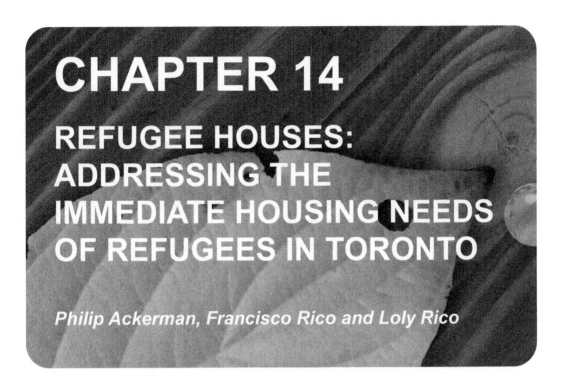

CHAPTER 14

REFUGEE HOUSES: ADDRESSING THE IMMEDIATE HOUSING NEEDS OF REFUGEES IN TORONTO

Philip Ackerman, Francisco Rico and Loly Rico

Case Study – Eva

Eva arrived in Canada with her two-year-old son and six months pregnant with her second child. She was a victim of gender violence in her own country, Kenya, and feared for her survival. As she entered Canada without proper identification, she and her son were placed in immigration detention, in conditions that she described as "unbearable." "I couldn't believe it," she said, "I have never felt so alone. I was so scared and upset ... I thought I was going to have my baby right there." As Eva's anxiety increased during her stay in the detention centre, her health began to deteriorate. The detention centre and members of Toronto Refugee Affairs Council (TRAC) agreed to move her to a local refugee house. "When I arrived at the house, that's the moment my life began to turn around. My son and I had our own room, and a hot meal waiting for us. We met other women and children, who were also refugees. It was in that house that I felt like I wasn't alone – I finally began to feel that I could overcome my ordeal."

Traveller, there is no road; the road is made by walking.
–Antonio Machado, Campos de Castilla

Introduction

Eva's story reflects the complicated trajectories of many individuals and families who come to Canada looking for refuge and safety. Over the years, concerns over multifaceted needs of these newcomers have lead to the inception of "refugee houses." Refugee houses comprise of select group of organizations with specific goal of offering shelter to refugees while serving as a gateway to an array of additional services from settlement to integration processes. The existence of refugee houses can be traced back to the early 1980s, thus with time they have evolved greatly to address the immigration and social services policy change in one hand and the ever changing needs of new refugees on the other.

While instability in reception patterns negatively affects settlement experiences of all immigrants, refugees often face additional barriers upon their arrivals in Canada. These challenges are shaped by pre-migratory experiences of oppression, violence, war, political instability, gender discrimination, and poverty resulting in their displacement and forced migration. Upon their arrival in Canada, refugees are further faced with stressful refugee process while continuing to experience discrimination based on their race, class, gender, language, religious belief and sexual orientation. Lack of access to appropriate and safe housing can exacerbate unforeseen challenges and trauma for refugees. In fact, a 2007 Canadian study reveals the direct relation between securing housing and successful integration (Sherrel, D'Addario, & Hiebert, 2007). Considering that forced displacement leaves little chance for refugees to plan or prepare their migration, it is not surprising to find that many refugees arrive in Canada as homeless. In addition, while all newcomers must learn English and navigate new legal process, employment, health and education system, refugees struggle with family separation and trauma caused by the situations from which they have fled.

The purpose of this chapter is to explore the link between the unique needs of refugees and the responses of refugee houses to such needs. We begin by outlining the history of refugee houses from their inception and ways in which they have evolved in response to changing political climates. This is achieved by first reflecting on refugee houses in Ontario, and second, through a careful analysis of the services offered by refugee houses in the Greater Toronto Area (GTA). It is important to note that very little empirical evidence is available about the history of refugee houses in Ontario. For this reason, we rely on oral histories and interview with those involved in the inception or in working at the refugee houses in the GTA.

Refugee Houses in Ontario: Historical Overview

The origins of refugee houses in Ontario can be traced back to the 1980s, when large numbers of refugees arrived in Canada from Latin America, Vietnam, and Cambodia. The needs expressed by these refugee populations led to the development of what are now referred to as "refugee houses." Currently there are more than a dozen refugee houses in Ontario, as well as few shelters that are specifically geared towards catering the needs of refugees. In effect, refugee houses have developed in response to the emerging settlement needs of refugees in order to overcome deficiencies in service delivery for newcomers.

It is vital to distinguish between a refugee house and a shelter. By definition, refugee houses belong to the sector of transitional housing, since they provide a balance of autonomy and support for refugees. They go well beyond the provision of basic lodging, as they also allocate comprehensive services for newly arrived populations, particularly those trying to navigate complicated immigration processes. However, refugee houses have not always been the arenas of support as they seem to be today. A careful examination of the refugee houses currently exist in Ontario will demonstrate how these entities have developed organically in response to the emerging needs of refugee populations in a Canadian context. Conversely, through this development, these organizations have suffered multiple limitations which bar them from achieving their full potential.

The Inception of Refugee Houses in Ontario: The 1980s

The post-Vietnam War era saw a greater number of refugees arriving from Vietnam and Cambodia, often referred to as "boat people." This phenomenon spurred profound changes in the attitudes of Canadians, who strove to be charitable and receptive to these populations. In fact, as a result of these efforts, the United Nations High Commission for Refugees (UNHCR) awarded Canada the Nansen Medal – the only "society" ever to be so awarded – "in recognition of their major and sustained contribution to the cause of refugees" (Canadian Council for Refugees, 2009). The sudden arrival of refugees fleeing violence and trauma caused many people in Canada to open their homes, initiating the welcoming spirit that has become a founding principle of many refugee houses. Many of the individuals inviting refugees into their homes were connected through faith-based communities, allowing the network of homes receiving refugees to grow (Ackerman, 2011b). The need for safe houses increased along with the idea of establishing houses with spaces specifically allocated for refugee claimants. For many, the first refugee house in Ontario was Casa El Norte, located in Fort Erie, which was originally formed to respond to the large influx of Salvadorian refugees entering Canada through Buffalo (Ackerman, 2011b).

At the time, the political climate in Canada was much more conducive for such endeavours. In 1989, the Immigration and Refugee Board (IRB) had an 84 percent approval rate of refugee claims, compared to 38 percent in 2010 (Showler, 2011). The receptiveness of both the Canadian government and individual activists fed the motivation to provide homes for refugees. Government policies were more open prior to the implementation of the Refugee Determination system, and Canada was arguably more progressive in its treatment of refugees (Ackerman, 2011b). Canada was, for instance, the first country in the world to issue Guidelines on Women Refugee Claimants fearing Gender-related Persecution (Canadian Council for Refugees, 2009).

At the turn of the decade, the number of refugees entering Canada began to rise. In 1990, there were 10,778 refugees accepted – a number that nearly doubled in 1991 (Showler, 2011). The combination of these factors resulted in the establishment of more refugee houses across the province, many of which were in the Toronto area. At the end of the 1980s and throughout the 1990s no less than six refugee houses were opened, including Casa El Norte (1989), Sojourn House (1989), FCJ Refugee Centre (formerly Hamilton House; 1991), Romero House (1992), Casa Maria (1994), Chez Marie (1995), and Matthew House (1998). These houses reflected the changes in the country of origins of refugees entering Canada. Additionally, many of the houses were founded through the contributions of religious groups, considered by some to be a double-edged sword. On the one hand, the charitable foundations of the religious communities were heartening for many people seeking refuge, but at the same time the religious model was seen as limiting and deemed exclusive by some. From these beginnings, the houses evolved in response to the emerging needs of refugees in Canada.

Refugee Houses through the 1990s

As the number of diverse refugees entering Canada grew during the 1990s, so did the demand for services tailored to address their multifaceted needs. This warranted a holistic approach to services covering translation to the provision of culturally-sensitive programs, legal information, and referrals to healthcare services, social assistance and other community agencies.

Despite the growing demand for services, refugee houses in Ontario faced mounting difficulties in accessing resources while attempting to retain their community-based values. The enduring challenges faced by refugee houses often serve to delay successful integration for many of the residents. Nevertheless, the houses continue to abide by their mandates and evolve in creative ways. The contemporary idea of a refugee house is that it has the capacity to foster the many facets of integration, especially those difficult for refugees to achieve. Integration services are described as those which "assist newcomers who intend to settle in Canada permanently" (Yu, Ouellet, & Warmington, 2007, p. 23). The current Canadian federal government now solely funds services that are "intended to facilitate permanent settlement and integration into Canadian society" (Yu, Ouellet, & Warmington, 2007, p. 23). Many settlement agencies that are funded through Citizenship and Immigration Canada are mandated to serve specific groups of refugee claimants and permanent residents.

Most of the refugee houses in Ontario provide services to anyone, regardless of their immigration status. Therefore, these houses need to find funding through other, often less sustainable means. This is a particular challenge for refugee houses that work with migrants with precarious status, which are often severely underfunded. Due to misconceptions about migrants with precarious status, who are often labeled as living here illegally, many funders do not want to support projects that may jeopardize their standing in public opinion.

Most refugee houses receive their base funding through their founding religious congregations, which barely fulfill base operations; any additional programs require external grants. Mary Jo Leddy, the founder of Romero House, explains the funding dilemma this way:

> The poverty of Romero House is both an obstacle and an asset. It is difficult to work with little funds. But I also think that poverty is important, because we are in almost the same situation as the refugees financially. I'm not sure what it would be like if we had financial security – I think it would profoundly change the attitude here. (Ryan & Woodill, 2000, p. 47)

With extremely limited financial stability, refugee houses are largely understaffed and rely on their volunteer support to operate. Although the spirit of volunteerism is fused with the mission of refugee serving organizations, reliance on volunteers may also be a hindrance when it denies the residents timely and stable service provision. Limitations in funding also cause additional consequences for refugee houses, including longer waiting periods, broad programs rather than ones targeting specific needs, language limitations, and superfluous and unnecessary external referrals.

Despite these limitations, many refugee houses have managed to survive for nearly two decades. Equally impressive is that more refugee houses have been established across the province. The resilience of refugee houses in light of tightened federal policies, severe funding cuts to the sector, and increasingly negative attitudes towards refugees speaks volumes about the impact of these houses on vulnerable populations.

Consider that these entities are termed "houses" rather than "shelters." Ryan and Woodill (2000) argue that providing shelter is not sufficient to end homelessness among refugees. Based on a holistic approach, refugee houses attempt to recreate the notion of "home" that was lost during the flight of the refugees through awareness, compassion, and support. This spirit lends itself to all aspects of the refugee houses, including an integrated approach to settlement that is the backbone of the houses.

The Housing Needs of Refugees: More than a House

Between 1989 and 2010, there were nearly 618,834 refugee claims in Canada (Showler, 2011), over 55 percent of them in Ontario (Citizenship and Immigration Canada, 2010). Many refugees who have been forcibly displaced due to persecution or high-risk conditions arrive in Canada with virtually nothing in their possession. These groups of refugees feel homeless and often lack a sound understanding of appropriate next steps. A 2000 study conducted by a refugee house in Toronto interviewed 49 refugees in order to explore what having a "home" meant for them. Many of the refugees expressed how they not only arrived here feeling homeless, but also that these feelings of homelessness continued in Canada despite being housed (Ryan & Woodill, 2000). The study concluded that homelessness "can be defined in terms of their loneliness, living far from their family and culture, physical and emotional isolation in Canada, a loss of security, and a lack of meaning in their life and a lack of hope for the future" (Ryan & Woodill, 2000, p. 5).

Refugees arrive in Toronto are already positioned to experience a multitude of systemic barriers. In their search for refuge they need to negotiate their relationship with a new society, while navigating a foreign immigration system. This proves quite burdensome for most refugees as they are forced to traverse various hurdles with little awareness of Canadian systems, few resources at their disposal, and often without family or community support. In many cases, refugee claimants are not received by anyone when they arrive in Canada, and need to rely on word of mouth for information on what to do next (Yu, Ouellet, & Warmington, 2007). The integration process for refugees is exacerbated as they are confronted with inequality based on their social identities, language barriers, racism, and economic disparity. These challenges contribute significantly to high level of housing stress as they strive to navigate the Canadian housing market.

Refugees face several challenges when they access the Canadian housing market. Toronto, for instance, is one of Canada's most desired destinations, but Toronto's rental market is notoriously expensive with limited vacancies. Refugees are often under-employed and are underpaid because of their status as refugees, lack of documentation to prove their education and employment history, and lack of Canadian work experience. As a result, newcomers have a high risk of homelessness (Paradis, Novac, Sarty, & Hulchanski, 2009). The combination of low income and high rent, according to Wayland (2007), results in refugees spending more than 50 percent of their incomes on rent. This is particularly significant for many newcomers who need to receive government assistance. Moreover, it is nearly impossible for someone on social assistance (such as the Ontario Works Program) to pay first and last month's rent The economic disadvantage felt by refugees is amplified by having to pay exorbitant refugee application fees in their quest for permanent residency, a cost which is a heavier burden for those with large families. All of these conditions compromise affordable and safe housing for refugees, forcing them to live in squalor, vicarious and exploitative housing conditions.

Refugee resettlement is fraught with discrimination stemming from immigration status as well as race, class, religion, creed, ethnic origins, gender, and sexual orientation hindering access to affordable and safe housing. A study by the Centre for Equity Rights in Accommodation (CERA) reveals pervasive discrimination in the rental market in Toronto, as many volunteer subjects were refused housing based on their accent or country of origin (CERA, 2009). These findings are supported by refugees interviewed by the Romero House, as many indicated that experiences of racism made them feel unwelcome in Toronto (Ryan & Woodill, 2000). The precariousness of refugees' resettlement experience is specifically salient for women, as the intersection of refugee status with gender ascribes additional barriers for refugee women. A 2009 study found that discrimination was the predominant reason for women being prevented from accessing housing; 31 percent of those surveyed stated that they faced discrimination by a landlord (Paradis, Novac, Sarty, & Hulchanski, 2009). Another notable group that experiences heightened discrimination are those lacking any form of legal immigration status. Precarious immigration status not only prevents people from accessing legitimate housing options, but also puts them at greater risk of exploitation and abuse at the hands of their landlords. These barriers further intersect with other elements such as family size, language, and knowledge of Canadian institutions as refugees attempt to access housing in Toronto.

Not all refugees face the same hurdles in the housing market. Some refugees may have a relative, community member, or family acquaintance who provide them with some form of lodging. However, besides being temporary in nature, these offers come with their own set of challenges. First of all, having this option available is quite rare for many refugees, as family members in Canada are often already involved in overcrowded living situations. Many people circumvent the exorbitant prices in Toronto by cramping large families into small living spaces, sacrificing privacy and basic comfort. Connecting with community members is also difficult for some refugees as there is often great division within certain ethnic communities, spurred on by complicated politics (Ryan & Woodill, 2000). This is noted by one refugee interviewed by the Romero House in Toronto, who says, "There is nothing wrong with inviting someone to stay with me. But you hardly see people do that…because the community is divided" (Ryan & Woodill, 2000, p. 28). Those who are able to connect with family or community members in Toronto often encounter greater barriers as they suffer from a lack of accurate and timely information. These people in turn may unconsciously make mistakes on their applications, miss deadlines, or fail to understand available recourses. The study by the Romero House notes that a refugee claimant was kept in hiding by family members in Canada and consequently missed the refugee hearing (Ryan & Woodill, 2000). Although having family, friends or community members may inherently provide more instruments for support, staying with friends and family is not always a viable option for newcomers.

The question is what options are then left for refugees, newcomers and migrants with precarious status who arrive in Toronto? Although many refugees already arrive in Canada "homeless," meaning that they are isolated and lack security and awareness, the numerous barriers they face put them at a higher risk of ending up on the street. It is well documented that various factors contribute to an increased risk of homelessness for refugees. This is evident in the case of refugees interviewed in Toronto (Ryan

& Woodill, 2000). Others spoke of their first night in Canada being left in the houses of strangers, or in a park, and later moving into a shelter (Yu, Ouellet, & Warmington, 2007). Shelter workers in Vancouver note that refugees are overrepresented in Canadian shelters (Sherrel, D'Addario, & Hiebert, 2007). Arriving at a point of entry, with little or no awareness of Canadian systems and limited resources, often forces refugees in Toronto to access the shelter system. Refugees are provided with shelter addresses by the immigration authorities or possibly by community members. Although there are a number of shelters in Toronto, they may lack available space or are not always a viable option for refugees, particularly for migrants with precarious status.

The existing shelters in Toronto may not necessarily cater to refugees for various reasons. For example, language barriers significantly reduces one's awareness of services available in the city, and further restricts the ability to gain access to necessary networks. In addition, most shelters are mandated to seek some of form of personal identification, which further diminish access to short term housing for migrants with precarious status. It is important to note that the situation has improved significantly in shelters since Toronto became a sanctuary city, and adopted recommendations to live up to this status. In recent years, the city has opened municipal services to anyone regardless of their immigration status. However, many workers continue to face difficulties as there remains a general lack of awareness of the changes or overall knowledge about the conditions perpetuating immigration precariousness. This leads to workers pushing individuals to take hasty steps to regularize their status, without fully understanding the legal and immigration system or the negative implications that may arise afterwards.

Among refugee communities, not mentioning the larger Canadian society, there is a great deal of stigma attached to staying in a shelter. Many refugees in Toronto who stayed in shelters felt that the atmosphere was "dangerous" as they were "with people who were alcoholic and used drugs" (Ryan & Woodill, 2000, p. 11). Finally, some shelters are ill-equipped to service refugees as they lack a sound understanding of their needs. Refugees arrive with specific, immediate needs such as requiring assistance in filling out immigration application forms and help with translation of their documents. For many, their fate hinges on their ability to complete applications thoroughly and in a timely manner. Overworked frontline workers in shelters are not always able to attend to refugee cases, which are subsequently lost in the shuffle. These cases are declared as abandoned by the client and at worse the applicant is at risk of receiving criminal charges for misrepresentation of information. Putting the distinctive requirements of refugee homeless populations on the back burner by lumping them in with the general population is a disservice that perpetuates their anxiety and the cycle of poverty.

This consideration of the multi-faceted needs of refugee populations is paramount when discussing their integration experiences. Having a roof over their head is only one, albeit significant, component in refugee resettlement in Canada. As already mentioned, for some the feeling of homelessness extends well beyond securing housing. As noted by Ryan and Woodill, "[t]he lack of social support, information, and supportive shelter upon arrival prolongs refugees' experience of homelessness and may create insurmountable obstacles to ever being at home in Canada" (Ryan & Woodill, 2000, p. vi). It is important to note that these feelings of homelessness are exacerbated for refugees with precarious immigration status, or no status at all, as they constantly need to move or are forced to go into hiding. All of these elements form the crux of the issue – essentially there are very few mechanisms in place that respond to the diverse needs of refugees. Canadian society has its own role to play to offset this issue; "most scholars and policy makers in Canada and elsewhere agree with a description of 'integration' as a 'dynamic, multi-faceted two-way process which requires adaptation on the part of the newcomers, but also the society of destination'" (Yu, Ouellet, & Warmington, 2007, p. 17). Many refugee advocates argue that in some ways Canada has fallen short of this responsibility, forcing individual organizations to rise up and fill this gap by providing a holistic reception for refugee populations.

The Integrated Response to Housing Needs

The settlement process is multi-faceted and reflective of the unique and diverse needs of individuals. Settlement goes well beyond offering basic shelter, as refugees need to rebuild their lives in the new environment. As previously noted, the increase in refugee houses and responsive to the settlement needs of refugees and precarious migrants is due to the adoption of an integrated holistic approach to settlement. To more aptly understand the unique features of this approach to refugee resettlement, we will examine the individual services provided at refugee houses in Toronto. A shared ideology among different houses is reflective of their endeavour to counter the disservices their clientele face during their integration into Canadian society. Although the individual houses diverge slightly in their mandates and provision of services, the shared framework in operating their facilities aptly demonstrate their far-reaching capacity to assist refugees.

We now turn to examine the effectiveness of the settlement-house model in championing the rights of migrants in Ontario as well as their alternative services to promote fair, accessible, and dignified treatment. The majority of refugee houses strive to ensure that refugee claimants and migrants will benefit from a community-driven and supportive environment. This approach provides a rich foundation for refugees and adequately equips to be productive members of society. An integrated approach builds on a balanced combination of orientation, skill development, innovation, peer-mentoring and networking in order to improve the conditions and lived experience of those uprooted from their homelands.

Housing and Orientation

Housing options in the Toronto area are limited. Most refugee houses have the capacity to offer shelter to approximately eight to 50 individuals and families, allowing them to stay until they feel ready to find a more permanent living arrangement. Meeting the exceptional needs of refugees, these houses diverge from the traditional concept of shelter by attuning themselves to the framework of transitional housing. At some houses, the residents pay rent and carry the same responsibilities that are expected of any resident of Toronto. This includes bringing in the mail, taking out the garbage, and co-operating with other residents to maintain the houses and yards. The benefits of this approach is twofold: the residents become empowered in taking an active role in their living environment, and at the same time, gain an active, hands-on understanding of the various Canadian systems in which they will be participating. This learning is facilitated for the residents as they are navigating these systems with other people going through similar experiences.

Independent living in refugee houses is complemented by a variety of client-centred programs that focus on integration. There are weekly workshops on eating nutritiously, budgeting, interview and job search skills, workers' rights, and dealing with bedbugs. These informative sessions also serve to reduce the anxiety of the residents and allow them to focus on other pressing issues such as their refugee applications and accessing clothing and food banks.

To meet the principles of transitional housing, it is important that the residents of refugee houses receive a well-rounded course of information and introduction to the Canadian experience. This includes providing the residents with appropriate and effective skill development to make sure they are able to be active and contributing members of society. For example, the Women's Community Economic Development Project at FCJ Refugee

Centre is a weekly project where women get together and create handmade jewellery and pottery. The women who participate in the program are then encouraged to sell their handiwork at craft venues, or possibly even start their own small businesses (FCJ Refugee Centre, 2011). Other refugee houses, such as the Sojourn House, provide assistance in identifying transferable skills for employment purposes (Sojourn House, n.d.). Additional programs include community kitchens that allow the residents to share their individual cultures, food, and customs; ESL classes run by trained teachers to help the residents overcome their language barriers; and cultural events and recreational fieldtrips to familiarize the residents with resources in the city. All of these programs have the express purpose of providing refugee populations with the support and awareness necessary to successfully navigate their new surroundings.

Residents of the houses often communicate their sincere gratitude for being connected with a refugee house instead of a shelter. Not only do they know everyone else in their house, as they operate on a much smaller scale, but everyone is enduring similar processes, allowing them to connect with each other on multiple levels. Participating in the programs while they are living in the houses empowers them to take an active role in their settlement process. The staff at these houses offer a range of services that are both comprehensive and inclusive. Some services extend beyond the house staff to include onsite case management and drop-ins, needs assessment, support, referrals, and follow-up, through appointments and over the phone, for migrants across the province. Essentially, refugee houses provide an overview of services to ensure that residents' needs are met and that they understand their rights, roles, and responsibilities in different areas, regardless of their immigration status.

Legal Information: The Case Study of FCJ Refugee Centre

One of the most significant challenges for the majority of residents in refugee houses is navigating through the complicated immigration and legal process. Although some refugee houses offer basic legal assistance, mainly through legal aid and referrals, others such as the FCJ Refugee Centre are unique in their capability to offer legal information at a fairly high level of competence. Some houses have legal support staff as well as an extensive network of volunteers and pro-bono law students who are able to meet the legal and bureaucratic needs of the large number of clients who access their services. Refugee houses are sometimes uniquely specialized in helping migrants with precarious status. These population experience vulnerability created by both the lack of any legal entitlement to be in Canada or because their immigration status is restricted by specific conditions. This creates the threat of being removed from Canada at any time without having any recourse to counter a deportation order. The FCJ Refugee Centre provides legal support in helping refugee claimants within Canada through every step of the refugee determination process. Support in navigating Canadian refugee and immigration processes has become more crucial since being overhauled in 2012. As a result of ongoing changes, migrants need to traverse more complicated processes in a shorter timeframe, with less recourse in the event of a negative claim. Direct assistance is offered in preparing for the refugee interview, the hearing, and the appeal process as well as the judicial review and Pre-Removal Risk Assessment (PRRA) and Humanitarian and Compassionate (H7C).

The FCJ Refugee Centre also supports the preparation of permanent resident applications, work/student/visitor permit applications or extensions, applications for family reunification and family sponsorship, sponsorship breakdown, assisting people who are detained, and helping migrants who are about to be deported.

Health and Emotional Support

Fleeing persecution, oppression and abuse is a common denominator among residents that quite often underpins the refugee experience. For many residents of refugee houses, their decision to come to Canada was fuelled by the need to escape situations of persecution, exploitation, abuse, violence, abject poverty, and discrimination. As a result of these experiences, many refugees arrive with some degree of emotional trauma that needs to be acknowledged during their integration process. To ensure that the residents are able to build a compelling case, it is imperative that they work through their traumatic experiences. To respond to the varying emotional needs of the residents, most refugee houses have trained counsellors or staff can refer cases to neighbouring health and social service agencies. Many houses offer timely and responsive counselling programs led by certified field volunteers and foreign-trained professionals.

The importance of providing counselling services at refugee houses is aptly described by Ryan and Woodill (2000), who provide examples of cases where refugees who have survived unbelievable trauma, torture, and sexual assault. For example, three people interviewed at Romero House were clinically depressed and attempted suicide (Ryan & Woodill, 2000). They need professional counselling to cope with their traumatic experiences. In conjunction with counselling on a professional level, refugee houses have the unique capability to offer peer support. Although the refugee experience is unique for each individual, there are shared elements that bind these people together. Different refugee populations can then offer appropriate support and empathy for one another, thereby reducing their anxiety and isolation.

Conclusion

The major developments throughout the history of refugee houses in the Toronto area have occurred in response to the emerging needs of refugees as well as immigration policy and legislative changes. The houses have grown from offering rooms strangers who arrive with nothing to a holistic system that expedites the integration process for refugees.

In order to stay afloat amidst funding cuts and lower refugee acceptance rates, refugee houses have learned to be resourceful and proactive. With limited access to other services for refugee claimants, the refugee houses have striven to offer comprehensive programs and services while adhering to best practices as described in the below box. Currently, refugee houses are burdened by multiple barriers across the sector, including reduced funding, service closures, and discriminatory attitudes toward refugees. To survive these difficulties and continue to serve multiple refugee populations, refugee houses have adopted accessible and anti-oppressive intake policies. In doing so, these houses are confronting the hierarchy of access that prohibits certain people from using services and gaining the assistance they need. Refugee houses have grown directly through community-driven, receptive support that has contributed to the transition from the difficult and often traumatic refugee experience. These houses have long been embedded with community-based support that has allowed them to circumvent government funding parameters and strict agency mandates; these constraints determine eligibility criteria that in turn often serve to stall the integration of newcomers. In the spirit of fairness and equity that fuels human services, why is everyone who arrives in Canada not afforded the same chances and opportunities? Instead of barring access to services, or forcing agencies to prioritize one client over another, the needs of the person should be paramount in this work.

The FCJ Refugee Centre: An Example of Best Practice

The FCJ Refugee Centre has supported uprooted people for more than 20 years. They maintain four houses in Toronto's west end, sheltering up to 40 women and 10 children each year. To offset the traumatic experiences of these individuals and families, and ease their introduction into Canada, the Centre provides living spaces that are comfortable and well maintained. While living in the houses the women are supported through the various application processes needed to achieve permanent residency. As these applications are notoriously complicated, this level of support is celebrated for anyone arriving Canada.

Beyond the bureaucratic processes embedded in the refugee experience, the FCJ houses offer a myriad of support services for residents. Such services include: responsive and timely counseling and emotional support, accessible and flexible ESL classes, peer mentoring and volunteer opportunities, educational workshops and awareness raising campaigns, clothing and food banks, and an array of community programming to encourage participation in Canadian society. Together these programs and services form an integrated model – an approach that is effective in helping refugees adjust and succeed.

Francisco Rico-Martinez, one of the Centre's co-directors explains it this way: "Really, what we're trying to do is reconstruct the kitchen table that refugees left behind." This is much more than providing a simple meal, or handing someone a pamphlet about language classes in the neighbourhood. We help to rebuild the community that was lost.

In many ways, Eva's situation with which we began this chapter exemplifies how refugee houses are in a unique position to respond to the plight of refugee populations. Eva arrived in Canada homeless, isolated from friends and family, without proper identification, and with no clear idea of what to do next. Her situation was exacerbated by the fact that she was pregnant and caring for a small child without adequate resources to do so safely. The stress and anxiety of her situation affected her health, causing her to fear that she might go into early labour. For Eva, a refugee house was the best option to provide for her unique needs – navigating a foreign society as a single mother with negligible resources.

continued...

Over the past two decades, refugee houses have collaborated with one another and forged pathways where otherwise limited options will be available for refugees. Moving forward in the current political climate, where restrictions are increasingly tightened for refugees and migrants with precarious status, refugee houses in Ontario need to continue to carve their own path. Ultimately the services offered through the refugee houses also benefit the receiving society of Canadians; as newcomers become better integrated, they will become neighbours and fellow Canadians. .

Develop your knowledge – Case study 1

You work at a refugee house located in Toronto. A young woman from Mexico is referred to your agency from a nearby organization. After speaking to the woman you discover that she was sponsored by her husband, who she met in her home city. After she arrived in Canada she soon realized that the dynamic of her relationship is changing. Her husband became abusive and threatened to break the sponsorship agreement if she raised any alarm. He went so far as to confiscate her passport to ensure he had full control of the situation. Things soon escalated as her husband began forcing her to engage in sexual acts with men she didn't know, which was all done under the threat of deportation. With the help of community workers she managed to leave the violent situation, but is unaware of what to do next.

1. How can a refugee house assist this woman?

2. What limitations would you face in applying an integrated approach to this situation?

Develop your knowledge – Case study 2

A young man comes to your refugee house from Uganda. During his stay you notice that he is very reserved and limits his involvement with other members of the house. As you begin to help him through the refugee process he withholds a lot of information, particularly the reasons why he fled Uganda. He does, however, speak frequently about a "partner" that he hopes to bring once he achieves permanent residency, although seems anxious when you ask for details. After some time you realize that the man becomes further anxious when ask to disclose certain information about his past. At this point the man is becoming progressively isolated.

1. How would you involve the integrated approach to foster community participation for this individual?

2. Can you foresee any ways in which a refugee house might fall short of holistic service provision for this case? If so, what referrals might be necessary?

Develop your knowledge – Ask yourself

1. In what ways do refugee houses provide an ideal model of integration for refugee populations?

2. How can we link the development of refugee houses to the changing socio-political climate in Canada?

3. How does popular media shape the experience of refugees in Canada?

Note

According to the Canada Housing and Mortgage Corporation (CMHC), the vacancy rate for the Toronto in April 2011 was 1.6 percent – one of the lowest in Canada (Canada Housing and Mortgage Corporation, 2011).

References

Ackerman, P. (2011a, September 21). Interview with "Laura." Resident of FCJ Refugee Centre.

Ackerman, P. (2011b, September 27). Interview with Co-Director Rico-Martinez.

Canada Housing and Mortgage Corporation (CMHC). (2011, June 9). *Canada's rental vacancy rate decrease.* Retrieved from http://www.cmhc-schl.gc.ca/en/corp/nero/nere/2011/2011-06-09-0815.cfm

Canadian Council for Refugees (CCR). (2009). *Brief history of Canada's responses to refugees.* Retrieved from http://ccrweb.ca.

Centre for Equity Rights in Accommodation (CERA). (2009). *"Sorry, it's rented:" Measuring discrimination in Toronto's rental housing market.* Toronto: CERA.

Citizenship and Immigration Canada (CIC). (2010, August 1). *Facts and figures 2009: Immigration overview: Permanent and temporary residents.* Retrieved fromhttp://www.cic.gc.ca/english/resources/statistics/facts2009/temporary/27.asp

FCJ Refugee Centre. (2011). Home page. Retrieved from http://www.fcjrefugeecentre.org

Teves, C. (2011, September 19). Interview with Director L. Hannigan, Ouellet, E., Warmington, A., & Yu, S. (2007). Refugee integration in Canada: A survey of empirical evidence and existing services. *Refuge, 24*(2), 17–34.

Paradis, E., Novac, S., Sarty, M., & Hulchanski, D.J. (2009). Better off in a shelter? A year of homelessness and housing among status immigrant, non-status migrant and Canadian-born families. In D.J. Hulchanski, P. Campsie, S.B. Chau, S.H. Hwang & E. Paradis (Eds.), *Finding home: Policy options for addressing homelessness in Canada* . Toronto: University of Toronto.

Pashang, S. (2011). The paradox of helping professions: Human service agencies and advocacy groups for the rights of non-status persons. In S. Pashang (Ed.), *Non-status women: invisible residents and underground resilience* (pp. 225–293). Toronto: Department of Adult Education and Counselling Psychology, University of Toronto.

Ryan, L., & Woodill, J. (2000). *A search for home: Refugee voices in the Romero House Community.* Toronto: Maytree Foundation.

Sherrel, K., D'Addario, S., & Hiebert, D. (2007). On the outside looking in: The precarious housing situation of successful refugee claimants in the GVRD. *Refuge 24*(2), 64–75.

Showler, P. (2011). *IRB refugee status determinations (1989–2010 calendar years).* Retrieved from http://www.cdphrc.uottawa.ca/projects/refugee-forum/projects/documents/RefugeeStatistics.pdf

Smith, N. (1995). Challenges of public housing in the 1990s: The case of Ontario, Canada. *Housing Policy Debate, 6*(4), 905–931.

Sojourn House. (n.d.). *Sojourn House.* Retrieved from http://www.sojourn-house.org

Wayland, S.V. (2007). *The housing needs of immigrants and refugees in Canada: A background paper for the Canadian Housing and Renewal Association.* Ottawa: Canadian Housing and Renewal Association.

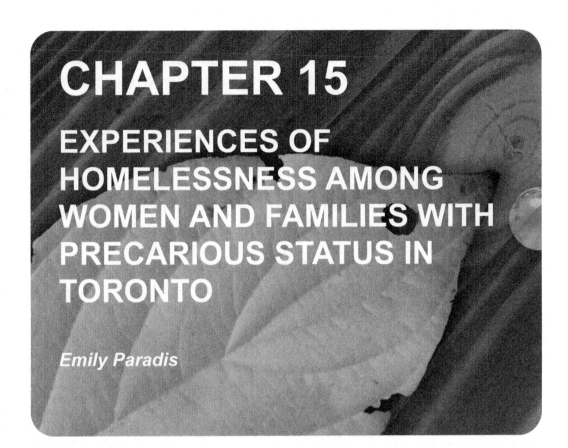

CHAPTER 15

EXPERIENCES OF HOMELESSNESS AMONG WOMEN AND FAMILIES WITH PRECARIOUS STATUS IN TORONTO

Emily Paradis

Introduction

I n this chapter I examine a phenomenon that is increasing in frequency in Toronto: homelessness among families headed by a mother with precarious status. Because mothers with precarious status may be threatened with detention and deportation if their status is exposed, there has been little research exploring the experiences of this very vulnerable group in Canada. Women with precarious status, and particularly mothers, are at heightened risk of exploitation related to their status, and their lack of access to services and supports affects not only their own well-being but that of their children as well. This chapter reports the findings of two studies that reveal the ways in which gender, racialization, immigration status, and homelessness intersect in the lives of mothers with precarious status. The first, a panel study comparing the experiences of immigrant and Canadian-born mothers in shelters, demonstrates that homelessness among families with precarious status is distinct from that of other groups in many ways. The second, a qualitative, participatory study in which homeless mothers with precarious status were interviewed by researchers who themselves had faced homelessness, immigration, and precarious status, draws upon women's own stories of migration, housing, and homelessness in order to better understand the complexities of these experiences.

(Re)defining Homelessness and Precarious Status in Canada

Homelessness is a relatively recent, and growing, phenomenon in Canada. Until the late 1980s, news media and research occasionally used the word "homeless" to refer to a very small number of people – mostly men in urban areas – who lived outside a family "home," whether in single-room-occupancy hotels and rooming houses, or more rarely, in shelters and on the street (Hulchanski, Campsie, Chau, Hwang, & Paradis, 2009). In the past three decades, though, homelessness has exploded across Canada, becoming a commonly used household word and an all-too-common experience of having no place of one's own to live. A recent national poll reported that one in nine Canadians have been homeless or have come close to it (Salvation Army, 2010), and research documents homelessness all across the country, in large and small cities, suburban and rural areas, and northern and First Nations communities.

There is no systematic collection of national data on homelessness in Canada, however, a recent comprehensive review of available data concludes that over 235,000 Canadians experience homelessness in a year (Gaetz, Gulliver, & Richter, 2014). Many cities conduct street counts and annual report cards to demonstrate the local extent of the problem. In Toronto, the most recent street needs assessment – including persons staying in shelters or on the street, and those with no fixed address residing in provincial institutions and violence against women (VAW) shelters – estimated that more than 5,000 people were homeless on a single night in 2013 (Toronto, 2013). City statistics in Toronto indicate that more than 16,000 different people used Toronto shelters in 2014 (Toronto, 2015).

A key challenge to estimating the prevalence of homelessness is that most data focuses on visible or absolute homelessness, and especially shelter statistics, thereby missing the much larger numbers of people experiencing hidden homelessness (including those with no place of their own who stay in vehicles, squats, or with family or friends), insecure housing (such as those living in situations of abuse, or facing the immediate threat of eviction due to inability to pay rent), and inadequate housing (for example, housing that is unaffordable, overcrowded, or in a dangerous condition). This leads to undercounting of specific groups, including women, who are more likely to have low incomes and to live in insecure, unsafe, and inadequate housing but less likely to resort to staying in shelters or on the street, especially if they have children (Callaghan, Farha, & Porter, 2002).

Homelessness does not affect all groups equally. Research consistently demonstrates that Aboriginal people and people with physical and mental health disabilities are overrepresented in homeless populations in all jurisdictions across Canada. Studies on family homelessness show that the majority of homeless families are headed by a lone mother, and that mothers who are Black, Aboriginal, and refugee claimants and those with disabilities including addictions, are overrepresented in family homelessness shelters (Paradis, Novac, Sarty, & Hulchanski, 2008).

As suggested by its relatively recent emergence, homelessness can be traced to economic and social changes of the past thirty years: free trade policies that have led to the loss of well-paying semi-skilled jobs in Canada through the relocation of the industrial and manufacturing sectors to the global South; the elimination of large-scale social housing programs by the federal and most provincial governments; the reduction of social assistance benefits and stagnation of minimum wages in most provinces; and cuts to health services, including deinstitutionalization programs in the mental health sector through which large numbers of psychiatric survivors were relocated from institutions into the community without the provision of adequate supports. Within this context of increasingly competitive job and housing markets coupled with diminishing financial and social supports, groups already disadvantaged by discrimination, violence, and exploitation – persons with disabilities, Aboriginal and racialized persons, immigrants and refugees, persons with low levels of education and income, lone parents, youth and older persons, queer and transgender persons, and especially women belonging to any of these groups – are at ever-increasing risk of homelessness.

Like "homelessness," "precarious status" is a neologism: a new term to describe an emerging social phenomenon. Though extensively documented in the United States, the existence of migrants without full legal status – usually described as "undocumented" or "illegal"– has been little discussed in Canada. Goldring, Berinstein, and Bernhard (2009) propose the construct of "precarious status" to describe the circumstances of increasing numbers of migrants to Canada under recent immigration policy. As they define it, precarious status refers to:

a confusing array of gradations of uncertain or "less than full" migration status ... marked by the absence of any of the following elements normally associated with permanent residence (and citizenship) in Canada: (1) work authorization, (2) the right to remain permanently in the country (residence permit), (3) not depending on a third party for one's right to be in Canada (such as a sponsoring spouse or employer) and (4) social citizenship rights available to permanent residents (e.g. public education and public health coverage). (Goldring, Berinstein, & Bernhard, 2009, pp. 240–41)

While some people with precarious status have entered or remained in Canada illegally (such as via trafficking, or overstaying visitor or student visas), precarious status is also a feature of many of the legal channels through which migrants enter Canada, including family sponsorship, refugee claims, and temporary worker programs (2009, pp. 248–51).

As with homelessness, recent policy changes have led to an increase in the proportion of people entering Canada who are vulnerable to having precarious status. Before the 1970s, Canadian immigration policy emphasized permanent immigration through which groups from designated racial and national origins could become Canadian citizens. Then, the elimination of preferred national and racial categories opened Canada's borders to immigration from countries of the global South and East, while at the same time the introduction of a "points system" and higher fees restricted immigration on the basis of education and income. In the past decade, the proportion of people immigrating with the opportunity to gain permanent status in Canada has declined in relationship to the proportion who enter Canada through temporary worker programs; since 2007, Canada has admitted more temporary than permanent residents each year (Nakache, 2010). Workers in temporary programs are mainly racialized people from the global South whose labour and social rights while in Canada are severely restricted, and most will never become eligible for permanent resident status (Sharma, 2006). Feminist scholars of immigration have also noted the gendered dimension of pathways into Canada, pointing out that categories such as Family Class immigration and the Live-in Caregiver Program make women particularly vulnerable to exploitation by sponsoring family members and employers (Thobani, 2001).

Critical analyses of both homelessness and precarious status call attention to the fact that they are actively *produced* by policies and programs. Such analyses argue against individualized explanations of homelessness and precarious status – for example, that they are the natural outcomes of an individual's decision to rely on welfare or migrate illegally – and instead, they examine how precarious status, precarious housing, and precarious work serve the interests of a hegemonic social and economic order. As suggested by the above historical accounts of economic and social changes leading to homelessness and precarious status, both phenomena have emerged in the context of neo-liberal globalization; that is, the recent proliferation of political and economic systems that favour the free global flow of money, goods, and labour, while systematically restricting or eliminating the rights of people who migrate, as well as the social rights and entitlements states provide to their own citizens.

Neo-liberalism has become a defining feature of Canadian policies and programs, with a direct impact on precarious status and homelessness that is often in contradiction to these policies' stated aims. For example, Sharma (2006) contends that neo-liberal immigration policies and border controls do not in fact function to protect "legal" immigrants and keep "illegal" migrants out of Canada. Instead, they ensure that migrants from the global South (themselves often displaced by the economic and political consequences of corporatist globalization in their countries of origin) are an easily exploited labour force having severely limited rights. Likewise, Peck (2001) points out that Ontario social assistance programs do not in fact provide access to dignified income and housing for those who are excluded from the labour and housing markets due to disability, parenting responsibilities, or other barriers. Instead, the welfare state of the past has become a neo-liberal "workfare state" which functions to push social assistance recipients back into the least-desirable sectors of the labour market and punish those who fail to become self-sufficient. In both cases, such policies diminish the social and legal rights of oppressed groups.

In Canada, policy and program changes based on a neo-liberal ideology have been implemented by successive governments at the federal and provincial levels, in spite of predictions, since realized, that they would increase levels of homelessness and precarious status. For example, in the lead-up to the new Immigrant and Refugee Protection Act of 2002, Thobani (2001) warned of how these changes would affect access to immigration, particularly for low-income racialized women from countries in the global South:

The current restructuring of the immigration program, which includes the introduction of the new act, will make immigration for permanent settle ment (with landed migrant status) from the countries of the South – and in particular, of poor and working women from the South – extremely restrictive. These restrictive measures can be expected to push many would-be immigrant women, who might otherwise have entered the country with landed status, into becoming migrants, whether legal or otherwise. As immigration for legal, permanent settlement into Canada is made more difficult for people from the South, we can expect an increase in extra-legal forms of migration. Likewise, the significant growth of unemployment globally and the expansion of the informal sectors, both of which have become key features of the restructuring of the global economy, will further escalate migrations from the South into the North. (pp. 31–32)

Similarly, when Ontario premier Mike Harris announced a 21.6 percent cut to welfare benefits in 1995, critics warned that it would lead to an increase in homelessness. As predicted, shelter use increased precipitously in the year following the cut.

If immigration policies have led to an increase in extra-legal migration by women from the global South while social policies have elevated the vulnerability to homelessness among disadvantaged groups, then we can expect to see more homelessness among women with precarious status. The remainder of this chapter documents this very outcome. The next section draws upon qualitative, longitudinal research to demonstrate how migrant women's pathways into and out of homelessness are distinct from those of women born in Canada and women with permanent resident status. This is followed by a detailed case study that illustrates the mutually reinforcing impacts of precarious status and homelessness on women. The chapter concludes with recommendations for policy and program changes that would mitigate these impacts and restore the rights of social citizenship for homeless women with precarious status.

Homelessness among Mothers with Precarious Status

The study "Immigrants, discrimination, and homelessness" (Paradis, Novac, Sarty, & Hulchanski, 2008) aimed to compare the experiences of Canadian-born and immigrant mothers in Toronto shelters for homeless families. We wanted to know the ways in which the experiences of immigrant women who are homeless differ from those of Canadian-born women. In what ways does discrimination contribute to family homelessness? We did not expect that the study's most important findings would respond to a question we had not even asked: How is homelessness different for families headed by a mother with precarious status? As it turned out, this became the first and only study in Canada to systematically compare the experiences of homeless families with precarious status to those of Canadian-born and status immigrant families.

The researchers recruited 91 women who were staying in family shelters with at least one dependent child. Of these, 50 were born in Canada and 41 had been living in Canada for between one and ten years. Each woman was interviewed three times between December 2004 and July 2007; at the time of recruitment, two months later, and one year later. Using a structured questionnaire, we asked mothers about their background, education, settlement experiences, housing history, history of homelessness, housing search, symptoms of stress, sense of belonging, dealings with people, experiences of discrimination, and income, as well as their children's health and happiness, childcare and school attendance, school performance, and episodes of separation from children. Survey responses were analysed using frequencies and simple correlations in SPSS statistical software, while open-ended responses were entered into a word processing file and analysed thematically.

By following these families over a year's time, the study was able to track how their circumstances, well-being, and perceptions changed as they survived their episode of homelessness and re-established housing in the community. We saw first hand the ways in which various systems – including the shelter, social housing, social assistance, child welfare, childcare, healthcare, and immigration systems – at times assisted families in achieving stability, and at times created further barriers to families' access to safe, decent, affordable housing. Because the interviews were conducted in English, this study did not represent the experiences of the many immigrant women whose English language ability is limited. The study also did not reflect the situations of mothers who separate from their children and enter the single women's shelter system when their family loses its housing, which is another common form of family homelessness.

At the time of the first interview, 20 of the immigrant women had no permanent status in Canada, while 21 were permanent residents or citizens. By the final interview, 57 women remained in the study: fifteen women without status, 17 status immigrants, and 25 Canadian-born. Because of participants' unstable living situations and circumstances of ongoing crisis, low retention rates are common in longitudinal research on homelessness. In this study, precarious status also contributed to our loss of contact with some participants – for example, when women went "underground" or were deported after their claims for refugee status were denied.

When we began to analyse the data, we were surprised to find that there appeared to be few statistical differences between immigrant and Canadian-born women. But when we broke down the results for the immigrant women into those who had achieved permanent resident status and those whose status was precarious, certain trends began to emerge. While there were many similarities between Canadian-born and status immigrant women, those with precarious status emerged as strikingly different from both other groups.

Women with precarious status who spoke with us – whether they were temporary workers, awaiting resolution of a refugee claim, or living "underground" – were extremely vulnerable, often living in conditions of deep poverty, housing instability, danger, and exploitation. They had limited access to social assistance, healthcare, and other social benefits, often relied on under-the-table employment, and drew on informal networks to secure housing. For these women, pregnancy and childbirth represented a crisis, making employment impossible, incurring healthcare costs, and disrupting precarious housing arrangements. When they entered family shelters, they were encouraged to try to regularize their status, although many would not qualify as refugees. Some were deported, while others would wait years and spend substantial sums on fees and legal counsel before they and their families could enjoy a life of stability. Though our sample is small, the experiences reported by this group of 20 women can help us understand the ways in which precarious status produces and maintains other forms of precarity and vulnerability.

Differences between Women with Precarious Status, Canadian-born Women and Status Immigrant Women

Due to their circumstances, women with precarious status in our sample differed significantly from Canadian-born women and status immigrant women across many dimensions, including their family status, housing and homelessness, education and income, and experiences of discrimination.

Demographics and Family Status

In keeping with the critical analyses above, women from the global South account for the vast majority of women with precarious status in this study. Of the 20 non-status women in the study, the majority (11, or 55 percent) were from the Caribbean, eight of these from St. Vincent; two were from Latin America, two from Europe, four from Africa, and one from Asia.

Non-status women had the fewest, and youngest, children of all groups: three out of four had only one child with them in the shelter, none had more than two children, and many had a baby under one year old. This suggests that for non-status women, homelessness is often precipitated by pregnancy and the birth of a child, which may prevent women from maintaining employment and may cause ruptures in precarious housing arrangements. Women with precarious status were also less likely than other groups to have lived with a partner before becoming homeless.

Distinct Profile of Housing and Homelessness

Non-status women were more likely than the other groups to report very unstable housing. Two out of three (65 percent) had lived in four or more places in the past two years, compared to 55 percent of Canadian-born women and 45 percent of status immigrant women. At the last place before they became homeless, non-status women had less housing security than the other groups. They were more likely to live in short-term, informal arrangements with acquaintances or extended family members, in which they lacked security of tenure, and were vulnerable to sudden eviction, exploitation, and invasion of privacy. In other words, their housing often resembled conditions of "hidden homelessness" more than it did a secure, permanent residence.

Low-income, racialized, and immigrant lone mothers are commonly discriminated against in the housing market and must often rely on precarious housing arrangements in which they are not the primary tenant. While they also face these forms of discrimination, women with precarious status are even more likely to be excluded from access to stable housing due to their status. For example, women who are living in hiding may lack bank accounts and other identity documents required by landlords, or may not wish to have their names recorded on a lease.

This group also cited somewhat different reasons for leaving home. The most common reason for becoming homeless overall was abuse: Thirty percent of all women in the study left home to escape abuse by partners, other family members, or landlords. But for women with precarious status, abuse was not the most common reason for leaving home. While one in five (20 percent) left home because of abuse, for almost one in three (30 percent), leaving home was related in some way to pregnancy or the presence of children. Further, almost all of the women in the study who left home for these reasons had precarious status. Some lost their jobs when they became pregnant, while others were told to leave their homes for this reason. The high number of young babies in this group of families is further evidence of the correlation between pregnancy and housing loss. Others were asked to move because their children were too noisy, hinting at conditions of overcrowding in their shared accommodations.

This intersects with another common precipitor of homelessness for non-status women: the sudden termination of precarious, shared housing arrangements. Many became homeless when they were simply told to leave by the people in whose homes they were staying; we did not always learn the reasons why they were kicked out. Though we did not ask about the citizenship status of women's cohabitants, these accounts of how women lost their housing indirectly suggest the desperate conditions of whole communities living in hiding with precarious status, trying to provide for each other while also protecting themselves, worried that noisy children would attract attention or that one more mouth would be impossible to feed.

Once in the shelter, non-status women stayed longer than any other group. More than one in four (27 percent) stayed in shelters for more than one year, whereas no status immigrant or Canadian-born women stayed this long. Only one in five women (20 percent) with precarious status stayed in the shelter for less than four months, compared to about one in three status immigrant women and one in two Canadian-born women. This is related to long processing times for refugee claims and Humanitarian and Compassionate (H&C) claims. Only once women have an active claim do they become eligible for benefits such as social assistance, the National Child Benefit and Supplement (NCBS), and subsidized housing. At this stage they are also eligible to apply for work permits, though many are refused. Without access to employment, welfare, social housing, or subsidized childcare, women have no choice but to remain in the shelter.

Finally, this group also had worse post-shelter housing than the other groups. More than two-thirds lived in one-bedroom apartments after leaving the shelter, whereas the majority of women in other groups lived in larger units. In contrast with their pre-shelter housing, women with precarious status were more likely than other groups to be the only adult in their post-shelter households. Unlike Canadian-born and status immigrant women, most non-status women said they were not satisfied with their new place. Common concerns included poor maintenance, disrepair, infestations, dangerous neighbourhoods, distance from amenities, and high cost. In spite of these problems, these women were more likely than other groups to stay in the first place they moved to after the shelter, suggesting that they had few other options. This is consistent with other research showing that women who are racialized, immigrants and lone mothers are forced into lower-quality and higher-priced sectors of the housing market, due to patterns of discrimination on the part of landlords (Callaghan, Farha, & Porter, 2002); those landlords who will "accept" these tenants know that they have nowhere else to go. It is also possible that for many, remaining in one place after leaving the shelter was related to the requirements and expense of claiming permanent residency.

Education, Employment, and Incomes

Due to the "points system" by which applications for immigration to Canada are assessed, recent immigrants tend to have higher rates of education than people of the same age born in Canada. However, it is surprising to note that women with precarious status had higher levels of education than both Canadian-born and status immigrant women in the sample. While about two-thirds of Canadian-born women and status immigrant women had no credentials, fewer than one-quarter of non-status migrant women had none. More than twice as many non-status women reported having vocational credentials (22 percent) and community college degrees (28 percent) than Canadian-born or status immigrant women (about ten percent each for community college, and less than ten percent each for vocational). For some, these credentials were earned in Canada, at private institutes that do not require proof of permanent residence. While credentials earned in Canada might improve women's job prospects and strengthen their claims to regularize their status, we also heard from a few that they had been lured by private institutes targeting new Canadians into paying exorbitant tuition fees for certificates that later turned out to be worthless. This scenario is another example of how precarious status contributes to women's vulnerability to exploitation.

Women with precarious status also had distinct patterns with regards to their sources of income. Contrary to the stereotype that most homeless people are dependent on social assistance, most families in the study had income from employment (whether earned by the mother or her partner) in the year preceding their episode of homelessness. Rates of employment declined across time overall, with fewer than half reporting income from employment at the final interview. Rates of full-time employment declined, while rates of casual employment and social assistance increased. For all mothers in the study, then, homelessness itself appeared to disrupt access to stable employment, and the effects of this disruption persisted after being re-housed.

For women with precarious status, this pattern was more significant and was related to their immigration status. Due to their status, most of these women had no legal access to social assistance; most also did not live with partners before becoming homeless. Almost half (40 percent) received income from full-time employment before losing their housing. Homelessness for many was directly precipitated by the loss of a job, often because of pregnancy or the birth of a child; however, none of those who had been employed full-time listed Employment Insurance as a source of income. Once in a shelter, most began the long and uncertain process of seeking permanent status in Canada; at different points in this process, claimants gain or lose eligibility for social assistance, work permits, and other benefits. By the time of the third interview, fewer than one in seven had full-time employment, while 40 percent reported casual employment, and more than half were receiving social assistance. In many cases, casual, under-the-table employment was likely the only option available to new mothers of infants with uncertain status and no work permits.

One important aspect of casual, under-the-table employment as the main or only source of income is its unpredictability, as demonstrated by one mother's situation: "My total income for the last month was $2,000, but it varies widely month by month. Some months I make as little as $600 or as much as $1,500 [cleaning houses], and my baby's father gives different amounts." Lack of legal access to employment makes workers with precarious status more vulnerable to exploitation by employers; however, as demonstrated by this quote, it also has the gendered effect of increasing women's dependence on the fathers of their children, making it even more difficult for women to leave situations of abuse.

Even though they were more likely to be employed full time before they entered the shelter, women without permanent status were also much more likely to report very low incomes than Canadian-born women or permanent residents. One out of three non-status women had annual incomes below $5,000.00, compared to only about one out of twenty permanent residents and Canadian-born women. Because groups in the study had different average family sizes, we also measured the relative depth of poverty of each family in relationship to the low-income cut-off (LICO), which is Canada's functional equivalent of a poverty line, set annually for families of different sizes in different locations. Nearly every family in the study had pre-shelter incomes that were below the LICO for their family size, but women with precarious status had the lowest incomes of all groups. Almost half (44 percent) had extremely low incomes of less than 25 percent of the LICO for their family size, compared to one in three Canadian-born women (33 percent), and one in ten status immigrant women (11 percent). The trend of very low incomes among non-status women held true for monthly incomes as well: Sixty percent of non-status women reported monthly incomes below $300.00, compared to 32 percent of Canadian-born women and only ten percent of permanent residents. By the time of the third interview, all non-status women still had incomes below the LICO for their family size, and one in three (33 percent) still had very low annual incomes below 25 percent of their family size LICO.

This data on employment and income corroborates the view that the lowest-paid, least-regulated, and informal sectors of the economy benefit from the availability of women with precarious status as a source of cheap, easily exploited labour. The state also benefits, for even though many workers with precarious status (such as temporary workers) contribute to Employment Insurance and pension programs, they are generally ineligible to receive assistance from these programs. Also significant is that women in the study who were fired as a result of pregnancy did not have recourse to human rights protections, which prohibit discrimination by employers on the basis of family status.

Experiences and Perceptions of Discrimination

Women with precarious status reported perceptions of discrimination and social exclusion that appear to be related to their status. For example, at the time of the third interview, a significant number said that they were regularly treated as though they were dishonest, while the other groups reported this type of discrimination at a much lower rate. Also at the third interview, more than one in three non-status women (much more than the other two groups) strongly agreed with the statement, "I feel that I am not given opportunities that are generally available to others." More than one in four strongly agreed that "I feel that I am consistently judged by society on the basis of things other than my abilities or personality." These rates of strong agreement represented a substantial increase from the previous interviews. These findings hint at the significant obstacles to employment and other opportunities women encountered due to their lack of status, as well as the barriers women were facing in attempting to regularize their status.

In addition to perceived discrimination, women with precarious status encountered incidents of overt discrimination in housing and employment that directly affected their loss of housing and prevented them from moving out of homelessness. At the first interview, almost one in three (30 percent) non-status women had been prevented from moving into an apartment in the previous year due to discrimination by landlords based on income, family status, and race. By the time of the third interview, the percentage of non-status women experiencing housing discrimination had increased to 40 percent – they were the only group whose rate of housing discrimination increased. Almost half of non-status women also reported discrimination in employment, usually based on status. Women's loss of jobs and housing due to pregnancy also represents prohibited discrimination on the basis of family status. Also of importance for women with precarious status – almost all of whom were racialized – is the finding that women of colour experienced higher rates of discrimination on all prohibited grounds, including gender, family status and source of income. This is consistent with research showing that landlords tend to discriminate more against people who are racialized on all grounds, not only race – or that they are masking racist discrimination with seemingly race-neutral explanations (Dion, 2001).

One Year Later

In the final interview, we asked women about changes for the better and for the worse in their lives over the past year. Though brief, the responses of women with precarious status demonstrate that their lives went on while they were moving slowly through the maze of applications, assessments, hearings, and appeals to regularize their status. Women went to school, found housing, formed relationships, got jobs, and expanded their families, all while living with changing eligibility for employment and social benefits as well as uncertainty about their long-term future in Canada.

The status of most had changed in the past year, and was still in flux. A few had been approved for permanent residency or had become citizens; several others had been denied at one stage of claiming status and were trying to become residents through a different process. At least one woman who did not complete the study was known to have been deported after her claim was denied, and we suspect that several others dropped out of contact with the study when they were forced "underground" by an unfavourable decision on their refugee claims.

The women's comments reveal the complexities of the process of attempting to regularize one's status in Canada. Some women were still in shelters since their lack of status restricted their access to social assistance, employment, subsidized housing, and childcare: "My situation is the same. I'm still in a shelter, I'm still a single mom, still waiting for my immigration. I can't work or go to school."

Once women's applications for refugee status had been registered, they were able to anticipate staying in Canada throughout the decision process. Also, with a claim under consideration, women became eligible for employment and some benefits: "My refugee claim was denied, but the Refugee Board is investigating to see if I qualify for government protection so I'm still here, have SIN [i.e., a Social Insurance Number], work permit, and OHIP [Ontario Health Insurance Program coverage]. I'm going to school for advanced computers, looking for a job. Now I'm eligible for, and receive, social assistance."

For some, attempts to formally regularize their status had resulted in an even more precarious situation than had been the case when they were living in hiding: "I'm moving into an apartment with my partner and children, still waiting for my Humanitarian and Compassionate Immigration hearing. They could deport me at any time, even before the hearing."

Even when women were finally accepted for permanent residency, they still faced financial barriers to obtaining needed documents. One mother, who was on welfare and living alone with an infant in a non-subsidized apartment, explained, "I was accepted as a refugee; now I'm waiting for my landed papers. It took me four months to save the $575 to get my permanent residency." Welfare barely provides enough to cover rent, food, and other necessities, but this woman was in an impossible situation: if she failed to pay the money and get the documents within a fixed number of months, her status would be revoked; but at the same time, any extra money she earned would be clawed back from her welfare cheque and would potentially place her entitlement at risk.

A few women achieved landed status and even citizenship during the course of the study, and were finally able to contribute fully to their communities and society without fear of being deported: "I got my landed immigration status! I have housing, started school to get my GED [General Educational Development], going to church. I'm in the choir." These success stories represented the end of a very long and uncertain journey.

Many mothers, regardless of their status, recounted life improvements that were poignant in their simplicity: Privacy, waking up in one's own room, and choosing children's meals or bedtimes are everyday comforts most housed parents take for granted. For women with precarious status who achieved permanent residency, this poignancy is amplified by the stark contrast between a life lived in fear of deportation, and a life lived secure in the right to stay where one chooses.

Case Study – One Woman's Story: Rose

In the "Diverse Family Homelessness" study, we conducted in-depth, semi-structured interviews with four groups of homeless mothers, including mothers with precarious status. Through these interviews, we hoped to gain a clearer understanding of some of the trends we identified in the previous study. The interviews were conducted by a pair of trained interviewers who themselves shared lived experiences of immigration, precarious status, and/or homelessness. The interviewers' expertise in these issues and the trust they cultivated with the research participants yielded stories that reveal not only the complex realities of living without status, but also women's thoughts and feelings as they confront the challenges of parenting without a stable home. This section presents one such story, that of Rose.

Rose came to Canada as a visitor in 1989. Though she was a young woman of colour from a Caribbean country with no legal status, she states that life was not too hard then. She was able to find work easily, shared an apartment with a friend, and saved her money. After five years in Canada she formed a relationship with a man, and together they bought a house. With a good job in a hospital, Rose's status barely affected her. It posed some financial disadvantages – like when she received bills for medical expenses after the births of their three children – but these were not onerous. Besides, her partner assured her that once they were legally married, she would get her status. She explains:

> When I was with the kids them dad he always promised I'm gonna get married to you so I'll sponsor you so you don't have to worry about that. So I said, well, you know, I'm okay, and we working, he working and I working—things would be okay. He promised but when his promise came for him to follow through he just changed his mind and said you are on your own.

In 2001, fleeing physical and verbal abuse, Rose took her children to a Violence against Women (VAW) shelter. She later

continued...

found out that if she had called the police, they would have evicted her partner, and she would have retained possession of the house. But as it was, with her status, she thought it safer to take her kids and leave everything else behind. Though women in shelters who are fleeing partner violence are given priority on the social housing wait list, Rose did not qualify because of her status. It took her nine months to find an apartment for her family. On the advice of a lawyer she made an application for refugee status, even though her country was not recognized as a "refugee-producing country." With an active claim, she became eligible for social assistance. Then her claim was denied, and she lost access to social assistance and the childcare subsidy. Her ex-partner never complied with a court order to sell the house and repay Rose her share of the life savings she had invested.

With no other source of income available, she went back to work to support her children, working extra jobs in order to afford the full cost of childcare. She began to file tax returns so that her children could receive the national child benefit, but was informed that she required a social insurance number in order to have the returns accepted. Then, in 2008, she was injured at work and subsequently hospitalized for over a month for complications from the injury. When she got out of the hospital, still too sick to work, she did not qualify for worker's compensation or employment insurance. Her landlord began to harass her, even though he had her last month's rent deposit. Knowing she could not work and would not be able to afford rent the following month, she gave notice, and moved her children, now aged 7, 10, and 12, to a shelter for homeless families. In the shelter, without access to Ontario's medical plan for low-income families, she struggled to get to medical appointments and cover the costs of her own medication and medicine for her son's attention deficit hyperactivity disorder (ADHD).

In analysing her own situation and the policies that need to change, Rose points out that her precarious status led directly and indirectly to her family's second episode of homelessness:

continued...

At that time [in the VAW shelter] if I did qualify for [subsidized] housing, I would've still been in the housing. The kids them would've been getting child tax benefit and the dad was ordered to pay child support. So if I was getting that and if I get sick and I went to the hospital, I know I was coming home to my home still. But because I wasn't qualifying for housing, social assistance, or anything like that ... but if I did have that opportunity I wouldn't be in the shelter. I would've still been able to be in my home.

While in the shelter, Rose received legal aid and hired a lawyer who filed a claim for Humanitarian and Compassionate status. The lawyer told her that if her first application had been for H&C instead of refugee status, it probably would have been accepted. She again qualified for social assistance, and found an apartment. The problem was that the rent cost the same amount as her monthly welfare cheque. She hoped the children's father would begin paying some child support so that her family could afford food while she waited for a green light from her doctor to go back to work.

As a woman with precarious status, Rose's social and economic rights – the rights to adequate housing and income, social security, health, and protection of the family – were consistently violated by a nation that has signed an international convention enshrining these rights for all who reside here. However, as she points out, this violation of the rights of social citizenship extended beyond her to her Canadian-born children:

It's a very hard road to travel down and especially when you have kids. They are Canadian born but still because of you they have no rights. They have a birth certificate that is Canadian, they have a health card but still they have no – they can't get no child tax benefit, they can't get no help from the government, no social assistance. Not even a drug plan ... So, it's really kind of affecting me and it affecting them in some way because things that they want, that they should be having, they can't have it because the parent is not a Canadian citizen.

Conclusion and Recommendations

In many respects, Rose's story is quite different from the profile in the previous section, in which many mothers who had been in Canada a shorter time lost precarious jobs and housing due to pregnancy. Shelter providers say that stories like Rose's are becoming more common since the 2008 recession: Family shelters are seeing an increase in mothers who have been in Canada many years and now have older children. Until the recession many were able to maintain employment and housing, but their precarious, under-the-table jobs disappeared with the economic crash. At the same time, tightening refugee regulations and longer processing times are further delaying their attempts to regularize their status, leading to even longer average shelter stays for this group as compared to in the past. As one administrator noted, "Refugee policy drives family shelter use."

Rose's story, and the profile of homelessness among women with precarious status in the previous study, both corroborate critical theorists' contention that a complex network of policies and practices produce and sustain homelessness among families with precarious status. Advocacy organizations such as No One Is Illegal and the Advocacy Centre for Tenants of Ontario call for sweeping changes that will enshrine rights to legal status, guaranteed income, and adequate housing for all who live and work in Canada. Certainly, these are the social transformations that are truly necessary for ending homelessness and precarious status.

At the same time, as Rose's story demonstrates, until these transformations can be achieved, simpler changes to numerous policies and programs at many levels would assist more families with precarious status in Toronto to avoid homelessness or to re-establish housing.

At the federal level:

1. **Canada Revenue Agency** must guarantee access to the Canada Child Benefit and National Child Benefit Supplement for all Canadian-born children of parents with precarious status.
2. **The Immigration and Refugee Board** must speed up processing time for the Letter of Referral, which is required to qualify for social assistance in Ontario.
3. **Citizenship and Immigration Canada** should automatically grant all work permit applications by status claimants: this will not only provide claimants with legal access to income, but will enable the government to collect income taxes and reduce other social spending associated with lack of access to income.

At the provincial level:

1. **The Ministry of Social Services** must guarantee access to the Ontario Child Benefit, the Trillium drug plan for low-income families, and social housing for all Canadian-born children of parents without status.
2. **The Ontario Works Act** should be amended to allow people with precarious status to apply for social assistance once they have registered an application for status, instead of requiring the Letter of Referral.
3. **The Human Rights Commission and Ministry of Labour** must ensure that workers with precarious status are aware of their human rights and have access to protection from discrimination in housing and employment.

At the local/municipal level:

1. **Non-profit organizations** in cooperation with municipal shelter administrations should develop dedicated transitional housing for homeless families with precarious status, so that children and parents can live in a home-like environment while parents regularize their status. Like provincially-mandated Violence Against Women shelters, these settings must be secure from intrusion by immigration enforcement and Canadian Border Services Agency officers.

Develop your knowledge – Ask yourself

1. Canadian law recognizes homelessness as a violation of human rights under the Charter of Rights and Freedoms.

   true   false

2. When a family with young children becomes homeless, they are immediately provided with a rent-subsidized apartment.

   true   false

Develop your knowledge – Ask yourself

As demonstrated by Rose's story, access to social benefits is highly complex for women with precarious status and their children. Shifting and sometimes arbitrary eligibility interferes greatly with families' access to stable housing. Using internet sources, determine which of the following benefits homeless families with precarious status have access to, and under what conditions.

Subsidized housing	yes	no	it depends
Work permit	yes	no	it depends
Welfare	yes	no	it depends
Healthcare for the mother	yes	no	it depends
Healthcare for the children	yes	no	it depends
Perinatal care for mother and baby	yes	no	it depends
Shelter	yes	no	it depends
Police protection from an abusive partner	yes	no	it depends
Employment insurance (regular and maternity)	yes	no	it depends
School for the children	yes	no	it depends
National child benefit and supplement	yes	no	it depends
Ontario child benefit	yes	no	it depends
Childcare subsidy	yes	no	it depends

How easy or difficult is it to locate this information? Do you find contradictory information? If you were serving a client in this situation, would you know how to refer them?

References

Callaghan, M., Farha, L., & Porter, B. (2002). *Women and housing in Canada: Barriers to equality*. Toronto: Centre for Equality Rights in Accommodation (CERA) and Women's Housing Program.

Dion, K. (2001). Immigrants' perceptions of housing discrimination in Toronto: The Housing New Canadians project. *Journal of Social Issues, 57*(3), 523–39.

Gaetz, S., Gulliver, T. & Richter, T. (2014). *The state of homelessness in Canada: 2014*. Toronto: The Homeless Hub Press.

Goldring, L., Berinstein, C., & Bernhard, J. (2009). Institutionalizing precarious migratory status in Canada. *Citizenship Studies, 13*(3), 239–65.

Hulchanski, D., Campsie, C., Chau, S. Hwang, S. & Paradis, E. (2009). Introduction: Homelessness: What's in a word? In: D. Hulchanski, P. Campsie, S. Chau, S. Hwang, & E. Paradis (Eds.), *Finding home: Policy options for addressing homelessness in Canada* (pp. 1-16). Toronto: University of Toronto.

Nakache, D. (2010, September). The Canadian Temporary Foreign Worker Program: Regulations, practices and protection gaps. Paper presented at the workshop of the Research Alliance on Precarious Status, Toronto, York University. Retrieved from http://www.yorku.ca/raps1.

Paradis, E., Novac, S., Sarty, M., & Hulchanski, D. (2008). *Better off in a shelter? A year of homelessness and housing among status immigrant, non-status migrant, and Canadian-born families*. Centre for Urban and Community Studies Research Paper, 213. Toronto: University of Toronto.

Peck, J. (2001). *Workfare states*. New York: Guilford.

Salvation Army. (2010). Poverty shouldn't be a life sentence: A report on the perceptions of homelessness and poverty in Canada. Retrieved from http://www.homelesshub.ca/Library/Povertyshouldn%E2%80%99t-be-a-life- sentence-A-report-on-the-perceptions-of-homelessness-and-poverty-in-Canada-48539.aspx

Sharma, N. (2006). *Home economics: Nationalism and the making of "migrant workers" in Canada.* Toronto: University of Toronto Press.

Thobani, S. (2001). Benevolent state, law-breaking smugglers, and deportable and expendable women: An analysis of the Canadian state's strategy to address trafficking in women. *Refuge, 19*(4), 24–33.

Toronto. (2013). 2013 street needs assessment results. Toronto: City of Toronto. Retrieved from http://www.toronto.ca/legdocs/mmis/2013/cd/bgrd/backgroundfile-61365.pdf.

Toronto. (2015). Staff report: Infrastructure and service improvement plan for the emergency shelter system. Submitted to Community Development and Recreation Committee, 9 March 2015. Toronto: City of Toronto.

PART 7

EMPLOYMENT

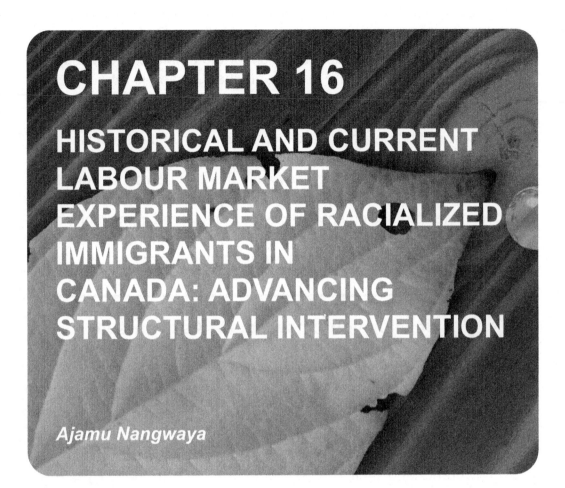

CHAPTER 16

HISTORICAL AND CURRENT LABOUR MARKET EXPERIENCE OF RACIALIZED IMMIGRANTS IN CANADA: ADVANCING STRUCTURAL INTERVENTION

Ajamu Nangwaya

Introduction

In this chapter I explore the historical and contemporary experience of racialized immigrants in the Canadian labour market. It is argued that the solution to eliminate inequalities in the labour market for racialized immigrants ought to address the systemic barriers engrained within the Canadian labour market as well as other major institutions. This inequality is rooted in Canada being a White settler-colonial society where race and racism have been used as organizing principles in regulating the use and treatment of the indigenous peoples and other racialized workers in the labour market. The challenges confronting racialized immigrants in accessing employment opportunities that match their educational attainment are informed by the racialization of their labour. By historicizing the labour experiences of racialized and immigrant workers the chapter makes it clear that the exploited and marginalized condition of racialized immigrant and racialized Canadian-born workers is not accidental or due to personal misfortune as is often perceived.

Their labour market reality is a very basic part of their racial subordination as a people and of the need of capitalism or the employers for cheap and readily available workers. The immigrants that Canada is attracting to its shores today are largely coming from global South countries of the Caribbean, Latin America, Africa, and Asia. These migrants are facing structural employment barriers that have long been a part of the Canadian experience for racialized people, including the indigenous peoples. Employment equity plans, employment equity laws, and the unionization of workplaces ought to play a larger role in the dialogue and proposed solutions about the employment-related settlement experience of racialized immigrants, especially in sectors of the job market where they are concentrated, such as the retail, healthcare, light industrial and transportation sectors.

Develop your knowledge – Ask yourself

As you read this chapter, ask yourself and reflect on the following questions:

1. What has been the historical experience of racialized immigrants and racialized workers in general in the Canadian labour market?

2. Who benefits from the racialization of immigrant labour and how does that affects the unity between white and racialized workers in the workplace?

3. What type of policies, laws, and initiatives are needed to deal with systemic and institutionalized forms of racism that are experienced by racialized immigrant and non-immigrant racialized workers?

4. How relevant are employment equity laws, the insertion of employment equity plans into collective agreements, or union contracts and workplace unionization to the labour market reality of immigrant and racialized non-immigrant workers?

Historical Context of Race, Immigration, and Settlement

Canada has a fabled history of welcoming immigrants to this country (Canadian Chamber of Commerce, 2009) and it is a much celebrated national myth that gives ideological reinforcement to its self-image as a fair, just, and tolerant political space. Many Canadians are familiar with the narrative of Canada providing refugee to enslaved Africans fleeing chattel slavery in the United States by way of the storied Underground Railroad (Hill, 1992; Mathieu, 2010). Generally, one will not find the same level of awareness of Canada's use of the enslaved labour of African and Indigenous peoples in Lower Canada and Upper Canada (Hill, 1992). Further, the narrative about Canada's legendary openness to newcomers is silent on the racist activities of the Canadian state and groups and individuals in society in preventing or severely restricting African Americans, African Caribbean people, and other racialized peoples from settling as homesteaders in Western Canada (Bolari & Li, 1988; Mathieu, 2010; Thomson, 1979).

Under provisions within the *Immigration Act* of 1910 the Canadian government "arbitrarily require that black immigrants possess $500 at the time of entry but wave in white American migrants with only $25" (Mathieu, 2010, p. 33). There were also instances where Europeans were given free passage to enter Canada. The aforementioned immigration legislation empowered the relevant minister to "prohibit for a stated period or permanently, the landing in Canada … [of] immigrants belonging to any race deemed unsuited to the climate or requirements of Canada" (Mathieu, 2010, p. 33). Yet the fact that enslaved Africans were able to live in the cold Canadian climate during two hundred years of enslavement never dawned on the architects and promoters of the exclusion of these prospective migrants from the United States and the Caribbean (Thomson, 1979).

While the government placed systemic barriers to limit the migration of African people to Canada as settlers, it nonetheless grudgingly accommodated their arrival as sleeping car porters with the railway companies, such as Canadian Pacific Railway and the Northern Alberta Railway. This apparent discrepancy was the result of the capitalist railway owners' need for a pool of compliant and wage-moderating labour that would receive lower wage rates than that paid to White workers. However this unfair wage system fulfilled racialized stereotypes of servile African workers being at the beck and call of affluent White customers (Mathieu, 2010). Even the trade unions that represented railway workers were in on the act of anti-African racism by excluding African workers from the ranks of their membership through racist exclusionary clauses in their constitutions (Grizzle, 1998). In 1908, the Canadian Brotherhood of Railway Employees inserted a clause into its constitution denying membership to African Canadians (Mathieu, 2010). The unholy alliance between White trade unions and capitalist bosses had the effect in both Canada and its southern neighbour of excluding African American and African Canadian men from skilled trades such as brakemen and firefighters on the railway (Grizzle, 1998).

The development of immigration schemes that welcomed the labour of racialized workers in Canada while placing a limit on the rapid growth in their population were also imposed against other peoples. Chinese migrant workers were invaluable to the construction of the Canadian Pacific Railway in the late nineteenth century, because of the limited supply of White workers in British Columbia (Bolari & Li, 1988). According to Bolari & Li, the significance of migrant Chinese workers may be deduced from the fact that "Between 1876 and 1880, for example, the number of Chinese arriving at Victoria by ship was 2.326, and the number rose to 13,245 for the period 1881–1883" (1988, p. 105). The access to Chinese workers was also useful to the capitalist employers because they were cheap and exploitable. However, in British Columbia these employers openly demonstrated their racist dislike for Chinese workers when lower wage rates were no longer an option, because White workers and their organization had forced the bosses to end the practice (Das Gupta, 1998). The employers gave the now better-paying jobs that were formerly occupied by Chinese workers to White workers.

However, once Chinese immigrant labour was seen as a source of competition to native White labour, racist attacks and initiatives emerged to curb migration to Canada. Trade unions and citizens' groups in British Columbia and the federal government found common cause by way of the *Chinese Exclusion Act* of 1923, which banned the migration of Chinese workers to Canada (Das Gupta, 1998). The legislation required all Chinese in Canada to register their presence with the federal government, which was affirmed by the issuance of a certificate (Bolari & Li, 1988).

Prior to the passing of the above-mentioned racist legislation, the federal government had passed the *Chinese Immigration Act* in 1885 that imposed a prohibitive head-tax of $50 on each Chinese immigrant entering Canada, and in 1903 this was later raised to $500 (Bolari and Li, 1988; Galabuzi, 2006). This measure was undertaken to restrict Chinese workers' entry into Canada and to satisfy the racist outcry against Chinese Canadians in British Columbia. The estimated $21 million dollars that was collected from the head-tax was "used to give land grants to European immigrants" (Lukas &

Persad, 2004, p. 7). It was quite instructive that the first head-tax law was only enacted after the Canada Pacific Railway (CPR) was built and the dire need for Chinese labour had passed (Bolari & Li, 1988; Galabuzi, 2006). Chinese Canadians did not have equal access to citizenship. Provincial legislation was passed that limited Chinese access to certain categories of employment and professions, the buying of government-owned land, participation in elections as voters, and banning their candidacy for various political offices (Bolari & Li, 1988). Other Asian workers (Japanese and East Indians) were also confronted with discriminatory and racist treatment in the labour market and the wider society.

Japanese workers and residents were subjected to British Columbian legislation, which restricted or eliminated their voting rights, and access to certain professions and employment on infrastructure or public works projects of the provincial government (Ujimoto, 1988). The fear of economic competition from racialized labour has a way of bringing out latent racist sentiments among White workers or within the general White citizenry. The opposition and agitation against Japanese migration into the province exploded in the form of a riot in 1907 in Vancouver by the White populace upon the persons and property of Japanese residents. A subsequent understanding or "Gentleman's Agreement" between Canada and Japan set an annual limit of 400 Japanese immigrants, and this accord was made so as to not cause problems for the alliance between Britain and Japan (Ujimoto, 1988).

Despite the racist immigration policy of the federal government, it was still responsive to the need for certain types of labour that could be procured from abroad to satisfy demand in the domestic labour market. The state had no reservation about going to countries with predominantly racialized people to get those cheap, exploitable, and available workers to do jobs that many native-born workers would not do. In this respect, the federal government-created the Domestic Scheme in 1955 that recruited largely African women from the Anglophone islands of Barbados, Trinidad and Tobago and Jamaica to work as live-in domestic workers for a mandatory one-year period (Makeda, 1989). These women's labour were on-call and super-exploited because of living in the same space as their employers, the low wage rates and benefits, and the servile nature of their employment. Racism and sexism confined many of the women who left this type of employment to jobs in the secondary labour market, and they also "found it much harder to assimilate into the larger society," which was not the case with their European counterparts from an earlier era (Silvera, 1989, p. 8). The Domestic Scheme was later replaced with the Temporary Employment Visa programme, which did

Develop your knowledge – Ask yourself

In recent years, many Canadians rely on live-in nannies to care for their children. While nannies make no more than $20,000-25,000 per year, many have reported being abused by their employers.

In your opinion what are some of the implications of live-in/live-out caregiving programs?

1. Why is government reluctant to enhance its publicly funded childcare program?
2. If these nannies are trusted to take care of children and elderly, what makes them un-trusted as permanent residence?
3. What options are provided to those who experience abuse or exploiation?

not maintain the granting of landed immigrant status to domestic workers after the stipulated one-year period of compulsory live-in domestic work (Silvera, 1988). The current scheme for migrant domestic workers is called the Live-In Caregiver/Live Out Program, but the critiques have essentially remained the same.

A migrant agricultural programme was created in 1966 to respond to the demand of the Canadian farm sector for cheap and readily available agricultural labour from the Anglophone Caribbean. The federal government developed a similar farm-labour arrangement with Mexico in 1974 (Bolari & Li, 1988). These workers are not treated with the same care and value as the agricultural products that they are producing for the tables of Canadians and others (Nangwaya, 2010). Further, most of these migrant farm workers do not have "a realistic chance to become permanent residents" after years of working in Canada (Nangwaya, 2008). They are also denied unemployment benefits despite the fact that payroll taxes are drawn from their salary toward Employment Insurance programme. Migrant agricultural workers do not have the right to join unions in most provinces, and cannot access the protective provisions of health and safety legislation.

The racist animus against racialized immigrants or workers entering Canada was eased in the 1960s with the introduction of the objective, "points system." Immigration reform bolstered the number of racialized people that entered The "points system" assigned a numerical value to prospective immigrants' suitability based on their education, training occupational skills, and prospect for immediate employment in Canada, one that was not based on the race criteria of prior legislation (Armstrong, 2000; Galabuzi, 2006; Tulloch, 1975). Many of these racialized workers were concentrated in lower job-classification occupations or secondary labour market jobs, and this was a reality for them even in unionized workplaces (Kholsa, 1989; Leah, 1989; Lukas & Persad, 2004).

The brief examination of race, racism, and Canada's immigration policy speaks to the fact that racialized immigrants have a historical experience with the labour market and settlement process that has been racially discriminatory. Their settlement difficulties were or are not the result of individual behaviour. The problems with which they must contend are the outcome of institutional and systemic forms of racism. It was important to examine the historical context of racialized labour in Canada so as to have a framework through which to understand the state of affairs of the current group of immigrants in the labour market and settlement process.

Immigrants and the Labour Market Today

The 2011 census in Canada revealed that 20.6 percent of the national population were foreign born and that Vancouver, Montreal and Toronto remain the magnet metropolitan areas for the majority of immigrants (63.4 percent) who are attracted to this country (CBC, 2013). In 2011, racialized people made-up 19.1 percent of the national population or 6,264,800 in that racial category (Statistics Canada, 2013), and this figure is certainly expected to grow beyond 20 percent in the 2016 census. About 250,000 immigrants are admitted to Canada each year and those in the category of investors, entrepreneurs, and skilled professionals constitute 64 percent of these newcomers (Keung, 2010). In 2013, Canada provided 258,619 permanent residencies to immigrants with 24,049 of them being refugees (Government of Canada, 2014).

The reality of being an immigrant and being racialized in Canada are now seen as interchangeable terms and realities Galabuzi (2006) elaborates on this turn of events:

In Europe as in North America, the term immigrant has been redefined to refer to non-Whites, especially Africans, Caribbeans, East Asian,

Canadians' Perspective on Immigration

- Canadians are aware of the economic benefits of immigration. A 2013-2014 tracking survey revealed that close to 80 percent were supportive of the idea that immigration was needed to facilitate economic development in Canada (Butler, 2014).

- A 2014 survey of 1,500 Canadian adults found only 55 percent of them were in agreement with the assertion that immigrants were "very important to building a stable Canadian economic future" (CBC News, 2014).

- Some Canadians are wary of the number of immigrants entering the country annually, but the percentage of their counterparts who are supportive of the current level of immigration has held firmly at about 50 percent for the last fifteen years (Butler, 2014).

- In the CBC poll, 30 percent of respondents were of the opinion that "immigrants take jobs from Canadians" (CBC, 2014). With such a sizeable group of Canadians holding negative views toward immigrants, some politicians are not averse to shamelessly pandering to this pool of potential supporters.

South Asians and Latin Americans, regardless of whether they are immigrants or born in that particular country. Immigrant status has been racialized, and the inferior status that is imposed on racialized peoples is now extended to immigrants. In consequence so much so that the quality of their human capital is called into question, with dire consequences for those with international qualifications (p. 83).

The settlement challenges that many racialized immigrants are experiencing in the labour market and the resultant precarious jobs that they are forced to take on comes, in part, from the devaluation of their internationally-obtained qualifications. Yet, their educational attainment was one of the primary reasons for their acceptance as immigrants to Canada.

Almost all of the countries in the global North are contending with a decline in their respective fertility rates, and the preceding state of affairs has resulted in a shrinking workforce. Statistics Canada had forecasted that by the year 2011, 100 percent of the net growth in Canada's labour force would come from immigration (Chamber of Commerce, 2009; Dugale, 2006). It is now anticipated that this level of dependence on immigration to grow the labour market will be achieved in 2015 or 2016 (Dean & Tory, 2011; Kustec, 2012). Canada has been able to maintain a positive population growth, because of its high rate of immigration.

Notwithstanding the views of many Canadians about immigration and the racialized immigrants who are coming into the country, Canada needs these newcomers to maintain its economic vitality. The need for skilled immigrants by employers was a factor in the introduction of the "points system" immigration scheme. There are astute observers who are very much aware of the potential and actual economic benefits of the type of immigrants coming to Ontario and Canada. Dean and Tory (2011) assert that "Quality immigration has been a huge blessing for Ontario and a huge contributor to our prosperity. We must continue to treat it that way and not allow it to become one more divisive political football. We have too many of those already." Canada will need to increase its immigration level to deal with the aging population phenomenon. Danielle Wong (2011) states, "A federal government backgrounder says Canada needs to increase immigration to almost 4 percent of our population from the current 0.8 percent to support our 'old-age dependency ratio.'" Canada will continue to depend on quality and highly-educated immigrants that it is largely sourcing from the global South.

The brain drain of highly educated people from the poorer global South countries to the richer global North is not a fanciful assertion on the part of observers of this experience. In the 24–54 age range, 31.8 percent of recent immigrants had a bachelor's degree in 2006, while only 16.1 percent of their native-born counterparts could make this claim (Zietsma, 2007). The education disparity between recent immigrants and Canadian-born workers with a graduate degree was also notable with 10 percent of recent immigrants had completed the requirements for a graduate degree in comparison to 5 percent of Canadian-born workers in 2006 (Zietsma, 2007). In spite of the higher levels of educational qualification of recent immigrants, "In March, 2011, Greater Toronto Area unemployment rates ranged from 5.4 percent for Canadian-born to 9.6 percent for immigrants, to 14.2 percent for immigrants who arrived in the past five years" (Dean & Tory, 2011).

Even when the employment situation for university-educated immigrants experienced a positive bounced as in the period 2010 to 2011 when their employment rate rose by 6 percent, the employment and unemployment gap with their Canadian-born counterparts was still troubling (Yssaad, 2012). In 2011, Canadian-born, university educated workers had an employment rate of 90.2 percent, while the rate for the immigrant equivalents stood at 78.7 percent. A university education is definitely not generating the same labour outcome for the university-educated immigrant as it is doing for the workers born in Canada with the same level of educational attainment.

The employment figures on how university-educated immigrants are faring are disturbing, and so too is the disparity with respect to their work-based income. A native-born Canadian with a university education earns, on average, over 300 percent ($61,904) of the income that his or her immigrant counterpart receives in employment income ($20,143) during the period 2001–2006 (Dean & Tory, 2011).

The racial status of immigrants is strongly associated with their likelihood of experiencing low income, which is the case for racialized immigrants (Palameta, 2004). The association of low income and being a racialized immigrant may be deduced by comparing the experience of non-racialized immigrants in Canada. Racialized immigrants in the early 2000s were considerably more likely that non-racialized ones to have low income, and this rate of occurrence remained the same irrespective of how long these two groups of immigrants had been in Canada (Palameta, 2004). The consistency of race as an explanatory factor in the incidence of low income may be seen from the fact that recent racialized immigrants and Canadian-born racialized people are more likely to go through "repeated (three or more years) rather than limited (one or two year) exposure" to low income when compared with non-immigrants and other Canadians "with similar characteristics who were not visible minorities" (Palameta, 2004, p. 16). Racialized workers who are Canadian-born have lower rates of incomes than their White Canadian counterparts (Jackson, 2005). With a racial earning gap as seen above, it is not a surprised that the racialization of poverty is gaining greater attention among anti-poverty advocates and researchers (Block & Galabuzi, 2011).

The low rate of acceptance by employers of the internationally-acquired qualifications of these highly educated immigrants is a contributing factor to the above situation (Drummond, 2010, Jackson, 2014). The prejudice against international credentials has nothing to do with their ability to match the academic or training standards found in Canadian educational institutions. In fact, the World Education Services Canada found that of the 7,300 credentials that it assesses yearly, 75 percent of them were consistent with those issued in Canada (Belford, 2009). A survey of 2,442 internationally and locally educated professionals carried out by the Office of the Fairness Commissioner (OFC) in Ontarian cities of Ottawa, London, and Toronto found that only one in four [immigrant] managed to obtain a licence in one of Ontario's 37 regulated professions, compared with 60 percent of Canadian graduates. And that licence may take two years to get, compared with less than a year for native-born Canadians (Keung, 2010).

The restrictive changes to the eligibility criteria for unemployment benefits, the percentage of one's prior employment income that is received under the Employment Insurance scheme, and challenges with getting training in the official languages of Canada are additional reasons for the low income experience of immigrant workers (Drummond, 2010). Structural factors such as racism (Jackson, 2014) and sexism are also at work in the low pay and poverty that are endured by today's immigrants.

Employment Equity Legislation and Breaking the Concrete Ceiling

The highly trained immigrants' access to jobs that match their education and training will not come about without the enactment of policies that dictate specific workplace-cum-labour market behaviour and outcomes. In Canada, employment equity is a concept and strategy that came out of the *Equality in Employment: A Royal Commission Report* of 1984, which was chaired by Judge Rosalie Abella. She asserted that employment equity is a proactive intervention strategy aimed at removing the undue discriminatory barriers that prevent certain groups in society from having equitable access to employment opportunities (Bakan & Kobayashi, 2000). However, even in cases where employment equity measures have been institutionalized, it will take commitment and strict enforcement accountability to create a level playing field for those who have been historically barred from certain types of jobs.

The federal government of Canada has enacted the *Employment Equity Act* that guides its employment practices. This legislation acknowledges four designated groups that face discriminatory employment barriers in the workplace. These equity-seeking groups are Aboriginals, people with disabilities, racialized workers or visible minorities (the official term), and women. Based on the workforce availability (WFA) statistics of all the federal civil service designated groups in 2010, racialized workers were the only ones whose employment figure was below their presence in the labour market (Sahoye, 2011). Racialized people were 9.8 percent of the federal workforce in 2010, but their workforce availability figure was 12.4 percent (Omidvar, 2010).

In the late 1990s, the federal civil service developed an *Embracing Change* programme that was implemented over a five-year period. It had an employment goal of one of every five new employees being racialized and 20 percent of its executive being from this group by 2005 (Goar, 2009). The employment equity project failed to achieve the targets on both initiatives, ending up with one of every ten new hires being racialized. Although racialized workers are concentrated in lower jobs classifications and certain departments, the presence of an employment equity programme has been a positive force for change. In 1999, racialized people were only 4.1 percent of all federal workers in spite of being 12.5 percent of the national population (Goar, 2009).

It took workplace activism from racialized federal employees and their trade union and communities to force the issue of a representative workforce on to the agenda of the government. But the federal government of Prime Minister Stephen Harper has decentralized the decision-making process around hiring and advancement and there are no serious accountability measures to ensure that employment equity is working for racialized workers (Goar, 2009). The government has actually ordered a review of its employment equity programme, because a White woman employee named Sara Landriault made a complaint about not having access to a job that was reserved for underrepresented racialized groups (Omidvar, 2010). It is interesting that the jobs set aside for racialized people represented less than two percent of the job vacancies in 2009 in the federal civil service.

In order for employment equity programmes to work for racialized immigrants in the labour market, employment equity laws are needed at the provincial level. There are employment equity policies established by provincial governments in Canada, but none of them are comparable to the *Employment Equity Act* of the federal government (Cornish et al., 2009). As problematic as the implementation of the employment equity programme is for racialized workers in the federal public sector, it has provided the foundation to challenge systemic barriers to employment. It is rather instructive that the private sector workplaces that are regulated by the federal government, or under the Federal Contractors Program with its employment equity requirements, have a higher representation of racialized workers in their workplaces than their counterparts that are not so legislated (Omidvar,

2010). Although there are people who claim that a business case for diversity ought to be presented to employers (Aulakh, 2010) so as to encourage them to remove the "concrete ceiling" facing immigrants and racialized Canadian-born women and men, such an approach has not worked so far.

The Collective Agreement and Employment Equity Plans

There is another approach to pushing employment equity in the workplace. It could come through the instrument of the collective agreement or contract that is signed between the employer and the employees in workplaces where trade unions are present. A collective agreement is a legal document that contains the negotiated terms and conditions of employment and a process for dealing with workplace disputes without workers going on strike or the employer locking out the employees (Kehoe & Archer, 1994). Trade unions have used the collective agreement to deal with workplace sexual and racial harassment and the provision of same-sex spousal benefits before laws were passed that covered these issues. This document may be used to advance issues that may be much more difficult to achieve in a political arena, where they may not be popular with the public.

Currently many trade unions representing civil service workers and those in the broader public sector have an employment equity clause in their collective agreement. The problem with these fine-sounding clauses is that the employer and the trade union will only work out a detailed employment equity programme after the signing of the contract. If the union and the employer are not mutually committed to employment equity, there will not be an incentive to prioritize and implement this particular clause in the collective agreement. However, if there are organized and mobilized constituencies for employment equity inside the respective trade union or a union leadership that is positive about the removal of structural employment barriers, they will invest the resources needed for pushing for a detailed employment equity plan in the bargaining proposal. This aforementioned document would be exchanged with the employer and vigorously bargained during the negotiation. If the employer agrees with having a detailed employment equity plan in the collective agreement, this would make it much easier to ensure that the parties are accountable for implementing it. If this approach is successful in challenging employment barriers in a unionized environment, it would have a greater likelihood of being emulated in non-unionized workplaces. A broad constituency could then be constructed to make employment equity legislation feasible as a public policy instrument, when it is being operationalized in a large number of workplaces in the public and private sectors.

Trade unions make the claim that they are social justice organizations that believe in social unionism; an orientation to unionism that goes beyond preoccupation with pay, workplace benefits, and working conditions. These working-class organizations celebrate the value statement of "An injury to one is an injury to all." Therefore, racist, sexist, ableist, and/or homophobic employment barriers ought to be of central concern to them. Unfortunately, trade unions are a part of society and are institutional spaces that too often perpetuate systemic forms of oppression. They are often wary of employment equity because they believe that it could negatively affect seniority rules. In today's workplace, seniority rules are institutional barriers to the rapid placement of groups that have experienced systemic exclusion into jobs that are higher up in the job classifications system. Trade unions and employers need to become more creative in applying seniority rules so that they do not remain as barriers to having a representative workforce.

Unionization, Trade Unions, and Solidarity for All

Trade unions have been able to act as a collective voice for the workers in unionized workplaces. Unlike non-unionized work environments, the single vulnerable worker does not have to face the employer alone when she or he has a workplace concern or seeks a raise in her or his compensation. Historically, jobs in trade union workplaces have provided workers with better wages, benefits, and working conditions that those without working-class organizations (Jackson, 2005). Trade unions have been able to improve the wages of bargaining units composed of lower paid workers (Jackson, 2005).

Unionization would benefit racialized immigrants and non-immigrant racialized workers given the lower wages they tend to earn relative to their respective counterparts. In Canada, trade unions had a history of keeping racialized workers outside of their membership during the period of industrialization throughout the later nineteenth century and up to the 1930s. Some trade unions went to the extreme of inserting a clause in their constitution that denied membership to racialized workers (Lukas & Persad, 2004). This type of exclusion led racialized workers, especially African Canadians, to view "white supremacy as an integral part of Canadian trade unionism" (Mathieu, 2010, p. 62).Today, the exclusion from membership is more systemic with regards to how vacancies in unionized workplaces are advertised or the weak commitment by trade unions to push for employment equity language and programmes in the collective agreement. However, "the continued marginalization of many workers of colour within unions remains a pressing issue" (Das Gupta, 2008, p. 148), and this state of affairs affects the ability of workers of colour to place their priorities on the bargaining agenda.

For the most part, the labour movement is not committing organizing resources to the hard-to-unionized sectors of the economy in which racialized people are employed. When the preceding reality is coupled with the systemic discriminatory employment barriers in unionized and non-unionized workplaces, it should not be a surprise that in 1999, a ten percent unionization gap existed between racialized and non-racialized workers (Jackson, 2005). A wage premium is evident for racialized workers who are unionized. In 1999, racialized workers in trade unions earned $7,724 or 20.9 percent more than their non-unionized racialized counterpart (Jackson, 2005). It is quite clear to racialized people that being a member of a union brings tremendous material benefits, especially in the public sector. In 1999, 84 percent percent of racialized union members maintain full-time status for the year, while only 71 percent of non-unionized racialized workers were so employed (Jackson, 2005). In a poll of non-unionized workers about their desire to join a union, 40 percent of racialized workers would like to do so, compared with 25 percent of non-racialized workers (Jackson, 2005).

The labour movement, immigrant settlement organizations and progressive civil society organizations ought to prioritize the issue of getting amendments to labour laws so as to make it easier for workers to unionize their places of employment. The provincial and federal governments have tilted the balance of power on workplace unionization toward the employer. The employers use all available methods to frustrate workers' attempts to form or join a union. Given the great advantages of being in a union in terms of job security, wage rates, benefits, and greater protection against arbitrary actions by the employer, immigrants and racialized workers would gain from having higher unionization rates in the workplaces of Canada. The current neo-liberal environment, with its emphasis on less regulation of corporations and pro-business governments, would make amendments to labour laws a challenge. Canada's capitalist sector would not likely be passive in the face of efforts from progressive social movements to change labour legislation in order to give workers a fighting chance. We must expect a vigorous and stiff challenge from business interests, which would be aided by the antiunion attitude that is usually found in the corporate-controlled media.

Actions toward Employment Equity and Workplace Justice

Below are a number of suggested actions that might be used by professionals to advocate and achieve equitable, anti-discriminatory employment policies and practices that affect racialized immigrant and non-migrant workers:

- Develop a broad understanding of the historical and current experiences of racialized workers in the workplace.
- Acquire a strong grasp of the resistance strategies and tactics that have been used by racialized workers and communities to fight institutional and systemic employment barriers and the lessons that may be drawn from them.
- Familiarize yourself with an employment systems review, which is a tool that thoroughly examines all aspects of the workplace's policies, processes, structures and practices to determine their fit with the strategic goals of the organization, e.g., employment equity.
- Develop your knowledge of the employment equity plan, which is the planning tool that outlines the course of action that will be methodically implemented to bring about an equitable employment practice throughout the organization. An employment equity should cover, at a minimum, the recruitment, interviewing and assessment practices, allocation of training and development opportunities, timelines to achieve goals, establishment of targets or measurable outcomes, provision of adequate resources, and a commitment to achieving a fair rate of employee retention among the protected groups, e.g., racialized and Indigenous workers.
- Utilize an integrative anti-oppression framework in your advocacy work and proposed solutions to the employment barriers faced by your clients. They experience multiple identities at the same time and these various intersecting identity markers could be implicated in their marginalization in the labour market or workplace, e.g., a racialized woman with a disability.
- Foster collective action and self-organizing among clients. Invest the time into encouraging and preparing clients to join or form groups that organize or mobilize around the problems that confront them.
- Reach out to existing community organizations and draw on their expertise, experience and other resources to help your clients. Historically, racialized communities have been important to the workplace struggles against racism and/or patriarchy or sexism.

- Develop a broad understanding of the role and operation of trades unions as advocates for unionized workers. Unions have resources that may be used to advance the cause of workers who are not unionized or covered by a collective agreement.
- Join coalitions, networks or alliances that are working for systemic or institutional change in society.
- Organize training and development programmes that provide your clients with the knowledge, skills and attitude to engage in social change. By building the capacity of people to shape the course of their own liberation, you are facilitating grassroots, participatory democracy and collective self-reliance of the socially marginalized. You are also sharing your power and developing an equitable relationship with your clients or the community.

Concluding Thoughts

The unfavourable employment experience of racialized immigrant workers in the labour market calls for activism from social movement organizations that are committed to achieving structural change. Racism, patriarchy and capitalism are all implicated in the exploited labour market condition of this group of workers. It generally takes organizing actions or resistance from below to improve the economic and social reality of racialized people in Canadian society. Oppressed groups do not normally achieve freedom or improved status without organized resistance or a struggle. Racialized people have organized independent trade unions, used public interests groups and community-based organizations, mobilized and organized within trade unions and other mainstream social movement organizations, and engaged the policy-making process to advance their material interests in society. A similar path will have to be travelled to achieve a substantive improvement in the labour market outcome for racialized immigrant labour.

The insertion of employment equity plans in collective agreements, the enactment of employment equity laws, as well as higher rates of unionization in areas of the labour market where racialized immigrants and non-immigrant racialized women and men are concentrated would bring about the desired change in their labour market experience. Racism is a major factor in the workplace experience of racialized immigrant and non-immigrant racialized workers. Given the systemic and institutionalized nature of the employment barriers faced by these workers, the labour market interventions ought to go after the root causes of their exploitative treatment.

References

Angus Reid Public Opinion. (2010, September 14). More Canadians are questioning the benefits of immigration. Retrieved from http://www.angus-reid.com

Armstrong, B. (2000). *Bromley, tireless champion for just causes: Memoirs of Bromley L. Armstrong.* Pickering, ON: Vitabu.

Aulakh, R. (2010, March 25). He created a job out of diversity. *Toronto Star.* Retrieved from http://www.thestar.com

Bakan, A. B., & Audrey Kobayashi, A. (2000). *Employment Equity Policy in Canada: An Interprovincial Comparison.* Ottawa: Status of Woman Canada.

Belford, T. (2009, January 15). Employers short-sighted in degrees. *Toronto Star.* Retrieved from http://www.thestar.com

Block, S. & Galabuzi, G-E. (2011). Canada's colour coded labour market: The gap for racialized workers. Ottawa: Centre for Policy Alternatives.

Bolari, B. S. & Li, P. S. (1988). *Racial oppression in Canada* (2nd ed.). Toronto: Garamond.

Brand, D. (1994). *Bread out of stone: Recollections, sex, recognitions, race, dreaming.* Toronto: Coach House.

Brennan, R. J. (2011, September 7). Hudak steps up attacks on Liberal plan for "foreign workers." *Toronto Star.* Retrieved from http://www.thestar.com

Butler, D. (2014, August 27). Canadians in the dark about immigration numbers: survey. Ottawa Citizen. Retrieved from http://ottawa citizen.com/news/national/canadians-in-the-dark-about-immigration-numbers-survey

CBC News. (2014, November 12). Canadian attitudes toward immigrants conflicted, poll says. CBC News. Retrieved from http://www.cbc.ca /news/canada/canadian-attitudes-toward-immigrants-conflicted-poll-says-1.2826022

Canadian Chamber of Commerce. (2009). *Immigration: The changing face of Canada.* Retrieved from http://www.chamber.ca

Cornish, M., Faraday, F. & Borowy, J. (2009). *Securing employment equity by enforcing human rights laws.* Retrieved from http://www.cava luzzo.com

Das Gupta, T. (1998). Anti-racism and the organized labour movement. In V. Satzewich (Ed.), *Racism and social inequality in Canada: Concepts, controversies and strategies* (pp. 315–334). Toronto: Thompson Educational.

Das Gupta, T. (2008). Racism/ANTI-racism, precarious employment, and unions. In M.A. Wallis & S.-M. Kwok (Eds.), *Daily struggles: The deepening racialization and feminization of poverty in Canada* (pp. 143–157). Toronto: Canadian Scholars' Press.

Dean, J. & Tory, J. (2011, September 20). Ontario's immigration debate is not getting the respect it deserves. *Globe and Mail*. Retrieved from http://www.theglobeandmail.com

Drummond, D. (2010, March 25). New Canadians, new workplace. *Toronto Star*. Retrieved from http://www.thestar.com

Dugale, V. (2006, October–November). The changing colour of Canada. *Our Times*, 25(5), 24–29.

Galabuzi, G-E. (2006). *Canada's economic apartheid: The social exclusion of racialized groups in the new century*. Toronto: Canadian Scholars' Press.

Goar, C. (2009, September 14). Diversity a low priority in civil service. *Toronto Star*. Retrieved from www.thestar.com

Grizzle, S., with Cooper, J. (1998). *My name's not George: The story of the sleeping car porters in Canada*. Toronto: Umbrella.

Government of Canada. (2014). Facts and figures 2013 – Immigration overview: Permanent residents. Citizenship and Immigration Canada. Retrieved from http://www.cic.gc.ca/english/resources/statistics/facts 2013/permanent/02.asp

Grizzle, S., with Cooper, J. (1998). My name's not George: The story of the sleeping car porters in Canada. Toronto: Umbrella.

Hill, D.G. (1992). *The freedom-seekers: Blacks in early Canada*. Toronto: Stoddart.

Jackson, A. (2014, June 13). Canadian-born visible minority youth face an unfair job future [Web log post]. Retrieved from http://www.broadbentinstitute.ca/en/blog/

Jackson, A. (2005). *Is work working for workers of colour?* Ottawa: Canadian Labour Congress.

Kehoe, F. & Archer, M. (1994). *Canadian industrial relations: Text, cases & simulations* (7th ed.). Oakville, ON: Twentieth Century Labour Publications.

Keung, N. (2010, March 30). Facts back up job-search frustration felt by newcomers. *Toronto Star*. Retrieved from http://www.thestar.com

Khosla, P. (1989). Profiles of working class East Indian women. In N. Gupta & M. Silvera (Eds.), *The issue is 'ism: Women of colour speak out* (pp. 58–69). Toronto: Sister Vision.

Kustec, S. (2012). The role of migrant labour supply in the Canadian labour market. Citizenship and Immigration Canada. Retrieved from http://www.cic.gc.ca/english/resources/research/2012migrant/index.asp

Leah, R. (1989). Linking the struggles: Racism, sexism and the union movement. In J. Vorst et al. (Eds.), *Race, class, gender: Bonds and barriers* (pp. 166–195). Toronto: Between the Lines.

Lukas, S. & Persad, J. V. (2004). *Through the eyes of workers of colour: Linking struggles for social justice.* Toronto: Women Working with Immigrant Women.

Mathieu, S-J. (2010). *North of the color line: Migration and Black resistance in Canada, 1870–1955.* Chapel Hill: University of North Carolina Press.

Nangwaya, A. (2008, April 4). A bitter reality for workers. Letter to the editor. *Toronto Star*, A5.

Nangwaya, A. (2009, April 7). Correcting flaws in nanny system. Letter to the editor. *Toronto Star*, A18.

Nangwaya, A. (2010, October 14). Farm workers: Dis is not slavery/just poverty/speaking to democracy. *Dissident Voice*. Retrieved from http://dissidentvoice.org

Omidvar, R. (2010, July 14). A place for equity policies. *Toronto Star*. Retrieved from http://www.thestar.com

Palameta, B. (2004, April). Low income among immigrants and visible minorities. In *Perspectives on Labour and Income*. Catalogue no. 75-001-XIE. Ottawa: Statistics Canada. Retrieved from http://www.statcan.gc.ca

Sahoye, J. (2011, October 5). Group wants level employment playing field. *Caribbean Camera*. Retrieved from http://www.thecaribbeancamera. com

Silvera, M. (1989). *Silenced: Talks with working class Caribbean women about their lives and struggles as Domestic Workers in Canada.* Toronto: Sister Vision: Black Women and Women of Colour Press.

Statistics Canada. (2013). Immigration and Ethnocultural Diversity in Canada. Ottawa: Statistics Canada. Retrieved from http://www12. statcan.gc.ca/nhs-enm/2011/as-sa/99-010-x/99-010-x2011001-eng.cfm#a4

The Canadian Press. (May 8, 2013). Canada's foreign-born population soars to 6.8 million, CBC. Retrieved from http://www.cbc.ca/news/canada/canada-s-foreign-born-population-soars-to-6-8-million-1.1308179

Thomson, C.A. (1979). *Blacks in deep snow: Black pioneers in Canada*. Toronto: J. M. Dent.

Treasury Board of Canada Secretariat. (2013). Demographic Snapshot of the Federal Public Service, 2013. Retrieved from http://www.tbs-sct.gc.ca/res/stats/demo13-eng.asp

Tulloch, H. (1975). *Black Canadians: A long line of fighters*. Toronto: NC.

Ujimoto, K.V. (1988). Racism, discrimination and internment: Japanese in Canada. In B. S. Bolari & P. S. Li, *Racial oppression in Canada* (pp. 127–160). Toronto: Garamond.

Wong, D. (2011, October 16). 10 myths about immigration. *Hamilton Spectator*. Retrieved from http://www.thespec.com

Yssaad, L. (2012). The Canadian Immigrant Labour Market. Ottawa: Statistics Canada. Retrieved from http://www.statcan.gc.ca/pub/71-606-x/2012006/part-partie1-eng.htm

Zietsma, D. (2007). *The Canadian immigrant labour market in 2006: The first results from Canada's labour market survey*. Immigrant Labour Force Analysis Series. Catalogue no. 71-606-XIE2007001. Ottawa: Statistics Canada. Retrieved from http://www.statcan.gc.ca

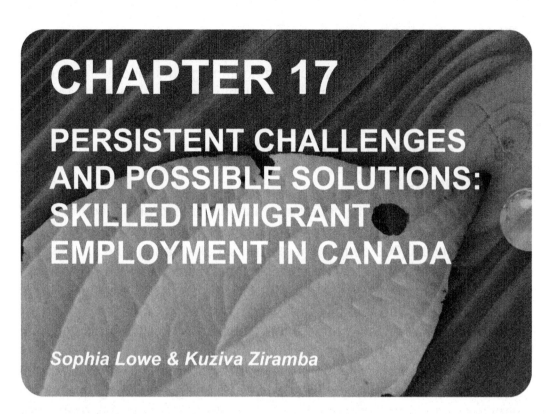

CHAPTER 17

PERSISTENT CHALLENGES AND POSSIBLE SOLUTIONS: SKILLED IMMIGRANT EMPLOYMENT IN CANADA

Sophia Lowe & Kuziva Ziramba

Introduction

International migration has been increasing globally. Approximately 60 percent of all migrants are now found in the world's more prosperous countries (GCIM, 2005, p. 6) and a significant proportion of global migrants are skilled and educated individuals. However, transferring the education and experience of skilled migrants into different systems is not always smooth.

Canada's immigration policy focuses largely on selecting and integrating immigrants with the qualifications and skills identified as necessary for the Canadian labour market. However, despite their calibre, as well as a vast array of integration systems and supports available, the actual labour market outcomes (the income and employment levels) of immigrants in Canada have not been at the level expected by policy makers and government.

This chapter focuses on the labour market integration of skilled immigrants[1] in Canada, looking specifically at continued challenges, mobilization and systemic changes, promising practices and initiatives, and recommendations for the future. We describe the organizing and learning that has and is taking place in Canada as the country's institutions and individuals become better at working together to address employment barriers facing skilled immigrants. By providing a current overview of what is being done to address labour market integration challenges for immigrants in Canada, we hope to inform practitioners supporting immigrants about the current resources and promising examples available, as well as engage them in helping immigrants succeed.

What's Canadian Immigration All About?

Labour Shortages

Canada has often been described as a nation of immigrants, and the reality of the demographics demonstrate that it is becoming more so. Every year, approximately 280,000 permanent residents make Canada their home, and about 20 percent of Canada's current population was born outside the country – in Toronto it's already as high as 50 percent (Statistics Canada, 2007a). It is projected that by 2031, all of Canada's population growth will be from immigration, and therefore its labour force growth will also depend on immigration (Statistics Canada, 2008a).

The Canadian fertility rate has fallen to approximately 1.68 per woman (Statistics Canada, 2011), and the population is aging, with a large proportion nearing or already in retirement. In this context, Canadians largely view immigration as a part of the solution for demographic and economic problems. Government considers filling the anticipated number of highly skilled occupations particularly important for Canada to remain competitive in the knowledge economy.

Canadian Attitudes

Canadians also hold a relatively positive view of immigration, with 81 percent agreeing or somewhat agreeing that immigration is "a key positive feature of Canada as a country." However, a strong majority of Canadians also believe immigration numbers should not increase, but should remain the same or decrease (Nanos, 2010). Following a recession, a 2010 EKOS Research Associates Survey showed that 67 percent of Canadians support current levels of immigration or higher, compared to 23 percent who thought there were too many immigrants (Reitz, 2011). Canadians generally have positive attitudes towards racialized groups, but the level of tolerance declines when specific questions that relate to the ways of life of racialized groups are posed. For example, 41.5 percent of respondents to the Environics Canada's 2010 Focus Survey thought Muslim women should be banned from wearing headscarves in public places and 77.8 percent believed that "Ethnic groups should try as much as possible to blend into society and not form a separate community" (Reitz, 2011).

Canada's Immigration Program

While Canada is a country that has been built on immigration, only relatively recently has immigration policy allowed those from non-European countries to freely enter Canada. In 1967, Canada moved from a discriminatory immigration policy based on race and country of origin to a merit-based points system that evaluates potential immigrants based on education and skills and attempts to match them with Canada's labour market needs. From that time on, a significant change in the source countries of immigration took place, with non-Europeans making up the bulk of immigrant entries. In 2007, Statistics Canada identified China, India, Philippines, and Pakistan as the top source countries of immigrants in Canada. Changes in source countries of immigrants has affected the ability of Canadian employers and institutions to effectively compare the value of the qualifications immigrants have with the standards they have set for employment, licensure, or admission to post-secondary education.

Today, Canada selects permanent immigrants under three broad classes: economic (66.6 percent), family (21.5 percent), and refugees (8.8 percent) (CIC, 2010). In addition, there are an increasing number of temporary workers and international students who enter Canada – some of who may have pathways to obtain permanent residency. The Federal Skilled Worker Program (FSWP), or points system, is Canada's economic immigration policy, with 42.5 percent of all permanent residents (applicants and dependants) entering through this program in 2010 (CIC, 2010). However, the FSWP is being largely replaced by immigration programs that are able to respond more quickly to the changing needs of employers and local labour markets, programs such as temporary worker programs and provincial immigration programs. In 2010, the FSWP admitted 119,339 skilled workers and their dependents (compared with 130,238 in 2005), while the Temporary Foreign Worker Program (TFWP) admitted 182,322 workers (compared with 122,694 in 2005). In 2005, only 8,047 immigrants and their dependants came through the Provincial Nominee Programs (PNPs), but by 2010, this had increased to 36,419. International student numbers are also on the rise, with 67,885 entering Canada in 2005, and 96,147 arriving in 2010 (CIC, 2010).

Launched in 2008, the Canadian Experience Class (CEC) is a new route to allow temporary workers and international students employed in skilled positions and with sufficient English or French language fluency the possibility of transitioning to permanent residency status while in Canada. Previously, those in Canada on a temporary basis who wished to stay permanently would apply through the FSWP from abroad. Temporary workers and international students who are working in jobs that are not considered skilled (based on HRSDCs National Occupational Classification Matrix) are ineligible for the CEC. However, PNPs have different eligibility criteria, some of which allow those who do not qualify under the CEC to stay through the PNPs.

The federal TFWP and the provincially directed PNPs are employer-driven and prioritized in the immigration system, and therefore able to quickly match skilled immigrants with in-demand occupations and to circumvent some of the barriers currently plaguing skilled immigrants. The PNPs are separate immigration programs that allow employers and provinces to nominate and expedite applicants for work in specific sectors and occupations – usually where there is a labour shortage of local residents – in certain provinces and territories. PNP applications have priority processing in the federal immigration system, meaning that provincial nominee (PN) applications are the first to be processed; the latter take between five to 31 months to process versus the FSWP in which applicants can wait up to 85 months (CIC, 2010). The TFWP functions at all skill levels, with over 36 percent of TFWs employed at the professional, managerial, and skilled levels in 2009 and 30 percent employed in positions defined by CIC as clerical, elemental and labouring positions, with the remaining unstated. TFWs can work in Canada, often for one employer, for up to four years (depending on the employment level) (CIC, 2009). Through many of the PNPs, as well as through the CEC, some temporary workers and students are eligible to apply for permanent residency should they be employed at a skilled level (CEC) or if the employer or province applies for them (PNP).

These policy changes mean that more immigrants will have had some labour market experience in Canada prior to becoming permanent residents, and therefore more likely to have immediate success in the Canadian labour market by avoiding the "no Canadian experience" conundrum. A drawback to some of these new immigrant categories is that an increasing number of people with "temporary" status will not be eligible for some of the program interventions described in this chapter (most federally funded programs). Indeed, newer migrants coming with temporary status may have unique support needs and challenges with regards to labour market integration, but they may not be able to use the many services and supports available.[2]

Though there is employer support for the TFW program, this program could squeeze out the skilled worker class. A two-step process reduces

Canada's competitive edge for attracting immigrants and delays settlement services, supports, and access to citizenship status that improves their prospects for successful integration into Canadian society. It also devolves the responsibility for selecting and initial settlement of Canada's future citizens to employers and post-secondary institutions, which may not be prepared to do this, or may not wish to play this nation-building role (Maytree, 2009). As such, a more pragmatic approach for Canada is to develop a citizenry base that will supply the labour market on a continuing basis.

What Are the Challenges?

Overview

Despite stringent selection criteria for skilled immigrants, there is a disconnect between immigration policy and labour market realities, as two thirds of recent immigrants are underemployed and yet professional jobs remain vacant. In 2006, 28 percent of recent immigrant men and 40 percent of women with a university degree held jobs which did not need university education (Statistics Canada, 2008b). The cost of the lack of recognition of skills and qualifications of immigrants has been estimated to cost the Canadian economy between $4.1 and $5.9 billion annually (Bloom & Grant, 2001, p. 21) and up to $15 billion, since immigrants are working far below their skill levels (Reitz, 2001).

Today, 70 percent of all recent working age immigrants (15 to 65 years of age) to Canada have at least some post-secondary education and 20 percent have a graduate degree, while only five percent of the Canadian-born do (Statistics Canada, 2007b). Despite immigrants' higher levels of education, almost 60 percent are not able to find jobs in their intended occupations (Statistics Canada, 2004). In 2006, the national unemployment rate for immigrants who had been in Canada five years or less was more than double the rate for the Canadian-born population (Statistics Canada, 2007b; Zietsma, 2007, p. 15). In addition, the gap between the unemployment rate of Canadian-born and immigrants has widened since the recession (Toronto Immigrant Employment Data Initiative [TIEDI], 2011).

Research shows that the most serious barriers to the labour market success of immigrants are lack of Canadian work experience, lack of recognition of foreign credentials[3] or work experience, language barriers, and discrimination (Zietsma, 2007, p. 13). All these barriers overlap, and "it is often unclear whether it is the immigrants' racial origin, gender or post-secondary degree that is being undervalued" (Li, 2001, p. 27).

Further, these barriers are complex and are two-sided, as both immigrants and Canadian society must adapt and change to address these issues. For example, correcting issues of cross-cultural communication and access to professional networks are issues that require the commitment of both Canadian society and immigrants if the issues are to be resolved. As such, we examine these issues and their solutions from a perspective that examines the relationships between immigrants and Canadian society at large.

The barriers to skilled employment, along with the responsibilities of providing for oneself and one's family, push many skilled immigrants into "survival jobs" – jobs well below their skill level, but which pay the bills. These immigrants often have an even harder time entering the labour market in positions consistent with their training, as their skills deteriorate or become out of date (Sweetman, 2005). In addition, the likelihood of immigrants leaving Canada increases if the return on their human capital is lower than what is expected in other countries competing for immigrants (DeVoretz & Ma, 2002). Recent Statistics Canada research shows that the rate of out-migration of immigrants is large (up to 35 percent) and that it occurs primarily during the first two years following entry. Therefore, the economic outcomes of immigrants during their initial years may be an important factor in determining the extent to which they remain in Canada (Picot, 2008).

In addition, due in part to challenges in transferring and utilizing education and experience obtained abroad, many adult immigrants are returning to school in Canada. Very recent immigrants aged 25 to 54 with a previous university degree are almost three times more likely than Canadian-born individuals to be enrolled in school or training programs (19 percent) in comparison to their Canadian-born counterparts (6.7 percent), with 73 percent of the former studying at the post-secondary level. Labour market outcomes for immigrants who obtain Canadian credentials are significantly higher than for immigrants with foreign credentials (Gilmore & Le Petit, 2008). In addition to the issue of poor credential recognition, immigrants are largely ineligible for student loans to help finance their studies in Canada, meaning that immigrants have to pay out of pocket or seek high-interest loans to get through post-secondary and bridge training programs as well as other short courses.

No Canadian Experience

One of the most frequently cited barriers to finding employment is the requirement of Canadian work experience. Immigrants are very often frustrated by this requirement, as there is no clear path to acquiring this experience and it is not obvious to them why it is required. In some cases, asking for Canadian work experience is a way of saying that the employer is not familiar with the immigrant's credentials or does not understand what their work experience means. It may also be a simple excuse for not wanting to hire an immigrant, or being concerned that they will not be a good "fit." There are times, however, when there may be a bona fide reason for requiring Canadian work experience; that is, are there laws, regulations, or country-specific knowledge that are required to perform the job. Regardless of the reasoning, this barrier is often cited as a "catch-22" because if employers are not hiring until immigrants gain Canadian experience, how then are they supposed to get that experience?

Credential Recognition

Recognition of qualifications in Canada is challenging since the federal, provincial, or territorial governments are each responsible for parts of the system, creating a complex structure that can result in mobility issues for everyone, including those who are Canadian educated. While all provincial and territorial governments in Canada have agreed to recognize the training, skills, education, and experience of all Canadians and immigrants in terms of regulation, licensing requirements and employment between provinces and territories under the 1994 Agreement on Internal Trade (AIT), the application of this agreement has yet to reach its full potential.[4]

For those with foreign credentials, the complexities are compounded. The procedures for evaluating and recognizing credentials and qualifications earned outside of Canada depend on many factors and differ based on whether the immigrant is trying to enter the labour market, pursue further studies, whether the chosen occupation is regulated or unregulated, and in what province or territory they wish to settle (Canadian Information Centre for International Credentials [CICIC], 2008). See Table 1 for an overview of regulated and non-regulated occupations in Canada. Employers, post-secondary institutions, and regulatory bodies want to ensure that credentials are legitimate, and to know what the Canadian equivalent would be and the quality of the granting institution. However, the issue of credential recognition, like that of "Canadian experience," has been critiqued as being a seemingly legitimate substitute for other forms of discrimination (Dietz et al., 2009).

There are multiple players involved in assessing and recognizing credentials. However, the lack of co-ordination between these diverse parties often means that immigrants are required to go through the cumbersome process of having their documents obtained and credentials assessed numerous

Table 1: What is the Difference between a Regulated and Unregulated Profession?	
Regulated	A "regulated" occupation is controlled by provincial and territorial (and sometimes federal) law and governed by a professional organization or regulatory body. This body governing the profession or trade has the authority to set entry requirements and standards of practice, to assess applicants' qualifications and credentials, to certify, register, or license qualified applicants, and to discipline members of the profession or trade. Some occupations are regulated in certain provinces and territories and are not regulated in others and requirements to practice may vary. You *must* have a license or certificate or be registered with the regulatory body for your occupation if you want to work in a regulated occupation and use a regulated title.
Non-regulated	A "non-regulated" occupation is a profession or trade for which there is no legal requirement (license, certificate or registration) or restriction on practice. Approximately 80 percent of occupations in Canada fall into this category. Sometimes non-regulated occupations will have voluntary certification or registration. Generally, applicants for non-regulated occupations will have to meet the requirements of individual employers in demonstrating that they possess the experience and training required for the job.

times for different purposes (Office of the Fairness commissioner [OFC], 2009). With the complexity of multiple institutions – provincial/territorial jurisdictions, government departments/ministries, regulatory bodies, provincially mandated assessment agencies, private assessment agencies, postsecondary institutions, employers, and non-governmental organizations (NGOs) – all playing a role in credential recognition, barriers for credential recognition in Canada are difficult to understand, let alone to address and resolve (Fernandez, 2006, p. 4).

Language, Communication and Cross-cultural Understanding

While knowledge of official languages, especially English, is associated with better labour market outcomes, and skilled immigrants are allowed entry into Canada in part based on their language abilities, language problems remained a serious problem for immigrants even four years after arrival (Statistics Canada, 2007a). Language barriers have been shown to have the largest impact on labour market outcomes of immigrants (Frenette & Morissette, 2003; Aydemir & Skuterud, 2004), and indeed, language training programs are some of the most important interventions for successful integration (TIEDI, 2010 July). Beyond the ability to communicate in official languages, immigrants also face challenges understanding and using Canadian nuances, communication styles, occupation-specific language and accents.

In addition to a potential language barrier, new immigrants to Canada are faced with other communication challenges in the labour market. These challenges are often related to cultural differences between employers and immigrants. At the recruitment and selection level, the challenges can arise from different norms involved in writing resume and cover letters. As well, there may be cultural bias inherent in behavioural-based interviewing style. For example, the interviewer may misinterpret the immigrant's body language to mean a lack of confidence in instances where the immigrant is actually being respectful according to his or her own culture.

After being hired, immigrants may continue to face communication challenges related to cultural differences. Every place of work has its own rules of behaviour and conduct that may not be communicated explicitly, either verbally or in writing. Success at the workplace may depend on figuring out these uncommunicated rules (Goldman, 2009). Managers sometimes communicate work instruction using the indirect approach, for example a manager may say, "I would approach this task this way," when he or she actually means, "This is how you must do it." The suggested approach may appear optional to the immigrant. Similarly, corrective feedback is often provided in an indirect manner, sometimes resulting in the immigrant not taking corrective action.

Professional Networks/Social Capital

Today's immigrants to Canada are more educated than immigrants in the past and on average, more educated than Canadian-born individuals, and so they seek more-skilled positions in the labour market (Alboim & McIsaac,

2007). Many have the education, experience and language skills to excel in the workforce but lack the social capital — the connections and networks — they need to increase the prospects of a successful job search. Recent research concluded that immigrants and Canadian-born use similar methods to find jobs. Most had found their current position either through networks of family or friends, followed by taking personal initiative (TIEDI, 2010, March). This conclusion points to the importance of social networks, in addition to strong English language skills, in making that crucial first connection to the job market. Given that this trend applies to both Canadian-born and immigrants, new immigrants who have not yet made as many social connections in Canada are at a disadvantage.

Mentoring is one way of addressing this problem. The idea is to connect the under-employed or unemployed skilled immigrant to a person employed in his or her profession. Mentors share their professional networks and offer guidance through the job search and/or licensing process, and the job-seeking immigrant gains a greater understanding of a specific occupational context and its trends. Programs in mentoring have been largely successful, with participants often finding work in their field of training. Based on a survey of program outcomes for The Mentoring Partnership,[5] 68 percent of the mentees in the program had found employment, 46 percent in their field (Alboim & McIsaac, 2007).

Discrimination

While the majority of Canadians support immigration, there are still challenges with regards to racial discrimination. However, it is very difficult to establish a causal relationship between racial discrimination and the economic outcomes of specific racial groups, as racial discrimination is not the only variable at play. Measuring the effect of race on economic outcomes is very difficult, partly since it is difficult to identify discrimination, and in order to attempt to measure it, it must be isolated from other variables that also affect economic outcomes. Not all variables are measurable or even observable.

In the case of credential recognition, credential assessment agencies may treat credentials from one country as more suited to Canadian standards than those obtained in another country. It is not always clear whether the difference in treatment of credentials is merely a matter of quality assurance or a matter of discrimination against the immigrant's country of origin. Either way, the economic outcomes of the person being discriminated against will be negatively affected.

In 1999, a decision of the British Columbia Council of Human Rights found that the distinction made by the College of Physicians and Surgeons of British Columbia between graduates of two categories of medical schools constituted discrimination on the basis of place of origin. In this case, candidates had differing requirements for licensure based on the country where they had attended medical school. The council found the correlation between place of origin and place of graduation to be high (Ontario Regulators for Access, 2004) and the distinction to constitute discrimination.

A recent study in British Columbia has attempted to isolate the effect of race from other factors using advanced statistical approaches to control for a number of other variables that can also influence economic outcomes of visible minorities. The research found that the earnings gap between Canadian-born visible minorities and the mainstream Canadian-born population has not eroded since the 1990s (Pendakur & Pendakur, 2011). Given that the majority of new immigrants to Canada are now visible minorities, racial discrimination must be understood as a significant factor in their process of settlement and integration, including labour market integration.

What's being Done?

History on Mobilization and Changes

In response to the barriers and challenges discussed above, governments, academic institutions, and community organizations have undertaken research, developed and implemented programs, and even introduced legislation to find systemic and practical solutions to credential recognition and labour market barriers facing immigrants. The roots of these programs go back many years, but in recent years specific attention has been given to assessing and recognizing international credentials.

In 1989, a landmark report entitled *Access!* was "the first major milestone in the Ontario movement toward better access to professions and trades" (Skills for Change & Centre for Research and Education in Human Services, 2001). However, recommendations from the report were never adopted as Ontario government policy, as they proved too costly. A few years later, in 1992, the Ontario government established an Access to Professions and Trades Unit (APT) and around the same time, many branches of government, organizations, and private foundations began funding community groups working to address these issues. Significant numbers of professional organizations and groups began mobilizing around credential recognition, and credential assessment services were set up in the late 1990s and early 2000s.

Another one of the first steps the province of Ontario took in response to this report was to fund a feasibility study to establish a credential assessment service in 2000. The report formed the basis for the government issuance of a Request for Proposal (RFP), and in 2001 it invited the foreign credential evaluation NGO World Education Services (WES) to set up an office in Ontario.

In addition, bridging programs and occupation-specific language programs began to be developed across the country during this time. In 2003, Toronto stakeholders came together to form the Policy Roundtable Mobilizing Professions and Trades (PROMPT), which became the voice for immigrant credential recognition concerns and helping to facilitate equitable access to professions and trades, to advocate transparent and fair licensing and registration processes, and to create an equitable system that would result in skills-commensurate employment for all (PROMPT, 2004).

Another response to labour market integration concerns has been the federal government's creation of the Foreign Credential Recognition (FCR) program and the Foreign Credentials Referral Office (FCRO) – both of which have tabled and institutionalized support for foreign credential recognition in Canada. As part of the government commitment to address credential recognition issues, in 2010, governments across Canada worked with HRSDC to develop the Pan-Canadian Framework for the Assessment and Recognition of Foreign Qualification to describe the ideal steps and proce-dures for various parties and jurisdictions across Canada to improve assess-ment and recognition processes. Recently, FCRO has embarked on educating employers on the benefit of employing immigrants.[6]

As a civic leadership response to the issue of immigrant employment, in 2003 the Toronto Region Immigrant Employment Council (TRIEC) was established. Envisioned as a multi-stakeholder response, employers, post-secondary institutions, community organizations, regulatory bodies, labour, immigrant professional associations, and all three levels of government were invited to join a leadership council to create and champion solutions to better integrate skilled immigrants into the local labour market. TRIEC focuses on three objectives:

1. to convene and collaborate with partners, creating opportunities for skilled immigrants to connect to the local labour market;

2. to work with key stakeholders, particularly employers, building their awareness and capacity to better integrate skilled immigrants into the workforce; and

3. to work with all levels of government, enhancing co-ordination and effecting more responsive policy and programs for skilled immigrant employment.

With leadership from the private sector, TRIEC has become a champion for promoting the value of immigrant expertise to employers. In 2007, ALLIES (Assisting Local Leaders with Immigrant Employment Strategies) was established to support similar local efforts across Canada to successfully adapt and implement programs that further the suitable employment of skilled immigrants. ALLIES provides resources and funding to immigrant employment councils.

Legislative changes have also taken place to address labour market issues for immigrants. In 2006, Ontario passed Bill 124, the *Fair Access to Regulated Professions Act*, to create the Office of the Fairness Commissioner (OFC) in order to advance equitable access to regulated professions in Ontario by assessing and monitoring the registration and regulation process and the compliance of regulators (Fernandez, 2006, p. 12). Other provinces have passed similar legislation and created similar institutions to advance fair access.

Credential Recognition

There are a number of services and initiatives to support the evaluation and assessment of credentials, qualifications, and skills. While all are important measures, questions around the effectiveness of these tools in the actual recognition process, and concerns about the potential for assessment processes to impose new barriers are ever present.

There are seven "third party" credential evaluation services across Canada, including five provincially mandated services and two other private services (see Table 2 for a list of services by province). All of these services have agreed to abide by provincial and territorial *General Guiding Principles for Good Practice in the Assessment of Foreign Credentials* and the *Recommendation on Criteria and Procedures for the Assessment of Foreign Qualifications* adopted in 2001 by the Lisbon Recognition Convention Committee. Credential evaluation services assess formal credentials by establishing the legitimacy of the institution, the authenticity of the documents, and the comparable credential in Canadian standards. They provide evaluation reports that are used for employment, further education, and licensure – though processes for obtaining an evaluation vary based on the purpose and jurisdiction.

Table 2: Credential Evaluation Services in Canada	
Agency	**Province/Territory**
Academic Credentials Assessment Service (ACAS)	Manitoba
Centre d'expertise sur les formations acquises hors du Québec (CEFAHQ)	Quebec
Engineers Canada3	Pan Canadian (Engineers)
International Credential Assessment Service of Canada (ICAS)	Ontario
International Credential Evaluation Service (ICES)	British Columbia
International Qualifications Assessment Service (IQAS)	Alberta, Saskatchewan & Northwest Territories
University of Toronto Comparative Education Service (CES)	Ontario
World Education Services (WES)	Ontario
Source: Canadian Information Centre for International Credentials (2011). http://www.cicic.ca/415/credential-assessment-services.canada	

For individuals, credential evaluation reports help them make informed decisions about applying for immigration, employment, education, training, and professional membership. Evaluation services also help end-users (employers, regulatory bodies, institutions, etc.) understand the value of foreign credentials in Canadian terms and provide assurance that supporting documents are legitimate. However, despite outreach efforts by evaluation services and governments, many employers are still unfamiliar with these services. In addition, the many stakeholders involved, the lack of awareness and understanding of the role of evaluation services, and the potential for inconsistent assessment outcomes by different service providers, can undermine efforts to improve credential recognition. As well, since credential evaluation services only assess formal credentials, they are only part of the solution in terms of addressing foreign credential recognition, as they do not address barriers in recognizing competency, work experience, or language abilities.

Useful and authoritative information on credential assessment and recognition is available through a number of websites. The Canadian Information Centre for International Credentials (CICIC) collects, organizes, and distributes information, and acts as a national clearing house and referral service to support the recognition and portability of Canadian and international educational, academic, and occupational qualifications. It provides over 200 occupational fact sheets that explain, in general terms, how to obtain assessment and recognition of foreign credentials and qualifications in Canada.[7] The FCRO website provides information, path-finding, and referral services to internationally trained individuals in Canada and overseas.

The FCR program funds an array of key programs and initiatives which support credential recognition. It aims to harmonize credential assessment and recognition processes across Canada into a pan-Canadian approach by providing strategic leadership in order to foster the development of consistent, national approaches to FCR. The *Pan-Canadian Framework for the Assessment and Recognition of Foreign Qualifications* sprung from this program in order to: develop common principles that guide the process of foreign credential recognition; establish standards for the timely handling of requests; and identify key occupations that will be the priority for developing recognition standards and help with pre-arrival information. At present, "there are internationally recognized general guiding principles for good practice in the assessment of international credentials," however, for the most part each assessment agency employs its own methodology when verifying document authenticity and in determining the academic comparability of education received outside of Canada (Johnson, 2008, p.7).

Recognition of Skills and Experience

Prior Learning Assessment and Recognition (PLAR) has been developed as a tool to identify, assess and recognize skills that cannot be reflected in formally obtained credentials. PLAR attempts to "identify and characterize the value of skills acquired through work experience, independent study, and forms of unrecognized training" (Duncan, 2008, p. 25). PLAR is a distinct procedure already in use in the Ontario college system; however the actual implementation differs from institution to institution, with some not practicing PLAR at all.

Related to PLAR is *Competency Assessment*, which is an assessment of credentials and non-credential knowledge and skills compared against the overall learning outcomes of a program or profession. Competency assessments emphasize learning rather than education (Divis, n.d.), and identify practical skills and gaps through written and practical skills demon-strations. Some sector councils, employers, and provinces and territories have developed competency assessments for specific professions.

Exemplary practice in credential and skills recognition requires an assessment of both academic (paper) credentials in conjunction with a competency assessment of workplace knowledge and skills and experience using various methods. However, these processes should not create more barriers for immigrants, and should be available to other groups, not only immigrants.

Starting the Process Overseas

In order to begin to successfully address immigrant integration issues in Canada, immigrants need to be provided with information and tools as early as possible in their immigration process, preferably prior to their arrival in Canada. Providing specific information that can help immigrants make informed decisions and identify and address any gaps before coming to Canada will enable quicker integration into jobs that appropriately reflect their academic background and work experience. In addition, the ability to have qualifications and skills assessed, and to access training and education are valuable at the pre-arrival stage.

Website portals can provide access to important tools and information that immigrants can access from almost anywhere in the world. Government portals such as the "Working in Canada" tool helps immigrants find out more about credentials, the labour market and the specifics related to their profes-sion and region (job duties, skill and qualification requirements, wage rates, etc.).[8] Provincial immigration websites are also valuable, as they provide a similar set of information, but with a focus on the region.[9] Further web-based resources are currently being developed, including the Orientation to Ontario project, aiming to streamline accessible informational resources for immi-grants.[10] In addition, specific pre-arrival steps to take before immigrating can be found in the Foreign Credential Referral Office's website,[11] and valuable settlement and planning information is located in the "Live in Canada" and "Work in Canada" sections of CICs website.[12] While these resources are valuable, there are concerns about the sheer amount of information results in these being both difficult to navigate and overwhelming, as well as whether, and to what extent, immigrants are able to process settlement infor-mation *before* they actually move (Owen & Lowe, 2008).

Workshops and orientation information offered overseas can also be helpful in preparing immigrants before they arrive. Providing information about credential evaluation, skills and language assessments, job search and resumé-building skills, and workplace orientation and counselling for options to bridge skills are essential in preparing immigrants for success in Canada. The Association of Canadian Community Colleges (ACCC) launched the Canadian Immigration Integration Project (CIIP), funded through the federal FCRO Program. The CIIP is currently running in the Philippines, China, India, and the United Kingdom to help immigrants and their spouses who have applied under the FSWP prepare for integration into the Canadian labour market while in the final stages of the immigration process. The program has both a one-day session on information and resources organized according to the destination province or territory, as well as one-on-one counselling interviews in which participants are helped to develop integration plans (Murray, 2007, p. 48). Through the CIIP, immigrants destined for Ontario get an immediate online credential equivalency provided through WES, which allows them to know where their credentials stand in Canadian terms. This assessment, in conjunction with face-to-face support, can help prospective immigrants identify any gaps that might exist in their skills and education, and so to begin addressing them as early as possible.[13]

Bridge Training

Bridge training programs identify and fill the gaps individuals have from their previous learning and work experience in order to meet Canadian standards in their professions. They provide training and Canadian workplace experience without requiring immigrants to redo all their education and training. Bridge training programs are successful because they incorporate occupation-specific language training, mentoring, and work experience. In addition, many programs are modularized, allowing immigrants to only take the relevant parts of the program – and not repeat unnecessary training. The Ontario Ministry of Citizenship and Immigration (MCI) funds the most extensive array of bridging programs for skilled immigrants in Ontario. Bridging programs are generally offered by not-for-profit organizations (NPOs) or educational institutions in collaboration with employers, regulatory bodies, and community organizations.[14]

Two-way Integration Strategies

In order to find jobs in their profession, immigrants must adapt to Canadian labour market requirements. At the same time, if employers are to find the skills they need to be productive and competitive, employers and society at large must adapt and become more effective in creating inclusive work environments that welcome diversity, including immigrant skills. The governments of Ontario and Canada fund both *immigrant* and *employer supports*. Notwithstanding many limitations to these supports, including the challenges of impact evaluation, there has been anecdotal evidence of successes, such as in the following story.

Case Study – Jennyfer Pacelo

In an ironic twist of fate for a risk manager, Jennyfer Pacelo's immigration papers were fast tracked after the devastating floods in the Philippines left her car submerged, her house destroyed, and no family to turn to for help. In April 2010, Jennyfer was reunited with her family in Canada.

While attending a job search workshop at ACCES Employment Services, Jennyfer learned about an American Express Canada Technologies hiring event for project managers, project management being a field she had worked in previously. She was hired a few months later.

Jennyfer realized that while she was getting her work done, her job evaluations were not entirely glowing. Jennyfer signed up for TRIEC's piloted workshop *Achieving Success in the Workplace*. "Right away I felt as though I wasn't alone," said Jennyfer. "The immigrants in my class were all experiencing similar challenges around the nuances of feedback."

Jennyfer could now pinpoint which of her responses she needs to flesh out during a performance review. "I know about constructive criticism," explains Jennyfer. "We were taught that too, but Filipino managers are more blunt. Now I know how and when to push a manager to be more direct with me."

The workshop also boosted her morale. "I'm now communicating more with my colleagues," said Jennyfer. "I'm building my interpersonal skills and asking for help when I need it."

The onus to adapt is not on Jennyfer alone. American Express Canada has sent staff to TRIEC's integration workshops to ensure that both immigrant employees and managers are equally informed and committed to new approaches to integration.

Immigrant Supports

Job search supports, funded by the federal and provincial governments, provide immigrants with counselling and workshops on navigating through a job search, and provide information about Canadian employer requirements regarding resume formats, interview styles, and the workplace. Job search support programs offer the necessary basic services leading to employment; but they often do not respond to the skill level of today's immigrants, and so need to be enhanced with more occupation-specific work experience elements.

Occupation specific language training (OSLT) teaches the communication skills needed in a specific occupation. It focuses on practicing dialogue and communication tasks commonly performed on the job in a specific field, sector, and occupation. Similarly, *enhanced language training* (ELT) combines occupation-specific language training with labour market supports, such as information on Canadian culture and the labour market, job search strategies, licensure preparation, and workplace experience.

A skilled immigrant may have all the academic credentials, language skills, and technical skills required to practice her or his occupation, but she or he may be lacking sufficient knowledge of the Canadian workplace; for example, of employment standards and occupational health and safety legislation, workplace cultural expectations and practices, organizational structures, or effective communication styles. *Work placements and internships* can be acquired through co-op placements, internships, job shadowing, and on-the-job training. Programs with workplace experience components generally demonstrate strong labour market outcomes for participants.

Mentoring brings together recent skilled immigrants and established professionals in occupation-specific mentoring relationships. Skilled immigrants entering these programs have the education, experience, and language skills they need to succeed in the labour market, but they need the social capital that supports effective labour market navigation. They need the local insights and access to professional networks that only a one-to-one professional connection with a mentor can offer.

Employer Supports

Human Resource Tools and Resources have been developed by a number of organizations serving immigrants for the benefit of employers to enhance their capacity to recruit, retain and promote skilled immigrants.[15]

What Still Needs to Be Done?

The following are recommendations on what can be done at the policy and practical level. The list is by no means comprehensive.

Public Investment in Supports for Immigrants

- Information and support to immigrants and potential immigrants at the earliest stage possible. This should include the assessment and recognition of credentials and other skills prior to emigration. Where possible, relevant service providers should offer online resources to individuals and professional bodies should offer the option to begin the licensing process overseas.

- Training programs that assess and upgrade required skills (e.g., bridging programs) are particularly helpful, but should be designed to provide full recognition for education and training already achieved, and offered in a modular and timely fashion. Where feasible, these should be offered pre-arrival.

- Language training at a level that provides proficiency in workplace communication. Labour market program interventions should be open to all who need them, including the unemployed, the underemployed, temporary workers, and international students.

- Make available low-cost tuition loans to provide access to upgrading and training programs.

- Programs that bring together immigrants and employers, such as mentoring and internships, that provide opportunities for immigrants to build their networks and to demonstrate their skills in real workplace situations.

Public Investment in Supports for Employers

- Increase employer awareness of the value of immigrant skills, education, and experience through public relations strategies, partnership development, and leadership development. Employers themselves provide the most powerful message in sharing and building momentum in hiring and investing in immigrants in the workplace. This process can best be supported by recognizing and highlighting champion employers and creating opportunities for employers to act as spokespersons in their industries regarding the value of immigrant skills.

- Develop and disseminate HR tools and resources for employers, with distinctive supports by industry and employer size.
- Create a simplified interface to help employers recruit skilled immigrants more easily and access resources available in the immigrant serving communities.

Credential Recognition

- Those assessing and recognizing credentials, including employers, should review their policies and procedures to ensure that they are objective, fair, and transparent. Governments should play a lead role in making sure that all agencies and institutions that evaluate credentials abide by procedures that are fair, objective, and transparent, and that adhere to international standards and best practices.
- In determining the comparability of foreign qualifications for eligibility to practice in a profession, consideration should be given to prior experience on the job, as well as to academic qualifications.
- Assessment agencies, professional licensing bodies, and academic institutions should collaborate to harmonize their requirements and procedures regarding credential assessment, with the goal of facilitating the portability of credential assessment reports. The government could assist in this process by facilitating the collection and verification of documents prior to immigration.
- Where the process of licensure or academic upgrading is lengthy for immigrants, consideration should be given to providing employment opportunities in related professions, so that individuals are able to gain related work experience.

Public Education

- Relevant stakeholders should engage in public education efforts to develop better understanding about the benefits and skills that immigrants bring, both to the economy and to Canadian society as a whole.
- There is also ongoing need for education among stakeholders about systems of education, credentialing, and work experience outside their own jurisdiction.

- Given that the majority of immigrants are from racialized communities, racial discrimination continues to adversely affect immigrants' experiences in the labour market and in society at large. In the short run, it is important to create public awareness through the media, of the value of immigration to the Canadian economy and society at large. In addition, long-term strategies are needed that embed diversity within existing structures. Employment equity legislation should also be revisited.

Each of these recommendations contributes to part of a broader opportunity that has the promise of creating meaningful employment for new immigrants in Canada.

Develop your knowledge – Ask yourself

As you read this chapter, ask yourself the following questions:

1. What percentage of recent immigrants are underemployed?
2. What are the most serious labour market barriers faced by immigrants?
3. What options would you suggest to a client who is having difficulty finding meaningful work?
4. How can credential evaluation reports help immigrants?
5. What is the difference between an unregulated and regulated profession?
6. After reading the case study, consider how the Canadian workplace can be different from a client's workplace back home, and how can you help a client understand those differences and support their success?

Notes

[1] This chapter is on the labour market integration of all immigrants, but we focus on those selected as economic immigrants.

[2] Social Planning Toronto's has a resource guide for immigrants without full status (permanent residency) available at http://socialplanning-toronto.org

[3] Credential recognition can narrowly be described as the assessment and recognition of formal academic credentials. However, the underlying dialogue and meaning of credential recognition relates to broader themes of immigration and labour market integration.

[4] Once an internationally-trained individual is certified to practice in a certain profession by a province or territory, this agreement stipulates that other jurisdictions accept that licensing decision. However, a coherent system for determining the recognition of international qualifications across Canada has not yet been realized. To meet this goal, governments across Canada have developed and committed to the A Pan-Canadian Framework for the Assessment and Recognition of Foreign Qualifications (http://www.hrsdc.gc.ca/eng/workplaceskills/publications/fcr/pcf.shtml)

[5] For The Mentoring Partnership, see www.thementoringpartnership.com.

[6] Recent FCRO videos showcasing employer best practices can be found at http://www.credentials.gc.ca/media/roadmap.asp.

[7] For Canadian Information Centre for International Credentials, see http://www.cicic.ca.

[8] For Working in Canada, see http://www.workingincanada.gc.ca.

[9] Ontario's website can be found at http://www.ontarioimmigration.ca.

[10] For the Orientation to Ontario project, see http://www.orientation ontario.ca.

[11] For the website of the Foreign Credential Referral Office, see http://www.credentials.gc.ca.

[12] For these sections of the CIC website, see www.cic.gc.ca

[13] For more information on the CIIP, see www.newcomersuccess.ca

[14] Working in Ontario is the MCI web portal that lists all bridge training programs in Ontario by profession; see http://www.ontarioimmigration.ca

[15] Examples of these tools and resources include: cultural competence training videos (see http://www.hireimmigrants.ca/tools/4); how-to HR resources (http://www.hireimmigrants.ca/index.php); an employer roadmap (http://www.hireimmigrants.ca/Roadmap/); immigrant employment best practices and case studies (http://www.hireimmigrants.ca); and

encouragement through recognition of promising practices (http://www. triec.ca/programs/is).

References

Adamowicz, K. (2004). *Developing integrated programming for immigrant professionals. Final report from Phase I: Developing a template for integrated bridging programs for internationally educated professionals.* Edmonton Mennonite Centre for Newcomers. Retrieved from http://www.emcn.ab.ca

Adams, T.L. (2007, Spring). Professional regulation in Canada: Past and present. In L. Hawthorne (Ed.), *Canadian issues: Foreign credential recognition* (pp.14-16). Retrieved from http://canada.metropolis.net

Alboim, N., & McIsaac, E. (2007). *Making the connections: Ottawa's role in immigrant employment.* Institute for Research on Public Policy (IRPP). 13(3). Retrieved from http://www.irpp.org

Aydemir, A., & Skuterud, M. (2004). *Explaining the deteriorating entry earnings of Canada's immigrant cohorts: 1966–2000.* Analytical studies. Catalogue no. 11F0019MIE2004225. Statistics Canada.

Bloom, M., & Grant, M. (2001). *Brain gain: The economic benefits of recognizing learning and learning credentials in Canada.* Ottawa: Conference Board of Canada.

Canadian Information and Networking Services. (2008). Home page. Available at http://www.canadainfonet.org

Citizenship and Immigration Canada (CIC). (2010). *Facts and figures: Immigration overview: Permanent and temporary residents.* Retrieved from http://www.cic.gc.ca

Canadian Information Centre for International Credentials (CICIC). (2008). *Foreign qualification evaluation and recognition in Canada.* Retrieved from http://www.cicic.ca

Canadian Information Centre for International Credentials (CICIC). (2011). *Credential evaluation, assessment and qualification recognition services.* Retrieved from http://www.cicic.ca

DeVoretz, D., & Ma, J. (2002, March 4). *Triangular human capital flows between sending, entrepot and the rest of the world regions.* Retrieved from http://www.iza.org

Dietz, J., Esses, J.M, Joshi, C., & Bennet-AbuAyyash, C. (2009). *The evaluation of immigrants' credentials: The roles of accreditation, immigrant race, and evaluator biases.* Canadian Labour Market and Skills Researcher Network. Working paper, 18. Retrieved from http://www.clsrn.econ.ubc.ca

Divis, J. (n.d.). *The international labour market: professional recognition of qualifications.* Dutch ENIC/NARIC. Retrieved from http://www.unesco.org

Duncan, D. (2008, January). *Improving bridging programs: Compiling best practices from a survey of Canadian bridging programs.* Ottawa: Public Policy Forum. Retrieved from http://www.uquebec.ca

Fernandez, S. (2006, August). *Who does what in foreign credential recognition: An overview of credentialing programs and services in Canada.* Prepared for The Alliance of Sector Councils and National Visible Minority Council of Labour Force Development. Retrieved from http://www.councils.org

Frenette, M., & Morissette, R. (2003). *Will they ever converge? Earnings of immigrants and Canadian-born workers over the last two decades.* Analytical Studies Branch Research Paper Series. Catalogue no. 11F0019MIE2003215. Ottawa: Statistics Canada.

Gilmore, J., & Le Petit, C. (2008). *The Canadian immigrant labour market in 2007: Analysis by region of postsecondary education.* Statistics Canada, Labour Statistics Division. Retrieved from http://www.statcan.gc.ca

Global Commission on International Migration (GCIM). (2005). *Migration in an interconnected world: New directions for action.* Report of the Global Commission on International Migration. Retrieved from http://www.queensu.ca

Goldman, L. (2009). *You're hired ... now what? An immigrant's guide to success in the Canadian workplace.* Toronto: Oxford University Press.

Hiebert, D. (2006, March). Skilled immigration in Canada: Context, Patterns and Outcomes. In B. Birrell, L. Hawthorne & S. Richardson (Eds.), *Evaluation of the general skilled migration categories.* Australian Government, Department of Immigration and Citizenship.

Human Resource and Skills Development Canada (HRSDC). (2006). National Occupational Classification System. Retrieved from http://www5.hrsdc.gc.ca

Johnson, K. (2008, December). *Pan-Canadian quality standards in international credential evaluation.* Prepared for the Alliance of Credential Evaluation Services of Canada (ACESC), Canadian Information Centre for International Credentials (CICIC) and Council of Ministers of Education, Canada (CMEC). Retrieved from http://www.cicic.ca

Li, P. (2001). The market worth of immigrants' educational credentials. *Canadian Public Policy, 27*(1), pp. 23-38.

Maytree. (2009, December). Policy in Focus, 10. Retrieved from http://maytree.com

Murray, K. (2007, Spring). Canadian immigration integration project: A switch in time. In L. Hawthorne (Ed.), *Canadian issues: Foreign credential recognition* (pp.47-49). Retrieved from http://canada.metropolis.net

Nanos, N. (2010, July–August). Canadian's strongly support immigration, but don't want current levels increased. *Policy Options/Options politiques*. Institute for Research on Public Policy (IRPP). Retrieved from http://www.irpp.org

Office of the Fairness Commissioner (OFC). (2009). *Study of qualifications assessment agencies*. Toronto: OFC. Retrieved from http://www.fairnesscommissioner.ca

Ontario Regulators for Access. (2004, May). *Business case: Rationale for improving access to professions by internationally educated and trained candidates.* Retrieved from http://regulatorsforaccess.ca

Owen, T., & Lowe, S. (2008, September). *Labour market integration of skilled immigrants: Good practices for the recognition of international credentials, Canada.* United Nations Educational, Scientific and Cultural Organization (UNESCO). Retrieved from http://unesdoc.unesco.org

Pendakur, K., & Pendakur, R. (2011). *Colour by numbers: Minority earnings in Canada 1996–2006.* Retrieved from http://www.sfu.ca

Picot, G. (2008). *Immigrant economic and social outcomes in Canada: Research and data development at Statistics Canada.* Catalogue no. 11F0019M-No. 319. Retrieved from http://dsp-psd.pwgsc.gc.ca

Policy Roundtable Mobilizing Professions and Trades (PROMPT). (2004). *In the public interest.* Retrieved from http://www.cassaonline.com

Reitz, J. (2001). Immigrant skill utilization in the Canadian labour market: Implications of human capital research. *Journal of International Migration and Integration, 2*(3), 347–378.

Reitz, J. (2011). *Pro-immigration Canada: Social and Economic Roots of Popular Views.* Institute for Research on Public Policy (IRPP). Issue 20. Retrieved from http://www.irpp.org

Skills for Change & Centre for Research and Education in Human Services. (2001). *Making a change together: Access to professions and trades for foreign trained people in Ontario.* Ministry of Training, Colleges and Universities. Toronto: Queen's Printer for Ontario. Retrieved from http://www.skillsforchange.org

Statistics Canada. (2003). *Longitudinal survey of immigrants to Canada: Progress and challenges of new immigrants in the workforce.* Catalogue no. 89-615-XIE. Retrieved from http://www.statcan.gc.ca

Statistics Canada. (2004). *Longitudinal Survey of Immigrants to Canada: Process, Progress and Prospects.* Catalogue no. 89-611-XIE. Retrieved from http://www.statcan.ca

Statistics Canada. (2007a). *Immigration in Canada: A portrait of the foreign-born population, 2006 Census: Findings.* Catalogue no. 97-557-XWE2006001. Retrieved from http://www12.statcan.ca

Statistics Canada. (2007b). Study: Canada's immigrant labour market. *The Daily.* Retrieved from http://www.statcan.ca

Statistics Canada. (2007c). Study: Immigration, citizenship, language, mobility and migration. *The Daily.* Retrieved from http://www.statcan.gc.ca

Statistics Canada. (2008a). *Canadian demographics at a glance.* Catalogue no. 91-003-X. Retrieved from http://dsp-psd.pwgsc.gc.ca

Statistics Canada. (2008b, December). *Immigrant's education and required job skills.* Perspectives. Statistics Canada. Catalogue no. 75-001-X. Retrieved from http://www.statcan.gc.ca

Statistics Canada. (2011). *Births and Total Fertility Rate.* Catalogue no. 84F0210X. Retrieved from http://www40.statcan.ca

Sweetman, A. (2005). Canada. In Niessen, J. & Schibel, Y. (Eds.), *Immigration as labour market strategy: European and North American perspectives* (pp. 13-46). Brussels: Migration Policy Group. Retrieved from http://www.migpolgroup.com

Toronto Immigrant Employment Data Initiative (TIEDI). (2010, July). *Language skills and immigrant labour market outcomes.* Analytical Report 11. By P. Kelly, N. Damsbaek, M. Lemoine, T. Fang, V. Preston, & S. Tufts. Retrieved from http://www.yorku.ca

Toronto Immigrant Employment Data Initiative (TIEDI). (2010, March). *Are immigrant wages affected by the Source of job search information?* Analytical Report 7. By T. Fang, N. Damsbaek, P. Kelly, M. Lemoine, L. Lo, V. Preston, J. Shields, & S. Tufts. Retrieved from http://www.yorku.ca

Toronto Immigrant Employment Data Initiative (TIEDI). (2011, July). *Economic recession and immigrant labour market outcomes in Canada, 2006-2011.* Report 22. By P. Kelly, S. Park, & L. Lepper. Retrieved from http://www.yorku.ca

Zietsma, D. (2007). *The Canadian immigrant labour market in 2006: First results from Canada's labour force survey.* Statistics Canada. Catalogue no. 71-606-XIE2007001. Retrieved from http://www.statcan.gc.ca

SUBJECT INDEX

AUTHOR INDEX

About the Authors

Philip Ackerman has worked extensively as an adult education instructor in Taiwan, Hong Kong and Canada. He holds a B.A. and has recently graduated from the Social Service Worker – Immigrant and Refugee Program at Seneca College. For the past few years, Philip has been committed to settlement work, assisting with workshops for the Canadian Council for Refugees, volunteering in various agencies throughout the sector, and participating with several projects. Currently, he is working in Research and Resource Development at the FCJ Refugee Centre.

Angie Arora is an activist and educator in the areas of violence against women, issues affecting immigrant and refugee communities, and pet loss bereavement. She has worked with organizations including Springtide Resources: Ending Violence against Women, Woman Abuse Council of Toronto, Ministry of Attorney General–Ontario Victim Services Secretariat, Council of Agencies Serving South Asians, Herizon House, and Humber College. She is currently a Professor with Seneca College's Social Service Worker - Immigrant and Refugee Program and operates her private practice, New Wave Consulting, where she provides professional development training to the non-profit sector and animal-care community. She completed her Bachelor of Social Work at Ryerson University, Masters of Social Work with York University, and Bereavement Education Certificate Program with Toronto Advanced Professional Education.

Amy Casipullai is Senior Policy and Communications Coordinator at the Ontario Council of Agencies Serving Immigrants (OCASI). In this capacity, she researches, develops and communicates public policy analysis informed by the experience of OCASI member agencies and community-based research to members, immigrant and refugee communities, academics, government, the general public and media. Amy has a background in social sciences and journalism. As a community activist and in her various jobs, she has worked on a broad range of social justice and equity issues, with a focus on the realities experienced by refugees, migrants, the racialized and workers. She has worked at various times in community-based research, journalism, popular education, and employment counselling, and mopping floors – all of which have shaped her awareness and activism.

Jennifer Clarke is an Assistant Professor in the School of Social Work at Ryerson University. Before joining Ryerson, Jennifer was the Research and Evaluation Specialist at the Toronto Community Care Access Centre (CCAC). She also worked for four years as the coordinator of community placements in the Urban Diversity Initiative at York University. In collaboration with Dr. Patrick Solomon, she piloted the Urban Diversity Model at the International University of the Caribbean in Jamaica. She is anti-racist educator whose research interests are in the area of settlement work, education and child welfare. Jennifer worked as a frontline settlement worker for many years in Toronto. She has a M.S.W. in Social Work and is currently completing her Ph.D in the Faculty of Education at York University.

George Sefa Dei is Professor of Sociology and Equity Studies at the Ontario Institute for Studies in Education of the University of Toronto (OISE/UT). Between 1996 and 2000 he served as the first Director of the Centre for Integrative Anti-Racism Studies at the University of Toronto. His teaching and research interests are in the areas of anti-racism, minority schooling, international development, anti-colonial thought and indigenous knowledges systems. Professor Dei has published extensively in the area of anti-racism education, minority schooling, African education, international development and Indigenous Knowledges. He is the recipient of "Race, Gender, and Class Project Academic Award" (2002); the "African-Canadian Outstanding Achievement in Education" from *Pride Magazine* in Toronto (2003); the "City of Toronto's William P. Hubbard Award for Race Relations" (2003); the "Canadian Alliance of Black Educators Award for Excellence in Education and Community Development" (2007); and the "Nile Valley Foundation Commission Award" (2009). Finally, in 2007, Professor Dei was installed as a traditional chief in Ghana in the New Juaben Traditional Area of Ghana.

Debbie Douglas is the Executive Director of the Ontario Council of Agencies Serving Immigrants (OCASI). Prior to arriving at OCASI, Debbie spent many years working in the non-governmental sector in direct service organizations as a manager, director and management consultant. In her latter role, Debbie designed and delivered anti-oppression workshops for a wide range of community-based organizations and public institutions. Debbie has been an active member of numerous boards and working groups including the Centre of Excellence for Research on Immigrant Settlement (CERIS–Ontario Metropolis

Centre); Women's College Hospital, and the Greater Toronto Civic Action Steering Committee. Debbie is the co-editor of *Ma-ka: Diasporic Juks*. In 2004, she was honoured with the prestigious YWCA Toronto women of distinction award in the area of social justice and action.

Avvy Go is Clinic Director of Metro Toronto Chinese & Southeast Asian Legal Clinic. Since becoming a lawyer in 1991, she has worked exclusively in the legal clinic system, serving the legal needs of low income individuals and families, the majority of whom are non-English speaking immigrants and refugees. Avvy is one of the recipients of the 2008 City of Toronto's William P. Hubbard Award for Race Relations. She was also the Recipient of 2002 President's Award of the Women's Law Association of Ontario. Avvy has given numerous lectures and educational seminars and published articles in various publications including law journals, law books, community as well as mainstream newspapers dealing with a variety of subject matters such as redress and reparations, constitutional litigation, and other legal and policy issues affecting immigrants and racialized communities. Apart from her legal practice, Avvy spends much of her time doing community organizing and advocacy work. In 2007, she co-founded the Colour of Poverty Campaign – a campaign to address the increasing racialization of poverty in Ontario.

Salah Hassanpour is an activist, journalist and instructor in Toronto. He received a B.A. from the Arts and Contemporary Studies program at Ryerson University and a M.A. from the Cinema Studies Institute at the University of Toronto. He is currently completing a doctoral degree at York University's Cinema and Media Studies department while teaching at Seneca College.

Nicole LaViolette was an Associate Professor at the Faculty of Law of the University of Ottawa. Her research and publications were devoted mainly to international human rights, international humanitarian law, and the rights of refugees. She was also interested in LGBT legal issues and transnational family law. She had published several articles on sexual minorities and the refugee determination system, and conducted professional development training for the Immigration and Refugee Board. She was a recipient of the Lambda Foundation Award for Excellence in Gay and Lesbian Studies for her work on the Canadian *Gender Guidelines* and their impact on sexual orientation and gender identity refugee claims, as well as the Germain-Brière Writing Prize for an article on the definition of torture in Canadian immigration and refugee law. On May 22, 2015, Nicole LaViolette lost her battle to cancer, however, her legacy and commitments towards refugee rights will never be forgotten.

Sophia Lowe is the Manager of Community Engagement and Knowledge Exchange at World Education Services in Toronto. The focus of her work has been on the nexus between immigration and student mobility in Canada, temporary migration, credential recognition and the academic and labour mobility of migrants. She has presented at a number of national and international conferences and has published on immigration in several education and policy papers, including Metropolis and UNESCO. Sophia received an M.A. from Ryerson University in Immigration and Settlement Studies and a B.A. from the University of Guelph in International Development, Gender Studies and Sociology.

Lisa Min is currently a third year student at Osgoode Hall Law School. She holds an Honours Bachelor of Health Sciences with a minor in Japanese Studies from the University of Western Ontario. During her undergraduate years, Lisa was actively involved in Japanese Students' Association and worked as a teaching assistant in the Department of Modern Languages & Literatures. While attending law school, Lisa was a caseworker at Community & Legal Aid Services Programme (CLASP) and cast member in Osgoode Hall's Mock Trial. In her second year, Lisa undertook clinical legal studies in the Intensive Program in Immigration and Refugee Law and completed her external placement at Guberman, Garson. Currently, she volunteers at Robin Seligman Barrister and Solicitor.

Cornelia Mazgarean is a law graduate from Romania, Cornelia Mazgarean also obtained a law degree from Osgoode Hall Law School. While at Osgoode, she was a division leader and then a senior division leader at the Community and Legal Aid Services Programme (CLASP). She is currently an LLM candidate and a supervising lawyer at CLASP. Cornelia also has her own private practice, focusing on Criminal, Immigration and Mental Health Law. In addition, she does work as a duty counsel lawyer, advising people arrested for criminal or immigration matters. Cornelia is a member of a variety of professional organizations. Apart from file work, Cornelia often delivers public legal education workshops in both criminal and immigration law, and is involved in community outreach and advocacy.

Ajamu Nangwaya is an instructor at Seneca College of Applied Arts and Technology and teaches courses in the areas of diversity/equity and social policy. He has a Ph.D in Adult Education and Community Development from the University of Toronto. Ajamu has held a number of leadership positions in the Canadian Union of Public Employees (CUPE) and is a former vice-president of CUPE Ontario. He is a community organizer and a public educator.

Geraldine Sadoway is a lawyer specializing in immigration and refugee law since her call to the Ontario Bar in 1983. She has been working as a clinical law instructor, adjunct professor and supervising lawyer at Parkdale Community Legal Services in Toronto since 1997. She regularly appears as legal counsel before the Immigration and Refugee Board and the Federal Court of Canada. She represented the Metro Action Committee on Violence Against Women and Children (METRAC) in the sponsorship debt recovery case of *Mavi et al v. M.C.I. and A.G. for Ontario* in the Ontario Court of Appeal and the Supreme Court of Canada. Geraldine is a well-published scholar and activist who has presented and written extensively on issues affecting refugees and immigrants in Canada. She is currently engaged in research at Osgoode Hall Law School, focusing on Canadian laws and policies that have a negative impact on immigrant and refugee children and their families.

Emily Paradis has worked for more than 20 years as an activist, researcher, advocate and service provider for women facing homelessness. As Research Manager at Cities Centre, University of Toronto, she has led participatory projects on homelessness among women and families, and has managed large studies of neighbourhood inequality in Toronto and other Canadian cities. As Research Consultant with the National Film Board of Canada, she has contributed to the development and production of HIGHRISE, a multi-year, multi-media, multi-disciplinary online documentary project exploring life in the high-rise neighbourhoods of the global suburbs. She has also taught Participatory Research at Ontario Institute for Studies in Education (OISE/UT). Dr. Paradis received her Ph.D in Adult Education (2009) from OISE/UT.

Siavosh Pashang is a criminal defence lawyer with the firm, Hicks Adams LLP. Siavosh attended the University of Ottawa, Faculty of Law, and graduated in 2013, receiving his Juris Doctor. During his time in law school, Siavosh interned with the Department of Justice: Research and Statistics Division, where he helped review decisions on third party records applications in sexual offence cases. The findings were published in *Victims of Crime Research Digest* (Department of Justice). Prior to law school, he obtained an Honours Bachelor of Arts degree in Political Science from York University and a Master of Arts degree in Political Science: International Relations from McMaster University. He previously taught at Seneca College, School of English and Liberal Studies in the areas of politics, ethnicity and race relations in Canada.

Soheila Pashang is a Professor and Co-ordinator at Seneca College, Social

Service Worker – Immigrants and Refugees Program. She has completed her Ph.D at the Ontario Institute for Studies in Education at the University of Toronto exploring the discourse of migration with specific attention to the lived conditions of illegalized women in Canada. For over two decades, Soheila has worked as a social worker/therapist with various organizations serving immigrants and refugees and has further served as Subject Matter Export (SME) on issues of mental health, trauma and gender violence. She writes poetry and has co-edited the book, *Roots and Routes of Displacement and Trauma From Analysis to Advocacy and Policy to Practice* with Sheila Gruner.

Donald Payne is a psychiatrist who graduated in medicine from the University of Toronto in 1963 and was certified as a specialist in 1971. Since 1979, he has performed psychiatric assessments on more than 1,500 refugees or refugee claimants from more than 90 different countries. He has testified at the Commission of Inquiry into the Actions of Canadian Officials in Relation to Maher Arar, the Supreme Court of Ontario and the Federal Court of Canada. He is a member of the Health Committee of the Canadian Centre for Victims of Torture (CCVT) and has served on its Board of Directors. He was the elected Canadian representative on the Council of the International Rehabilitation Council for Torture Victims (IRCT) from 2003 to 2006. Since 1982, he has been National Coordinator of the Health Network of Amnesty International, English Section. He has written articles on human rights issues and is the editor of the Amnesty International, Canadian Section bulletin *Health Care and Human Rights*.

Loly Rico is a Founder and Co-director of FCJ Refugee Centre responsible for the Settlement Programme. She is also teaching at Seneca College, Social Service Worker – Immigrant and Refugee Program. Loly is a recipient of 2004 Constance E. Hamilton Award of the City of Toronto and Peace Medallion of the YMCA. In 2010, she received the Trever Bartaun Award from CCVT for her work around the issue of trafficking of women, and achieved a plaque of recognition from the Salvadorean Canadian Association of Toronto (ASALCA) for her relentless work for refugee rights in Canada. Currently, Loly is a Vice-President and Chair of Anti-Trafficking Sub-committee of Canadian Council for Refugees (CCR). She is a past President of the Board of Ontario Council of Agencies Serving Immigrants, member and founder of the Coalition of Services Providers for Refugee Claimants (CSPRC).

Francisco Rico has an M.A. in Economics from Costa Rica and a Law Degree (J.D.) from El Salvador. In El Salvador he was a law professor at the National

University, writer, political analyst, human rights advocator and investigator for the Archbishop office of San Salvador. He was also an advisor for the Jesuit Refugee Service in El Salvador. In Canada, Francisco is a Co-director of FCJ Refugee Centre that strives to meet the diverse needs refugee claimants and people without status and is a member of the Editorial Group of the *Refugee Update Newsletter*. He is the Toronto Regional Director of Ontario Council of Agencies Serving Immigrants (OCASI) and past president of the Canadian Council for Refugees (CCR). Francisco has received the Community Leadership in Justice Fellowship of the Ontario Law Foundation for 2007, the 2001 City of Toronto William P. Hubbard Race Relations Award and the YMCA Peace Medallion of 2006.

Kuziva Ziramba was Program Coordinator for Toronto Region Immigrant Employment Council's Employer Initiatives, responsible for planning and co-ordinating workshops and events aimed at building employer capacity to effectively recruit and integrate skilled immigrants in the Greater Toronto Area labour market. He also supported the Intergovernmental Relations Committee by conducting research on issues pertaining to immigrant integration. Previous to this, Kuziva served as Chief Economist, public sector expenditure for the Ministry of Finance in Zimbabwe. Kuziva has an M.A. in Economics from the Centre for Development Economics, Williams College, Massachusetts.

CPSIA information can be obtained
at www.ICGtesting.com
Printed in the USA
LVOW02s0044130216

474770LV00008B/17/P